MEDITATION
& LIGHT VISIONS
A NEUROLOGICAL ANALYSIS

Philip T. Nicholson

Library of Congress Control Number LCCN 2009904424

Cataloging-in-Publication Data

Nicholson, Philip, 2010

Meditation & Light Visions: A Neurological Analysis / Philip Nicholson

  Includes bibliographical information and index.

  ISBN 1-4392-4033-7

  1. Neurology. 2. Brain Science and Religion. 3. Anthropology.

Front Cover Photo (by Carlye Calvin): © University Corporation for Atmospheric Research
Book Design: Tita Young, WordScribe.com

Printed in the United States of America

ACKNOWLEDGEMENTS

I'd like to thank Michael Witzel, editor of *The Electronic Journal of Vedic Studies*, and Steven Fahrion, editor of *The Journal of Subtle Energies and Energy Medicine*, for their support in publishing my early work and their generosity in granting me permission to use material published first under their auspices. Dr. Witzel, Professor of Sanskrit and Indian Studies at Harvard University, was particularly helpful, offering sage observations about early Indian mysticism which ranged from insights about the etymologies of obscure Sanskrit words to observations about Vedic sources and about the research strategies that were most likely to prove productive. The comments of Carol Schneider, Paul Firnhaber, and Lance Farrar helped shape the evolution of these ideas, and the editorial revisions suggested by my daughter, Noelle, have been incorporated throughout the book.

The late Robert Goldman, M.D., Director of the Department of Psychiatry at Boston University School of Medicine and my psychotherapist during the strange and disorienting events described in this book, provided care and counsel that proved invaluable at the time and that continue to inspire my affection, admiration, and gratitude.

No one knows better than a person who engages in the solitary pursuits of research and writing that the most important and most rewarding moments in life come from loving—and being loved by—the people with whom one shares the intimacies of daily life: for their affection, support, and frequent forbearance, I want to thank my wife, Elizabeth; my three daughters, Virginia, Noelle, and Melina; my parents, Philip W. and Pauline Nicholson; and my siblings, Jack Nicholson and Paulette Harp, who always welcome new ideas.

Finally, I'd like to thank the University Corporation for Atmospheric Research in Boulder, Colorado, and photographer Carlye Calvin for granting me permission to use the dramatic photograph of lightning that appears on the front cover.

Philip T. Nicholson
Boulder, Colorado

TABLE OF CONTENTS

1

WHY LIGHT VISIONS ARE IMPORTANT FOR NEUROSCIENCE

INTRODUCTION

Decoding the Hidden Clues

The fundamental obstacle impeding progress in the scientific study of meditation is not a dearth of empirical data—there are many correlation studies that document changes in the brain during meditation—but there is still no comprehensive *causal* theory that can explain meditation in terms of the sequential activation of specific brain mechanisms. In this book I show that important clues about the identity of these neural mechanisms are *hidden in the data that have already been published.* The reason why investigators continue to overlook these hidden clues is that they do not have access to a conceptual framework that can reveal how new developments in the neuroscience of sleep, vision and epilepsy—developments that are generally regarded as unrelated to meditation—can be realigned to provide a simple, comprehensive and vertically-integrated causal theory of how the meditative state is installed and maintained. The key that makes it possible to reframe the conceptual landscape and to decode the hidden clues is a systematic, neurologically-grounded analysis of internally-generated light visions ("geometric phosphenes") that begin to flow spontaneously during the kind of "empty-mind" meditation practiced by experienced adepts in India and Tibet.

The sacred scriptures and yoga meditation treatises of India and Tibet describe these meditation-induced light visions as having predictable features that evolve in a predictable progression and culminate in ecstatic visions of lightning-like flashes. The importance of understanding this phenomenon is underscored by the fact that many of the prominent scientific studies of expert meditators published in recent years have recruited Tibetan lamas as subjects. Often subjects are selected for their reputed mastery of the meditation techniques of "Highest Yoga Tantra" (*maha-anuttara-yoga*), and, to be more specific, on their ability to generate the phenomenon of "psychic heat" (*phumo*) that provides researchers with a clear and convincing physical sign of meditative prowess. The practice of Highest Yoga Tantra is based on a systematic cultivation of the same sequence of meditation-induced light visions that is the subject of the present investigation, a sequence that eventually produces lightning-like flashes and paroxysmal sensorimotor symptoms. This epileptiform outcome suggests the possibility that expertise in Highest Yoga Tantra instigates a neuronal kindling that gradually lowers the seizure threshold of those neuron assemblies in the visual pathways and in the temporolimbic complex that are regularly induced to fire in concert during meditation. If scientists are not aware of the mental strategies that the monks use in their advanced meditations, they are likely to encounter serious problems when it comes time to interpret their results and to compare their results with the findings reported by other studies that use different kinds of meditation techniques, especially if the subjects are novice meditators.

This book offers detailed, empirically-oriented descriptions of the spatial and temporal characteristics of meditation-induced light visions and proposes to answer this question: What kinds of neuronal events must take place at each stage of vision-processing in order for a phosphene image with the specified features to appear in the visual field of a meditator? The results of this investigation are dramatically more definitive than anyone might reasonably have expected at the outset—and I doubt that these results could be extrapolated by an independent review of the existing research literature.

The Neural Correlates of Light Visions

In recent years several books have been published in which scientists discuss science and meditation—books like James Austin's *Zen and the Brain* [MIT Press, 1999], Andrew Newberg and Eugene d'Aquili's *Why God Won't Go Away: Brain Science and the Biology of Belief* [Ballantine Books, 2001]; Richard Davidson and Anne Harrington's *Visions of Compassion: Western Scientists and Tibetan Buddhists Examine Human Nature* [Oxford University Press, 2002]; John Horgan's *Rational Mysticism: Dispatches From the Border Between Science and Spirituality* [Houghton Mifflin, 2003]; B. Allan Wallace's *Buddhism and Science* [Cambridge University Press, 2003]; Richard Dawkins' *The God Delusion* [Houghton Mifflin, 2006]; Daniel Dennett's *Breaking the Spell: Religion as a Natural Phenomenon* [Viking: 2006]; David Coming's *Did Man Create God: Is Your Spiritual Brain at Peace with Your Thinking Brain?* [2007]; and Beauregard and O'Leary's *The*

Spiritual Brain: A Neuroscientist's Case for the Existence of the Soul [2007]; and Anne Harrington and Arthur Zajonc's *The Dalai Lama at MIT* [2008]. All of these books address the subjects of brain science and religious mysticism in an interesting and informative manner, but none of them examines the particular phenomenon of meditation-induced light visions in any detail. If understanding light visions is the key that makes it possible to decode the nature of the brain mechanisms involved in meditation, as I propose, then all of these books have missed out on the most important and revealing phenomenon.

It is worth taking special notice of a comment by John Horgan, author of *Rational Mysticism*, who points out that only one of the many scientist-authors that he interviewed—all of whom are leading researchers in the field of neuroscience and religion—could actually say that he had himself experienced the kind of mystical event that was the subject of his scientific research. That single author is neurologist James Austin, author of *Zen and the Brain*. He describes his own mystical experiences in great detail and also ranges widely in his discussions of various mystical phenomena, but there's a catch. Since he practices Zen Buddhism, and since Zen actively discourages the cultivation of light visions, Austin's own experiences do not incorporate this particular phenomenon. While he does discuss light visions in passing, he can only rely on an outsider's perspective and thus is able to add little beyond what has already been written.

Reverse-Engineering the Author's Experiences

I'm a medical writer who specializes in writing technical videos for the continuing education of physicians. For many years I practiced meditation at irregular intervals, and often I would see two sets of geometric phosphenes, one following after the other in a predictable manner. These same phosphenes might also appear spontaneously if I were relaxing in bed, waiting for sleep to come. But if this were all I saw, I would not have begun the research that produced this book: what startled and intrigued me was a dramatic elaboration of the light vision sequence that occurred on one occasion when I inadvertently triggered a paroxysmal progression of phosphene images.

I had been suffering from insomnia—an unusual experience for me—and, as a result, I'd accumulated a substantial sleep deficit. I can be quite sure about the timing because I knew precisely when I got in bed and when I got out, and, by this criterion, I could not have slept for more than four of the preceding thirty-six hours. The night when the paroxysmal episode occurred, I found myself still awake and alert at four o'clock in the morning. I decided to get in bed and to meditate in the hope that this would induce enough relaxation for me to fall asleep. When I concentrated my attention in this sleep-deprived condition, the familiar light visions begin to flow. I noticed that the phosphenes seemed to be unusually bright, but then suddenly everything changed: the familiar geometric phosphenes I'd seen on so many occasions were eclipsed by light visions that were much more dramatic and attention-riveting. These light visions evolved in an elaborate progression that culminated in lightning-like flashes, loud sizzling sounds, paroxysmal sensorimotor symptoms and an "ecstatic" emotional accompaniment.

This prolonged progression of light visions is seen only rarely and then only by religious mystics who are more interested in the metaphysical significance of the visions than in the neurological origins. So it is rarer still—and perhaps even unique—for someone with a scientific background and with no sectarian commitments to see these same visions. I can testify that the emotional experience was as powerful as the mystical texts suggest, but what caught my attention was the paradox that an ecstatic visionary rapture highly prized in the mystical traditions of India and Tibet had to be some kind of seizure. Was this really a *seizure*, and, if so, what kind of seizure? How it is possible for someone who has no symptoms of epilepsy to learn how to trigger this kind of ecstatic seizure and to do so at will? Do meditators who induce these light visions suffer any deleterious effects, and, if so, at what point does self-harm begin? Why is there little or no discussion of this paradoxical aspect of meditation in the medical research literature?

I prepared a set of schematic drawings to illustrate the salient characteristics of these internally-generated "phosphene" visions—their shapes, colors, movements, timing intervals and the order of appearance. Then I studied the latest research in the neuroscience of vision, sleep and epilepsy and used what I found to subject each phosphene image to a "reverse engineering" analysis. By systematically matching the structural characteristics of these phosphene images with the known activation patterns of various brain mechanisms, I was able to identify the precise mechanisms that would have to be activated in order for phosphene images with those characteristics to appear in the visual field. Based on this analysis and on the hypotheses it produced, I can now propose a simple, concrete and comprehensive *causal* theory that explains the neural origins of the behavioral state of meditation and of the phosphene images that appear during meditation. This theory generates a number of predictions amenable to empirical testing and also explains many of the contradictory and otherwise anomalous findings reported in the existing studies of meditators.

Reasoning that meditation must activate the same set of brain mechanisms no matter when or where it is practiced, and recognizing too that I needed to demonstrate that my own experiences were not merely idiosyncratic, I began to study the ancient yoga meditation texts of India and Tibet and autobiographical narratives of contemporary Hindu mystics. My prediction was that I'd find evidence of the same phosphene progression in most of the important meditation-related texts, and this was indeed the case—in Hindu and Tibetan sources [Nicholson, 2002a-c], in Chinese Daoist sources [Nicholson, 2008; Pfister, 2008], and in the literature on shamanistic practices, past and present [Nicholson, 2008; Nicholson and Firnhaber,

2003]. Having a template of neurologically grounded drawings to serve as a standard for comparison, it becomes possible to decode references to self-induced light visions in textual passages and iconic representations that experts in the field have regarded too opaque and ambiguous to permit confident interpretation.

Methodological Issues in the Study of Meditation-Induced Qualia

This investigation must confront several methodological problems. First, introspective self-reports are generally regarded—with good reason—as being notoriously unreliable. Also, the subjective, "felt" qualities of a person's experience—the *qualia* of that experience—are generally considered to be epistemologically private and thus inaccessible to an "outside" observer. Finally, a serious methodological problem is posed when someone offers *ad hoc* (after-the-fact) explanations of any phenomenon: there are often several different, competing explanations that might conceivably account for the observed outcome, and the only scientifically-acceptable way of choosing among these alternatives is to conduct a disciplined hypothesis-testing program to sift the good explanations from the bad.

Unfortunately, all three of these methodological problems converge in this inquiry: I rely on *ad hoc* reasoning about introspective reports to generate my hypotheses, and I am not in a position to test the hypotheses myself. I also claim that my own subjective experiences of phosphene phenomena can be equated with written descriptions of visions which always involve some indeterminacy, and, what's worst, these descriptions were written by people who spoke different languages and lived in different cultures and historical epochs. In contemporary neuroscience, this kind of study would probably not be accepted for publication in a mainstream journal, even if it could somehow be compressed into an article-length format. How, then, can I reasonably expect that scientists will pay serious attention to the analyses I present in this book?

In the earliest stages of research in a scientific field, circumstances sometimes arise which require a relaxation of generally-accepted methodological standards in order to find ways to progress beyond the obstacles that pose barriers to further progress. Research on meditation, which is still in its infancy, falls within this exception. I've already mentioned one reason why that is so—the lack of a theoretical framework—but equally important is the fact that the most precise measuring instruments currently available have significant limitations when applied to meditation research. In particular, these instruments have not yet achieved the resolution needed to probe effectively into the complex and intricately-interconnected circuits of the very small neuron assemblies that have been implicated by my phosphene analysis as key participants in establishing a meditative state, for example, the lateral geniculate nucleus (LGN), the thalamic reticular nucleus (RTN) and the hippocampal complex. And there are other problems as well, including these issues noted by Dr. Andrew Newberg, the radiologist responsible for organizing many of the more advanced and well-regarded studies of meditators that use radionucleide imaging:

> There are other more global problems that affect the ability to interpret the results of all functional neuroimaging studies. The most important of these is how to be certain what is actually being measured physiologically and how it compares to various subjective experiences. There are already potential problems addressing what a particular scan finding means in terms of the actual activity state of the brain. . . . A bigger problem is trying to compare the observed physiological changes to the subjective state. With regard to religious and spiritual experience, it is not possible to intervene at some "peak" experience to ask the person what he or she is feeling. Therefore, . . . how will the researcher know which scan findings it relates to? In addition, there are typically a number of changes in the brain with varying degrees of strength. It is not clear what degree of change should be considered a relevant change—10 percent? 20 percent? [Newberg and Lee, 2005, p. 477].

The analysis of meditation-induced phosphenes provides a way of side-stepping the limitations in the resolution of neuroimaging instruments and in the interpretation of the results. This analysis focuses the attention of researchers on certain specific neuronal circuits, and it moves far beyond what would be possible using radionucleide imaging by revealing how neuronal events evolve over time—how pre-ictal events potentiate lowered seizure thresholds; how different kinds of paroxysmal activity are triggered and how they propagate; and how the variety of post-ictal sequelae provide retrospective evidence about what kinds of excitotoxic damage must have been caused by the meditation-induced ecstatic seizure.

As for the question of whether or not it is legitimate for scientists to study the neural correlates of consciousness by analyzing subjective qualia, I'd like to cite the comments of neuroscientist Gerald Edelman, creator of the influential theory of Neural Darwinism, who writes that "It is our ability to report and correlate while individually experiencing qualia that opens up the possibility of a scientific investigation of consciousness [Edelman, 1992, p. 115]." Reports of qualia can be "discriminated in terms of modality, intensity, continuity, or their temporal or spatial properties," and these kinds of discriminations can provide useful information about "the actual mechanisms by which qualia arise [Ibid., p. 116]." My investigation of the shapes, colors, movements, timing intervals and sequences of meditation-induced light visions, all of which are generated by wholly internal processes, constitutes a good example of what can be accomplished by following Edelman's advice.

That a seizure-like event is implicated here may present a special advantage. In an article entitled "Consciousness, epilepsy and emotional qualia," Monaco et al. [2005] suggest that seizure-associated qualia represent "a privileged window into the neural bases of consciousness" because many qualitative aspects of seizure-driven experiences are associated with specific kinds of neuronal events that are known to be localized in the temporolimbic system. Epileptiform tempo-rolimbic discharges are often proposed as likely causes of the anomalous psychic and emotional experiences documented in the literature of religious mysticism. Research psychologist Michael Persinger [1987] was an early proponent of the theory that many kinds of psychic phenomena and mystical religious experiences are the products of "temporal lobe transients." More recently psychiatrists Jef-frey Saver and John Rabin [1997] have proposed a "limbic marker hypothesis" as the most likely explanation for a variety of anomalous experiences that are com-monly regarded as "mystical:" in their view, the contents of a person's perception, cognition, and emotion at some specific time can be suddenly and dramatically transformed by momentary eruptions of abnormal discharges in the temporolim-bic system that have the effect of "tagging" those erstwhile ordinary experiences with a sense that these events, far from being ordinary, were exceptional and deeply meaningful. This emotional embellishment of the contents of everyday experience is then preserved in the person's memories of the event. The limbic marker thesis can explain why many of the psychic symptoms described by religious mystics are also known to be associated with temporal lobe disturbances:

> The core qualities of religious and mystical experience . . . are the noetic and inef-fable—the sense of having touched the ultimate ground of reality and the sense of the unutterability or incommunicability of the experience. Frequent additional features are an experience of unity, an experience of timelessness and spacelessness, and a feeling of positive affect, of peace and joy. We suggest that the primary substrate for this experience is the limbic system. Temporolimbic discharges can produce each of these components in fragmentary or complete form: distancing from apparent reality (depersonalization, derealization), timelessness and spacelessness (autoscopy, time distortion), or positive affect (ecstatic auras) / The limbic system integrates exter-nal stimuli with internal drives and is part of a distributed neural network that marks stimuli and events with positive or negative value. . . . Moreover, in addition to simple positive or negative valence, limbic discharges can produce experiences that are in-termediate between customary divisions between affects and cognition. For example, "a sense of familiarity" arises in the limbic system as a quasi-emotional marker of experience. Usually the limbic familiarity jibes with explicit recall, but it can appear discordantly, producing déjà vu or jamais vu experiences. We suggest that, similarly, limbic discharges may mark experiences as (1) depersonalized or derealized, (2) cru-cially important and self-referent, (3) harmonious -indicative of a connection or unity between disparate elements, and (4) ecstatic - profoundly joyous. This limbic activ-ity underlies certain psychic seizure auras, near-death experiences, and religious and mystical experiences of normal individuals [Saver and Rabin, Ibid., p. 204].

The two psychiatrists predict that researchers will soon be able to detect the presence of these abnormal temporolimbic perturbations as newer instruments capable of making more refined measurements of internal brain processes become available. But what can neuroscientists hope to accomplish while they're waiting for the advent of this new technology? And when those new instruments become available, where in the brain are the scientists most likely to find what they're looking for?

Information produced in the analysis of the structural and temporal characteristics of meditation-induced phosphenes can help neuroscientists plot a research strategy that maximizes the chances of making important new discoveries. The phosphene analysis presented in this book identifies the precise nature of the abnormal temporolimbic activity that Saver and Rabin predict will be identified once new technology becomes available—and the phosphene evidence is available now. The "reverse-engineering" of the meditation-induced phosphene images reveals that the final event in a predictable progression is the outbreak of a simple partial seizure of hippocampal (temporolimbic) origin accompanied by psychic symptoms that definitely qualify as "ecstatic," even under the most restrictive definition of that label. But what makes the phosphene analysis especially valuable is the insight it provides into *how events at the neurological level unfold as time elapses*: as the subject begins to meditate, the initial changes in brain wave patterns associated with a tranquil meditative state give way to brain wave patterns associated with an outbreak of abnormal discharges, then further changes in phosphene elements allow the spread of paroxysmal activity to be traced from thalamocortical circuits to the hippocampus and then through the subregions of the hippocampus and out into the adjacent mesotemporal cortices. These insights are otherwise unobtainable, given existing equipment, and they will almost certainly continue to be invaluable in the future, even after better equipment becomes available, for those researchers who design empirical studies of meditation.

The Sleep Rhythm Theory of Meditation

The theory I propose, based on my analysis of phosphene imagery, is that meditators learn how to manipulate the neural mechanisms that normally govern the transition from waking to slow wave sleep. In normal circumstances the activation of the synchronous sleep rhythms of "stage 2" non-rapid-eye-movement sleep (NREMS) would induce the familiar loss of consciousness that begins at sleep onset, but meditators can learn how to manipulate eye position and attentive focus so that they keep visual consciousness intact. As the synchronous sleep rhythms of stage 2 NREMS are relayed through the visual cortices (as would happen even if consciousness had been lost), the meditation-stimulated neurons in the primary visual cortices receive and process these signals as if they were afferent visual signals—and, as a result, the meditator sees a phosphene image.

When meditation is restricted to calm contemplation, the phosphene images are generated by synchronous sleep rhythms reverberating back and forth between the thalamus and the visual cortices, but meditators can learn to provoke a destabilization of sleep rhythm oscillators that triggers a sudden, discontinuous change in the kinds of phosphene images they see: instead of the "sleep rhythm" phosphenes, they see images that display a more forceful, "driven" quality and that are accompanied by paroxysmal sensorimotor symptoms. I trace this shift in phosphene imagery to the outbreak of hypersynchronous activity in corticothalamic circuits similar to what happens during absence seizures, but the incipient absence-like seizure does not generalize in this situation (probably because inhibitory mechanisms remain intact in the normal brain). What happens next is a build-up of rhythmical activity in the hippocampus driven by the hypersynchrony in corticothalamic circuits, and this build-up of rhythmical activity eventually triggers an outbreak of paroxysmal discharges that the phosphene evidence attributes to a specific and spatially-restricted region of the contralateral hippocampus. The analysis of phosphene imagery shows the evolution of these events, second-by-second, revealing where paroxysmal discharges begin inside the hippocampus and how they propagate from one intrahippocampal circuit to the next. The culminating event that underlies the ecstatic visions of lightning-like flashes, strange sensorimotor currents, and psychic symptoms of euphoria and ecstasy is a rare type of simple partial temporolimbic seizure of hippocampal origin.

If my theory is correct in explaining what takes place in the temporolimbic structures of the brain when meditators claim to have induced a "peak ecstasy," then one should be able to find evidence of a shift to paroxysmal activity in the published studies of advanced meditators. Does such evidence exist? I'm confident that it does, especially in the more recent EEG studies that generate topological maps of dominant brain wave frequencies—and the book contains a chapter dedicated to exploring this claim.

The possibility of a link between slow wave sleep and meditation has begun to attract the attention of neuroscientists. In a recent study of hypnotized subjects, Rainville et al. [2003] used PET scans in conjunction with a cortical EEG to compare the changes in cerebral activity measured by these different instruments. The researchers found significant increases in blood flow to the occipital cortices at a time when delta activity was prominent in the scalp EEG, "a pattern similar to the results obtained in slow wave sleep [Rainville et al., Ibid., p. 116]." Based on their findings, they propose "a state theory of hypnosis in which occipital increases in rCBF and delta activity reflect the alteration of consciousness associated with decreased arousal and possible facilitation of visual imagery [Ibid., p. 110]." This is the first PET study that I'm aware of which identifies slow wave sleep rhythms as potentially important in the generation of hypnotic trance states, but if my sleep rhythm activation theory is correct, this will be only the first of many.

Is There a "God Module" in the Brain?

A provocative question was posed to an audience of neurologists at the annual meeting of the Society for Neuroscience in New Orleans in 1997: V. S. Ramachandran suggested that humans may have "specialized neural circuitry for the sole purpose of mediating religious experience," a comment that led journalists who attended the meeting to report that neurologists were speculating about the existence of a "God module" [Bower, *Science News* 2001;159(97): 104 – 106]. The Ramachandran experiment that gave rise to this remark was a minor one: it was a demonstration that patients with temporal lobe epilepsy who listened to words with religious connotations had stronger galvanic skin responses than did normal volunteers [Ramachandran and Blakeslee, 1997]. The researchers were not in a position to identify the specific brain mechanisms involved based on their data.

My analysis of meditation-induced phosphenes suggests that there is a set of neural mechanisms that can occasionally function as a "god module," but the analysis reveals that these mechanisms, as they manifest in clear light visions, are not "specialized . . . for the sole purpose of mediating religious experience," as Ramachandran suggested, but rather these are the very same mechanisms that put humans to sleep at night. This insight demonstrates that the mundane can be transformed, temporarily, into a vehicle of transcendence—into a "god module."

2

LIGHT VISIONS IN INDIA, CHINA, AND TIBET

LIGHT VISION METAPHORS IN ASIAN TEXTS

Cross-Text Comparisons

The metaphors used to describe meditation-induced light visions in India, China, and Tibet are remarkably similar. In this chapter I'll give a brief overview of how light visions influenced the evolution of the Hindu, Buddhist, and Daoist religious traditions, and, to facilitate cross-text and cross-cultural comparisons, I'll present a number of charts that list the light vision metaphors used in each text. In the Indian tradition we'll examine texts that span 3,000 years of history, beginning with the Indo-Aryan *Rig Veda* (circa 1500 BCE), then moving on to the *Upanishads* (ca. 800-500 BCE), the *Yogasutras* (ca. 100-200 CE), and various Tantric texts (ca. 700-1400, CE). Descriptions of meditation-induced light visions can also be found in the autobiographies of modern Hindu mystics like Muktananda, Gopi Krishna, and Lahiri Mahasay, and I'll include excerpts from their works to demonstrate that contemporary meditators continue to see light visions similar to those recorded in the ancient texts.

In the Buddhist tradition I'll review the visionary experiences of the founder, Gotama Sakyamuni, a Hindu renunciate whose Awakening (*Buddha*) came when he was meditating in an all-night vigil: Gotama saw his familiar vision of "a limited light-manifestation" suddenly change into "a boundless light-manifestation" [*Majjhima-Nikaya* 128.III.161, in Gonda, 1963, p. 310]. I'll also describe how Buddhist ideas about light visions evolved in different directions after Gotama's death. In the Theravadan tradition of Southeast Asia, the first appearance of light visions is tolerated as a sign of meditative prowess—as the "beginner's attainment"—but from then on the meditator who wants to make further progress is counseled to disregard light visions as a seductive form of illusory reality that is likely to distract the seeker from the true path of Insight. As a representative of the Theravadan tradition, I'll include an excerpt from Buddhaghosa's *Visshuddhimagga*, an early Pali text written in Ceylon (ca. 400-500 CE) that provides very graphic descriptions of light visions at the same time it instructs meditators to ignore them. In the Mahayana tradition that evolved in Tibet, called *Vajrayana* Buddhism, the contrast with Theravadan practices could not be greater: in Tibet the cultivation of light visions is considered to be the most expeditious vehicle for attaining Enlightenment in a single lifetime and is reserved for monks who can demonstrate their mastery of less demanding techniques. To examine visionary experiences in the Vajrayana Buddhist tradition, I'll examine the metaphors used to describe meditation-induced light visions in Naropa's *The Epitome of the Six Yogas*, an anthology of meditation treatises on "Highest Yoga Tantra" (*maha-anuttara-yoga*).

The examples of light mysticism that I've cited above are all drawn from cultures that are closely related to one another; to demonstrate that similar descriptions of light visions can also be found in other cultures before they were subjected to influences from India or Tibet, I'll look at Daoist and pre-Daoist meditation texts written in early China from the 3rd Century, BCE, to the 4th Century, CE. The metaphors used to describe light visions in these early Chinese texts differences are dramatically different from those used in the Indo-Tibetan traditions, but it is clear from the characteristics shared by those different metaphors that they are intended to refer to a phenomenon that is essentially the same. The practice of inducing light visions reached its peak in China during the 3rd century, CE, when Daoist masters of the Shangqing "Highest Clarity" school wrote *The Book of the Yellow Court, The Upper Scripture of the Purple Texts Inscribed by the Spirits*, *The Book of Great Profundity*, and *Three Ways to Go Beyond the Heavenly Pass*.

Key excerpts of light vision descriptions from all of the Chinese and Indo-Tibetan texts I've identified in this preliminary overview are presented in a series of charts that that accompany the text and that employ a similar layout in order to facilitate cross-text comparisons. Readers who are already familiar with the historical evolution of light vision mysticism in India, China, and Tibet, or who are more interested in getting to the analysis of neurological mechanisms and thus want only the most expeditious survey of traditional light vision metaphors, may want to

Figure 1. A preliminary overview of the kinds of metaphors typically used to describe light visions in the ancient source texts from India, China, and Tibet and the sequences in which they are said to appear. The text metaphors are juxtaposed with my schematic drawings of light visions I've seen, images that will be examined in detail during the course of this investigation.

Overview of Light Vision Metaphors Used in Asian Texts

1
WHEELS, HALOS

EYE OF PEACOCK FEATHER

ORBED PHOSPHORS

2
FLAME-ARROWS

SMOKE, FOG

PURPLE HAZE

REVOLVING AURORAS

3
EYES

A BRIGHTER RING WITHIN

FIERY PEARLS INSIDE THE PURPLE ENERGY

4
FIREFLIES

DAZZLING SPARKS

THE FORM OF THE 10,000 THINGS

5
A CLOUDLESS SKY

AN INNER, CONSCIOUS DAWN

THE GREAT OCEAN OF ENERGIES

6
NIPPLE

SWOLLEN UDDER

POINT OF A GOAD

TURTLE'S HEAD

MOON

7
STREAMS

DAZZLING MESH SPREAD AFAR

SWAN

COBRA HEADS REARING UP

BEAMS OF LIGHT

8
LIGHTNING

OCEAN OF LIGHT

FIRE-BURSTS

BRIGHT, VASCILLATING RADIANCE

skip the exposition and simply study the charts. It is important, however, for readers to acquire some familiarity with the metaphors used to describe light visions in the traditional sources before moving into the image-specific neurological analyses. The historical material often differs from popularized accounts that are available in modern bookstores which are usually more prescriptive and metaphysical than the strictly empirically-oriented approach I've used in this book. Also, it's important for readers to appreciate that the descriptions of meditation-induced light visions I've presented in this book are not just my own idiosyncratic inventions, that they conform closely with the metaphors used to describe light visions in the ancient meditation guides and other source texts.

Readers who would like more detailed information—about the meanings of particular words or phrases, about individual mystics mentioned in passing, or about the historical evolution of light vision mysticism—should consider consulting articles I've published elsewhere that typically contain cross-cultural comparisons of light vision imagery [Nicholson, 2002a-d, 2003, 2006, 2009]. Some articles are available as PDF files that can be downloaded from the websites listed in my biographical sketch at the end of this book. It is also worth noting that I'm working on a less technical book for general audiences that explores how antecedent events in the lives of the world's most influential mystic seers prepare them for seeing visions and how the evolution of their ideas is shaped by the interaction of personality, neurology, and culture.

AN OVERVIEW OF VISIONARY EXPERIENCE IN INDIA

Empty-Mind Consciousness

Inexperienced meditators don't start out seeing light visions. First they have to learn how to control their mental processes to achieve a state of mind called *turiya* in Hindu India, *dhyana* in Buddhist countries. Here I'll refer to this state as "empty-mind consciousness" or "empty-mind meditation." Novice meditators are initially taught to relax while keeping their attention focused on their breathing or on some evocative external object (or a mental image of such an object)—on a flickering flame, for example, or the intricate patterns of mandala painting. The goal of this preliminary practice is to learn how to induce "one-pointed concentration." After meditators become proficient at one-pointed concentration, they are taught more advanced skills designed to help them shed the novice's reliance on mental imagery. The goal is to remain detached from the thoughts, images, and emotions that flow in and out of the untrained mind and threaten to distract the meditator's concentration. When meditators master this, they are able to enter into "empty-mind meditation," and it is in this state that meditators begin to see phosphene phenomena. The first meditation-induced light visions to appear are described as "wheels," "rings" or "halos." These threshold visions are said to be followed by an elaborate progression of light visions that eventually culminates in an ecstatic rapture and a vision of white light that looks like the sun or like flashes of lightning illuminating a stormcloud from within.

Indo-Aryan Roots: Mind-Bending in the Rig Veda

During migrations that took Indo-Aryan tribes from their ancestral home-lands in the steppes of southern Russia to the Indus Valley, migrations thought to have taken place between 1500 and 1200, BCE, poets in many different tribes were composing eulogies to the gods who granted them victories. These oral hymns were recited for centuries before they were compiled and rendered in written form to create the *Rig Veda* (RV), the world's oldest written scripture. In these hymns, eulogists celebrate the luminous visions which first appeared to their ancestors, visions which they now seek for themselves, visions of the *dhitayah*, the "lightnings and flame-arrows" of Agni, god of fire. The importance of these luminous visions is well-documented by the Dutch scholar, Jan Gonda, in his *Vision of the Vedic Poets* [1963], and it is worth taking some time to consider Gonda's analysis of Vedic hymns because they constitute the foundation on which all of the Indo-Tibetan traditions have been erected. The basic idea behind the *dhitayah*, the "lightnings and flame-arrows" of Agni, is that there can be a "breaking through of a stream of the great and fundamental power called *rta-*, of a sudden influx of sacredness, of an extraordinary insight into the reality beyond the phenomena of this world [Gonda, Ibid., p.172]." The *dhitayah* that "begin to glow spontaneously in a secret place" represent "a stream or 'fountain' of transcendental truth (*dhara rtasya*) [Gonda, 1963, pp. 172-3]." The source of these luminous visions is "beyond human reach, knowledge and understanding, and those who receive them may be said to glow or shine themselves," Gonda writes, citing RV 8.6.8: "When the visions which are concealed glow spontaneously, the *Kanvas* [seers] (begin to glow) by the stream of rta [Ibid., p. 172]." But the streams of rta do not intrude into consciousness unless a person learns how to summon them: ". . . the man to whom *dhitayah* come is not idle. It is on the contrary expressly stated that he must fashion them, give them a definite form. This activity is compared to the carpenter or cartwright [Gonda, Ibid., p. 184]." To obtain this vision, the celebrants must look inward and exert mental effort: "[T]he poets are said to make the god favourably disposed merely by means of their faculty of sight. The image used is that of the felly [i.e. wheel-rim] which is bent; they 'see' this felly with their inner 'eye' and thereby they bend it, i.e., they exert their influence upon the god (*nemim namanti caksasa*) [Gonda, Ibid., re RV 8.97.12, p. 33]."

The Vision of the Radiant Wheels

The first vision to appear is said to be a radiant "chariot," but the descriptions in many verses make it clear that this is a vision of "radiant wheels," which

16

is like a chariot in that it is a vehicle that can transport the viewer into the sky. The verse emphasize that this is not an ordinary chariot, because it is said to have *three* wheels (or, in some verses, *one* wheel), which would distinguish it from the two- or four-wheel chariots used in the Vedic era. Similarly, the hymns state that ". . . this three-wheeled car . . . traverses the firmament without horses, without reins [RV 4.36.1-2, Wilson, 1888]." The vision of radiant wheel-rims seem to "move away from the seer [Gonda, Ibid. p. 165, 168]," and in at least one verse the wheels are described as being green [i.e., "verdant," in RV 3.44.1-2, Wilson, Ibid.]. The vision of the Asvins' chariot wheels is preceded by a tell-tale buzzing that sounds like a fly or bee (*maksika*), so the priests are encouraged to listen for the buzzing as a sign that they are about to mount the chariot that will eventually lead them to an auspicious vision called Soma: "To you, O Asvins, that *maksika* betrayed the Soma [RV 1.119.9, Wilson].

The Vision of Swirling Smoke

The hymns of the *Rig Veda* contain many references to "flame-arrows" (*dhitayah*) sent by Agni, god of fire, which are "many-colored" [RV 10.91.5] and "smoke-like" [RV 1.27.11; 5.11.3; 7.2.1; 1.3.3]. These visions are said to arrive like water bubbling up from "a hole in the ground abounding in water from which one may draw the desirable liquid [RV 1.67.7; 3.10.5; Ibid., p. 172]," or, in another formulation, they are said to "assemble like the streams of water into holes [RV10.25.4; Ibid., p. 173]," a phrase that suggests the smoky light swirls around, shrinks in size, and then vanishes. The meditator who sees the threshold vision of the radiant light-wheels and the swirling flame-arrows will begin to encounter new visions that are said to be more auspicious—visions of Usas, the goddess of Dawn, and visions of Soma, god of the drink that makes men into gods, visions that are harbingers of the ultimate attainment, which is seeing Indra's lightning.

The Vision of Inner Dawn

Usas (or Ushas), the goddess of dawn, sends the seer a vision of a gradual brightening and bluing that resembles a natural dawn but lasts longer:

> Many are the days that have dawned before the rising of the sun, on which thou, Ushas, has been beheld like a wife repairing to an inconstant husband, and not like one deserting him. / Those ancient sages, our ancestors . . . discovered the hidden light, and, reciters of sincere prayers, they generated the Dawn [RV 7.76.2-3, Wilson].
>
> * * *
>
> [O]ur mortal forefathers departed after instituting the sacred rite, when, calling upon the dawn, they extricated the milk-yielding kine . . . / . . .when they found the light, and were thus enabled (to worship him) with holy ceremonies . . . / . . . then they glorified the conscious dawns, and the purple dawn appeared with the radiance of the sun. / The scattered darkness was destroyed; the firmament glowed with radiance; the lustre of the divine dawn arose . . . [RV 4.1.11-17, Wilson]

The celebrant who sees this vision of the inner dawn can expect that a vision of Soma is about to appear—and that the appearance of Soma is an auspicious sign that the culminating vision of Indra's lightning-bolt is not far behind.

The Bulbous Vision of Newborn *Soma*

This most auspicious of all visions is "newborn" *Soma*. The word "Soma" is ambiguous in that it can refer to three different things: to a type of plant (of a species still unknown) called soma that was used by the Indo-Aryans to make an exhilarating drink that made men feel like gods, or to the soma drink, or to a *vision* of the god, Soma, who is responsible for imbuing the soma plant and the soma drink with transforming properties [Nicholson, 2002a-c]. For present purposes, it is only the *vision* of Soma that will concern us, and this vision is invariably described by reference to metaphors that share a bulbous shape— "udders," "stalks (*amsu*)," "navels," "bull's horns," "penises," "waterskins," and "bolls of wool." The Soma vision is said to have a white color like milk or wool. Many verses also note that the bulbous Soma vision protrudes and then pulls back like a bull's horn being rubbed against a tree or like the head of a warrior raised furtively to catch a glimpse of an enemy and then quickly pulled back.

The Vision of Purified *Soma* Expressed in Streams

The peculiar back and forth movement of the pale, bulbous light vision of newborn Soma described above gives rise to another metaphor that often appears in the Vedic hymns—that the priestly seers who induce the vision use their minds like "fingers" to "express" milky fluid from the divine udder. When the seers "express" the Soma, it shoots out of the bulbous image as a "purified" liquid divided into thin white streams that look like jets of milk expressed from a cow's udder. The streams of white liquid are also described as having been forced through a "wooly filter." The milky streams of purified Soma shoot out "as rapid as thought [RV 9.100.3, Wilson]" and soar into the dark space of the mind like birds in flight, "spreading" apart as they rise to form "oblique angles." This verse contains a typical description of the purified Soma streams: "The filtre of the burning [Soma] has been spread in heaven's home. Its dazzling mesh was spread afar . . . They climb the back of the heaven in thought [RV 9.83.2, Bhawe, in Wasson, 1971, p. 54]." A number of verses mention that the purified Soma is first expressed in only *three* streams: "The fingers press the Soma, they squeeze it glittering like a water-skin; *its juice becomes three-fold* . . . [RV 9.1.8 Wilson]." When the purified Soma is fully expressed, it lowers itself like a bird "alighting" on the edge of a nest: "The Soma . . . purified, he passes through the sheep's fleece, to alight on the water-moistened seat like a hawk (on its nest)" [RV 9.82.1, Wilson]." In some verses the streams of purified Soma are described using a sexual metaphor—they are said to "penetrate" into the belly of the god, Indra, like an ejection of purified white semen:

Soma, being purified, alights on the vessels; putting his seed (in the vessels) as in a heifer . . . [RV 9.99.6, Wilson]

* * *

[P]ut the Soma juice into Indra [RV 9.11.5-6, Bhawe, in Wasson]

* * *

The penis, men, take the penis and move it and stick it in [RV 10.101.12, Doniger/ O'Flaherty, 1971]

The Vision of Indra's Lightning-Bolt

Indra, the god of storms, drinks in these rising Soma streams and is so exhilarated by the power of Soma that he manifests himself as a full-blown lightning storm that fills the mind of the seer with "firebursts" that "cloth the back of heaven like a spread-cloth" [RV9.71.9, Bhawe, in Wasson, p. 38]. This ecstatic vision is "bright-like-lightning" [RV 10.177.2, Gonda, Ibid., pp. 178-9], so bright that the seer becomes "sun-eyed (*svarcaksa*) [RV 9.97.46, Bhawe, in Wasson, p. 47]." The hymns chanted by the priestly seers beg the gods to give them this vision ("milk heaven and earth for us as lightning (milks) the clouds [RV 9.69.5, Bhawe, in Wasson, p. 40; RV 9.76.3, Wilson, Ibid.]"), and those who receive the vision feel that they've been transformed into gods themselves: "We have drunk the Soma; we have become immortal; we have gone to the light; we have found the gods [RV 8.48.3, Doniger/O'Flaherty]."

This account of light visions in the *Rig Veda*, the oldest of all sacred texts and the foundation on which Indo-Tibetan light mysticism is based, demonstrates that as early as 1500, BCE, the Indo-Aryan tribes were aware that meditation could trigger a predictable series of light visions and that this vision-sequence, if it reached its full culmination, would erupt in an ecstatic rapture that closely resembled a dramatic lightning storm. A summary of the light vision metaphors used in the *Rig Veda* appears in Figure 2.

Light Visions in the Upanishads

Between 800 to 500, BCE, hundreds of treatises were written to explain and embellish ideas that had been introduced in the *Rig Veda* and the other Vedic collections. Eventually ten treatises, called *Upanishads*, were recognized as being the most influential and important. In his translation of the ten Upanishads, Radhakrishnan [1992] points out that the Sanskrit word means "sitting down near,"

Figure 2. Metaphors used to describe meditation-induced light visions in the oral hymns of the Indo-Aryan *Rig Veda*, dated by scholars at about 1500, BCE. All excerpts cited here are from the English versions of the *Rig Veda* cited here by the initial of the last name of the translator: RV/B = translated by Bhawe as quoted in Wasson, 1971; RV/W = by Wilson, 1888; RV/G = by Griffin, 1889; RV/GN = by Gonda, 1963; RV/O = by O'Flaherty/Doniger.

Light Vision Metaphors in the Indo-Aryan *Rig Veda*

1

3 wheels form a radiant "chariot" with no horses that moves away from the viewer [RV/W: 4.36.1-2; Vala 10.3; RV/G: 8.22.4 & 10.85.16]

The rims of these wheels are bent by the mind [RV/GN: 7.34.1]

These radiant wheels are "verdant" [green] [RV/W 3.44.1-2]

2

Agni's "flame-arrows" look like smoke or like water pouring into holes and they have many colors [RV/GN: 1.27.11, 5.11.3, 1.67.7, 3.10.5, 10.25.4]

3

4

5

Many are the days that dawned before the rising of the sun . . . our ancestors discovered the hidden light and created the Dawn [RV/W: 7.76.2]

They glorified the conscious dawns . . . and the purple dawn appeared [RV/W: 4.1.11-17]

6

The vision of newborn Soma looks like an udder swollen with milk, or, as in other verses, like a navel, a waterskin, a boll of white wool, a bull's horn, a phallus . . . [RV/W: 9.70.7, 9.87.7, 9.1.8; RV/GN: 10.64.12; RV/B: 9.79.4, 9.74.4, 9.12.4, 9.86.3]

7

In jets, the pressed Soma is clarified [RV/B: 9.72.5]

Its juice becomes three-fold [RV/W: 9.1.8]

The filtre of the burning has spread...Its dazzling mesh afar . . . [RV/B: 9.32.2]

The Soma...passes through the sheep's fleece & then alights like a hawk (on a nest) [RV/W: 9.82.1]

8

This inspired thought which is bright-like-lightning, a *dhih* [vision] of the light of heaven and the seat of *rta* [RV/GN 10.177.2]

Soma...milk heaven and earth for us as lightning (milks) the clouds [RV/W: 9.76.3]

He has clothed himself in the fire-bursts of the sun [RV/B: 9.71.9] which suggests these works were probably written by teachers who instructed small groups of disciples [pp. 19-20], so it is not surprising that some of the verses refer to practicing meditation. Meditators who want to experience the primordial radiance of Brahman that undergirds all phenomenal reality are advised to find a place that's clean, level, and hidden from view, where they can practice holding their bodies erect and orienting their attention inward on the correct method of breathing [e.g., *Svetasvatara Upanishad*, 2: 2, 10; Radhakrishnan, Ibid., p. 721]. By exercising self-discipline and concentration, meditators enter into a "fourth" state of consciousness called *turiya* said to exist somewhere beyond the familiar states of waking, sleeping, and dreaming:

> "[Turiya] is not cognitive, not non-cognitive. Unseen, incapable of being spoken of, ungraspable, without any distinctive marks, unthinkable, unnameable, . . . the non-dual, such, they think, is the fourth quarter [*Mandukya Upanishad*, 7; Ibid., p. 698; also see verse 12, p. 701].

Upon entering turiya, yogis are told they will see the "Brahma-light" begin to flow spontaneously, manifesting first as "tranquil" lights but then in the end as an "abounding" light [*Maitri Upanishad*, 6: 36; Ibid., p. 849]." Brahman is the source of this "bright power that has its place in the heart that casts forth light . . . [that looks like] smoke rises to the sky in one column and follows afterwards one branch after another [*Maitri Upanishad*, 7: 11, Ibid., p. 858]."

The verses of the *Upanishads* provide only cursory descriptions of light images: "Fog, smoke, sun, wind, fire, fireflies, lightning, crystal moon, these are the preliminary forms [*Svetasvatara Upanishad*, 2: 11, Ibid., p. 721]." Another verse describes a light that looks like a "lotus" blossom with small, dark space at its center and advises the meditator to concentrate on that inner core [*Chandogya Upanishad* 8: 1, 1.; Ibid., p. 491].

The light vision mentioned most frequently is described by metaphors which all share a bulbous shape—manifesting as a "nipple [*Taittiriya Upanishad*, 1: 6.1; Ibid., p. 533]," as a "flame without smoke" which is about "the size of a thumb [*Katha Upanishad* 2: 1, 13 & 3, 17; Ibid., pp. 634-5 & 647]," or as a light which has the size and shape "of the point of a goad [*Svetasvatara Upanishad*, 5: 9; Ibid., p. 740]." This bulb-shaped light is called the *atman* or *purusha*, which means the inner "self" or "person" that "dwells in the heart of man." The basic idea of the atman/purusha that a fragment of light is split off from the primordial

---

Figure 3. **The metaphors used to describe the paradigm sequence of meditation-induced light visions in a collection of commentaries on the Vedas called the *Upanishads*, which scholars date to about 1000, BCE. The excerpts listed here are from a translation by Radhakrishnan [1992]. The specific texts contained within the larger collection are identified here by the following abbreviations: the *Brhadaranyaka Upanisad* (BU); *Chandogya U* (CU); *Katha U* (KU); *Taittiriya Upanishad* (TU); *Svetasvatara U* (SV); and the *Maitri U* (MU).**

Light Visions Metaphors in *The Upanishads*

1 The nature of the ether within the space (of the heart) is the same as the supreme bright power. . . . In the breathing, that (bright power) has its place in the heart that casts forth light.　　　　[MU 7:11]

2 Fog, smoke . . . are [among] the preliminary forms which produce the manifestation of *Brahman* in Yoga　　　[SU II:11]

In inner space the bright power sends light that looks like smoke, like bubbles rising in heated butter, and that dissolves like salt in water
[MU: 7:11]

3 One sees a small lotus flower; within it is a small space. What is within should be sought, for that, assuredly, is what one should desire to understand
[CU: 8:1:1]

4 Fireflies . . . are [among] the preliminary forms which produce the manifestation of *Brahman* in Yoga　　　[SU II:11]

5

6 This is the space that is within the heart: therein in the Person consisting of mind, immortal and resplendent. That which hangs down between the palates like a nipple
[TU: 1: 6.1]

The person the size of a thumb resides in the middle of the body, like a flame without smoke
[KU: 2: 1, 13]

He is of the measure of a thumb, of appearance like the sun, . . . And the self he seems to be the size of a point of a goad
[SU: 5: 9]

The form of this person is . . . like white wool
[BrU: 2: 3, 6]

7 The form of this person is . . . like a white lotus [blossoming]
[BrU: II: 3,6]

The [Brahma-Light] is a bird of golden hue, a diver-bird, a swan of surpassing radiance
[MU: 6:34]

8 *Brahman* who sparkles like a wheel of fire
[MU: 6:24]

Why is it said to be lightning? Because it lights up the whole body
[MU 7:11]

That which is the sunhood of the sun is the Eternal Real, the prevader. That is the bright . . . Of the bright power that pervades the sky, it is only a portion, which is, as it were, in the midst of the sun, the eye [*cakus*], and in the fire. That is *Brahman*. That is immortal, that is splendor. . . . That is the ocean of light. In it, indeed, the worshippers become dissolved like salt. . . . It is the oneness with *Brahman* for in it are all desires contained.　　　[MU: 6:35] radiance of Brahman, the original "Self" of the Cosmos, and hidden "in the heart" of every human. This splinter of light yearns to be reunited with its original source. When meditators enter turiya and eventually begin to see the vision of this splinter of light—their inner self, the atman—they are well on the way to reuniting the light of the atman with the "abounding" Brahma-light, and in so doing they help restore, albeit temporarily, the primal unity that is the True Reality of the cosmos.

The *Upanishads* report that when this "abounding" Brahma-light arrives, it looks like lightning ("why is it said to be lightning? Because in the very moment of going forth it lights up the whole body [*Maitri Upanishad* 7: 11; Radhakrishnan, Ibid., p. 858]"), and the vision of lightning as the atman merges with Brahman is said to be the "Realization of the Self." For a human being, this rapture is the ultimate attainment:

> That is *Brahman*, that is immortal, that is splendor. . . . That is the ocean of light . . . the worshippers becomes dissolved like (a lump of) salt. . . . He who knows this is the knower, . . . having grasped the oneness, he becomes identified with it. It is the oneness with *Brahman* for in it are all desires contained [*Maitri Upanishad* II: 35, Radhakrishnan, Ibid., p. 847].

Light Visions in Patañjali's Yogasutras

The first practical guide for meditators was a collection of verses attributed to an author named Patañjali who is thought to have written his *Yogasutras* during the lst or 2nd century, CE, midway between the compilation of the *Upanishads* (800 - 500, BCE) and the Hindu Tantras (ca. 700-1400, CE) [Kinsley, 1993]. The verses of Patañjali's *Yogasutras* are aphoristic in style and so succinct that they are rendered inherently ambiguous. The meanings of many verses, especially verses in the final chapter on *Kaivalpa* ("Aloneness") which describes the experiences that lead up to the eruption of the Brahma-light, can be parsed in many different ways, even when commentators agree on the literal translations of the Sanskrit words. Because of this inherent ambiguity, there are many extant translations and commentaries that claim to provide an authoritative interpretation of Patañjali's *Yogasutras*; unfortunately, the translations and commentaries that I've read in English translation all share a common failing: while they present intelligible versions of the verses in the first three chapters, verses dealing with lifestyle changes and how to achieve one-pointed meditation, upon arriving at the final chapter on *Kaivalpa* these translations all fail in the same way—they suddenly shift from a practical, experiential perspective to recitations of conventional Hindu metaphysics, which is to say, they give up trying to describe the experience itself and instead present their interpretation of what it *means* to have that experience. In particular, the extant translations do not make sense of the words that clearly refer to *visual* discriminations. To provide an alternative, "experience-near" translation that preserves the meanings of the individual Sanskrit words, making references to visual phenomena explicit and consistent with what is described in the Hindu texts that preceded the *Yogasutras*—the *Rig Veda* and the *Upanishad* commentaries which would have served as the models for Patañjali's own meditation practice—I studied a literal word-by-word translation of each verse in the *Yogasutras* by Feuerstein [1989]. Drawing on that source, I composed my own "experience-near" translation of the verses that describe the advent of *Kaivalpa*:

4.22. Seer and seen merge in the colored light.

4.23. Those countless speckles that strike—they have a purpose.

4.24. Once the flux ends, the *atman* comes.

4.25. That bending image (*nimnam*)—behind it lies *Kaivalpa*.

4.26. That cut (*chidescu*)—from it yet more forms arise.

4.27. All of these forms cease.

4.28. For one wholly free of desires, consciousness is filled by the Raincloud of Cosmic Truth (*dharma-megha-samadhi*).

The metaphor of a raincloud evokes an image that would be familiar to anyone who lives on the Indian subcontinent—the image of dark, towering nimbocummulus clouds arriving in the afternoon during the monsoon season and moving overhead as sheet lightning reverberates within the dark billows. This new, alternative translation of which reveals the explicit references to visual images brings the *Yogasutras* in line with the other important texts of the Indo-Tibetan yoga meditation tradition, as shown in Figure 4.

Light Visions in the Indian Tantras

During the 7th century, CE, the traditional Vedic religion of India with its emphasis on caste duties and priestly rituals began to be transformed from within by new ideas and new practices which are now regarded as integral aspects of Hinduism. There were many new religious movements: sects that emphasized devotional worship (*bhakti*) over the old formulaic rituals; sects dedicated to single gods such as Shiva or Vishnu who had played only minor roles in the original Vedas; schools of philosophical speculation that created elaborate metaphysical systems based on ideas inspired by the original Vedas; and teachers of the *Tantras* ("Looms") who proclaimed a radically new doctrine—that every man and woman, not just those who belonged to one of the three "twice-born" castes of the traditional Hindu hierarchy, could achieve Self-Realization within a single lifetime if they practiced certain rituals and chants which were said to have magical efficacy [Kinsley, 1993, pp. 11-21].

Light Vision Metaphors in Patanjali's *Yogasutras*

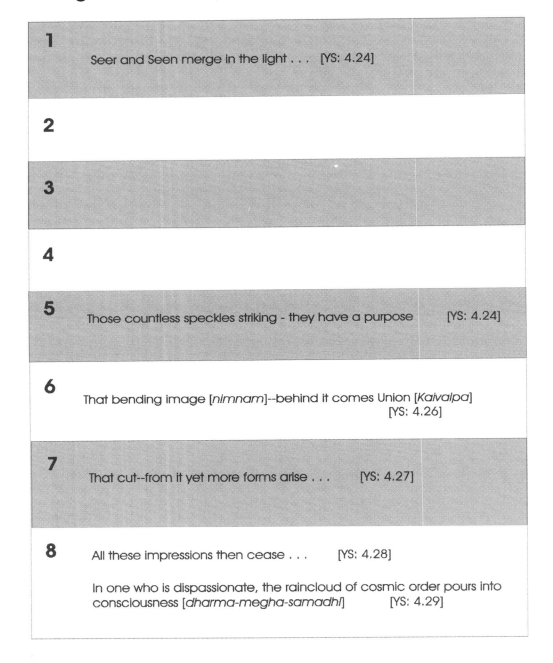

1

    Seer and Seen merge in the light . . .   [YS: 4.24]

2

3

4

5

    Those countless speckles striking - they have a purpose   [YS: 4.24]

6

    That bending image [*nimnam*]--behind it comes Union [*Kaivalpa*]
                [YS: 4.26]

7

    That cut--from it yet more forms arise . . .   [YS: 4.27]

8

    All these impressions then cease . . .   [YS: 4.28]

    In one who is dispassionate, the raincloud of cosmic order pours into
    consciousness [*dharma-megha-samadhi*]   [YS: 4.29]

Figure 4. List of metaphors used to describe light visions in the *Kaivalpa* chapter of Patañjali's *Yogasutras*, dated by scholars to about the 1st or 2nd Century, CE.

The Tantric teachers wrote yoga meditation treatises with vivid descriptions of meditation-induced light visions. To explain why light visions appear in a predictable sequence, the Tantrists elaborated the traditional Vedic concept of the atman—the concept that a tiny portion of Brahman's radiant energy is split off from its source in the Self and hidden in the human body, not in the physical body but rather as part of a "subtle" or spiritualized nervous system that infuses and surrounds the physical body. The spiritualized energy is called *kundalini* because it rests in latent form in a reservoir (*kunda*) aligned with the lower trunk and the genital system. When meditators enter the fourth state of consciousness called *turiya*, they can begin to stir and agitate the kundalini energy, causing it to flow up through a network of nerve-like conduits (*nadis*). If meditators achieve their goal, the kundalini energy rises to the crown of the head where all the streams converge to generate a bulbous light vision called the *Brahmarandhra*, which can be translated as either the "Egg" or "Aperture" of Brahman (or, as I prefer, as the "Egg/Aperture of Brahman," since it looks like an egg and serves the function of releasing the kundalini so that it can reunite with Brahman). The *Brahmarandhra* is a Tantric reworking of the tradition concepts of a light within—of the "newborn Soma" in the *Rig Veda* and the atman/purusha in the *Upanishads*. As the kundalini energy rises, it encounters a series of gates or "energy centers" that can be "opened" by a skilled meditator. When these energy centers open, they emit a light said to have a certain specific color. The Tantrists call these light visions and the subtle energy centers that emit light by the same name—*cakras,* which means "wheels" and which also implies an association with the inner "eye" of humans (*caksus*), the faculty that allows humans to see the divine light of the cosmos.

The Tantric writers are much more explicit than their predecessors about the kinds of light visions that meditators can expect to see as they make progress toward Self-Realization. In this analysis I'll examine light vision metaphors used in three Tantric treatises—Abhinavagupta's *Tantraloka*, Goraksanatha's *Amaraughasasana*, and Ksemaraja's *Shivasutravimarshini*, all available in an English translation of research published by Silburn [1988]. The descriptions of the earliest light visions are merely cursory in these texts, presumably because the authors assume that aspirants will be studying under the tutelage of a guru who has already introduced them to the initial steps in the raising of kundalini. In the *Tantraloka* treatise, Abhinavagupta states that the kundalini energy will first manifest in the energy center of the heart (*hrdaya-cakra*) as a green light [Silburn, Ibid., p. 28], then appears next in the brow-cakra (*bhrumadkya*). In Goraksanatha's *Amaraughasasana*, these first visions are said to look like "fiery effulgences" and like "the tapering flame of a candle" hanging in the middle of the vault of the palate [p. 10-11; Silburn, Ibid., p. 128]." When the kundalini shines in the brow-cakra, there is a second type of light that glows within the greater light, which is "cognitive energy subtler than the hundredth part of the tip of a hair." Goraksanatha warns the meditator that once this "cognitive energy" in the brow-cakra is concentrated into its most intense and purified form—into a tiny, shimmering star or dot (*bindu*)—there will be an explosion that sends shattered flecks of light in all directions, and then these flecks of light become transformed into yet another vision which manifests as a white, bulb-shaped light: "When the *bindu* explodes and shatters, it expands immediately and forms the *mastaka* (that is, the *brahmarandhra*), similar to the triangular fruit of the water-chestnut [*Amaraughasasana*, p. 10-11; Silburn, Ibid., p. 128]." Another Tantric writer, Ksemardaja, describes an experience which would seem to have similar explosive qualities: there comes a time, he writes, when there is a "churning" and a "continuous whirling movement until there appear dazzling sparks . . . . [*Shivasutra*, 3: 3; Silburn, op. cit., p. 42-43]."

Many different metaphors are used by the Tantric writers to describe the bulbous image that follows the vision of exploding sparks: Abhinavagupta describes it as looking like a "uvula," like "the stomach of a fish," or like a sexual congress of the gods in which the meditator sees a linga (penis) that protrudes and withdraws (lit., "unfolding and retracting") [*Tantraloka*, 5: 54-58; Silburn, Ibid., pp. 56 - 57]." Abhinavagupta calls this protrusion of the bulbous linga-vision the "consummation of the flow of virile capacity (*virya*) and of Kundalini's ascent [*Tantraloka* 3: 68-69, 137-141; Silburn, Ibid., p. 21]." Goraksanatha also relies on sexual metaphors to describe this light vision with a bulbous shape: he calls it a "supreme *linga*" (penis), a "*lampika*" (uvula), a "*gharba*" (womb), and a "*rajadanta*" (ivory tusk) [*Amaraughasasana*, p. 10; in Silburn, Ibid., p. 126]. And all of these authors refer to the vision of the *Brahmarandhra*, which connotes a bulbous, white image. The vision of the *Brahmarandhra* is the highest of the subtle energy centers, and, as such, it presents the final barrier that meditators must penetrate if they are to free the kundalini energy within so that it can merge with the primordial radiance of Brahman. Abhinavagupta calls this penultimate task the "Serpent-piercing" because when it happens a meditator sees the *Brahmarandhra* disappear and, in its place, there is a vision that looks like a "five-hooded cobra" rearing into view. This is not the vision of the "Supreme Emission" but rather the "supreme-non-supreme emission." It manifests as a "Triple Emission," as three streams of light "spreading through the movement of the point (bindu)" [*Tantraloka*, 3: 141; Silburn, Ibid., pp. 20-21]," and these three streams of light form a "trident" (*trisula*). Abhinavagupta says that the trident image undergoes a duplication and its duplication then rotates to form the image of a six-pointed star, the *satkona* [Silburn, Ibid., pp. 31-33, 131-2]. Then the "supreme-non-supreme emission" gives way to the "Supreme Emission," and the seer is enveloped in lightning:

> This supreme energy blossoming into bliss is *adorned like a five-hooded cobra* as she rises from the inferior to the superior center. Thus her five-fold aspects are witnessed . . . . / When this energy endowed with five modalities draws herself up from the *brahman's* (lower) seat and enters the *brahman's* (higher) seat, *she flashes forth like lightning* in the former and then dissolves into the latter. Having thus penetrated, let her pierce the body, let her discover the Self. Such is the so-called

serpent piercing, as described in the *Bhairavagama* [*Tantraloka*, 29: 248-251; in Silburn, Ibid., p. 97; emphasis added].

When the meditator is caught up in this blissful vision of the Brahma-light, an observer can see external signs of the internal ecstasy: these signs include an "attitude of surprise" (*cakitamudra*) in which the mouth drops half-open, the eyes stay half-shut, and the breathing stops [Silburn, Ibid., p. 74], plus there are quivering nostrils [p. 53], shaking legs [p. 53n], and a piloerection of hair on the surface of the skin (*pipilaka*) [p. 66]. And there are other signs which are only experienced by the meditator and cannot be detected by an onlooker: there are orgasmic spasms of the muscles at the base of the meditator's penis [pp. 57-58], buzzing sounds [p. 75, 96], and a sensation called *ghurni* which means a "mystical whirling" or a sensation of "dizziness or reeling" [Silburn, Ibid., pp. 59, 74].

There are some interesting autobiographical accounts of seeing kundalini light visions by religious mystics living in the modern era. These descriptions show the continuing vitality of the ancient Tantric meditation practices we've just discussed. Table 1 lists excerpts from a diary written by Shyama Charan Lahiri Mahasay, a clerk in the Bengali Military Engineering Service who lived from 1828 to 1895. Mahasay practiced meditation every morning just before dawn for many years until in 1961, at the age of 89, he reported having attained the ecstatic rapture and sun-like visions that constitute Realization of the (Cosmic) Self in the Hindu mystical tradition [Satyeswarananda Giri, 1991]. Table 2 contains descriptions from the autobiography of Swami Muktananda [1978]: born in Mangalore in 1908, he chose to become a wanderer at the age of 15. It was not until 1947, at the age of 39, that he sought and received initiation into the Siddha mystical tradition. The guru who administered the initiation, a Swami Nityananda, advised Muktananda to retire to an isolated hut where he could practice meditation for long hours, day and night, without being disturbed. After nine years of rigorous meditation practice, Muktananda attained a blissful, paroxysmal vision of the Cosmic Self. After developing a prosperous ashram in India, he emigrated to the United States, recruited disciples, and formed a large organization known as SIDDHA. He died in 1982. Table 3 contains excerpts from the autobiography of Gopi Krishna, born in 1903, who was a 40-year-old Kashmiri clerk working for the Directory of Education when he inadvertently triggered a visionary experience that was exciting and awesome but also unexpected, overwhelming and deeply disorienting. He was accustomed to meditating every night just before dawn, and it was during one of these pre-dawn meditations that he was surprised to be overtaken by the ecstatic vision [Krishna, 1971; also see White, 1988]. Among New Age mystics, Gopi Krishna's experiences are considered to be examples of a "spontaneous rising of kundalini," described as a rare and dangerously destabilizing phenomenon which only occurs when the ecstatic vision of rising kundalini erupts in someone who has not previously submitted to the care, tutelage and protection of a traditional guru. Krishna's autobiography is also notable, first, for his attempts to give empirically

Light Vision Metaphors in Tantric Yoga Meditation Treatises

1	Like the tapering flame of a candle, the fiery effulgence shines [AM, Silburn, 1988, p.128]	The heart bindu [colored green] is seen first . . . [TL, Silburn, p.28]
2	The fifth center, bhrumadhya, is between the eyebrows [Silburn, p. 28]	
3	In bhru . . . rests a cognitive energy subtler than the 100th part of a tip of a hair. Above this [i.e. After this] . . . dwells the dot, *bindu* [AM, Silburn, p. 129]	
4	When the *bindu* explodes, it immediately expands . . . [AM, Silburn, p.128]	The churning...must be performed with whirling force until there appears the dazzling sparks [SS: II:3, Silburn, p.42]
5		
6	The Egg-of-Brahma looks like a uvula, a womb, an ivory tusk, a linga (penis), or like the stomach of a fish . . . [TL: 5: 54-58, Silburn, p. 56-57; AM, Ibid., p.126]	When the bindu explodes, it immediately expands to form the mastaka...[that looks like] the water chestnut [AM: Silburn, p. 128]
7	From the [bulbous] navel arises a trident (trisula), whose points . . . reach a cosmic *dvadasanta* [TL: 15, in Silburn, p. 82]	Supreme energy blossoms . . . like a five-hooded cobra as she rises . . . [TL: 29: 248, in Silburn, p. 97] The swan of dazzling whiteness [appears]. . . [AM: 136, in Silburn, p.146]
8	When this [cobra] energy rises . . . she flashes forth like lightning. . . . Having thus penetrated, let her pierce the body, let her discover the Self. [TL: 3: 248-52, Silburn, p. 97]	An eminent splendor...brighter than the sun and the moon.../...a 1,000-spoked wheel, the *sahasrara* [TL: 4:132, Silburn, p.144]

Lahiri Mahasay (c. 1828 - 1895)

To practice pranayam at 4 o'clock in the morning is good
[Satyeswarananda, 1991, p. 93]

When the air of breath is held tranquil, the six centers are seen in bright Light but it does not stop at the centers   (p. 108)

OM is radiant Light. . . . spread throughout the body [Ibid., p. 208]

I saw a blue color in the light; in the blue, I saw a white spot; and in the white spot, I saw a man . . .   (p. 211)

Beyond the five senses there is mind . . . ; beyond the mind there is buddhi, that is bindu, or spot; beyond the bindu, Brahma (p. 212)

It seems there is another uvula above the uvula   (p. 99)

First the dazzling sign or penis (Jyotir Lingam) is seen, then it disappears into Voidness or Silence. . . . [Author's Note: This line of text is illustrated by a reproduction of Mahasay's hand-drawn sketch of a thumb-like shape, p. 108]

The sun is the form of OM   (p.111)

I am Mahapursusa. In the sun I saw that I myself am Brahma, the ultimate Self   (p. 210)

Table 1 (this page). Excerpts from the diary of Shyama Charan Lahiri Mahasay (ca. 1828 - 1895) describing some of his visionary experiences at age 89 [Satyeswarananda Giri, 1991].

Figure 5 (opposite page). The metaphors used to describe meditation-induced light visions in several Tantric texts that were written between 700 and 1400, CE, including Abhinavagupta's *Tantraloka* (TL), Goraksanatha's *Amaraughasanana* (AM), and Ksemaraja's *Shivasutravimarshini* (SS). All of the excerpts used here are from Lillian Silburn's *Kundalini: Energy of the Depths* [1988], translated into English by Jacques Gontier.

Swami Muktananda (1908 - 1982)

[T]he pupils of both my eyes became centered together. I began to see one thing with two eyes. . . . After this happened, a blue light arose in my eyes [Muktananda, 1978, p. 125].

[A] light came in meditation, like a candle flame without a wick, and stood motionless in the ajna chakra, the two-petaled lotus between the eyebrows [Ibid., p. 128].

The blue akasha, an expansion of blue color, began to appear, and with it, the neela bindu, the Pearl of infinite power. As I watched it, I felt as if my eyes were going to burst. . . . The blue light came and went, came and went [Ibid., p. 135]

It was not the Blue Light or the Blue Pearl, but a blue star. Though it looked small, it was large enough to contain me . . . [Ibid., p. 149]

As I sat, the blue star appeared, and for some reason I felt compelled to go and sit in it. . . . [and] the star at once took me back at immense speed to the place where I was meditating and exploded. Its fragments spread throughout the vast spaces of the sahasrara. There was no star in front of me now, but just an ambrosial white light [Ibid., p. 150]

Sometimes . . . an egg-shaped ball of radiance would come into view. This is the vision of the radiant thumb-sized Being, who is described as follows in the Shvetashvatara Upanishad: . . . "The inner soul always dwells in the heart of all men as a thumb-sized being" [Ibid., p. 136]

The wonderfully radiant Blue Pearl . . . came closer to me and began to grow. It assumed the shape of an egg . . . .[Ibid., pp. 169-170]

I have already described the Sphere of Unmanifest Light found in the *sahasrara*. One day it opened up and its light was released, and the brilliance of not one or two thousand but millions of suns blazed all around. . . . .That brilliance had drawn me toward itself, and as I gazed at it, I lost consciousness. . . . As I fell, I urinated involuntarily, . . . / I lay in this unknown state of consciousness for about an hour or an hour and a half, and then, as a man rises from sleep, I got up and laughed to myself, saying "I just died, but now I'm alive again." I got up feeling very much at peace, very happy and very full of love. . . . I realized that death is nothing but this condition. Once I had seen that Sphere of unmanifest Light I lost all fear. This is the state of liberation from individual existence [Ibid., p. 175-6]

Table 2. Excerpts from the autobiography of Muktananda (1908 - 1982) describing his visionary experiences at the age of 48 [Muktananda, 1978].

Gopi Krishna (1903-1984)

I sat breathing slowly and rhythmically, my attention drawn towards the crown of my head, contemplating an imaginary lotus in full bloom, radiating light [Krishna, 1971, p. 11]

Whenever I closed my eyes I found myself looking into a weird circle of light, in which luminous currents swirled and eddied, moving rapidly from side to side (p. 49)

I tossed restlessly from side to side without being able for hours to bring my agitated mind to the degree of composure needed to bring sleep. . . . I found myself staring fearfully into a vast internal glow, . . . always in rapid motion as if the particles of the ethereal luminous stuff crossed and recrossed each other, resembling the ceaseless movement of wildly leaping lustrous clouds of spray rising from a waterfall which, lighted by the sun, rushes down foaming into a seething pool (p. 49)

I never practiced yoga by Tantric methods. . . . If I had done so with a firm belief in the existence of the lotuses, I might well have mistaken the luminous formations and the glowing discs of light at the various nerve junctions along the spinal cord for lotuses, and . . . might even have been led to perceive the letters and the presiding deities . . . suggested by the pictures already present in my mind (p. 174)

Sometimes it seemed as if a jet of molten copper . . . dashed against my crown and fell in a scintillating shower of vast dimensions all around me. . . . Occasionally it resembled a fireworks display of great magnitude. As far as I could look inwardly with my mental eye, I saw only a brilliant shower or a glowing pool of light (p. 50)

When completely immersed, I again experienced the sensation [at the base of the spine], . . . the sensation again extended upwards, growing in intensity, . . . with great effort I kept my attention centered around the lotus. Suddenly, with a roar like a waterfall, I felt a stream of liquid light entering my brain. . . /. . . The illumination grew brighter, the roaring louder, I experienced a rocking sensation and then felt myself slipping out of my body, entirely enveloped in a halo of light. . . . I felt the point of consciousness that was myself growing wider, surrounded by waves of light . . . . I was now all consciousness, . . . immersed in a sea of light (pp. 12-13)

Table 3. Excerpts from the autobiography of Gopi Krishna (1903 - 1984) describing a "spontaneous rising of kundalini" that occurred when he was meditating just before dawn at the age of 40 [Krishna, 1971; see also White, 1988].

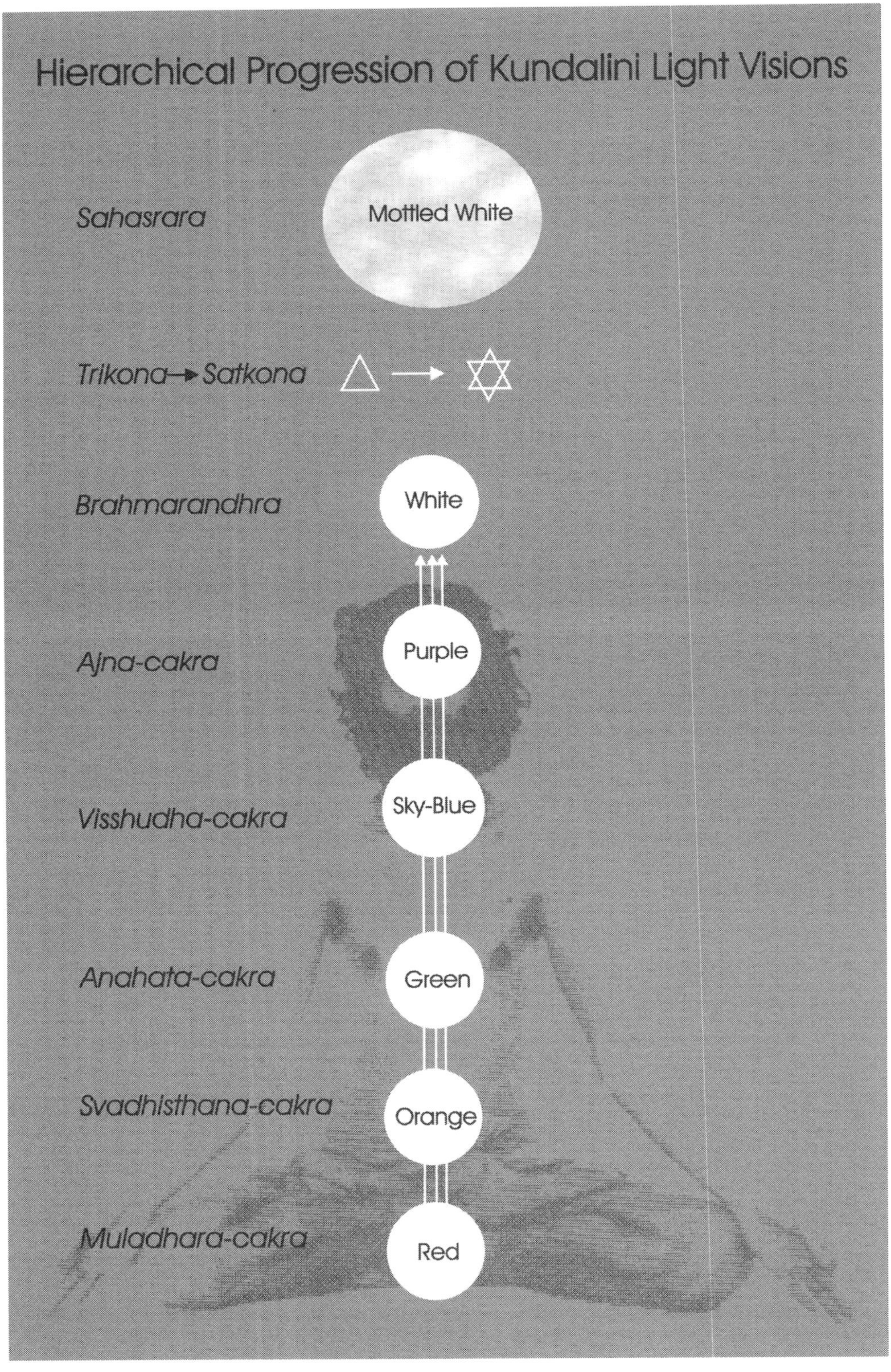

Hierarchical Progression of Kundalini Light Visions

Sahasrara — Mottled White

Trikona → Satkona — △ → ✡

Brahmarandhra — White

Ajna-cakra — Purple

Visshudha-cakra — Sky-Blue

Anahata-cakra — Green

Svadhisthana-cakra — Orange

Muladhara-cakra — Red

oriented descriptions of what he actually saw, and, second, his disappointment that, despite a dedicated search, he could not find any guru or siddha in India who was able to provide any insights about his experience. Krishna, who spent much of his later life trying to publicize the idea that kundalini was a type of evolutionary energy that could change and benefit humankind, died in 1984.

The sequences of meditation-induced light visions described in the ancient Tantric texts we've examined here—Abhinavagupta's *Tantraloka*, Goraksanatha's *Amaraughasanana*, and Ksemaraja's *Shivasutravimarshini*—differ in important respects from contemporary popularizations of kundalini yoga and its associated cakras. These popularizations also differ from important Tantric texts that are fundamental to meditation practice in Tibetan Buddhism, for example, Naropa's *Epitome of the Six Yogas* which we'll examine in this chapter. The contemporary popularizations add several new light visions to the older list and also describe the light visions as appearing in a different serial order. Figure 6 illustrates the hierarchical progression of cakras and their associated light visions as described in most contemporary books on the subject. Instead of a progression that begins with green lights or green-colored light-rings, this contemporary account specifies that the first light vision will be red, the next orange, and then comes the green light. Continuing

Figure 6. Schematic drawing of the conventional Tantric concept of kundalini as popularized in modern Hindu, Buddhist, and New Age texts. The basic idea is that a type of "subtle" or spiritualized energy called *kundalini* is stored in all human bodies in a "subtle" reservoir (*kunda*) associated with the base of the trunk, i.e., the perineal region. A meditator can learn to activate the kundalini energy which causes it to begin rising up through a channel of three "subtle" nerves (*nadis*), represented here by the three straight vertical lines. Once the kundalini energy begins to rise through the *nadis*, it encounters a heirarchical series of "subtle energy centers," each of which must be activated before the kundalini can rise any further. These subtle energy centers are called *cakras*, a Sanskrit word that means "wheels." Each cakra emanates a "subtle" or spiritualized light that is said to have certain characteristics that distinguish it from the lights of other cakras—for example, each cakra is associated with light of a distinctive color. This drawing depicts the sequence of colors in the cakra hierarchy as envisioned by contemporary popularizations of the kundalini concept. When a meditator sees the tell-tale light begin to shine, this signals that the cakra involved no longer interposes a barrier to the further rise of the kundalini energy. Eventually the energy ascends to a point in the crown of the head where the three subtle nerves are said to converge to produce a psychic protrusion called the *brahmarandhra*, which means the"egg" or "aperture" or "egg/aperture" of Brahman. When the meditator's concentration "pierces" this egg/aperture, the "Divine Eye opens" and consciousness is filled by a vision of the *sahasrara* ("the lotus of thousand petals" or "the Abounding Brahma-Light"). The hierarchy of kundalini cakras portrayed in this popularized version of the kundalini concept differs in important respects from the descriptions of meditation-induced light visions in the traditional Indian and Tibetan Buddhist texts that are featured in this analysis, especially in the different characterizations given to the first light visions in a paradigm sequence: the traditional sources specify that the first light visions are ring-like and green in color, whereas the contemporary popularizations specify red and orange lights.

on, this approach describes a sky-blue light that comes before the amorphous swirls of the dark blue or purple light. Usually there is little, if any, description of what the remaining cakras actually look like as opposed to their meaning, that is, to what they signal about the spiritual progress of the meditator and about the imminence of the culminating vision and the ecstatic merger into Brahman. If the empirically-oriented, neurologically-grounded analysis of light visions presented in this book is correct, the contemporary popularizations of kundalini have to be mistaken in some important respects. In view of the possibility that some scientists might consider using these contemporary accounts as models for designing research projects, I thought it might be useful to present a brief critique.

While it's true that meditators do see visions of red light—I see them myself if I've just finished exercising or am resting after sexual intercourse, and I've been told by one person that he sees a dark red ring whenever he meditates with the assistance of a binaural beat audiotape—but the characteristics of the red ring that I see are quite different from any of the ring-images that I describe in this book. When I see a red ring, it is stationary, centered in the visual field, and already well-formed when it effloresces. It does not, in my experience, appear as one image in a sequence of visions but rather as an isolated phenomenon. As regards the orange light, in my experience this appears only when I happen to meditate in a place with bright ambient light which penetrates the skin of the eyelids: in this kind of situation, the visual field takes on a pink or orange color, and the orange hue becomes more pronounced once the meditation-induced phosphene images begin to flow and interact with signals from the external light source. A final critique is that the claim that the sky-blue light (*Visshudha-cakra*) appears before the purple light (*Ajna-cakra* or *Bhru-cakra*) is definitely mistaken, a claim that I make based not only on my own experience but also on the testimony of the ancient treatises we're examining in this chapter. I suspect that these contemporary popularizations of kundalini cakras are based on the work of meditation gurus whose goal was to demonstrate their mastery of the tradition by including every type of light vision that had ever mentioned by any meditator into a single, comprehensive, and authoritative hierarchy, and that, in the process, they did not take care to discriminate among visions that appear in different kinds of situations. To conduct an empirically-oriented analysis of meditation-induced light visions, it is wise to retain a critical approach to claims about visionary experiences found in the conventional popularizations of kundalini cakra heirarchies.

THE VISIONS OF THE BUDDHA AND HIS FOLLOWERS

Gotama's Enlightenment

In the 6th Century, BCE, a young Hindu prince named Gotama became so depressed that he felt compelled to abandon everything he formerly valued—the luxuries of life in his father's court and his wife and child—and to search for some way to find "release" (*moksha*) from his painful feelings. He looked for a spiritual teacher but was unable to find anyone who inspired him with confidence. He decided retire to the forest and to follow an ascetic tradition which taught that punishing the body with severe austerities would help strengthen his spirit and eventually free it. Seven years later Gotama realized that he was no closer to his goal and that his health was extremely precarious, so he left the forest in even greater despair than he'd entered it. He walked to the outskirts of a small village and sat down in the shade beneath a big tree, vowing that he would remain in that place meditating continuously until he either attained Release or died in the attempt.

What happened next is the subject of many hagiographies that recount myths of miraculous supernatural events that would challenge the credibility of a modern reader, but there are also other texts that claim to preserve Gotama's own words about his experiences beneath that tree. In Jan Gonda's translation of the *Majjhima-Nikaya,* an important text in the Buddhist canon, Gotama reports that for most of that first night of mediation he "perceived a limited light-manifestation (i.e., a light-manifestation in regard to a limited object of meditational exercise) and saw a limited (number of) material shapes," but then, just before dawn, suddenly everything changed: Gotama was overtaken by "a boundless light-manifestation and saw a boundless (number of) materials shapes," a vision that is said to have lasted for "a whole night and a whole day" [*Majjhima-Nikaya* 128.III.161, in Gonda, 1963, p. 310]. In the *Samyuda Nikaya,* another text in the Pali canon, the Gotama uses traditional Hindu concepts when he explains that the "Divine Eye opened (*caksus uppada*)" and flooded his consciousness with the abounding Brahma-Light:

> Coming to be! Coming to be! At the thought, there arose in me, brethren, things not taught before vision (lit. eye [*caksus uppada*]; 'knowledge with the sense of vision'), there arose in me knowledge, insight, wisdom ('as meaning penetration'), light (as meaning radiance or luminance') arose [*Samyuda Nikaya* 12, 1, 10, in Gonda, Ibid., p. 306].

It is worth pointing out Gotama's use of the word, *caksus*, which, as we discussed earlier in this chapter, refers to an inner, spiritual eye, so that a literal translation of the phrase, *caksus uppada*, would be "Eye arose," or, put another way, that "the Divine Eye opened." In the *Anguttara-Nikaya,* another text in the early Buddhist canon, Gotama is said to have "become vision (eye)[*caksus*], he has become knowledge, become dhamma, become Brahma . . . . [*Anguttara-Nikaya* 10, 115 (5, 226), in Gonda, Ibid., p. 311]." Note that Gotama's "Blissful Awakening" (*Buddha*) refers to a *literal* enlightenment, in the sense that his vision was flooded with light, and also to a *metaphorical* Enlightenment, in the sense that this vision of light automatically implanted a new knowledge of Ultimate Truth. Gotama called his experience of Blissful Awakening an "extinction" (*nirvana*) because he thought it was a release that terminated all of the karmic entanglements he had accumulated during his life in much the same way that a sudden burst of wind can extinguish the flame of a candle.

One aspect of his Awakening that surprised Gotama was that he did not see visions of an inner "self" (*atman*) or a cosmic "Self" of the sort that would match what he'd come to expect based on the traditional Hindu teachings; he saw only an "unlimited light-manifestation" in ceaseless flux devoid of anything that could be said to be a permanent soul-substance. Having concluded based on his own experiences that the traditional concepts needed modification, Gotama began to preach a new doctrine of *an-atman*, or "non-self," which claims that the human sense of self is merely another form of illusory experience with no more inherent reality than the temporary aggregations of energy that create other phenomena in the natural world. Gotama's teaching that all phenomena are inherently illusory (*maya*) is accepted as a fundamental principle in all Buddhist sects.

The History of Early Buddhism

After the death of the Gotama the Buddha, the new religious movement he had begun continued to flourish: monasteries were built, missionaries were sent in all directions, and new ideas were developed from the founder's original concepts. Where Buddhist communities were primarily monastic, monkish ideals began to prevail over the pursuit of unmediated ecstatic experience. It became more important for an ambitious monk to demonstrate "scholarly learning/insight (*prajña*)" and "behavioral purity (*sila*)" than to pursue the kinds of visions seen by Gotama. In a scholarly study of the early history of Buddhism in India, Ray [1994] explains how the exigencies of monastic life tend to undermine the practice of meditation:

> [A]lthough many classical texts—both Buddha-word and commentaries—recommend meditation as a necessary component of the Buddhist path, in monastic tradition, meditation has remained a primarily theoretical ideal, followed more in the breach than in the observance. . . According to the great spokesman of monastic Buddhism, Buddhaghosa, the institution of the settled monastery, along with its characteristic environment, tends to inhibit the practice of meditation owing to its many inhabitants, its noise, the necessary duties of communal life, obligations to the laity, the arrival of visitors, and other interruptions [Ray, 1994, p. 18]

The ideals of learning and purity were especially strong in the monastic communities of Ceylon and Southeast Asia. This version of Buddhism came to be known as *Theravadin* Buddhism. This tradition is also known as *Hinayana* Buddhism, which means "The Lesser Vehicle," but this pejorative name assigned by a rival Buddhist movement which called itself *Mahayana*, "The Greater Vehicle," is avoided by most scholars for reasons that should be obvious.

The Mahayana sect also established monasteries, but, by contrast with the Theravadin, Mahayana monks did not remain aloof from society; they taught lay people how to live by Buddhist precepts without isolating themselves from their social duties. Mahayana missionaries were especially active in the far northwestern reaches of the Indian subcontinent—in Kashmir and Gandhara—and they also moved into Tibet, Central Asia, and, emigrating along the Silk Road with merchant caravans, they eventually reached China. These different patterns of movement by Theravadin and Mahayana monks became critically important for the future evolution of Buddhism in the 11th century, CE, when Muslim armies invaded the Indian subcontinent and destroyed all the Buddhism monasteries in their path. After this catastrophe, Buddhism in the Theravadin tradition survived in the monasteries of Southeast Asia, and Mahayana Buddhism survived in a proliferation of sects scattered throughout Tibet, Central Asia, China, and Japan, but the Buddhist religion essentially disappeared from the Indian subcontinent (although many Buddhist ideas had already been nm incorporated into Hindu religions).

Light Visions in Theravadan Buddhism

Theravadan Buddhists with their emphasis on monasticism regard meditation-induced light visions as yet another form of apparitional reality, inherently no different from the illusory *maya* of the natural world. Experienced meditators are advised to shun light visions as seductive distractions, but the Theravadans also recognize that learning how to induce a state of empty-mind consciousness is an important prerequisite for advancing on the path to True Insight, and since one of the best signs that meditators are able to induce empty-mind consciousness is that they begin to see lights, the initial appearance of these visions is accepted even though it is is disparaged as representing no more than a "beginner's insight." The earliest articulation of the Theravadan view of light visions appears in a famous 5th-century Pali text from Ceylon, Buddhaghosa's *Visshuddhimagga* ("Path of Purification") [Nanamoli, 1991], which devotes a single paragraph to the subject of "illuminations." One might regard these vivid descriptions of light visions as being especially authoritative since the author is trying to warn his audience against devoting undue attention to this phenomenon:

> When the several truths, aspects of the dependent origination, methods, and characteristics have become evident to him thus, then formations appear to him as perpetually renewed . . . . And they are not only perpetually renewed, but they are also short-lived like dew-drops at sunrise . . . , like a bubble on water . . . , like a line drawn on water . . . , like a mustard seed on an awl's point . . . , like a lightning flash . . . , And they appear without core, like a conjuring trick . . . , like a mirage . . . , like a dream . . . , like the circle of a whirling firebrand, like a goblin city, like froth, like a plantain trunk, and so on. . . . . With the attainment of this he is known as a 'beginner of insight' [*Visshuddhimagga* 20: 104, in Nanamoli, Ibid., pp. 655-656].

Buddhaghosa describes the cultivation of "illuminations" as one of "Ten

Imperfections of Insight," warning that meditators who continue to induce light visions will likely to become attached to the emotional serenity that accompanies them and to be led astray, concluding incorrectly that this is a sign they have attained a state of spiritual elevation when in fact this play of inner light, like other apparitions, should be regarded as "impermanent, painful, and not-self." A meditator mistakes "what is not the path to be the path and what is not fruition to be fruition [*Visshuddhimagga* 20: 106-107, in Nanamoli, Ibid., pp. 656 - 657]." For Buddhaghosa, the correct approach to illuminations is to regard them as a flux of apparitional light forms which is no less impermanent, conditionally arisen, and subject to cessation than other natural phenomena: "Having investigated it thus, he sees the illumination as 'This is not mine, this is not I, this is not my self.' . . . . Seeing thus, he does not waver or vacillate about the illumination [*Visshuddhimagga* 20: 127; Nanamoli, Ibid., pp. 660]." The metaphors Buddhaghosa uses to describe meditation-induced light visions are listed in Figure 7.

Light Visions in Tibetan Tantric Buddhism

Other Buddhist traditions reached different conclusions about the spiritual value of meditation-induced light visions. When Mahayana Buddhist missionaries emigrated from India and established schools in the northwestern kingdoms of Kashmir and Gandhara, they encountered students who'd been exposed to many

Light Vision Metaphors in Theravadan Buddhism

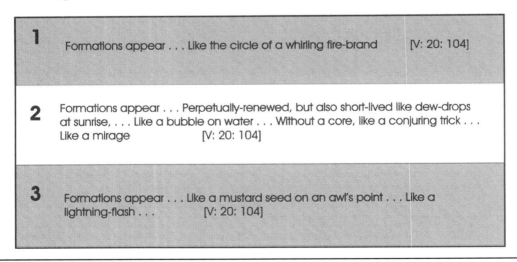

1	Formations appear . . . Like the circle of a whirling fire-brand [V: 20: 104]
2	Formations appear . . . Perpetually-renewed, but also short-lived like dew-drops at sunrise, . . . Like a bubble on water . . . Without a core, like a conjuring trick . . . Like a mirage [V: 20: 104]
3	Formations appear . . . Like a mustard seed on an awl's point . . . Like a lightning-flash . . . [V: 20: 104]

Figure 7. The metaphors used to describe meditation-induced light visions in Buddhaghosa's *Visshuddhimagga* ("Path of Purification"), an important text of the Theravadan school of monastic Buddhism written in 5th Century Ceylon. These excerpts are from the English translation by Nanamoli [1991].

cosmopolitan influences: merchants, traders and soldiers from many different lands with many different cultures passed through these cross-road kingdoms. To appeal to these audiences, Mahayana missionaries adopted an eclectic mix of religious ideas and practices, including ideas from the Hindu Tantras and Tantric meditation practices. A Buddhist teacher named Naropa who lived in Kashmir compiled an anthology of Tantric treatises on yoga meditation, *The Epitome of the Six Yogas* [Evans-Wentz, 1958]. One of Naropa's students, a Tibetan named Marpa, translated the *Six Yogas* and carried it back with him when he returned to his native land. Eventually Marpa and his fellow missionaries were able to establish a uniquely Tibetan version of Buddhism called *Vajrayana* as the dominent religion. *Vajra* means lightning, so Vajrayana means "Vehicle of the Thunder-Bolt," a name that expresses the belief that this approach to Buddhism can slash through the mental obstacles to Enlightenment like a bolt of lightning can instantly split a rock. In the Vajrayana tradition, the most expeditious method for attaining Enlightenment in a single lifetime is said to be the practice of "Highest Yoga Tantra" (*maha-anuttara-yoga*). Naropa's *Six Yogas* is one of the basic texts used in that practice; it emphasizes one aspect of Highest Tantra Yoga, called "The Path With Forms" or "The Tangible Path" (*Hdsin Lam*) [see Chang, in Evans-Wentz, Ibid., pp. xxvii-xxviii], in which the cultivation of meditation-induced light visions is described as an efficacious vehicle for attaining the "Final Realization" that all phenomena are inherently empty and lacking in substantial reality.

In Naropa's *Six Yogas*, a treatise entitled "The Yoga of the Psychic Heat" advises the meditator to begin by paying attention to the old and often-cited verse that a vision of "wheels" will appear:

> 'Meditate upon the four wheels,
> Each shaped like an umbrella,
> Or like the wheel of a chariot'
> [v. 1: 66, Evans-Wentz, Ibid., p. 190].

What do these wheels look like? Their shape is said to resemble an "umbrella" or a "chariot wheel." Many contemporary commentators interpret this to mean that the light-wheels have internal spokes, but there is another interpretation that is much more likely: the light-wheels are said to resemble umbrellas because, like umbrellas, the wheels are seen to collapse in diameter like an umbrella that is collapsed after the rain passes, and the light-wheels are said to be like chariot wheels because they move away from the viewer (and no doubt also because the original *Rig Veda* stated that these visions looked like chariot wheels). This alternative interpretation is a better fit, not only with the other texts in the Indo-Tibetan tradition, with my own experiences (and with the neurological analysis), but also with other evidence gleaned from the Tibetan Highest Yoga Tantra tradition. For example, Marpa the Translator described this threshold vision in a meditation-induced sequence as being a halo of light that manifests itself five times: "First one experiences the hallucination-like sign / That arises with the halo of five lights. . . . " [Nagabodhi's *Elucidation of the . . . Five Stations*, in Mullin, 1996, p. 167].

Meditators who enter *dhyana* ("empty-mind consciousness") experience many different light visions along with other unusual sensations like psychic heat and bliss:

> By retaining in the psychic-centres the vital-force,
> Something akin to heat is produced at first;
> Secondly, blissfulness is experienced;
> Thirdly, the mind assumeth its natural state;
> Then the forming of thoughts ceaseth automatically,
> And phenomena, appearing like *smoke, mirage,* and *fireflies,*
> And something resembling the *light of dawn,*
> And something resembling a *cloudless sky* are seen.
> [*The Yoga of Psychic Heat,* 1: 98-99, p.195; emphasis added]

This summary passage does not specific the sequence in which these visions appear, but that omission can be remedied by turning to other texts in the Highest Yoga Tantra tradition. The most interesting of these is Karma Lingpa's *The Natural Liberation of Seeing: Experiential Instructions on the Transitional Process of Reality-Itself* which was incorporated in an anthology of meditation treatises assembled by a Tibetan monk named Karma Chagmé in the 17th century, CE [Chagmé, 2000]. Like Marpa, Lingpa describes the first light visions to appear as "halos" which are "lamps of pristine absolute space [Chagmé, Ibid., p. 164]." Lingpa then describes a sequence of light visions, one "inside" the other, which is his way of saying that one vision is located *inside* the border of another or, alternatively, that one vision comes *after* another:

> [B]etween your eyebrows there is the 'lamp of the pristine absolute space' [i.e., the halo]. It appears like the *colors of a rainbow or the eye of a peacock feather.* Inside it is the so-called 'lamp of the empty bindus,' and it is like the *concentric circles of ripples* when you throw a stone into the pond. *Inside a form like the round plates of a shield there appears a bindu about the size of a mustard seed or a pea. Inside that are the so-called 'vajra-strands of awareness,' which are like knots tied in a strand of a horse's tail, like a string of pearls, like an iron chain, like a lattice of flowers moving with the breeze, and so on.* All those appear in combinations of two or three, and so on, and they are called the "sole bindu of the strand of your own awareness" [Lingpa, in Chagmé, Ibid., p. 164; emphasis added]

In the *Six Yogas*, Naropa mentions the vision of "a yellow radiance," also called "The Flaring," which is one of the Supernormal Visions that comes later in a meditation-induced progression ["Yoga of the Psychic Heat," 1: 123-124, in Evans-Wentz, Ibid., p. 198]. Elsewhere he refers to "The Ignition" which looks like "apparitional fireflies" ["The Yoga of the After-State" 5: 15-16; Evans-Wentz, Ibid., pp. 235 -236]. These metaphors recall the Tantric Hindu references to "dazzling sparks" and the "shattering" of a tiny dot of light and the "immediate expansion" of its shattered pieces.

The Flaring gives way to "something resembling a cloudless sky" [*The Yoga of Psychic Heat*, 1: 98-99, p.195], and then, as the kundalini rises to its highest level at the crown of the head, the energy exerts a pressure that causes a white, bulbous image to "protrude" out of the background vision of the cloudless sky. It is said that this "psychic protrusion" is engorged with white "moon-fluid," a euphemism for the Tantric concept that male semen has been spiritually transmuted to form the kundalini energy ["The Yoga of Psychic Heat," Ibid., pp. 196, 201]. This bulbous vision is also called "The Pure Illusory Body" which is said to look "like a fish leaping out of a pond, like the moon's reflection in water, like the Buddha-form which rises as if it were awaking from sleep ["The Yoga of the Clear Light," 2: 19-20, 4: 34, p. 230; "The Yoga of the Illusory Body," 2.14 et. seq., in Evans-Wentz, Ibid., pp. 230, 212]." As its name suggests, The Pure Illusory Body is considered to be an apparition (*maya*), but it is a potent and auspicious apparition— "The Maya of the Perfected State" —and its appearance signals the likelihood that a meditator will attain The Final Realization: "By entering into it, the Goal becometh nearer [Yoga of the Illusory Body, 2: 14 et. seq.; Evans-Wentz, Ibid., p. 212]." Tibetan monks believe that yogis must see the Pure Illusory Body if they are to escape the cycle of rebirth and existence: "If the vision is not experienced, the practice has not been perfect [Evans-Wentz Ibid., p. 213, note 3]."

As the pressures of kundalini energy inside the Pure Illusory Body build, suddenly the protrusion ruptures, ejecting streams of white fluid that "floweth upward to the crown of the head." This is the vision in which the meditator becomes a "Wielder of the Thunderbolt." The bolts of lightning release a flood of moon-fluid which pours into consciousness and fills it completely with a bright white light:

> [T]he upper extremity of the median-nerve is set into overwhelming vibration (of a blissful nature). / And thus is produced the *invisible psychic protuberance* on the crown of the head. / *When the protuberance becometh filled with the vital-force of the transmuted seminal fluid, one attaineth the transcendental boon of the Great Symbol, and realizeth the State of the Great Vajra-Dhara* ["Wielder of the Thunderbolt"]. Simultaneously with this realization, *the white-fluid issueth in an intensified manner from the base of the organ of generation and floweth upward to the crown of the head and permeateth completely* . . . . ["The Yoga of the Psychic Heat," 1: 143-146, Ibid., pp. 201-202; emphasis added]."

The meditator who becomes a "Wielder of the Thunderbolt" also becomes a master of the "Very Bright and of the Enduring" and, in the process, is able to restore, albeit temporarily, "The Uncreated, Primordial Mind, . . . the abode of inexhaustible *samadhi* ["Yoga of the Psychic Heat," in Evans-Wentz, Ibid., p.201]." Tibetan Vajrayana Buddhists believe that this ecstatic vision also instills a recognition of the truth of a principle considered fundamental in Mahayana Buddhism, which is that all phenomena are merely apparitions, inherently empty of permanent substance. A summary of the light vision metaphors described in Tibetan Buddhist yoga meditation texts is presented in Figure 8.

Light Vision Metaphors in Tibetan Vajrayana Buddhist Texts

1	Meditate on 4 wheels, each like an umbrella [YPH: I:66, p. 190]	5 halo-like signs are first appear [Marpa in TSY, p.167]	Between your eyebrows is the "lamp of pristine absolute space,"…[that looks like] the eye of a peacock feather [NSL, p. 164]
2	Phenomena like smoke or mirages appear [YPH: I: 98, p. 195]	[Next comes] the "lamps of empty bindus" which look like: ripples in a pond, or like the round plates of shields [NLS: p. 164]	
3	Inside the "empty" bindu is a second, pea-sized bindu in which appear vajra-strands. These strands look like knots tied in hair, like a string of pearls, like leaves fluttering in the wind . . . [NLS: p. 164]		
4	Phenomenon that look like fireflies [YPH: 1; 98-99]	The internal sign looks like apparitional fireflies. This is the time of the Ignition [YBS: 5: 15-16]	The Flaring will appear as a yellow radiance [YPH: 1: 123]
5	Something resembling the light of dawn, and something resembling a cloudless sky is seen [YPH: I: 98, p. 195]		
6	The Pure Illusory Body looks like a fish leaping out of a pond, like the moon's reflection in water, like the Buddha-form which rises as if it were awaking from sleep [YCL: IV: 34, p. 230] And thus is produced the invisible psychic protuberance...which is filled with transmuted seminal fluid... [YPH: I: 144-5, p. 201]		
7	The transmuted white seminal fluid issues forth in an intense flow upward to the crown of the head which it permeates completely [YPH: 1: 143-146]		
8	The whiteness completely permeates the head [YPH: 1: 143-146] One thereby attains the Great Symbol & the State of *Dorje-Chang*, "Wielder of the Thunder-bolt" [YPH: 1: 143-6] When illusory forms contact the Formless, . . . / And one gains understanding of the Pervading and the Real, / And mastery of the Very Bright and of the Enduring, and of the Siddhi of Transformation [YCL: 4: 35-36]		

An Overview of Visionary Experience in Ancient China

Two Methods of Daoist Meditation: Shou-i *and* Cun-jian

Long before Buddhist missionaries arrived in China, Chinese seekers evolved their own native meditation techniques designed to "draw down" visions of "celestial light" for use as an alchemical agent to transmute the meditator's body into the pure light of a Perfected Being who would live on as an Immortal amid the stars of the night sky [Pruett, 2002]. Two types of meditation were practiced in China: "Guarding the Light of the One (*shou-i*)," where the meditator induces a state of empty-mind consciousness using essentially the same practices described in the Indo-Tibetan texts that we've just discussed, and "retentive visualization (*cun-jian*)," where meditators begin by imagining that colored lights are moving through their bodies with the hope that their efforts will ignite light that flows spontaneously, a pure, spiritualized light that is released from heavenly bodies—from the sun, moon, and stars. In retentive visualization, meditators begin by visualizing colored lights that they direct into particular regions of their body. They do not claim to actually see their own internal organs (although it can often sound as if this were the case); rather, they direct their self-generated lights into specific way-stations located in a symbolic, spiritual landscape aligned with the physical body. The fundamental idea in retentive visualization is that "similar things attract," so that by visualizing light as it moves through a mythical landscape, a meditator hopes to attract the attention of celestial deities associated with each of the way-stations that the meditator bathes with light. The goal is to get the celestial gods to respond by blessing the meditator with "returned views" (*fan-kuang*), that is, to get them to release the flow of a pure light from the heavens to replace (or blend

Figure 8. The metaphors used to describe the paradigm sequence of meditation-induced light visions in the Tibetan Buddhist practice of *anuttara-yoga* ("Highest Yoga Tantra"), as described in several key texts. Many of the excerpts listed here are from Naropa's *Epitome of the Six Yogas*, an anthology of Tantric Buddhist meditation treatises written in northwestern India and later imported into Tibet. The excerpts listed here are from an English translation by Evans-Wentz [1958]. The selections from Naropa's Six Yogas are identified by the names of the anthologized treatises: "The Yoga of the Psychic Heat (YPH);" "Yoga of the Clear Light (YCL);" "Yoga of the Bardo State (YBS);" and "Yoga of the Illusory Body (YIB)." One of the excerpts comes from a commentary on Naropa's anthology by Tsong Khapa, a famous abbot and founder of the Gelupa sect, entitled *Six Yogas of Naropa* (TSY), translated into English by Mullin [1996]. Finally, there are a number of quotations from *The Natural Liberation of Seeing* (NLS) by Lama Karma Lingpa whose treatise on meditation was included in an anthology by a monk named Chagmé entitled *Naked Awareness: Practical Instructions on the Union of Mahamudra and Dzogchen*. The Karma Lingpa quotations are from an English translation by Gyatrul Rinpoche and Wallace [Chagmé et al., 2000].

with) the light produced by the meditator's own visualizations [Robinet, 1993, p. 61; Schipper, 1993, pp. 171 - 172]. The outcome of a successful visualization is when the meditator sees light visions continuing to appear even after he has stopped visualizing. In *The Elegies of Chu* (*Chu-ci*), a text written in the 3rd Century, BCE, the author describes how visualizations launched him on a "far-off journey" (*yuan-you*): "I look within . . . to find the place where life's energy rises," Chu writes, and then goes on to say that this looking inward placed him in an "empty and tranquil" darkness; once there, he sees a "flow of energy, rising ever upward . . . All dazzling essence, flashing back and forth." Chu imagines that he "eats the six energies" of the sun, ingesting its pure light and letting it circulate. By "guarding the purity of the spirit light within," he is transported into "a Great Brightness" where he sees "Yang in its gentle flashes, not quite bright," where he "wander[s] on the floating waves of steady mist," where he "traverse[s] fresh blue clouds . . . floating freely [Kohn, 1993, pp. 251 - 257]."

The second type of meditation, "Guarding the Light of the One (*Shou-i*)," is described in a 1st Century, BCE, text: *The Scripture of Great Peace* (*Taiping jing*), :

> With prolonged practice . . . you will be able to see within your body. The physical body will become lighter, the essence more brilliant, and the light more concentrated. . . . / To practice guarding the light of the One, when you have not yet attained concentration, just sit quietly with your eyes closed. There is no light seen in the inner eye. / *Practice guarding the One like this for a long time and a brilliant light will arise* [Kohn, 1993, pp.194 – 195; emphasis added].

The Vision of Circling Green Light

The Scripture of Great Peace describes light visions as a form of the "energy" or "breath" that animates the universe, called "chi (*qi*)," and it specifies that the first chi-lights to appear to a meditator "Guarding the Light of the One" will be wheels of green light:

> The *splendor of yang starts to shine and spreads its light* within the Original Beginning, soaking all the heavens; *its breath* [chi] *turns and circles like the wheels of a chariot* [Translated in Robinet, 1993, p. 110; emphasis added].

An explanation for why the initial lights in a meditation-induced sequence are yellowish-green is presented in *The Book of Great Profundity (Ta-tung ching)*, a text written by adepts in the Highest Purity (*Shangqing*) school of the 4th Century, CE: it explains that the Original Father, who lives in the head, sends a green "breath" (*qi*) down into the body at the same time that the Original Mother, who lives at the base of the trunk, sends a yellow "breath" upward, and when these two breaths meet in "The Yellow Court of the Heart," they blend to form the yellowish-green color that illuminates the inside of the adept's body [Robinet, op. cit., p. 102]. Another text in the Highest Purity tradition (*Shangqing yupei jindang taiji jinshu*) describes this light as a "Jade Girdle" (*yupei*), and it advises the meditator to begin the search for this vision by using his own imagination, to "visualize the energy of the Jade Girdle [as it] descends from the Nine Heavens and encircles his or her body.[Little, 2000, p. 205]." Jade is often (but not always) green in color, so the metaphor of a Jade Girdle points to a green light that surrounds the meditator's mind and shrinks in from all sides to form a tight binding. References to circular images and green colors also appear in other texts from the same school, for example, in *The Upper Scripture of the Purple Texts Inscribed by the Spirits*, where it is said that the early visions manifest as "Orbed Phosphors" and "Green Glares."

The Vision of Purple Clouds with Bright Pearls

Daoist texts also describe light visions that look like purple clouds and sometimes these purple clouds acquire a small ring of bright, opalescent light surrounding a dark central space, a combination that looks like a disembodied eye:

> *[W]ithin the sunlight auroras there will be also a purple pneuma* [chi], *as large as the pupil of your eye,* but wrapped in several tens of layers and *flashing brilliantly* . . . . This is called the flying root of solar efflorescence, the jade placenta . . . . [Bokenkamp, op. cit., p. 315; emphasis added].

Some Daoist texts suggest that meditators stare intently at this celestial vision of the light of the "inner eye," because this causes the eye to act like a mirror that can reflect the beams of celestial light arriving in the meditator's head (in the "Upper Cinnabar Field") down into the internal organs (into the "Lower Cinnabar Field") where the light can trigger the "inner alchemy" that will eventually release the ultimate vision of the One [Schipper, op. cit., pp. 105, 171 - 172; Robinet, op. cit, p. 61]. Another metaphor used to describe the bright node of light gleaming inside the purple cloud is "fiery pearl," as, for example, in this passage from *The True Lord of the Supreme One Who Dwells in the Cinnabar Palace (hsüan-tan):*"

> [C]oncentrate on the pole star. A *purple breath descends* from it which enters into my hsüan-tan palace. . . . / I then concentrate on the sun which enters into my hsüan-tan palace. It fills the palace and *penetrates to the center of the purple breath. Then I see it as a fiery pearl within the darkness.* [Maspero, quoted in Robinet. op. cit., p. 130; emphasis added].

The pearl metaphor also appears in *The Scripture of Immaculate Numen (Su-ling ching)*. As the celestial light descends, it moves through nine "cavities" in the head, awakening the spirits that reside in each; when a meditator sees lights that are green and lights that are purple, these are the spirits that guard the gate to the first cavities, but when the light reaches the fourth cavity, the meditator will see "The Palace of the Moving Pearl" (*liu-chu kung*) [Robinet, op. cit., p. 129]. All of the metaphors I've mentioned so far give good descriptions of the earliest of the light visions in a meditation-induced sequence.

For meditators who want to progress to the next stages of visionary experience, the Daoist texts advise them to build up a sleep deficit: "Stay awake, day and night," advises *The Book of the Yellow Court*, "and you will be immortal [Schipper, op. cit., p. 135]." The transition from visions of calm contemplation to ecstatic raptures includes passes through an intermediate stage of paroxysmal experiences.

The Vision of a Fiery Wind

In *The Book of Great Profundity* (*Ta-tung ching*), meditators who have learned how to draw down the celestial light energies are advised to "fuse" the celestial light with their own self-generated visualizations using the technique of "inner alchemy," a fusion which, if successful, will bring on the image of the "Emperor One:" "by the fusion of the One (*hun-i*), one is born into the light of the (celestial) Emperor [Robinet, op. cit., pp. 104 - 105]"). To catalyze this alchemical fusion, a meditator must be able to stir up a "whirlwind" (*hui-feng*): "the whirlwind brings about fusion with the Emperor [Robinet, p. 109]"). This whirlwind experience is triggered by attention to the twisting patterns of the purple light visions:

> The breath [*qi*] is then transformed into a purple cloud which goes through the same circulatory process finally "whirling" (*hui-lun*) and "twisting itself" into the form of the Emperor One, ... which brightens everything "like a white sun" [Robinet, op. cit., p. 110; emphasis added].

In another Daoist text, the *Chen-kao*, the whirlwind is described as *piao*, which can mean either a "violent or wild or fiery wind" or a "fast chariot" [Robinet, op. cit., 113 - 114]; combining these two metaphors into one, the *piao* whirlwind experience suggests that meditators see visions of wind-blown sparks, a metaphor that recalls the references in Indo-Tibetan texts to visions of "dazzling sparks" and "apparitional fireflies" that appear at an intermediate stage on the path to the culminating vision of lightning flashes. The meditator who experiences the *piao* whirlwind is buffeted about "like a cloth fluttering in a strong wind," so that he "twirls around like a falling leaf, [and] abandons himself to things and is spontaneous [Robinet, p. 116]." The whirlwind is a vision in which there is said to be a "dispersal" of "ten thousand things," which again recalls the Indo-Tibetan image of sparks and fireflies.

The Vision of the Great Ocean of Energies and a Turtle's Head

When the whirlwind is over, the meditator sees a "tranquil" vision which brightens everything—a vision called "the Miracle of the Emperor One:"

> The Ta-tung . . . makes [the primordial breath] revolve (*hui-hsün*), purifies the spirits and rejoins with the Tao, causes a propitious wind to blow and guides the dance within the void. Suddenly (*hu*), the respiration *disperses the form of the ten thousand things* and, at the height of movement, there is *tranquility again -*

obscurely, all around, the Miracle of the Emperor One. This is what is called the *Whirlwind of the Unitive Fusion* [Robinet, op. cit., p. 116 - 7; emphasis added].

Daoist scholar, Karl Schipper, in his commentary on the passage in *The Book of Great Profundity* that states the vision of the Emperor One "brightens everything 'like a white sun'," explains that the sense of the text is that the meditator's consciousness is filled with a vision of light reflecting off a blue expanse— "The Great Ocean of Energies" —that contains only one differentiating feature: a bulbous protrusion that looks like the head of a turtle protruding up as it swims in the ocean:

> We now arrive in the watery lower world. Here again sun and the moon are found, this time in the kidneys. They cast their light on *the Great Ocean of Energies (ch'i-hai), which covers the whole* of the lower body, and *wherein a large turtle swims* [Schipper, op. cit., p. 106-7; emphasis added].

This account of a blue ocean with a bulbous figure protruding out recalls the descriptions of the intermediate sequence of light visions in Indo-Tibetan texts— the vision of a sky-blue dawn which eventually acquires the superimposed vision of a pale, thumb-size nipple that seems to protruding out of the blue surface. Schipper notes that the bulb-shaped vision emerging out of the Great Ocean of Energies is described in some texts as a sacred mountain called *K'un-lun*:

> In the middle of the ocean rises the K'un-lun, the sacred, *inverted* mountain with its narrow base widening towards the top, giving it the outline of a *mushroom.* The mountain has a *hollow summit (the navel),* which gives access to the deepest recesses of the ocean [Schipper, op. cit., pp. 106 – 107; emphasis added].

It is hard to imagine what this vision of K'unlun mountain might actually look like based on Schipper's account, but we can turn to a description of the sacred K'unlun mountain in *The Record of the Ten Continents* [*Shizhou ji*]) which states that the vision is "shaped like a *hanging bowl* [Kohn, op. cit., p. 55; emphasis added]." And the K'unlun vision is also called "The Tortoise Mountain" [Bokenkamp, op. cit., p. 344]. If we return to Schipper's account bearing these last two images in mind, we find that Schipper combines references to three different bulbous shapes; if we were to separate each of these three references, and if we were to assume that the viewer's angle of gaze in all these instances is looking up from beneath the figure, then it becomes possible to conform each of the three references, considered individually, to the kind of bulbous figure described in the other Daoist texts just mentioned ("tortoise head," "hanging bowl") and to the Indo-Tibetan texts discussed earlier. The first image would be looking up at a mountain with its peak pointing downward, i.e., looking up at an inverted cone. The second image would be looking up from below at a mushroom as it rises, widening and eventually expanding to form the flat top characteristic of some Chinese mushrooms, i.e., the viewer is looking up at another inverted cone. Third, Schipper refers to the

Light Vision Metaphors in Early Chinese Daoist Texts

1

A green light descends from the head and mixes with a yellow light . . . (TT: Robinet [1993], p. 102)

The Purple Palace rides on green phosphors . . . (DP: Bokencamp [1996], p. 173)

Orbed Phosphors / . . . Green (Rainbow) Glare, . . .Revolving Auroras (PT: Bokenkamp [1997], p. 314)

2

Glinting and luminous, . . . a purple haze   (HJ: Kroll [1996], p. 15)

Concentrate on the Pole Star. A purple breath (*chi*) descends   (TLS: Maspero, in Robinet, p. 130)

3

The sun . . . penetrates to the center of the purple breath [*chi*]. Then I see a fiery pearl in the darkness.   (TLS: Maspero, in Robinet, p. 130)

Within the sunlight auroras, there will also be a purple pneuma [*chi*], as large as the pupil of your eye, but wrapped in layers and flashing brilliantly. This is . . . the flying root of solar efforescence (PT: Bokenkamp [1997], p. 315)

4

Suddenly, the respiration disperses the form of the ten thousand things and . . . (TT: Robinet, p. 116-117)

5

. . . the form of the ten thousand things and, at the height of movement, there is a tranquility again - obscurely, all around, [one sees] the Miracle of the Emperor One. (TT: Robinet, p. 116-117)

It is this Emperor One who exhales the breath of the Whirlwind which brightens everything 'like a white sun.'   (Robinet, p. 110)

We now arrive in the watery lower world. . . . The great Ocean of Energies . . . (HJ, Schipper [1993], p. 106)

6

In the middle of the ocean arises K'un-lun, the sacred, inverted mountain with its narrow base widening towards the top, [like] a mushroom.   (HJ, Schipper, p. 106)

Essence of Yang, and Fetal Germ Stored in Heaven and Hidden in the Moon. / You should envision the moon at the time it is newly emerged.   (PT: Bokenkamp [1997], p. 318)

The moon now wanes, now waxes. / The luminous essence glows . . . (PT: Bokenkamp, p. 320)

7

The luminous essence glows within, / Then spurts forth as a bridge across dark waters (PT: Bokenkamp, p. 320)

Concealed in the moon, / The Five Numinous Ladies / Let fly their beams of light . . . / To illumine my Muddy Pellet [i.e., Head].   (PT: Bokenkamp, p. 321)

8

Last, meditate on the Passgate Star. This is the Heavenly Pass of Mysterious Yang, the great brightness of Vascillating Radiance.   (TG: Kohn [1993], p. 264)

"It may be said that the exertion of the adepts who practice the Great Purity exercises ends with an imaginary self-cremation. . . . everything turns into fire;. . . Body and fire become one substance. Inside and outside, all is light."   (Robinet, p. 169) mountain as being like a "navel" because it is an inverted triangle that is hollowed out from its base, i.e., the viewer is looking up at a navel-like protrusion. To this melange of bulb-shaped images we can add yet another metaphor: *The Purple Scriptures* describe a vision that looks like the white moon. The white color reveals that this bulbous protrusion is filled with transmuted semen ("yang-essence").

The Vision of White Beams

The Purple Scriptures report that the vision of the white, bulbous moon "gives birth" to another vision in which "beams" of light "spurt" out against a dark background, with the first appearance consisting of *three* light beams ("The circling yin joins thrice"):

> *Moon essences, phosphors of the night,* . . . high in the Dark Palace . . . . May the fetus fly in; May the newborn babe gradually emerge. The *circling yin joins thrice, It's beams* mystically darkening in all directions. / * * * / . . . *the moon now wanes, now waxes.* The *luminous essence glows within, Then spurts forth as a bridge across dark waters.* . . . I now feed on lunar efflorescences, [j]oining thereby with the Perfected. / * * * / Bring to me the waters of lunar efflorescence, . . . Stored in heaven, concealed in the moon, The Five Numinous Ladies *Let fly their beams of light in nine paths, To illumine my Muddy Pellet* [Bokenkamp, op. cit., pp. 319-320; emphasis added].

The Vision of Self-Immolation

The culminating light vision, as described in an early Daoist text from the Great Peace movement, *Three Ways to Go Beyond the Heavenly Pass* (*Tiganguan santu*), is "the Heavenly Pass of Mysterious Yang, the *great brightness of Vascillat-*

Figure 9. Metaphors used in early Chinese Daoist texts to describe the qi ("chi") energies that manifest as light visions. Most of the material listed here (but not all of it) is excerpted from treatises written by masters of the Shangqing school of "Highest Clarity" or "Highest Purity" Daoism that flourished in central China during the 4th-Century, CE, just before Buddhist ideas became influential in this region. The excerpts come from a variety of sources: from the Tiganguan santu (TG), "Three Ways to Go Beyond the Heavenly Pass," as translated in Kohn [1993]; from the Ch-uci (CC), "The Elegies of Chu," as translated in Kohn [1997]; from several texts analyzed by Robinet in Taoist Meditation [1993], including the Ta-tung jing (TT), "The Book of Great Profundity," as translated in Robinet [1993], the Su-ling jing, "The Book of Immaculate Numen" (SL), and one excerpt from "The True Lord of the Supreme One Who Dwells in the Cinnabar Palace (TLS), originally translated by Maspero and quoted in Robinet; from "The Declarations of the Perfected" (DP), as translated in Bokenkamp [1996]; from the "Upper Scripture of the Purple Texts Inscribed by the Spirits" (PT), also translated by Bokenkamp [1997]; from the Daode jing (DJ), "The Book of the Way," as translated in Schipper [1993], and also from Schipper's interpretations of Huang-ting jing (HJ), "The Book of the Yellow Court; from (SY)= Shangqing yupei jindang taiji jinshu [Little, 2000].

ing Radiance. Here the Tao Lords of the Highest Jade Emperor reside [Kohn, 1993, pp. 264]." One translation of Lao-tzu's *Dao-de ching*, the progenitor of all Daoist texts, has Lao-tzu urging his students to seek for a state of mind that is beyond all cognition in which consciousness is filled by all-encompassing white light: "Can you, by Non-Knowledge, let the *white light* penetrate all regions of the (inner) space? [Schipper, 1993, p. 139]."

The pioneering Daoist scholar, Isabelle Robinet, in her monograph on Shangqing "Great Purity" Daoism, concludes that the ultimate goal of meditators in this tradition was to be consumed by a fiery light and thereby transmuted into a wholly spiritual Perfect Being. It is, she writes, a form of "imaginary self-cremation:"

> [T]he exertion of the adepts who practice the Great Purity exercises ends with an imaginary self-cremation. Thus adepts see "a red breath envelop their bodies and *everything turns to fire; the fire engulfs their bodies. Body and fire become but one substances. Inside and outside, all is light.*" This is called "purification (or "refining," lien) by the sun and moon" or "dying and living again" [Robinet, op. cit., p. 169; emphasis added].

By the end of the 4th Century, the influence of "Great Purity/Highest Clarity" Daoism was waning as Buddhist influence was on the rise. The new forms of Daoism that emerged during this period were eclectic and often incorporated Buddhist ideas in their work. After the 4th Century it becomes more difficult to distinguish meditation practices unique to Chinese Daoism. A list of the metaphors used to describe light visions in the ancient Chinese Daoist texts appears in Figure 9.

3

SLEEP RHYTHM PHOSPHENES, I: SHRINKING RINGS

PHENOMENOLOGY

Inducing Empty-Mind Consciousness

If I want to induce a trance, I lie down on the floor with my eyes closed and my arms at my side and give myself silent instructions—"let yourself relax," "concentrate on your breathing in and out"—and if I discover that I'm a bit tense, I use progressive relaxation techniques of the sort developed by Jacobson [1938]: I tense a group of muscles, for example, the muscles of the feet and legs, for a count of 10, then I let them relax and concentrate all my attention on the sensations of release while telling myself that I am myself becoming more and more relaxed at the same time.

After these preliminaries, I speed the process of dissociation by manipulating attention and eye movements in a stereotyped manner: I converge my eyes, pointing them toward the tip of my nose, stare intently at the visual field, then experiment with shifting my angle of gaze higher—for example, straight forward, or, slightly higher, to the level of the forehead—searching for which angle of gaze produces the kind of proprioceptive response that I'm hoping to induce. The responses that I'm looking for are, first, a sense of "pressure" or "fullness" inside the eyeballs, and, second, a faint tinnitus that is part sound, part vibration, and could be described as a "buzzing" or, even better, as a "fluttering of bird wings" or a "sputtering campfire." The sensation of pressure in the eyeball and the fluttering sound signal that the process of dissociation has already begun and is rapidly intensifying.

I make sure that this process continues by keeping my mind free of distractions. To accomplish this, I tell myself to be passive, to acquiesce in whatever happens, and to disregard any thoughts, emotions, itches, or pains that intrude into consciousness, treating their arrival with indifference, allowing them to drift freely in and out of consciousness. The paradoxical result of giving up any attempt to control one's thoughts is that the flux of mental content dissipates, leaving in place the charcoal gray of an "empty" visual field, the *eigengrau* generated by the random metabolic discharges of retinal neurons.

As the mind clears and then continues to watch itself, waiting with an expectation that something will appear (but without trying to force anything), the physiological arousal drops to a level typically experienced in falling asleep—but I don't fall asleep and my visual awareness remains acute. This is the state of "empty-mind consciousness" that is the prerequisite for my seeing light visions, and which is, I believe, the same state that Hindu meditators call *turiya*, that Buddhist meditators call *dhyana*, and that Daoist meditators call *Shou-i*. Having achieved the state of empty-mind consciousness, the meditator must often wait patiently (and passively) for some time before the first light visions to appear.

If the meditator is adept and the trance is well-established, the first phosphene image to appear is usually a yellowish-green ring of light that is shrinking steadily in diameter from the moment it effloresces in the visual field. For the seer, the green ring seems to "recede" toward some distant point in 3-dimensional space. Several light-rings appear, one after another, and then they stop automatically. In this chapter I'll begin the neurologically-grounded, "reverse-engineering" analysis of the spatial and temporal characteristics of meditation-induced phosphenes by focusing on the threshold images of green light-rings.

The Vision of Shrinking Light-Rings

When I meditate in a dark room with eyes closed, the first geometric phos-

Figure 10. Schematic drawings of the threshold phosphene image of a shrinking ring. This image originates in the influx of a dark, barely-perceptible, ring-shaped wave that sweeps into the visual field from all 360° of the peripheral rim and then suddenly efflorescences as a green phosphene ring upon reaching a position between 80° to 60° of isoeccentricity. Once it has illuminated, the phosphene ring continues to shrinks steadily in diameter at the same rate as its dark predecessor, and this movement creates the illusion that the ring is "receding" away from the viewer in a 3-dimensional space toward some distant point. The image disappears abruptly, as if it had evaporated, after a total elapsed time of 4 seconds. There is a 1-second refractory interval in which the visual field remains vacant, then another ring effloresces and begins the centripetal trajectory. That means the interval between successive rings is 5 seconds. About halfway into the trajectory (i.e., 2 seconds), the empty space in the ring suddenly fills in—at first it filled in with green phosphene, but after about a year of intermittent induction the fill-disk abruptly changed over the course of three meditation session to dark blue. Once the green ring fills in with this dark blue disk, it looks exactly like the irridescent eye of a peacock's feather. The volley of shrinking light-rings almost always ends abruptly after the third rings. My schematic drawings do not capture the elusive, ever-changing, hazy and translucent qualities of these phosphene rings, qualities that remind me of well-formed smoke-rings floating through space.

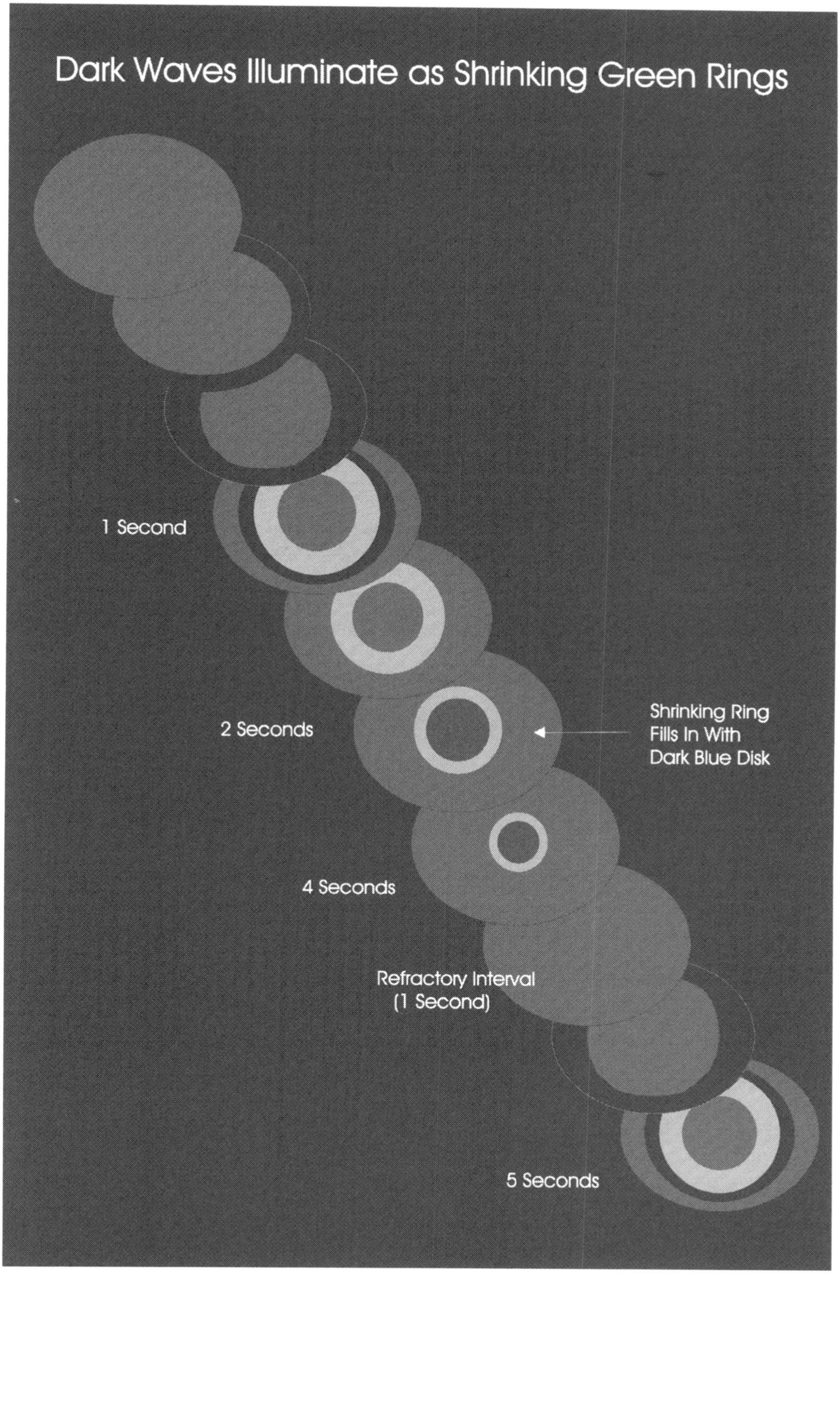

Dark Waves Illuminate as Shrinking Green Rings

1 Second

2 Seconds

Shrinking Ring
Fills In With
Dark Blue Disk

4 Seconds

Refractory Interval
(1 Second)

5 Seconds

phene image I see is a barely perceptible sensation of a dark wave that sweeps inward from the perimeter of the visual field and then suddenly effloresces as a phosphene sensation while it is still located in the peripheral visual field between 80° to 60° of isoeccentricity. The phosphene is a translucent green ring, and after its efflorescence it continues to shrink steadily in diameter along the same concentric trajectory initiated by the influx of the dark wave. The drawings in Figure 10 illustrate the key features of this phosphene ring image. The shrinking movement of the ring creates the illusion that it is "receding" in 3-dimensional space, pulling one's attention along with it, but then the image suddenly disappears as if it had evaporated. A ring remains in the visual field for 4 seconds, based on my count of "1001, 1002...." After a ring disappears, I count a 1-second interval before the next ring illuminates, so the interval between the onset of successive rings is about 5 seconds, or 0.2 Hertz (Hz). This sequence is clock-like, and terminates automatically after only three or four rings have completed their trajectory. Sometimes I see a few more rings, but I've never seen more than 6—and these longer sequences occur when there is some momentary distraction that interrupts my meditative focus. Once a sequence of rings ceases, it does not recur for the remainder of that meditation session.

This same ring image can appear spontaneously in other circumstances. For example, if I'm lying in bed, feeling very relaxed and just about to fall asleep, I sometimes see a volley of green phosphene rings. I've also seen the same ring images appear spontaneously while listening to hypnosis-induction audiotapes (as part of an appetite control program) that were seeded with binaural beats timed at intervals that mirror the frequency of delta-band brainwaves (0.5-4.5 Hz). And I often see a sequence of light-rings while I'm having a therapeutic massage to relieve shoulder pain. I should also mention my wife's experience after she broke her wrist: she had always been sceptical that there could be any such thing as light-rings, but one evening after taking a codeine pill for her wrist pain, she was relaxing on the couch and watching television. She became much more relaxed than normal—and at that point she saw a sequence of receding light-rings. The fact that the the same light-rings can appear not only during meditation but also in other circumstances like sleep onset, self-hypnosis, therapeutic massage, and drug-induced drowsiness suggests that all of these responses might be generated the same neural mechanisms and that those mechanisms are associated somehow with sleep onset.

I should mention that my description of these green phosphene rings is based on my usual practice of meditating in a dark room with my eyes closed. On the few occasions when I've attempted to meditate outside in direct sunlight, the threshold phosphene was dramatically different: the visual field filled with a bright orange light that initially appeared to be undifferentiated, but the orange quickly organized itself into discrete bands with slightly different textures and with a very small, black pupil-sized space at the center. The borders between bands were faint and only barely perceptible.

The Acquisition of a Blue Fill-Disk

When I first saw the receding green rings, the empty space within the ring would fill in with a disk of green phosphene when the ring was about halfway through its 4-second trajectory. After I'd induced light visions for about one year, I saw a dramatic change in the color of the fill-disk. The first sign of a change coming was that I saw a few tiny flecks of blue flash out in the green disk as it filled it. On the next occasion when I meditated, I saw many more of these blue flecks in the green fill-disk, and then, the time after that, I saw the empty space in the green ring fill suddenly with a beautiful, well-formed, dark blue disk instead of the green disk that had appeared in the past. From then on, the dark blue fill-disk always appeared at precisely 2 seconds when the shrinking green ring was midway through its 4-second trajectory. The dark blue disk surrounded by the yellow-green ring looks remarkably like the irridescent eye image that shines at the top of a peacock's feather (which is one of the metaphors used to describe this threshold light visions in the Tibetan yoga meditation texts discussed in Chapter 2). Ever since this change occurred, the light-rings have always filled in with a dark blue disk except in one unusual situation that I'll discuss next.

MRI-Driven Anomalies in Light-Ring Sequences

An unusual sequence of receding light-rings appeared when I had a magnetic resonance imaging (MRI) test. When the MRI technician fastened me to a platform and slide it into the claustrophic confine of a narrow tube, I felt a bit anxious. To keep calm, I used the same behaviors I often used to relax and meditate: I concentrated on my breathing, kept my eyes closed, stared at the empty visual field, and told myself to relax, but I didn't think about trying to induce phosphenes. Nevertheless, when I heard the loud clanking, whirring sounds that signaled the MRI machine had been activated, I soon began to see a stream of green light-rings. I noticed immediately that these light-rings were not the same as what I normally saw: this MRI-related variant did not terminate after the "normal" sequence of 4 rings but instead kept on flowing into the visual field for as long as the clatter of the MRI equipment continued to sound. And these light-rings flowed at a dramatically faster rate: counting the passing seconds, I found that each ring completed its inward trajectory in 2 seconds, *half* the "normal" duration of 4 seconds. A third difference in this MRI-related series was that the accelerated light-rings filled in with *green* disks, not with the dark blue disks that I'd long ago become accustomed to seeing. These three changes—the change in the color of the fill-disks, the change in speed, and the continuation of the light-rings beyond a normal volley—suggest the inference that light-rings can be driven by a bombardment of MRI radiofrequency beams, an hypothesis that I'll examine in more detail later in this chapter. The anomalies observed in the MRI-related light-rings suggests that the neural mechanisms responsible for generating the fill-disks can produce different colors depending on how long the ring image remains in the visual field—a dark blue disk if the ring trajectory is a normal 4 seconds, and a green fill-disk if the ring trajectory ends before 2 seconds.

The Analgesic Effects of Meditation

On some occasions I've used meditation-induced phosphenes to defray the pain caused by minor irritations (like headaches) or minor medical or dental procedures. For example, I used this method of dissociation when I had to have an infected cyst removed from my back when the doctor did not have any local anesthetic available. I also used it while a dermatologist was using a laser to reduce keloid scars. On several occasions I've used phosphene induction to hypnotize myself while I'm waiting in the dentist's office for a procedure that I know will involve some pain. To achieve this kind of analgesic effect during meditation, it is important to add a new behavior, a variant of the passive, indifferent attitude that I mentioned earlier. Most people are familiar with the involuntary tensing of muscles that occurs in anticipation of a painful stimulus. I've learned to counter these instinctive and involuntary reactions by meditating and by silently telling myself during the meditation that this pain that I'm feeling (or that is about to arrive) is not actually attached to my body, that I can choose to let it flow away, that I can, in effect, "give the pain away" by visualizing that it is streaming out of the top of my head and dispersing in all directions.

Having adopted this attitude toward the pain, there is no longer an urgent need for me to take action to escape from the situation, nor any need to tense my muscles in an attempt to avoid the painful stimulus. This meditation exercise constitutes, in effect, a deliberate abandonment of the vigilance one would normally maintain towards external stimuli that have some important behavioral significance. The result is a sudden, precipitous drop in apprehension and, with that, a corresponding drop in muscle tension which restores the relaxed state that formerly had formerly existed. This re-relaxation occurs immediately after the muscles tense involuntarily in response to the painful stimulus. Keeping relaxed helps diffuse the pain sensations and the anxiety about pain. The anticipation that relaxation (and the relief it brings) can be quickly restored after the next painful stimulus creates confidence that events are not out of control, and that, therefore, it is not necessary to divert one's attention from the focus on the visual field in order to take some kind of remedial action. For me, this strategy is only partially effective—the analgesia that I induce is as not complete as the accounts published by gurus who give public demonstrations of their indifference to pain—but the combination of feeling in control of events and feeling confident that I don't need to take remedial action is surprisingly effective as a technique for ameliorating pain.

A particularly interesting example of phosphene-induced analgesia occurred on one occasion when the dentist had to abrade the surface of six teeth with damaged enamel in order to create a strong bonding surface. This experience with hypnotic analgesia is particularly interesting because it involves an induction of sleep-onset phosphenes that succeeded despite the fact that it took place when I was in a state of high physiological arousal and was anxious because I'd arrived a bit late and thus had no time to prepare, as I would typically do, by hypnotizing myself in the waiting room; instead, on this occasion I had to begin my phosphene induction *after* the dentist had already begun to work on the first tooth. I could feel the sharp pain sensations from the application of the dentist's instrument and was naturally apprehensive, so that each application of the device elicited an involuntary tensing of the large muscles in my body, but I persisted in keeping my eyes converged and my attention focused on the center of the visual field, hoping for the best. I soon noticed that whenever the dentist stopped abrading the surface of the teeth, the apprehension would vanish and my muscles would relax with a dramatic suddenness. The alternation between the muscle tensing that occurred whenever the abrading began again and the precipitous relaxation that occurred as soon as the drill was withdrawn induced a deep hypnotic trance by the time the dentist finished the second tooth. I began to see the familiar phosphene images—light-rings and amorphous nebulae—which continued even while the dentist was still using the drill. I was amazed that this alternation of high physiological arousal and precipitous relaxation induced an hypnotic trance as deep, if not deeper, than my normal meditation techniques, and that it induced this trance state in much less time. This unexpected and paradoxical observation—that painful stimuli can drive the emergence of a dissociated state that confers some measure of analgesia even though the pain also raises the level of physiological arousal far above what would normally be associated with a meditative state or sleep onset—suggests that the same neural mechanisms that trigger a transition from waking to sleep when the body is in a state of very low arousal can also be activated by certain kinds of external stimuli that increase the level of physiological arousal. This reminds me of a passage I once read in Peter Levine's book, *Walking the Tiger* [1997], in which he describes the rapid dissociation that overtook prey animals that had been captured by a predator: sometimes the predator's attention was redirected and the prey animal survived the initial trauma, but then the lucky survivor had to stand and shake itself vigorously to dissipate its mental and physiological dissociation; if this shaking did not happen, the animal soon died.

NEUROLOGICAL ANALYSIS

Slow Wave Sleep: A Review of Recent Research

I've described how, in my own experience, the same sequence of phosphene images that appears spontaneously just before sleep onset also appears in a number of behavioral states that, like sleep, are characterized by a state of deep physiological relaxation and an inward orientation of attention: during meditation, self-hypnosis, hypnosis induced by playing audiotapes of a hypnotist's voice, and therapeutic massage. It is reasonable, then, to predict that the neural mechanisms that generate the transition to the first nightly episode of slow wave sleep must also be activated during these other behavioral states that resemble sleep, so I'll begin my "reverse-engineering" analysis of the first phosphene image—the green light-rings—with a review of what neuroscientists know about the neural mechanisms that govern sleep.

Stage 1 Non-Rapid-Eye-Movement Sleep (NREMS)

Important breakthroughs in the neuroscientific understanding of sleep occurred in the 1990's and produced a consensus scenario about the identity and operation of the neural mechanisms that govern the nightly transition from waking to slow wave sleep [Steriade and McCarley, 1990; McCormick and Pape, 1990; Steriade et al., 1993a; von Krosigk et al., 1993; Steriade, et al., 1993b]. In this consensus scenario, the transition to sleep is orchestrated by an interaction of three brain rhythms that oscillate in the reciprocal neuronal circuits linking the thalamus and the neocortex. The transition from waking to slow wave, non-rapid-eye-movement sleep (NREMS) begins with a relaxed and drowsy state of consciousness that is conventionally designated as "stage 1 NREMS." This transitional state is sometimes called "hypnagogic consciousness." During stage 1 NREMS, large numbers of cortical cells begin to discharge in synchrony, generating an oscillating wave with a very slow rhythm of less than one wave per second (<1 Hz). Because these synchronous waves have not yet become dominant, the scalp EEG continues to register intermittent desynchronizations whenever sensory signals and mental thoughts momentarily disrupt the subject's relaxed, drowsy state of consciousness. The cortical slow wave is transmitted to the thalamus where its pulses evoke a change in the firing patterns of the thalamic reticular nucleus (RTN). This change in RTN firing patterns signals the start of stage 2 NREMS.

Stage 2 NREMS

The RTN is a thin sheet of GABAergic cells that forms a sheath covering most of the lateral posterior portions of the thalamus where the sensory relay nuclei are located. The efferent axons of sensory-relay cells that project to cortical targets must pass through the RTN's thin sheath of neurons en route, and when these axons enter the RTN matrix, the RTN neurons impose inhibitory synapses on the efferent axons of sensory-relay cells. This network of inhibitory synapses enables the RTN to regulate the flow of sensory signals leaving the thalamic sensory-relay nuclei en route to the neocortex.

When a person is awake, the RTN cells facilitate the accurate relay of sensory signals by firing single spikes, but this firing pattern changes dramatically when stage 1 gives way to stage 2 NREMS. The shift occurs when the synchronous pulses of the cortical slow wave are referred back to the thalamus where they push the polarization of thalamic cell membranes down to the threshold level of Vm = – 60 mV. At that point, the RTN neurons suddenly shift from firing single spikes to firing in synchronous bursts. When the waves generated by these synchronous spike-bursts reach the scalp EEG, they produce a distinctive waxing and waning pattern that looks like an old-fashioned spindle of yarn, hence the nickname, "spindle bursts" or "sleep spindles." Each spindle burst lasts from 1 to 3 seconds, and successive bursts are fired with clock-like regularity at a rate of one burst every 3 to 10 seconds (0.3 to 0.1 Hz). In the EEG, the spindle waves register as sigma band frequencies of 7 to 10 Hz. The conventional criterion for determining the end of stage 1 NREMS and the onset of stage 2 is the appearance of synchronous spindle bursts globalized across the cortical mantle.

Once stage 2 NREMS begins, the relay of sensory signals through the thalamic nuclei is largely blocked because the synchronous firing of the RTN cells imposes successive waves of inhibition. As a result of this blockage, the person usually succumbs to sleep and loses conscious awareness of external events. Stage 2 NREMS does not last very long; it only takes a few spindle bursts to induce to stage 3: in a study of normal young adults, Uchida et al. [1994] found that the shift to delta activity required a minimum of 3 spindle bursts but not more than 7 with a mean of 4.78 ± 1.62. The number of spindle bursts required to induce stage 3 NREMS was the essentially the same for each subject on successive nights, although there were differences in the number of bursts needed to produce this shift in different subjects.

Stage 3 NREMS

During stage 2 NREMS, the cortical slow (<1 Hz) wave continues to oscillate while the RTN fires synchronous spindle bursts. The interaction of these two synchronous sleep rhythms pushes the polarization of thalamic cell membrances down from Vm = - 60, the level of hyperpolarization at the time the spindle bursts begin, to VM = - 75 mV. At this second threshold, intrinsic calcium currents begin to flow in the sensory relay cells. These currents stimulate the cells to fire single "calcium spikes," and large numbers of cells release their calcium spikes in response to the receipt of the pulse of the cortical slow wave. The interaction of RTN spindle bursts, the cortical slow wave, and the calcium spikes released by sensory relay neurons pushes the polarization of thalamic cell membranes even lower to Vm = - 90 mV. At this threshold, the RTN neurons automatically stop firing synchronous spindle bursts, ending stage 2 NREMS. What happens next is determined by the interaction of the synchronous cortical slow (<1 Hz) wave and the calcium spikes fired by sensory-relay cells: together these events generate a sleep rhythm that registers in the scalp EEG as delta waves with frequencies of 0.5 to 4 Hz [Steriade et al., 1993a, 1993b; Uchida et al., 1994]. The conventional EEG criterion for determining the beginning of stage 3 NREMS is the disappearance of spindle waves and their replacement by synchronous delta waves globalized across the cortical mantle. The EEG power spectra for both sleep spindles and delta-waves reach their highest levels during the *first* episodes of stage 2 and stage 3 NREMS [Ferrillo et al., 2000a, 2000b].

Spindle Bursts and Light-Rings Have Similar Timing Intervals

The green light-rings enter the visual field at a rate one every five seconds (0.2 Hz), and the RTN fires spindle bursts at a rate of 0.1 to 0.3 Hz, that is, one every three to 10 seconds; therefore, the timing of the light-rings is consistent with the timing interval of the RTN spindle bursts. There is another parallel as well: I see a volley of 3 to 4 light-rings before the automatic termination, and the average number of spindle bursts required to induce a shift from stage 2 to stage 3 NREMS ranges from 3 to 7 spindle bursts (4.78 ± 1.62) [Uchida et al., 1994]. Other analogies suggesting a link between light-rings and spindle-bursts are summarized in Table 4.

There is no other brain rhythm that oscillates in the reciprocal cortico-thalamo-cortical circuits of the visual pathways which has the same timing as RTN spindle bursts. This suggests that, based on timing alone, it is reasonable to infer that RTN sleep spindles are responsible for generating the phosphene ring-images as an epiphenomenon. But the hypothesis of spindle wave etiology can be further strengthened by showing that the *shape* of the phosphene image and its *movements* can also be explained by reference to RTN spindle bursts and their effects on vision-relay cells in the thalamus.

Shape and Movement as Artifacts of LGN Anatomy

The lateral geniculate nucleus (LGN) is the thalamic structure responsible for relaying the vision-related signals generated in retinal receptors to the visual cortices. Retinal signals transmitted by ganglion cell axons from both eyes are reorganized at the optic chiasm where the two optic tracks converge: all axons transmitting visual signals that represent the *right* half of the visual field are collected together and then that reconstituted optic track projects to the *left* LGN, and, similarly, all axons transmitting visual signals that represent the left half of the visual field are collected and sent to the right LGN. (The importance of this anatomical detail will become evident later in the investigation when we begin to trace the origins of phosphene images that appear in the right side of the visual field.)

The LGN is composed of six thin sheets (laminae) of thalamocortical neurons. The laminae fold over a central hilus to form a structure that has characteristics similar to a half-dome, as shown in the drawings in Figure 11: the first drawing shows a frontal view of the outer (dorsal) surface of a monkey LGN, the second a schematic view of what the LGN would look like if sliced horizontally [Le Gros

	PHOSPHENE RINGS	RTN SPINDLE BURSTS
Average Number	I usually see 4 phosphene rings before the ring stop appearing	The average number of spindle bursts required to put a normal adult to sleep is 4.87 (± 1.6) spindle bursts. The RTN spindle bursts terminate automatically.
Duration & Extension	Thin band (≈ 0.5 - 1.5 cm); Each ring visible for 4 seconds	A spindle burst lasts 1 to 3 sec
Periodicity	A new ring enters the visual field every 5 seconds	The RTN fires spindle bursts at 3 to 10 sec intervals
Direction	A black ring sweeps into the visual field from 360° and shrinks steadily in diameter, efflorescing as a phosphene ring between 80° and 60° of isoeccentricity. The ring continues shrinking in diameter at the same rate.	Spindle waves flow ventro-dorsally through RTN matrix, so the waves of rebound spikes fired by vision-relay cells in the LGN also flow in a ventro-dorsal direction through the geniculate laminae.
Speed	Constant speed over 4 seconds	Unknown
Signal-to-Noise Ratio	High (i.e., bright phosphene)	High (Short intense bursts that block sensory signal-processing)

Table 4. Summary of the similarities between the characteristics of RTN spindle bursts and the meditation-induced phosphene rings

Clark, 1940-41]. The rest of the drawings are adaptations from an anatomical study by Connolly and Van Essen [1984] in which they physically detached each lamina in a monkey LGN, flattened the 3-dimensional structure into a 2-dimensional plane, then adjusted the shape of that 2-dimensional plane by imposing a grid of retino-topic coordinates based on data collected in experiments by Malpelli and Baker

[1975]. In Figure 11C-E, I've adapted their drawings for the largest and most dorsal lamina, designated as number 6. This new map of lamina 6 with its retinotopic and visuotopic grid makes it possible to identify the location of vision-relay cells in the LGN that represent different regions of the visual field, where a position in the visual field is represented in terms of equidistance from the centerpoint ("isoeccentricities"). It is important to remember that this map pertains to lamina 6 in only one of the two LGNs, so the vision-relay neurons located in the lamina shown here represent only one-half of the visual field.

When the RTN begins firing spindle bursts, a wave of excitation moves through the RTN matrix, inhibiting the axons of vision-relay cells that project to the primary visual cortex. After the spindle wave moves on, many of the vision-relay cells that have just been released from spindle wave inhibition fire "rebound" spikes [Coulter, 1997]. These waves of rebound spikes reflect the spatial distribution and direction of movement of the spindle wave that just stimulated their release. The RTN has a retinotopic organization that parallels the retinotopic organization of the LGN, so a wave of RTN spike-bursts will "influence the lateral geniculate nucleus retinotopically, with little regard to visual functional streams [Ulrich et al., 2003]."

Figure 11. Anatomical drawings of the primate lateral geniculate nucleus (LGN). A. Saggittal section of a monkey LGN in silhouette, adapted from Le Gros Clark [1940-41], that shows six sheets ("laminae") of vision-relay neurons layered and folded over a central hylus to form a shallow dome. In the human LGN the hylus is less pronounces so the dome is flatter, but in other respects the two structures are comparable. Retinal signals transmitted via the optic track enter the LGN through the rostrodorsal surfaces (i.e., through the front and top) and then form one-to-one synapses with the target thalamocortical that relay those signals with one-to-one fidelity to the primary visual cortices. The axons that project from vision-relay neurons extend out through the ventrocaudal (i.e., back and bottom) surfaces of the laminae and collect to form the optic radiations that extend to the primary visual cortices. As the efferent axons of vision-relay cells exit the LGN, they are intercepted en route by a matrix of inhibitory neurons that wraps around the posterior portions of the thalamus; this matrix, called the thalamic reticular nucleus (RTN) governs the transmission of sensory signals from the thalamus to the primary visual cortex. **B.** A schematic drawing (adapted from Le Gros Clark) of the *anterior* surface of the LGN which is formed by the most dorsal lamina (labeled #6). **C-D.** This drawing, adapted from Connolly and Van Essen [1984], show how these researchers extracted the individual laminae from a monkey LGN—including the dorsal lamina #6, shown here—and then flattened its 3-dimensional, curved structure into a 2-dimensional sheet with a triangular shape. **E.** Retinotopic and visuotopic map of geniculate lamina 6. This drawing, also adapted from Connolly and Van Essen, shows how the researchers adjusted the triangular shape of the flat lamina 6 and used data from an earlier experiment by Malpelli and Baker [1975] to construct a visuotopic grid that accurately reflected the position of vision-relay neurons in lamina #6 that represented different regions within that one-half of the visual field innervated by each of the two LGNs.

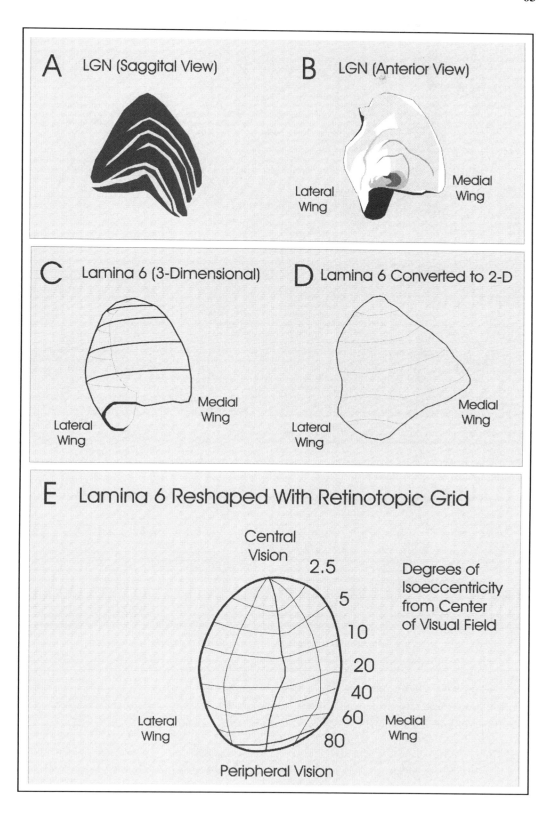

A LGN (Saggital View)

B LGN (Anterior View)

Lateral Wing

Medial Wing

C Lamina 6 (3-Dimensional)

Medial Wing

Lateral Wing

D Lamina 6 Converted to 2-D

Medial Wing

Lateral Wing

E Lamina 6 Reshaped With Retinotopic Grid

Central Vision

2.5
5
10
20
40
60
80

Degrees of Isoeccentricity from Center of Visual Field

Lateral Wing

Medial Wing

Peripheral Vision

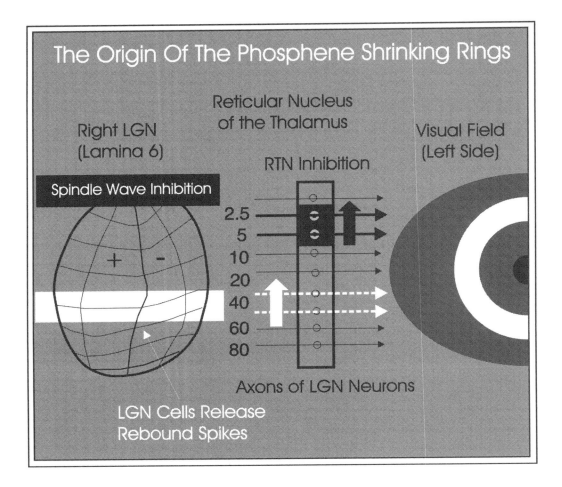

The Origin Of The Phosphene Shrinking Rings

Right LGN
(Lamina 6)

Reticular Nucleus
of the Thalamus

Visual Field
(Left Side)

RTN Inhibition

Spindle Wave Inhibition

2.5
5
10
20
40
60
80

Axons of LGN Neurons

LGN Cells Release
Rebound Spikes

Figure 12. The neural mechanisms responsible for generating epiphenomenal phosphene images of shrinking green rings. When a spindle burst during stage 2 NREMS ascends ventrodorsally through the RTN matrix, it consists of a relatively thin, coherent spatial wave that imposes inhibition on the efferent axons of of vision-relay cells in the LGN—only lamina #6 is shown here—which blocks the normal relay of visual signals to the primary visual cortices, including those signals generated by random metabolic discharges in the retinae that generate the charcoal background color of the visual field; this wave of inhibition generates an image of a dark ring shrinking in diameter in the visual field, but this ring is barely perceptible, if at all, because it is black-on-charcoal. As the spindle wave moves higher up the RTN matrix, it releases the inhibition on that band of vision-relay cell axons that it had suppressed only a moment before, and in response the vision-relay cells in the disinhibited band fire "rebound spikes." The spatial distribution of the rebound spikes mirrors the bandwidth of the spindle wave that triggered them, and when these waves of rebound spikes reach the higher visual cortices, neurons there respond as if these internally-generated signals were actually veridical visual signals from the retinae. These signals register in consciousness as a ring of internally-generated light formed by fused half-rings contributed by the right and left LGN, each of which innervates the ipsalateral visual field.

We are now in a position to identify how the phosphene image of a ring with a shrinking diameter is generated by the interactions of the RTN sleep spindles and vision-relay cells in the LGN. In order to generate a phosphene ring with the characteristics I've described, the RTN spindle waves have to flow in a direction that would trigger vision-relay cells in lamina 6 to fire waves of rebound spikes that begin in the most ventral regions of the LGN (where vision-relay cells representing peripheral vision are located) and that move steadily upward in a ventrodorsal direction (where vision-relay cells representing central vision are located). In Figure 12, I use the retinotopic map of lamina 6 developed by Connolly and Van Essen [1984] to plot the ventrodorsal ascent of a spindle wave and its effect on vision-relay cells in lamina 6. While the spindle wave is imposing its inhibition, the vision-relay cells affected by that inhibition are prevented from forwarding any signals whatsoever, not even the signals from the retinae that are generated by random metabolic discharges—the signals that generate the distinctive charcoal color of the visual field. It is because of this blocking of signals generated by random activity in the retinae that the first image generated by the spindle wave as it begins in the most ventral region of the RTN matrix is the sensation, which is often only subliminal, of a dark ring that sweeps into the periphery of the visual field from all 360° and then shrinks steadily in diameter. The dark ring is barely perceptible, if at all, even for someone who knows what to look for, because it moves against the dark background of the visual field, because it moves very fast, and because it is quickly eclipsed by the sudden efflorescence of the bright green phosphene ring once the dark ring shrinks past 80° of isoeccentricity. For most people who are meditating or who are lying in bed and hovering on the cusp that separates stage 1 and stage 2 NREMS, the dark ring itself will remain subliminal even as it generates a sensation of subtle movement ("optic flow").

The sudden effloresce of phosphene light occurs because the passing of the spindle wave releases the inhibition imposed on vision-relay cells—the inhibition that generated the dark ring—and those cells fire rebound spikes. The waves of rebound spikes released in the wake of the spindle waves are forwarded to the visual cortices where they are processed as if they were normal visual signals generated by retinal receptors. Figure 12 shows how a band of rebound spikes from lamina 6 in one LGN will eventually register in consciousness as a phosphene image of half of a ring. Since this interaction between RTN spindle waves and the rebound spikes of vision-relay cells in the LGN takes place simultaneously in both right and left hemispheres, the contributions of both LGNs will fuse to create a single, integrated image, just as signals from both eyes are fused to produce images of external objects, and the result of that fusion is that the meditator will see one green light-ring. Since spindle bursts ascend the RTN matrices in a ventrodorsal direction, the waves of rebound spikes in each LGN will follow the same pattern, moving from the most ventral regions of the laminae, where the cells represent peripheral vision, toward the most dorsal regions, where the cells represent central vision, and, as a result of this ventrodorsal movement, the phosphene ring will appear first in the more peripheral regions of the visual field and will shrink toward the more central regions, creating the illusion of a light-ring that seems to be "receding" in 3-dimensional space.

Before proceeding with this "reverse-engineering" analysis of meditation-induced light-rings, it is important to discuss the merits of a potential challenge to the hypothesis that I've just presented. Some might object that it would be possible to generate the image of a light-ring with the same characteristics I've described by converging the eyes as strongly as possible, or, alternatively, by pushing a finger against the eyeball to deform the retina and discharge the outermost receptors, but there are a number of reasons why these behaviors would not be effective. It is unlikely that someone could converge the eyeballs with enough force to discharge retinal receptors, but even if this were possible, there is no reason to suppose that the discharges would be distributed in a thin band along the peripheral rim of the retina, as would be required to generate the image of a symmetrical ring. The same can be said for pressing a finger against the eyeball. But even if it were possible to mechanically trigger a symmetrical ring along the rim of the retina, there is no reason to suppose that the wave of discharges initiated in this manner would propagate along an inward trajectory that would preserve the symmetry of the ring in the phosphene image that resulted; it's much more likely that the wave of discharges would propagate in an amorphous and unpredictable manner. Moreover, the deformation hypothesis cannot explain the clock-like timing intervals of the green light-rings nor the filling-in of a dark blue disk at precisely 2 seconds into the 4-second trajectory of the light-ring. Any one of these reasons provides sufficient grounds for rejecting the mechanical deformation hypothesis, but, as it happens, there is also a recent study that supports this conclusion. When researchers asked a group of yogis to press their fingers hard against their eyeballs, some subjects reported seeing a "central circular area filled with yellow color that was surrounded by patches of many colors as if the whole retina glowed [Pandey Vimal et al., 2007]," but none of the yogis reported seeing thin green rings that appeared with clock-like regularity, that shrank steadily in diameter while retaining their symmetry, and that acquired a dark blue fill-disk at precisely 2 seconds after the light-ring entered the visual field. It is reasonable to conclude, therefore, that given the spatial and temporal features of the meditation-induced light-rings, these images are generated as an visual epiphenomenon of a meditator's activation of RTN spindle bursts usually associated with onset of stage 2 NREMS.

Ring and Disk Colors as Functions of LGN Anatomy

The activation of spindle waves can also account for the distinctive yellowish-green color of the light-ring and the dark blue color of the fill-disk. So far I've traced the effect of spindle wave inhibition on only one of the six lamina contained in the primate LGN. The six laminae differ not only in size but also in the types of vision-relay cells they contain, which means the vision-relay signals generated by spindle wave inhibition are substantially more complex than what I've described above. It is these differences in laminar size and cell composition that explain why the light-rings are yellowish-green in color and why the disk that fills the center of the light-ring at the midpoint of its inward trajectory has a dark blue color.

The primate retina has four kinds of light receptors: three different kinds of cone receptors, each designed to respond to light with specific wavelengths, and one type of rod receptor that responds to the brightness of a light ("luminance") but not to wavelength. Retinal signals that encode information about the wavelength and luminance levels of the ambient light energies (and about other visual features like orientation, movement, stereopsis, and the like) are processed by a hierarchy of vision-processing centers in the neocortex. Centers located earlier in the hierarchy extract information about specific features encoded in the signals, centers located later in the chain synthesize the extracted features, and eventually the visual signals are combined with other kinds of information to form a complete percept. Neuroscientist Semir Zeki has proposed a particularly useful phrase to describe the integration of vision-related signals: he calls this process the composition of a "cortical lightness record" [Zeki, 1993].

Understanding color perception is notoriously difficult, and, to make matters worse, there is still much about this subject that remains unknown, but I found that it was possible to account for the green color of the light-rings and also for the dark blue of the fill-disk by making a set of relatively simple calculations. This analysis is highly speculative, but the similarities between the colors predicted by these speculative calculations and the observed colors are remarkable. I'll begin with some background information on color-processing in the primate brain.

Some cones vary in that some respond to long wavelengths (L-cones), some to medium wavelengths (M-cones), and some to short wavelengths (S-cones.). The cone responses are collected by ganglion cells which have very long axons that extend all the way to the thalamus where they make their first synapse with individual vision-relay neurons located in one of the six laminae of the LGN. The responses of two types of cone receptors (L-cones and M-cones) are linked in the retina by "spatially-opponent" circuits that combine the two sets of responses and encode them as paired signals—as "red-on/green-off" (L+/M-) signals or as "green-on/red-off" (L-/M+). When these combinations of L-cone and M-cone signals reach the LGN, they are received by vision-relay neurons in two laminae—in the most dorsal lamina (6) and its neighbor, lamina (5). By contrast, *S-cones are not organized in a spatially-opponent circuit, so their signals are forwarded to the LGN via their own dedicated set of ganglion cells.* The S-cone signals are processed only in the two intermediate laminae (4 & 3), called the "koniocellular" laminae. Finally, the responses of rod receptors that encode the brightness (luminance) of a light stimulus are sent exclusively to the two innermost laminae (2 & 1).

Figure 13. Phosphene color as a function of differences in the sizes and composition of the six geniculate laminae. A. A schematic drawing of the primate LGN that illustrates the differences in the sizes (and hence the ventral extension) of the six laminae and also differences in the types of visual signals relayed by the neurons located in each lamina. This drawing is based on Connolly and Van Essen's 2-dimensional visuotopic map of LGN laminae introduced in Figure 11. The far periphery of the visual field is represented in only 2 of the 6 laminae—in the most ventral lamina (#1) which relays visual signals that encode brightness information (luminance) but not color-related information (wavelength), and also in the most dorsal lamina (#6) which encodes color-related (wavelength) signals but only those that signals that were encoded in the retina as spectrally-opponent combinations—signals that encode either "red-on/green-off" (+L/-M) or "green-on/red-off" (-L/+M), but do not encode "blue-on" (+S) signals. By contrast, once a spindle wave has ascended farther up the RTN matrix so that its inhibition affects vision-relay cells representing the visual field from 20° of isoeccentricity inward, vision-relay cells in all 6 laminae will participate in firing rebound spikes. As a result, the visual signals relayed to the primary visual cortices will contain contributions from both of the intermediate "koniocellular" laminae (#3 and # 4) that encode S-cone "blue-on" signals, from both of the magnocellular laminae (#1 and # 2) that encode luminance signals only, and from both of the parvocellular laminae (#5 and #6) that encode spectrally-opponent wavelength signals, "red-on/green-off" (+L/-M) or "green-on/red-off" (-L/+M). B. This chart of spectral sensitivity curves, adapted from Marks et al. [1961], shows the response patterns of retinal cone receptors to stimulation by external light of different wavelengths. In the text I use the maximal response rates for all three types of retinal cone receptors and retinal rods to calculate the average wavelength that would result if all vision-relay cells in all LGN laminae were to discharge simultaneously at maximal levels, as they might be expected to do in response to the spindle wave repression. These *hypothetical* calculations suggest that light sensations produced waves of rebound spikes from the most ventral regions of the LGN will be green in color while those from the most dorsal regions of the LGNs will be blue. If vision-relay cells in the LGNs fire waves of rebound spikes in the wake of spindle wave inhibition, what kind of cortical lightness record will be generated by this process, given that it is wholly internal and not driven by an external light source? To answer this question, we need to find out which of the six laminae will be affected by the spindle wave inhibition at various stages as the wave moves up through the RTN matrix, because some laminae are longer than others, so that their ventral regions extend well below the ventral regions of other laminae, and it is these most ventral extensions that will be impacted first when a spindle wave begins its ventrodorsal trajectory up the RTN matrix. The drawing in Figure 13A (adapted from the anatomical study by Connolly and Van Essen [1984] we discussed earlier in this chapter) shows the relative sizes of the six laminae in a primate LGN and the types of wavelength signals processed by the vision-relay cells in each lamina. The more peripheral regions of the visual field (i.e., from 80° to 50° of isoeccentricity) are represented in only two laminae: in lamina #1 which only relays signals that encode luminance information, and in lamina 6 which relays signals encoding the spectrally-opponent combinations, "red-on/green-off" (+L/-M) and "green-on/red-off" (-L/+M). The koniocellular laminae that relay S-cone "blue-on" signals do not have the same ventral extension and thus would not participate in the release of rebound spikes while the spindle wave is still moving through the most ventral regions of the RTN matrix. If I see light-rings suddenly effloresce at about 80° of isoeccentricity, this means that the band of rebound spikes that eventually registers in consciousness as the perception of a light-ring must be generated in the only two laminae that contain vision-relay neurons representing the more peripheral region of the visual field, and of these two laminae, dorsal lamina #6 is the only one that relays wavelength signals that generate color sensations, and it relays the spectrally-opponent combinations of "red-on/green-off" (+L/-M) and "green-on/red-off" (-L/+M). If these are the only wavelength signals that contribute to the composition of the "cortical lightness record," what color sensation will a subject perceive?

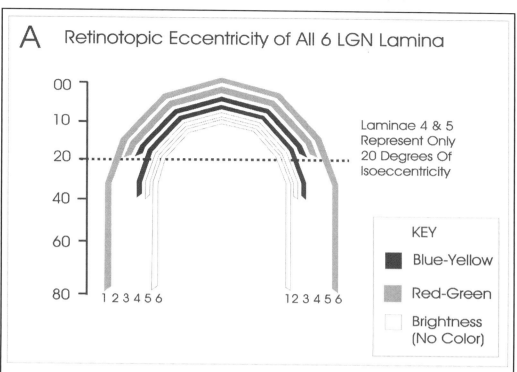

A Retinotopic Eccentricity of All 6 LGN Lamina

Laminae 4 & 5
Represent Only
20 Degrees Of
Isoeccentricity

KEY

Blue-Yellow

Red-Green

Brightness
(No Color)

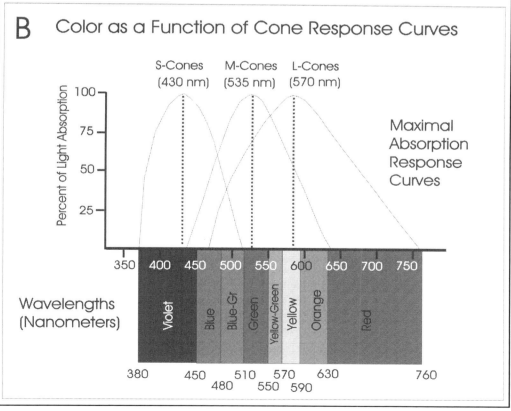

B Color as a Function of Cone Response Curves

S-Cones
(430 nm)

M-Cones
(535 nm)

L-Cones
(570 nm)

Percent of Light Absorption

Maximal
Absorption
Response
Curves

Wavelengths
(Nanometers)

Violet Blue Blue-Gr Green Yellow-Green Yellow Orange Red

If vision-relay cells in all six laminae of both LGNs fire waves of rebound spikes in the wake of spindle wave inhibition, what kind of cortical lightness record will result from this internally-generated activation? Because two of the laminae are much longer than others, their ventral skirts extend well below the ventral regions of the other four laminae; as a result, once a spindle wave begins its ventrodorsal trajectory up the RTN matrix, it will trigger its first effects only in the two laminae with the most ventral extensions. The drawing in Figure 13A adapted from the anatomical study by Connolly and Van Essen [1984] depicts the relative sizes of the six laminae in a primate LGN and the types of wavelength signals processed in each of the six lamina. This drawing reveals that the more peripheral regions of the visual field (from 80° to 50° of isoeccentricity) are represented in only two of the six laminae: in lamina 1, which only relays luminance information, and in lamina 6, which relays wavelength signals generated by spectrally-opponent combinations—by the "red-on/green-off" (+L/-M) and "green-on/red-off" (-L/+M) combinations. The koniocellular laminae that relay S-cone "blue-on" signals do not extend as far in the ventral direction as do laminae 1 and 6, so vision-relay cells in the koniocellular laminae will not fire rebound spikes at a time when the spindle wave is still moving through the most ventral regions of the RTN matrix. Based on these considerations, we can make the following inference: if I see a light-ring suddenly effloresce at about 80° to 60°of isoeccentricity, the color of the light-ring will be determined by waves of rebound spikes that originate in laminae 1 and 6, with lamina 6 being the more likely source since it not only has enough ventral extension to represent images in the peripheral visual field but also has the capacity to encode wavelength signals which lamina 1 lacks.

Since almost all vision-relay cells in the band just released from spindle wave inhibition will discharge at about the same time, the cortical lightness record will be composed by equal contributions of spectrally-opponent "red-on/green-off" (+L/-M) and "green-on/red-off" (-L/+M) signals. We can estimate what color lightness record will result by referring to the spectral sensitivity chart in Figure 13B, a chart adapted from Marks et al. [1961]. Assume, for the moment, that all of the vision-relay cells representing peripheral vision (i.e., that portion of the visual field extending from 80° to 50° of isoeccentricity) fire their rebound spikes at *maximal* rates, just as they would if the cone receptors in the retinae were being discharged at maximal rates. In the spectral sensitivity chart of Figure 13B, the maximal responses of retinal L-cones occur at wavelengths of 570 nanometers (nm), the maximal responses of retinal M-cones occur at wavelengths of 535 nm; and the maximal responses of retinal rods occur at 511 nm. If we calculate the average for these maximal response rates, what color sensation would result?

In making this calculation, we will encounter two issues which cannot be conclusively resolved given the current state of research, so we will have to make two alternative calculations and then check to see if both calculations produce results that are consistent with the colors reported by meditators. The first problem is whether or not to include maximal rod responses in our calculation, given that rods do not encode wavelength information. The second problem, which turns out to be related to the first, is whether or not L-cone and M-cone signals will end up cancelling each other's contribution because of their spectrally-opponent organization, in which case only the rod-based luminance signals will determine the composition of the cortical lightness record. A cancellation of wavelength-sensitive signals because of their spectrally-opponent organization will not result in a total absence of color but will generate sensations with green or blue-green colors:

> The stimulus that is located in color space at the intersect of the cardinal axes does not elicit a response from either of the spectrally opponent cell classes because all the spectrally antagonistic inputs cancel each other . . . This chromatic-null hypothesis, when plotted on a chromaticity diagram, is far from the region of achromatic stimuli and *would appear as a somewhat desaturated G or BG [green or blue-green]* [Abramov, 1994, p. 457; emphasis added].

Since I cannot determine which of these is the correct position, I plan to make two alternative calculations. For the first calculation, assume that the responses of three types of receptors (L-cones, M-cones, and rods) participate in determining the color sensation when a spindle wave triggers rebound spikes in the most ventral regions of the two longest laminae, lamina 1 and lamina 6. If we add the maximal responses of retinal L-cones, M-cones, and rods, then divide that sum by 3 (because there are 3 types of receptors contributing to the composition of the cortical lightness record in this calculation), we get an average wavelength of 539 nm: 570 nm + 535 nm + 511 nm = 1616 nm ÷ 3 = 538.66. In the cone spectral sensitivity curves shown in Figure 13B, light with a wavelength of 539 nm has a *green* color. For the alternative calculation, assume that signals from cells with spectrally-opponent organization cancel out each other's contribution, so the cortical lightness record will be determined solely by rod-based luminance signals from lamina 1 which produce a maximal response to light with wavelengths of 511 nm. In the cone spectral sensitivity curves of Figure 13B, light with this wavelength has a *blue-green* color. These alternative calculations produce a similar outcome: both predict that the cortical lightness record for the phosphene ring image moving through the far periphery of the visual field will be in the green spectrum—a solid green or bluish-green, not a red, orange, yellow, blue, or violet color.

When the light-ring reaches the mid-point of its centripetal trajectory, it fills-in with disk that has a dark blue color. The same kind of calculation that identified green as the color generated by stimulation of the most ventral regions of laminae 1 and 6 can also explain the dark blue color of the fill-disk if we take into account the fact that, once the spindle wave begins triggering rebound spikes in the more dorsal regions of the LGN, more laminae will begin to contribute signals, an addition that produces dramatic changes. When the vision-relay cells that represent central vision begin to fire rebound spikes (i.e., the vision-relay cells that represent that portion of the visual field extending from 20° of isoeccentricity inward), all six laminae will contribute to the composition of the cortical lightness record, including both koniocellular laminae which are the exclusive source for the relay of S-cone "blue-on" signals. The maximal responses of S-cones are evoked by light with wavelengths of 430 nm, so we need to adjust our calculation of the average wavelength to include this new figure. The inclusion of S-cone "blue-on" signals requires another adjustment as well: a study by De Valois et al. [2000] found that S-cone signals relayed from the LGN get augmented in a non-linear fashion as they arrive in the primary visual cortex. The researchers report that only 10% of the vision-relay neurons in the LGN responded to the receipt of S-cone signals from the retina but in the primary visual cortices 19% of neurons responded. To adjust for this phenomenon in calculating the average wavelength, the contribution of S-cone "blue-on" signals should be double-weighted. Moreover, De Valois et al. also found that there was a significant *delay* in the cortical processing of the S-cone "blue-on" signals relative to the processing of other visual signals, a delay they attribute to the circuits that perform the intracortical amplification of those signals: "Because this S input is also often delayed relative to the inputs of cells from the L/M systems [Cottaris and De Valois, 1984], we have speculated that the S_o signal from the LGN might be inverted, and delayed, by a circuit within the striate cortex (p. 6)."

Now we can calculate the average wavelength that will appear in the cortical lightness record generated when vision-relay cells in all six laminae participate, and here, as before, we will have to make alternative calculations because we don't know whether or not the L-cone and M-cone responses will cancel each other out. First assume that the responses of spectrally-opponent L-cones and M-cones do not cancel each other out: then the average of maximal responses for the rods, all three types of cones, and the amplification of S-cone input in the primary visual cortex is 2476 nm, divided, in this case, by 5 (which is the sum of the four types of retinal receptors and an extra representation for the cortical amplification of S-cone input): 570 nm + 535 nm + 511 nm + 2 (430 nm) = 2476 nm ÷ 5 = 495.2 nm. In the chart of cone sensitivity curves presented in Figure 13B, light with this wavelength would have a *blue-green* color. This is close to the color of the fill-disk that suddenly effloresces in the center of the shrinking light-ring, but that is not actually the same color that I observed. For the alternative calculation, assume that the spectrally-opponent L-cone and M-cone signals cancel each other out, in which case the composition of the cortical lightness record will determined by 3 inputs—by rod signals, S-cone signals, and the cortical amplification of S-cone input, as follows: 511 nm + 430 nm + 430 nm = 1371 nm ÷ 3 = 457 nm. In the chart of cone sensitivity curves in Figure 13B, light with a wavelength of 457 nm produces a *blue* sensation, which is the color of the fill-disk that I see. While in this case the alternative calculations have produced slightly different results, both averages fall within the blue spectrum, broadly defined.

The blue fill-disk only began to appear after I had practiced inducing phosphene images on many occasions; before that, the fill-disk was the same green color as the light-ring. This change from a green to a blue color can be explained by reference to the longer latency required to process S-cone "blue-on" signals [De Valois et al., 2000] combined with the prospect that frequent induction of phosphene light-rings would likely reduce that delay over time. We know, based on my observations of light-rings, that the latency for blue signals had to have been cut in half—that in the beginning the delay must have lasted more than 4 seconds (so that the "blue-on" signals did not have time to register in the cortical lightness record before the green ring disappeared), but then the delay was shortened to only 2 seconds (so that the "blue-on" signals registered fast enough to appear when the light-ring was only halfway into its trajectory). The frequent repetition of a set of behaviors stimulates the growth of connections linking those neurons that discharge in concert, reorganzing the neuronal circuits to be more efficient in processing similar signal-sets reappear in the future. This longterm potentiation of neuronal circuits, which is precisely what one would expect to happen when a meditator keeps on inducing phosphene ring images, would decrease the time required to amplify S-cone "blue-on" signals in intracortical circuits, and it is reasonable to infer that, in this case, it cut that time in half.

In the case of the MRI-driven light rings, these rings remained in the visual field for 2 seconds, not enough time for the registration of S-cone "blue-on" signals, even after I'd induced a reorganization of neuronal circuits that cut the processing time in half. The MRI machine used in my test was an older, 1990-vintage machine in which the interval between the successive radio pulses was preset at 2 seconds, an interval considered to be optimal for the machine to be able to recapture the energy released by the body's atoms as they returned to their former, pre-bombardment state ("precessional relaxation") [Edelman, 1990; Newhouse and Wiener, 1991]. Apparently the energy released by precessional relaxation flowed through the RTN, the anatomical structure that regulates the flow of all sensory signals through the thalamus, and its flow produced essentially the same effect as a spindle wave generated by wholly endogenous processses—the image of a phosphene ring—but the 2 second interval of the radiobeam pulses drove the wave of excitation up through the RTN matrix at a much faster rate than a normal spindle wave—at 2-second intervals rather than the 5-second intervals associated with an endogenous spindle burst. Therefore, the MRI-driven light-rings completed their inward trajectory in less than 2 seconds and disappeared before the S-cone "blue-on" signals had time to register in the cortical lightness record. In this case, the cortical lightness record was composed of signals from rods, L-cones, and M-cones—the combination that generated a green color in our speculative calculations.

It is interesting to note that in this MRI scenario the RTN functions as kind of "resonator," which is to say, as a structure that can be driven by different kinds of energy. The existence of just such a resonator was proposed many years ago by

Max Knoll, one of the first researchers to conduct experimental studies of phosphene generation. When Knoll's team induced phosphene images by applying electric stimuli calibrated at different frequencies to the heads of volunteer subjects, they found that specific types of images—including phosphene rings—could be induced in individual subjects by stimulation with specific frequencies, a regularity that implied the existence of a resonating circuit that the researchers were unable to identify at the time with the instruments available [Knoll et al., 1963]. The inference that the RTN can function as resonator capable of transmitting energy that originates in abnormal processes is interesting because it offers a possible explanation for why some people who have near-death experiences as a result of severe bodily injury sometimes report that they see themselves moving through a "dark tunnel" that transports them toward a bright light—a subject that we'll want to revisit when we discuss the onset of paroxysmal phosphene visions.

Retaining Consciousness During Sleep Rhythms

In a normal transition to NREMS, the volley of synchronous spindle bursts that marks the onset of stage 2 NREMS "overwhelms" the normal firing pattern of thalamocortical cells, preventing them from relaying afferent sensory signals, and, as a consequence, imposing a loss of consciousness [Contreras and Steriade, 1995]. But the loss of consciousness cannot be timed precisely using only the cortical EEG; the thalamus is too remote for the onset of spindling to be reliably detected by the scalp electrodes [Steriade, 1993]. In experiments with cats that had electrodes implanted in the thalamus, *researchers found that spindling often reached peak levels of activity in the thalamus—the level of activity which is thought to mark the transition to stage 2 NREMS—at a time when the cortical EEG was still showing intermittent desynchronizations, a pattern characteristic of the drowsy stage 1 transition [Lancel et al., 1992].* There is a short period of time in which the synchronous rhythms of stage 2 NREMS are installed in the thalamus but have not yet reached the cortex, so that cortical neurons remain in a condition that allows them to depolarize in response to the receipt of afferent sensory signals. This suggests one explanation for how it might be possible for meditators to retain consciousness even though synchronous spindle bursts are already active in the thalamus: if meditators can learn to prolong the duration of this time lag between the onset of synchronous spindle bursts in the thalamus and the installation of synchronous activity in the cortex, prolonging the time in which cortical cells can continue to depolarize in response to the receipt of vision-related signals, then this would enable meditators to retain enough conscious awareness to keep processing signals from the LGN as if they were visual signals that had originated in the retinae.

If meditators are indeed able to prolong vision-sensitive awareness, what would cause this to happen? There are several micro-behaviors that meditators typically use to induce a state of empty-mind consciousness, and these behaviors—convergent eye movements, attentive fixation, and an attitude of expectancy—produce dramatic increases in the excitability of neurons in the visual cortices. For example, converging the eyes releases a type of ponto-geniculo-occipital (PGO) wave called an "eye movement potential" (EMP). By contrast with the PGO waves associated with rapid-eye-movement sleep (REMS) which are emitted throughout a REM episode, eye movement potentials last only as long as the eye movement itself [Steriade and McCarley, 1990; Datta, 1995], but the EMPs trigger the same kinds of desynchronizations in visual neurons as the PGO waves associated with REMS—and in both instances the result of these desynchronizations is an increase in neuron responsivity in the LGN and also in the primary visual cortices [Wurtz and Mohler, 1976; Steriade and McCarley, 1990; Steriade, 1991; Datta, 1995]. The combination of eye convergence and attentive fixation produces increases the excitability of a special set of light-sensitive neurons located in area PG of the posterior parietal cortex [Bazier et al., 1991]: in experiments with monkeys trained to fix their attention on a screen and to keep on fixating even when no targets appear, the excitability of these neurons increased by as much as 350% [Mountcastle et al., 1981]. Angle of gaze, which is another behavior that meditators use when inducing trance states, can also enhance the responsiveness of the light-sensitive neurons, especially those located in area PG of the posterior parietal cortices [Andersen et al., 1987; Andersen et al., 1990]. Increases in the responsivity of light-sensitive neurons in area PG are important because this is the first processing center in the visual pathways that contains individual neurons that respond selectively to signals evoked by large stimuli extending into both sides of the visual field and moving in opposite directions in the right and left visual field ("opponent vector motion")[Motter et al., 1987; Steinmetz et al., 1987; Andersen et al., 1989; Andersen et al., 1990]. A large light-ring covering both sides of the visual field and shrinking in diameter would generate opponent vector motion. The recurring desynchronizations of visual neurons triggered by EMPs and the increases in the excitability of visual neurons could explain how meditators are able to retain consciousness despite the activation of synchronous sleep rhythms: the meditator's induction behaviors must keep neurons in the visual pathways desynchronized and hyperexcitable, and, as a result, the cortical neurons, rather than being entrained into synchronous rhythms by the arrival of waves of rebound spikes, react instead as if the afferent signals were veridical visual signals of retinal origin, which is to say, they process those signals from the LGN as they would process normal visual signals.

Indirect evidence that a meditator's eye movements, attentional manipulations, and attitude of expectancy combine to produce dramatic changes in the excitability of neurons in the primary visual cortices is provided in a PET study of mental imagery by Kosslyn et. al. [1995]: before the experiment began, the researchers took baseline measurements while their subjects were resting in a reclining position with their eyes closed and following instructions to "keep it black in front of your eyes." When the researchers examined their data, they found that while the subjects were performing the experimental task, which was to create mental pictures of familiar objects that had just been shown to them shortly before, there were significant increases in neuronal activity in the secondary visual cortices (as expected) but no increases in neuron activity in the primary visual cortices (also as expected). However, they discovered an anomaly in their data that surprised them: before the experiment began, while baseline measurements were being taken, and at a time when the subjects were relaxing and following instructions to "keep it black in front of your eyes," there was a different pattern of activity—an increase in the activity of visual neurons in the primary visual cortices. This increase must have been generated by wholly internal mechanisms that become active when subjects close their eyes and stare intently at an "empty" visual field with an attitude of expectation, essentially the same strategy used by meditators to induce empty-mind consciousness.

Sleep Rhythm Phosphenes and Hypnotic Analgesia

If meditation-induced light-rights produce an analgesic effect, as I've suggested, what neural mechanisms might be responsible for modulating that response? In a theoretical article on the neurophysiology of hypnosis, psychologists Crawford and Gruzelier [1992] propose that the variations in hypnotizability found in the human population are probably a function of variability in the efficiency of the frontolimbic (anterior) attentional system. In this view, high-hypnotizables would be better able to sustain focused attention on a task and to ignore extraneous stimuli than low-hypnotizables. In a related empirical study, Crawford et al. [1993] compared the use of attention by subjects with high versus low hypnotizability: they found that "highly hypnotizable persons *continue to show physiological reactivity while cognitively not perceiving the painful stimuli. . . .* Through disattentional processes, they can dissociate themselves from the awareness of pain [emphasis added]."

For a sensation to be perceived as painful, two kinds of signals must be integrated. First, there are *nociceptive* signals that are generated by cutaneous receptors to encode the location and intensity of a noxious stimulus. These nociceptive signals are sent to the thalamus and then relayed on to somatosensory cortices dedicated to the processing of the "sensory-discriminative" aspects of pain perception [Coghill et al., 1994]. But before these sensory-discriminative signals register in a person's consciousness as a painful perception, they must be forwarded from somatosensory cortices to the limbic system. The limbic input adds an affective dimension to the sensory-discriminary content, activating *memory-based emotional associations* that endow that particular pain stimulus with meanings that it acquired at some past time in the life of the person who's now being subjected to a similar noxious stimulus. Studies of brain metabolism reveal that this linking of somatosensory information with limbic associations takes place in the anterior cingulate and in the anterior insula [Jones et al., 1991; Talbot et al., 1991; Coghill et al., 1994].

Visual signals from the retinae are also referred to the anterior cingulate where they acquire memory-based emotional associations. In PET studies by Corbetta et al. [1991, 1993], the researchers demonstrated that the anterior cingulate is activated when subjects shift their spatial attention in response to expectations as to where stimuli will next appear. A meditator's shifting of spatial attention in response to expectations as to where phosphenes will appear is essentially the same behavioral state. Since the visual signals and nociceptive signals both have to receive limbic enhancement before they can register in consciousness, and since this enhancement requires access to the anterior cingulate, the two types of afferent sensory signals will often have to compete for access. In a theoretical article on the mechanisms of attention, Posner and Rothbart [1994] propose that visual signals can interfere with nociceptive signals by blocking access to the anterior cingulate. As behavioral evidence, they cite studies showing that young infants making distress calls can be distracted by the presentation of a new visual stimulus:

> We have shown the evidence of such control at about three months. Orienting to visual events can be employed to quiet or calm negative vocalizations. However, the distress appears to be maintained and reappears when the infant's attention to the stimulus is reduced. Caregivers also report the use of visual orienting to block overt manifestations of distress at about this age [Posner and Rothbart, Ibid., p. 197].

Also, a meditator's manipulation of attention—the intense focus on the "empty" visual field and the attitude of expectation, combined with a relative neglect of external stimuli—may actually reduce the numbers of nociceptive signals that get forwarded to the anterior cingulate: in a PET study by Drevets et al. [1995], researchers found that the mere *anticipation* of a touch at a specific cutaneous site *increased* the flow of blood to neurons in the somatosensory cortices that are linked with that particular cutaneous site, while at the same time the flow of blood *decreased* to those neurons linked with cutaneous sites where the touch was not expected. It seems likely, based on Drevets et al., that meditators who focus exclusively on the "empty" visual field in the anticipation of seeing phosphenes will produce an analogous shift in cerebral blood flow, that is, an *increase* in blood flow to neurons in the visual cortices and a *decrease* in blood flow to neurons in the somatosensory cortices. If so, then the nociceptive signals sent from cutaneous receptors to the somatosensory cortices will activate fewer neurons than in normal circumstances and, as a result, fewer nociceptive signals will be forwarded to the anterior cingulate—and therefore fewer of these signals will acquire the emotional associations they need to surface in consciousness.

Meditation-induced dampening of neuronal activity in the somatosensory cortices is not the only mechanism that has the potential to interfere with nociceptive signals: meditation also has important effects on the thalamus that might impede the relay of those signals. The thalamus does relay nociceptive signals [Jones et al., 1991; Talbot et al., 1991; Coghill et al., 1994; Lenz et al., 1997], so if a meditator is able to activate slow wave sleep rhythms, the onset of this synchronous activity in the thalamus will block the relay of nociceptive signals from cutaneous sites. In this regard, it is interesting to note that a study by Steriade et al. [1997] found that there was a close resemblance between the slow wave sleep rhythms they recorded during NREMS and the EEG activity they recorded during certain types of anesthesia.

The synchronous activity that blocks afferent nociceptive signals will also block the thalamic relay of other kinds of sensory signals, including the relay of afferent visual signals, but here it is important to remember that the signals that generate meditation-induced phosphene rings are *not* visual signals that originated in the retina and thus that have to be relayed through the thalamus in order to register in the cortical lightness record; rather, these signals are themselves integral components of the synchronous sleep rhythms, consisting of waves of rebound spikes discharged by vision-relay cells in response to the release of inhibition imposed by spindle waves ascending the RTN matrix. The waves of rebound spikes are able to flow unimpeded from the LGN to the primary visual cortices at a time when visual signals that originated in the retina would be blocked at the thalamic relay by the synchronous activity in the LGN, the same activity that generates the rebound spikes.

A meditator's focus of attention on the dark visual field might also interfere with the processing of nociceptive signals because the activation of RTN spindle bursts can reinforce the effects of attention. Researchers report that burst firing of RTN neurons of the sort that generates sleep spindles can also appear during waking states, although the spike-bursts that occur during a waking state are arhythmical rather than synchronous [McAlonan and Brown, 2000]. These arhythmical spike-bursts are discharged in the RTN's initial response to the receipt of afferent sensory signals: "These burst responses comprise the initial cellular response to visual stimulation and thus may provide a form of signal amplification that allows relay cells to signal the cortex about the presence of a stimulus of potential behavioral importance (Sherman, 1996) [McAlonan and Brown, Ibid., p. 303]." In another, related experiment [McAlonan et al., 2000], two different stimuli were presented simultaneously to a rat—a visual stimulus and an auditory stimulus—after which the rats were sacrificed so that the researchers could perform a postmortem exam of sensory-specific subsectors in the rat's RTN. When they measured the relative number of Fos proteins in the sensory-specific subsectors, proteins that serve as markers of neuron activity, they found that Fos proteins were much more numerous in the vision-specific subsector of the RTN than in the audition-specific subsector, thereby demonstrating that the rat had been attending to the visual stimulus and neglecting the auditory stimulus. The researchers conclude that the RTN must interact with attention networks during waking states to control which sensory signals become conscious:

> These demonstrations of selective activation in the sector of [RTN] associated with attended stimuli support the view that *this structure is not a component of the sensory relay but rather acts as an attentional gate, or filter, modulating the flow of information between the thalamus and cortex* [McAlonan et al., Ibid., p. 303; emphasis added].

If RTN burst firing during waking states is a neuronal mechanism that can amplify some sensory signals while impeding the thalamic relay of other sensory signals, as the McAlonan experiments suggest, and if it is attention that determines which signals get amplified by RTN spike-bursts, then we can explain how staring at sleep rhythm phosphenes helps meditators ameliorate the perception of pain by reference to this mechanism of RTN gating in addition to, or perhaps in combination with, the other mechanisms discussed above. The two other mechanisms were (1) an attention-related increase in neuronal activity in the visual cortices that produces a dampening of neuronal activity in the somatosensory cortices, and (2) the induction of synchronous sleep rhythms in the thalamus that then block the relay of afferent nociceptive signals and at the same time produce signals that register in consciousness as phosphene images. This combination of processes might explain why meditators who are able to manipulate attention and use it to induce phosphene imagery can ameliorate the effect of nociceptive signals that would normally register as acutely painful.

Light-Rings and the Sleep Rhythm Activation Theory

This neurologically-grounded, "reverse-engineering" analysis of light-ring characteristics supports the hypothesis that light-rings are generated by the onset of RTN spindle-bursts usually associated with stage 2 NREMS. This simple hypothesis can account for (1) the *number* of light-rings; (2) the *timing*; (3) the *durations* of individual light-rings and of a complete volley of light-rings; (4) the *automaticity* of light-rings; (5) their *movements*; (6) their *yellowish-green color*; (7) the belated acquisition of a *fill-disk* and the blue color of the fill-disk; and, (8) the *2-second latency* of the fill-disk. The hypothesis that light-rings are generated by activations of the RTN burst-firing mechanism can also explain why light-rings can appear as a spontaneous phenomenon at sleep onset but also as an induced phenomenon associated with behavioral states that resemble sleep, such as meditation, self-hypnosis, third-party hypnosis (induced by hypnotherapists or audiotapes), deep tissue massage, and some drug-induced reveries.

4

SLEEP RHYTHM PHOSPHENES, II: EYE-LIKE NEBULAE

PHENOMENOLOGY

The Vision of the Amorphous, Expanding Wave

When the volley of light-rings terminates automatically, there is a refractory interval in which no images appear, then a new image with very different features appears: an amorphous, expanding "cloud" of dark blue or purple phosphene suddenly efforesces in one side of the visual field, usually about mid-range, as shown in Figure 14. The leading edge of the wave expands with a swirling motion toward the center of vision (as if it were igniting neurons not yet activated) while the trailing edge of the wave evaporates (as if neurons already activated were now in refractory mode). Once it arrives at the center of the visual field, the phosphene cloud hovers there for several seconds. I can't be more specific about timing: I've tried to count the passing seconds to estimate the duration of a typical wave or the interval between successive waves, but the waves disappear if I divert even a miniscule amount of attention to observing my observations. What is most predictable about the amorphous expanding waves is their unpredictability—unpredictable shapes, unpredictable duration, and unpredictable timing intervals. By contrast with the light-rings that terminate automatically, the amorphous, expanding waves can be evoked indefinitely so long as the meditative focus is maintained.

The color of these cloud-like images can vary between dark blue and reddish purple. In the full-color panel on the back cover there is an insert that compares these two colors. When I'm meditating and see the amorphous phosphene clouds after the volley of light-rings, I usually see dark blue waves, but if I wake up in the middle of the night and see clouds of amorphous phosphene arriving spontaneously as I wait for sleep to return, the waves have a purple color.

The Acquisition of an Inner "Eye"

The amorphous cloud usually develops an inner node in which the phosphene is the same color as its surroundings but much brighter and more fine-grained in appearance. The smooth, opaque sheen of this inner node reminds me of molten

Figure 14. The vision of amorphous phosphene expanding waves. A. A wave of dark blue or purple phosphene suddenly illuminates in the middle-range of the visual field (i.e., within 40° of isoeccentricity), then drifts toward the center of the visual field, expanding and shrinking at the same time and swirling slowly like a small, wispy cloud when it first begins to coalesce and expand in otherwise empty sky. The image seems to move across the visual field, but this is because the leading edge of the wave is moving forward at the same time that the trailing edge of the wave is evaporating. When the cloud of phosphene reaches the center of the visual field, acquires a disk-like or amoeboid aspect, and it continues to hovers in that central position until disappears after a few seconds. The clouds borders are always amorphous and undergoing continuous fluctuations while it remains in the visual field. B. When meditator can sustain this image of amorphous clouds for longer intervals, the cloud can acquire a central node of brighter, more fine-grained (and hence opaque) phosphene which looks like it is about the diameter of a small pencil eraser. The fluctuations of this bright central node are mezmerizing: the bright phosphene ebbs away from its center to open up a dark "pupil-like" space, transforming the bright phosphene node into a ring-shape that looks like the "iris" of a disembodied eye—a vision of a "third eye" that might account for the many references to such an entity in the mystical literatures of world religions. This "eye" image is constantly being transformed back into the former image of a bright node within a cloud of duller phosphene: this happens because from the moment of its first appearance the dark pupil-like space begins to fill back in with promontories of bright light that shoot down into the dark space from the ring of bright iris-like phosphene. As these strips of light coil about and merge with neighboring promontories, the dark pupil quickly fills back in with the bright phosphene; then the process begins again—the bright phosphene begins to ebb away from the center of the node, restoring the pupil-like space at its center. C. One the one occasion when I inadvertently triggered a paroxysmal episode while meditating, I saw the amorphous cloud-like phosphene with its bright central node condense into a tiny "star-like" image that seemed to "twinkle" at the center of the dark visual field. This star-like phosphene is composed of a tiny cluster of very thin and very densely-packed phosphene filaments that flash into view and then instantly disappear only to be replaced by other flashing filaments. These filaments appear to be white in color, sometimes with a bluish tinge added. D. Inset: Close-up of the bright central node in an "eye-like" constellation. E. Inset: Close-up of an amorphous cloud with its bright central node condensing into a star-like phosphene.

The Vision of Amorphous Expanding Waves

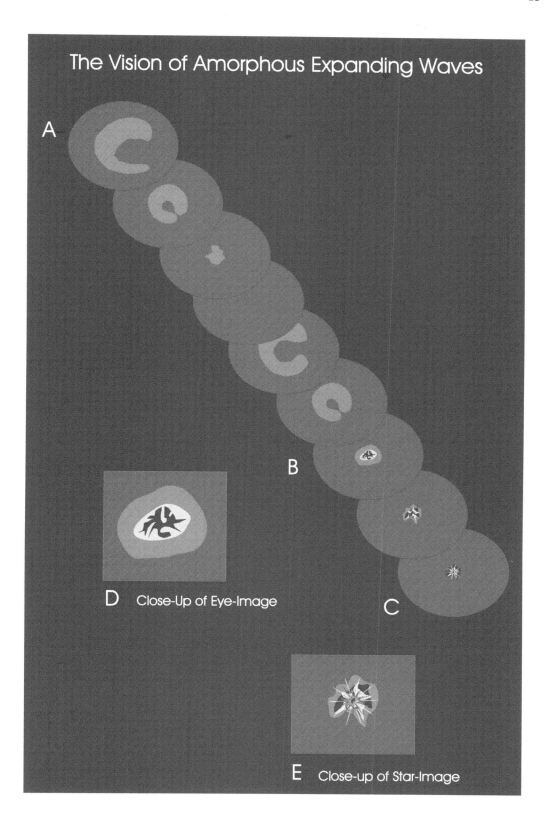

A

B

C

D   Close-Up of Eye-Image

E   Close-up of Star-Image

metal or of a ball of mercury that has escaped from a thermometer. Like the duller phosphene cloud that surrounds it, the bright central node is always changing its shape: the bright, "molten" phosphene keeps pulling back from the center to open up a tiny, dark space that looks uncannily like a dark "pupil" surrounded by a ring-shaped "iris" which is itself surrounded by the cloud of duller phosphene. But as soon as it appears the dark "pupil" is probed by tiny promontories of the bright, molten phosphene that shoot out of the ring-shaped "iris." These tiny protrusions coil and twist about, merging with other promontories so that they refill the dark "pupil" space, reconstituting a disk-like node for only a moment before the bright, molten phosphene once again pulls back from the center to open up another dark "pupil" space, and once again the promontories of bright phosphene shoot into that space, coil about, and fill it back in. The drawing in Figure 14D gives a static view that approximates the image of a disembodied "eye" formed by the inner node of brighter, more opaque phosphene. The fluctuations of this "inner eye" are quite dramatic, compelling the attention of a meditator so long as they appear in the visual field.

Some of the metaphors used in the ancient texts to describe the eye-like image with its two-toned phosphene are interesting and worth revisiting here because they're particularly apt. A verse in the *Rig Veda* describes lights that swirl around in a funnel motion, "assembl[ing] like the streams of water into holes [RV10.25.4, in Gonda, 1963, p. 173]." A verse in the *Upanishads* states that "here in this city of *Brahman* is an abode, a small lotus flower; within it is a small space. What is within that should be sought, for that, assuredly, is what one should desire to understand [*Chandogya Up.*, 8: 1, 1, Radhakrishnan, 1992, p. 491]." The Tibetan monk, Karma Lingpa, describes a vision in which a smaller light moves about within the larger cloud of light that surrounds it:

> Inside a form like the round plates of a shield there appears a bindu about the size of a mustard seed or a pea. Inside that are the so-called 'vajra-strands of awareness,' which are find like knots tied in a strand of a horse's tail, like a string of pearls, like an iron chain, like a lattice of flowers moving with the breeze, and so on. All those appear in combinations of two or three, and so on, and they are called the 'sole bindu of the strand of your own awareness [Lingpa, in Chagmé, Ibid., p. 164]

Daoist texts in the Shangqing tradition also describe light visions that look like purple clouds containing within a small ring of bright, opalescent light surrounding a dark central space: ". . . there will be also a purple pneuma [chi], as large as the pupil of your eye, but wrapped in several tens of layers and flashing brilliantly . . . . This is called the flying root of solar efflorescence [Bokenkamp, op. cit., p. 315]," and "A purple breath . . . enters into my hsüan-tan palace. It fills the palace and penetrates to the center of the purple breath. Then I see it as a fiery pearl within the darkness [Maspero, quoted in Robinet. op. cit., p. 130]."

The Condensation of the Star-Image

On the one occasion when I experienced an evolution of light visions be-yond the familiar light-rings and eye-like nebulae that I've just described—an event that I'll describe in some detail in subsequent chapters—the transition from my familiar sequence of light visions to the new and overtly paroxysmal visions was preceded by a shrinking and condensing of phosphene cloud with its bright inner "eye" that culminated in the formation of a tiny star-like image that seemed to "twinkle" like the real stars one sees in the night sky. The "star" seemed to "twinkle" because it consisted of a cluster of thin and intensely-bright phosphene filaments that would flash into view and immediately disappear as other flashes took their place, as shown in Figure 14C and 14E. Some of the filamentous flashes were white and others were blue.

As the tiny and intensely-bright image of the "twinkling star" hovered at the center of my visual field, the rest of the visual field seemed much darker than the normal eigengrau, and I felt a strong vortex pulling my attention into that central point. I've only seen this star image on one occasion—on the night when I inadver-tently triggered a paroxysmal episode and the elaborate series of light visions that accompanied it—but some of the texts I cited in Chapter 2 seem to regard the vi-sion of the star-like *bindu* as a natural outcome for expert meditators, as something that they might see regularly after inducing a series of eye-like phosphene nebulae. However this may be, the unique positioning of this star-like phosphene between the sequence of "tranquil" phosphenes and the sequence of paroxysmal phosphenes implies that it might function as the triggering event for self-induced epileptiform activity.

NEUROLOGICAL ANALYSIS

Cortical Slow (<1 Hz) Waves and Phosphene Nebulae

Our analysis of the spatial and temporal features of the green light-rings in the previous chapter determined that they are most likely generated when the RTN shifts to firing the synchronous spindle bursts normally associated with stage 2 NREMS. Since the amorphous, expanding waves appear shortly after the green light-rings, it would seem likely that these dark blue nebulae are generated by the predictable shift from stage 2 to stage 3 NREMS, but it is not necessary to rely on serial order alone: there is abundant evidence that the cloud-like phosphenes are generated by the slow wave sleep rhythms normally associated with stage 3 NREMS.

In the discussion of the consensus scenario about the nature of the cellular mechanisms that govern the normal transition from waking to NREMS, I described how activation of stage 2 spindle bursts pushes the polarization of thalamic cell membranes ever lower, and that, when a threshold level of hyperpolarization is achieved, the RTN automatically stops firing spindle bursts. Once this happens, the cortical slow (<1 Hz) wave, which was the mechanism originally responsible for initiating the transition from wakefulness to sleep—the mechanism responsible for evoking the drowsy transitional state designated as stage 1 NREMS—and which continues to oscillate throughout the volley of spindle bursts, is now the only synchronous wave still oscillating, so it becomes the dominant influence in shaping what happens next. When the pulse of this cortical slow wave gets transmitted back to the LGN (and other sensory-relay nuclei in the thalamus), it causes large numbers of vision-relay cells (and other sensory-relay cells) to fire their individual calcium spikes in unison upon receipt of that pulsation [Steriade et al., 1993a, 1993b; Uchida et al., 1994]. The waves of calcium spikes triggered by receipt of the cortical slow wave are then transmitted by the vision-relay cells (and other sensory-relay cells) to their target neurons in the neocortex. The interaction of the cortical slow waves and the waves of thalamocortical calcium spikes generates brain waves in the scalp EEG in the delta frequency range of 0.5 Hz to 4.0 Hz. The EEG criterion for determining onset of stage 3 NREMS is detection of synchronous delta waves distributed all across the cortical mantle. Given this sequence of events, it is reasonable to expect that the spatial propagation patterns of the cortical slow wave will determine the distribution of the calcium spikes in the LGN and their subsequent propagation patterns; it is important, therefore, to determine what is known about the propagation patterns of cortical slow waves.

The cortical slow wave is one example of a generic pattern of neuronal excitation that often occurs when large networks of neurons are linked by local projections. An experiment by Maeda, Robinson, and Kwana [1995] found that networks of locally-connected neurons generated "spontaneous, periodic, synchronized bursts" of calcium transients that propagate as an expanding spatial wave across cellular networks linked together by many local interconnections. To learn more about these spontaneous, periodic, synchronized bursts, the researchers prepared cultures of dissociated cortical neurons and allowed them to mature for several days *in vitro*. After 3 to 4 days of maturation, concentrations of extracellular magnesium decreased to the point that electrodes began to detect spontaneous, synchronized bursts of low frequency calcium transients (i.e., between 0.1 and 1 Hz). These spontaneous, synchronized bursts originated at intervals ranging from 10 to 20 seconds at different locations in the sheet of cells and then spread across the sheet of cells at a relatively slow speed that averaged at 50 mm/second. The researchers could not predict where the expanding wave would originate ("successive burst events originate in different regions of the network") or where it would expand ("the direction of burst propagation is constantly shifting"), but the pattern of propagation was not wholly random; rather, they found that the propagation "occurs sequentially from electrode to electrode, as each local group of neurons 'charges up' its neighboring, nonrefractory areas, rather than in a random sequence of regions . . . . [Maeda et al., Ibid., p.6843]." The probability that a burst will occur, and the probability that it will spread in a particular direction, were found to be determined by the level of excitability of neurons in a particular location within the sheet of locally-connected cells. Maeda's team concluded that periodic bursts are most likely "produced by spatial and temporal summation of a continuous random background of synaptic inputs, including 'miniature' spontaneous synaptic events [Ibid., p.6843]." They note that synchronous slow waves with this distinctive propagation pattern have been detected in rat hippocampus *in vivo* and also in the cortical networks of cats, two sites which contain continuous sheets of locally-connected neurons, which leads the researchers to add this comment:

> It appears to be a stable mode of firing towards which these neuronal networks 're-lax' following perturbations, for example, by electronic stimulation or by drugs. Moreover, the synchronous bursting can undergo long-lasting changes that apparently involve plasticity of neuronal connections . . . . [Maeda et al., Ibid., p. 6844].

There is another characteristic of these "spontaneous, periodic, synchronized bursts" that is relevant for our analysis: the researchers observed refractory periods lasting from 5 to 10 seconds during which no bursts occurred, even when they experimented with applying an electrical stimulus. The refractory intervals in the cultured sheets of cells lasted slightly longer than similar refractory intervals reported in *in vivo* experiments involving intact brains where the interval typically lasted from 2.5 to 4 seconds . It is also worth noting that, in the network of cultured cells, the refractory intervals between successive bursts became significantly shorter as cultures matured (i.e., after left alone for more than 30 days), and in some instances the matured cells became so insensitive to inhibition that they continued to fire spike-bursts even after extracellular concentrations of magnesium returned to the relatively high levels that normally would extinguish any activity.

Based on the research by Maeda et al. defining the characteristics of spontaneous, periodic, synchronized bursts in locally-connected networks of cortical cells, we can make a number of predictions about the propagation patterns that will characterize any phosphene image generated by the interaction of cortical slow waves and thalamocortical calcium spikes: (1) the phosphenes will appear in the visual field at unpredictable times and at unpredictable locations; (2) the phosphene will emerge in the form of an expanding wave that moves at a relatively slow speed (about 50 mm/sec) and that creates unpredictable, asymmetric spatial patterns; (3) these phosphenes will disappear while the neurons involved enter refractory intervals that last at least as long as 2 to 4 seconds; and, finally, (4) these phosphene waves can keep on reappearing for as long as the hyperpolarization of the thalamic cell membranes remains at the level required for maintaining stage 3 sleep rhythms. The spatial propagation patterns of the amorphous, expanding nebulae that I've described display all four of these characteristics associated with activation of spontaneous, periodic, synchronized bursts in locally-connected cortical neurons. It is reasonable to conclude that phosphene nebulae are generated by cortical slow waves that would normally be associated with stage 3 NREMS.

The schematic drawing in Figure 15 illustrates how the spatial propagation pattern of a cortical slow wave, when referred back to the LGN, will cause the vision-relay cells to fire their individual calcium spikes in a wave that mirrors the propagation pattern of the cortical slow wave that evoked this response. In the meditator whose behaviors keep the neurons of the visual cortices in a hyperexcitable state, this wave of calcium spikes discharged by vision-relay cells in the LGN will be received by neurons in the primary visual cortices of the meditator as if it were a set of veridical signals that originated in the retinal receptors—and it will eventually register in the cortical lightness record as a wave that mirrors the characteristics of the cortical slow wave, that is, as an amorphous, expanding wave with spatial propagation patterns and timing intervals that are, for the most part, unpredictable.

The Bright Node as an Artifact of Cone Density Patterns

The eye-like node of brighter, more opaque phosphene always appears to hover near the center of the visual field, the region of central, foveal vision. In the retinal fovea, cone receptors are densely packed: as shown in the drawing in Figure 16, the relative density of cone receptors peaks near the center of the retina (except for that tiny region at the very center of the retina which does not contain any retinal receptors) and then drops off sharply so that relatively few cones are located outside 20° of isoeccentricity. Similarly, the relative density of retinal ganglion cells—the neurons that transmit the cone signals to the LGN—peak at about 7° to 10° of isoeccentricity, then drop off sharply, maintaining only minimal levels after 40° of isoeccentricity. Since color perception depends primarily on visual signals that encode wavelength, and since wavelength is encoded in the retina by cone-based ganglion cells that only extend out to 40° of isoeccentricity, it is reasonable to expect that the dark blue or purple phosphene cloud-image will appear within this ambit. The very brightest parts of the phosphene cloud will be generated by the most densely-packed cones which are arrayed within 5° of isoeccentricity. What happens, then, when these cone signals arrive in the LGN for relay to the

Figure 15. The relationship between the spatial propagation patterns of the cortical slow (<1 Hz) wave associated with delta band activity in corticothalamic circuits during stage 3 NREMS and the spatial propagation patterns observed in the amorphous expanding nebular phosphenes. During stage 3 sleep rhythms, large numbers of vision-relay cells in the LGN release calcium spikes in unison upon receipt of the pulse of the cortical slow wave referred to the thalamus through back-projections from the primary visual cortices. The propagation patterns of synchronous slow (<1 Hz) waves in the locally-connected neuronal circuitry of the primary visual cortices have been identified by Maeda et al. [1995] and are discussed in more detail in the text.

Origin of the Amorphous Phosphene Images

The Propagation Patterns of Cortical Slow (<1 Hz) Waves
in the Visual Cortex, When Referred Back to the LGN,
Drive LGN Vision-Relay Cells To Fire Calcium Spikes
in Patterns that Mirror the Cortical Slow Waves

Primary Visual Cortex

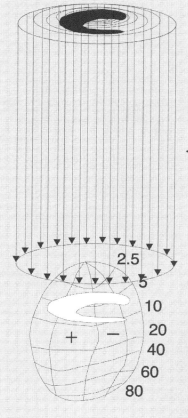

Corticothalamic
Back-Projections

2.5
5
10
20
40
60
80

LGN Lamina 6
(Retinotopic Grid)

Visual Image

visual cortices? If we refer to the visuotopic map of geniculate lamina #6 that was introduced in Chapter 3 (Figure 11), we see that almost 33% of the dorsal lamina is dedicated to vision-relay neurons that represent the very center of the visual field (that extends out as far as 5° of isoeccentricity) and almost 50% of the dorsal lamina is dedicated to vision-relay cells that represent the surrounding central regions of the visual field that extends out as far as 10° of isoeccentricity. It is no wonder, then, that when the pulse of the cortical slow wave stimulates vision-relay cells to fire calcium spikes in lamina #6, that wave of calcium spikes will contain many more signals that represent central vision (i.e., extending out to 5° or perhaps 10° of isoeccentricity) than signals representing more peripheral regions of the visual field. Therefore, the cortical lightness record for central vision will consist of many, many more points of light per unit of surface area in the very center of the visual field than in more peripheral regions (beyond 10° of isoeccentricity). Given this distribution of cone densities, it becomes clear why the tiny ring at the center of the phosphene cloud appears to be brighter and more opaque than the dull phosphene surrounding it, since that ring is composed of many more signals per unit of space than the dull cloud. Just like a digital camera or a television set produces a more fine-grained, sharper image if each unit of space is illuminated by more light-bearing pixels than a competing model, the central region of the visual field is composed of many more cone signals per unit of space than the more peripheral regions occupied by the duller phosphene cloud.

Why the Eye-Like Nebulae are Blue or Purple

The colors of the amorphous nebulae can vary between dark blue and purple, the hues shown in the full-color drawings presented on the back cover. Since dark

---

Figure 16. The relative diameters of the phosphene cloud-image and its central node compared to the distribution of vision-relay cells representing foveal vision in lamina 6 of the primate LGN. **A.** A schematic drawing of a typical example of an amorphous nebular phosphene with a bright central node shaped in an eye-like formation. **B.** A chart showing the relative densities of cones, rods and ganglion cells in the primate retina. Note that the diameter of the phosphene cloud extends out to about 20° of isoeccentricity. If this image is compared to the distribution of retinal cells contributing visual signals to represent that region of the visual field, the cloud image is subserved by a relatively large number of retinal ganglion cells, certainly a larger number than in those areas falling outside 20° of isoeccentricity. Similarly, the diameter of the bright central node within the larger cloud extends out to about 5° to 7° of isoeccentricity, a region of the visual field subserved by a large number of retinal ganglion cells which happen to be those that convey signals generated in that area of the retina where cone receptors are most densely-packed. The dark pupil-like space that keeps reappearing at the very center of the visual field occupies a region that is not innervated by any retinal receptors, suggesting that the observations of the continual fluctuations that take place at the very center of the visual field—the alternation between a filling-in of bright phosphene and an ebbing back to form the eye image—most likely represents the kind of perceptual "filling-in" process documented in psychophysical experiments.

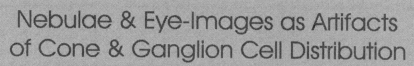

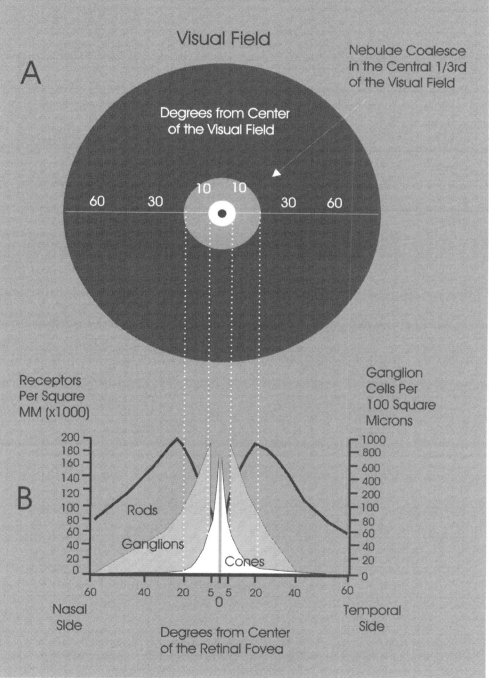

blue or violet is also the color of the phosphene disk that fills in the shrinking green light-rings, it seems likely that the blue and purple hues colors of the amorphous nebulae would be generated by the same cortical processes. As regards the dark blue fill-disk, we found that the two LGN laminae that are dedicated to the relay of S-cone "blue-on" signals—the intermediate or koniocellular laminae—do not extend as far in the ventral direction as dorsal lamina #6 (see Figure 13A, Chapter 3); as a result, a spindle burst ascending the RTN matrix will cause "blue-on" vision-relay cells to fire rebound spikes only after that spindle wave ascends to within 40° of isoeccentricity, in which case it triggers rebound spikes in one koniocellular lamina, and only after it ascends farther—to within 20° of isoeccentricity—will "blue-on" signals in *both* koniocellular laminae be forwarded to the visual cortices and included in the composition of the cortical lightness record. This anatomical constraint explains why the dark blue or purple nebulae swirl into view in the central region of the visual field and remain there for the duration. If seers shift their angle of gaze, the nebulae move so as to preserve their central position.

Origins of the Star-Image

The Significance of Antecedent Events

If a meditator continues to fixate on the amorphous, expanding waves and the bright inner "eye" within, the eye-like nebulae can, in some circumstances, condense in size and increase in intensity, forming the image of a tiny, "twinkling star" hovering at the center of a visual field that becomes noticeably darker. The star image feels vaguely ominous because it seems to pull all of the seer's attention into a vortex. I only saw this image of a twinkling star on one occasion, but since its appearance occurred immediately before the onset of a paroxysmal episode, it is obviously important to examine what kinds of neuronal events would have to take place in order for this image to appear in the visual field—and to determine if the condensation of this star-like image constitutes the formation of a transient epileptogenic focus in a brain that is otherwise intact. Before we begin the neurological analysis, it will be useful to address the convergence of several circumstantial factors that may have served as predisposing events.

Two days before the onset of the paroxysmal episode, I'd flown from east from California to Boston, crossing three time zones, and, as a result, I was still adjusting to the usual circadian disturbances ("jet lag"), with my symptoms being fatigue and, most notably, insomnia, a condition that I would otherwise seldom experience. By the night of the second day back, I had only slept four out of the preceding forty-four hours. (I'm confident about this assertion, notwithstanding the notorious unreliability of self-reports about the length of time spent sleeping, because in this instance I can rely on some objective measures: I was not sleepy the first night back home and did not even get into bed until two o'clock in the morning, and I got up the next day at 6:30 a.m. because it was my responsibility to wake up our three daughters, cook them a hot breakfast, and then drive them to school by eight o'clock in the morning, and this I did, despite my fatigue from not having had enough sleep. To my surprise, the insomnia continued into the second night back: I was still wide awake at 4 a.m., pacing around in the kitchen, ruminating about an earlier argument with my wife, distracting myself by listening to blues music playing loudly. I was also feeling very depressed, and this brings up another subject that's relevant for explaining this episode. At this stage in my life, it was not unusual for me to feel depressed, and I'd been diagnosed as having "atypical dysthymic depression" secondary to chronic posttraumatic stress disorder (PTSD). I was in psychotherapy with a psychiatrist who'd earlier prescribed the anti-depressant, phenelzine, a MAO-inhibitor that elevates mood by blocking the uptake of neurotransmitter, but I'd been taken off that medication about six months before I took the California trip. The significance of these circumstantial factors is that, on the one occasion when I experienced a sudden shift from my normal meditation practice to the outbreak paroxysmal visual and sensorimotor symptoms, there was a convergence of three factors known to increase a person's vulnerability to epileptiform activity: a sleep deficit, depression, and circadian disturbances.

Lack of sleep for a term of thirty-six hours or more has been shown to be associated with a lowered seizure threshold [Gunderson et al., 1972; Rajna and Veres, 1993; Lorenzo et al., 1995; Bettendorff et al., 1996; Brunner et al., 1997; Hesdorffer and Verity, 1997; Leproult et al., 1997; Wolf, 1997]. Sleep loss is also associated with a decrease in the amount of time that elapses before the onset of the stage 2 NREMS spindle bursts [Daurat et al., 1997]. The epileptogenic effects of sleep loss can be aggravated by co-existing factors like emotional stress or depression [Friis and Lund, 1974; Friis, 1990; Loiseau, 1997], and there is evidence that even the lesser condition of transient sadness may have the effect of increasing the excitability of neurons in the thalamus and mesotemporal cortices [George et al., 1995].

Another consideration to be taken into account is that medical researchers have recently identified two new diagnostic categories, "subictal-dysphoric disorders" and "interictal dysphoric disorders," both associated with mood depression, as their name implies [Blumer et al., 2004]. In these conditions, the symptoms tend to be intermittent and can vary dramatically on different occasions. What's important, for our purposes, is that the subictal and interictal dysphoric disorders can both involve "paroxysmal excessive neuronal activity" which occurs without any overt evidence that a seizure is taking place; indeed, the symptoms of dysphoria caused by occult epileptiform activity can be so subtle that it often takes a long time, the occurrence of many episodes, and a gradual exasercbation of symptoms before a person realizes something is amiss. There is no evidence that suggests I have some kind of subictal dysphoric disorder, but given the sequence of events that we're investigating—the presence of depression and the onset of a seizure-like event—it would be premature to dismiss an etiology that might be relevant.

Finally, the fact that I'd been diagnosed with PTSD points to another vulnerability that might affect the outcome of our investigation. PTSD is often associated with neuron loss in the hippocampus, especially damage to the right hippocampus [Myslobodsky, 1993; Bremner et al., 1995; Rausch et al., 1996; Magariños et al., 1997]. Both extreme stress and chronic stress have been found to produce elevated levels of cortisol which is associated with neuron damage in the hippocampus. Since patients who experience recurring epileptic seizures are often found to have substantial neuron loss in their hippocampal regions, there is clearly the potential for some hippocampal issues to be relevant in the case of someone with PTSD who also experiences a seizure. Medical researchers are still debating whether the loss of hippocampal neurons in these cases occurred before the seizures, so that it was a pre-existing condition, or whether the neuron loss is the result of the patient having suffered recurrent seizures. Both alternatives will warrant further investigation in chapters on the neural mechanisms that generate the final set of paroxysmal phosphenes in a meditation-induced progression. But let me emphasize here, as I just did in reference to the subictal and interictal dysphoric disorders, that there is no clinical evidence suggesting that I am one of those people with PTSD who has hippocampal damage—the issue has never been tested—so the point to remember is that if such damage did pre-exist this visionary experience, the loss of neurons would likely increase the vulnerability to hippocampal seizure. Now let's return to the chronology of events on the night when the paroxysmal visions appeared.

At 4 o'clock in the morning, with dawn only an hour away, having accumulated a substantial sleep deficit over the past two days, I decided to get into bed even if I didn't feel sleepy and to use my usual meditation techniques to induce phosphenes, hoping that this focus would produce enough relaxation that I'd fall asleep while I was watching the flow of the internally-generated light sensations. This was a strategy I'd used to good effect on many occasions, but from moment I closed my eyes and began to concentrate I noticed that something was different: I was surprised to see that the phosphene images began to flow immediately without my having to engage in the usual induction behaviors, which typically took some time to achieve the intended effect, and light visions also seemed to be more "intense" and "vibrant" than usual, with the blue, eye-like nebulae appearing much earlier than I would have expected based on past experience. But I was even more surprised at what happened next: a wave of amorphous phosphene with the bright, eye-like ring within suddenly condensed in size so that it looked like a "twinkling star." This "twinkling" effect occurred because the phosphene image had changed into a cluster of very small, very thin, and intensely-bright phosphene filaments that flashed existence and then almost instantly disappeared. A static, 2-dimensional drawing of this star image is presented in Figure 14 (C & E). Most of these flashing filaments were white, but it also seemed as if some had a blue color. As this tiny and intensely-bright image of the "twinkling star" hovered at the center of my visual field, the rest of the visual field seemed to become much darker than the normal eigengrau, although I can't be sure that this actually happened, but I do know that I felt a strong vortex pulling my attention into the star.

The Star as a Transient Epileptogenic Focus

What kinds of neuronal events would have to take place in the primary visual cortices and/or the LGN to generate a phosphene image with these characteristics? If the eye-like nebulae that appear just before the star-image and that seem to evolve into the star-image result from the interaction of the cortical slow (<1 Hz) wave and calcium spikes in the LGN, as I've proposed here, is it possible for this same interaction to produce the image of a "twinkling star" hovering in an unusually dark background and exerting a strong sensation of optic flow? It might seem that we should look elsewhere for causation, because the presence of delta wave activity has been shown to *inhibit* the onset of absence-like generalized seizures [Nobili et al., 2001], so we have to explain how recurring phosphene images generated by delta waves could trigger a shift to hypersynchronous activity. For a tiny cluster of flashing filaments to appear at the center of the visual field amid darkened surroundings, excitatory signals must be reverberating back and forth between a small number of neurons in the LGN and in the primary visual cortices that represent the center of the visual field. In the LGN, the excited neurons must be located in the dorsal apex of the six laminae. In addition, there must be some inhibition imposed on neurons that subserve the rest of the visual field.

To induce the star-image, a meditator keeps attention focused on the center of the visual field, and this attentional fixation affects the activity of neurons in both the primary visual cortices *and* the thalamus. In a study examining the "top down" transmission of excitatory signals from the primary visual cortex to the thalamus, Montero [2000] found that *an attention-driven increase in excitatory discharges originates in the primary visual cortices but is then referred down to the thalamus where it enhances the responses of vision-relay cells in the LGN that are associated with the object of attention. Equally significant, for our investigation, is that attention also enhances the activity of neurons in the RTN matrix, the neurons that control the relay of sensory signals from the thalamus to the cortex.* Montero proposes that "attentional modulation of vision-relay transmission is a main function of corticothalamic pathways to sensory relay nuclei [p. 95]," and the enhancement of the RTN's inhibitory activity plays in important role in this process since the cortically-driven stimulation of RTN inhibitory neurons can suppress visual signals other than those relating to the object of attentional interest:

> The retinotopic organization of V1 innervation of [the RTN] and LGN, and of [RTN] projections to LGN, is ideally suitable to influence geniculocortical transmission in a spatially discrete manner. The results are thus consistent with the hypothesis that a focus of attention in V1 generates a core of enhanced geniculocortical transmission via direct corticogeniculate inputs, and surround regions of depressed geniculocortical transmissioon via cortico-reticulo-geniculate pathways [Montero, Ibid., p. 102].

If we apply Montero's hypothesis to my account of having fixed my attention on the image of a tiny, filamentous "star" at the center of the visual field, an image that is no larger than the tip of a ballpoint pen, it is reasonable to infer, first, that excitatory signals were flowing back and forth through reciprocal projections linking a relatively small number of neurons in the primary visual cortices with a relatively small number of neurons in the LGN, and, second, that the attention focused exclusively on the star-like image also excited RTN neurons to inhibit the relay of visual signals from areas of the visual field that were not being attended, an effect which would likely produce a darkening of all areas of the visual field other than the "twinkling star."

If a meditator continues fixating on the star-image, generating a positive feedback loop of excitatory signals linking a small number of neurons in the LGN and the primary visual cortices, it is reasonable to expect that this attention-driven feedback will eventually have some kind of destabilizing effect. In a study of conditions preceding the outbreak of hypersynchronous seizures in animal models of human epilepsy, Meeren et al. [2002] found that the coupling of cortical and thalamic activity might vary in its direction during the first 500 milliseconds preceding a seizure, sometimes initiated by cortical cells, sometimes by cells in the thalamus, but that *if this interaction evolved into a seizure, it was always a cortical focus that fired first and thus was responsible for triggering the seizure.* This finding is supported by the findings of an experiment by Blumenfeld and McCormick [2000]: these researchers used intact slices from LGN and RTN tissue to study how an enhancement of corticothalalmic input to the RTN and LGN can trigger a sudden shift in which the RTN stops firing in normal patterns and begins firing hypersynchronous spindle bursts. To administer an excitatory input to the sensory relay nuclei of the thalamus, they stimulated the corticothalamic back-projections with single shocks that were very brief (0.1 msec), shocks that "mimic normal cortical firing," and then they followed this by re-stimulating the same corticothalamic back-projections with short bursts of six shocks at 200 Hz, shocks which "mimic abnormally enhanced cortical excitability." As they increased corticothalamic input to the RTN and sensory-relay nuclei (including the LGN) in this manner, Blumenfeld and McCormick produced changes in the activation of GABAergic cells which then caused the RTN to shift from firing in normal patterns to firing hypersynchronous spindle bursts, the kind of spindle bursts that register as hypersynchronous spike-waves in the cortical EEG. This is a critically-important finding, for our purposes, because in the next chapter, when we begin to analyze the origins of the dark, fast-moving rings that create a tunnel-like effect, we'll find that this image is generated by hypersynchronous spike-waves.

These studies show how a meditator's fixation of attention on the eye-like nebulae can establish a positive feedback loop of excitatory signals in which only a small number of neurons subserving central vision participate, and also show how the same attention-driven can impose a strong inhibition on the relay of all other visual signals; this scenario explains why the star-image has the characteristics I've described and also why it is surrounded by an unusually dark visual background. The same studies also show that this "top-down" pattern of neuronal activity can eventually trigger the onset of a hypersynchronous seizure. This outcome can occur even if a meditator's cortical neurons are not already hyperexcitable, so it is reasonable to expect that this outcome would be even more likely to occur if cortical neurons were already in a hyperexcitable state before the meditation began.

My account of the star-like phosphene is limited by the fact that I saw it on only one occasion, but it is worthwhile noting that a similar evolution of events is described in some of the ancient source texts: for example, in Tantric Hindu texts (see Figure 7), there are references to a tiny *bindu* ("dot") vision that shatters and expands, and in Tibetan (Tantric) Buddhist texts, there are also references to an explosive inner event called "The Ignition" or "The Flaring" which is said to produce a vision that looks like "apparitional fireflies." In the autobiography of a contemporary Hindu mystic, Swami Muktananda [1978], there is a more complete descriptions of blue nebular lights evolving bright inner nodes that look like "blue pearls" which then condense into a blue star: Muktananda is pleased to see the auspicious vision of "The blue akasha, an expansion of the blue color, . . ., and, with it, the *neela bindu*, the Pearl of infinite power," and even more pleased to see the next vision which was "not the Blue Light or the Blue Pearl, but a blue star [p. 149]," then the star exploded and he was caught up in the ecstatic vision that he so fervently desired and had pursued for so long:

> [T]he blue star appeared, and for some reason I felt compelled to go and sit in it. I don't know how I did this or who was controlling me. . . . / . . . the blue star passed within me into my *sahasrara* and exploded. It's fragments spread throughout the vast spaces of the *sahasrara*. There was no star in front of me now, but just an ambrosial white light. Then I passed into Tantraloka, . . . The blue star, which became your vehicle and took you there, is the only way of traveling to it [Muktananda, Ibid., pp. 150-1]."

Cortical Slow Waves and Amorphous "Bubble" Phosphenes

There is another type of phosphene image that we can now discuss, an image that involves an amorphous, expanding wave and that is even more evanescent and unpredictable than the eye-like nebulae, an image generated by the same neural mechanisms as the eye-like nebulae. The reason I've delayed writing about this image is that it occurs in a different context than the eye-like nebulae—it occurs earlier in the sequence of meditation-induced phosphenes—but it would have been confusing to discuss it in the chapter on the threshold image of shrinking light-rings, since the etiology of the two phosphenes in so different; that's why I've chosen to append the description and analysis of this phosphene at the end of the chapter on amorphous, expanding waves.

I often see faint, fleeting efflorescences of yellowish-green phosphene "blubs," "curtains," or "bubbles" in three circumstances: (1) when I'm just beginning to induce a meditative state before the light rings appear; (2) when I'm lying down in a dark room, relaxed but not trying to meditate, and I'm staring up at the dark ceiling; or (3) when I'm having a therapeutic massage for an injured shoulder muscle, in which case I see these phosphene "bubbles" continue to appear even when the massage becomes painful. These "bubbles" of light erupt at unpredictable locations in the visual field and usually disappear almost immediately, like water bubbles rising to the surface of a boiling pot. In some instances—especially in the context of therapeutic massage—the phosphene waves expand beyond the bubble-shape, forming larger, more long-lived "blobs" or "curtains" of yellow-green light that drift across the visual field. Sometimes these phosphenes remind me of the aurora borealis slowly unfurling in the night sky.

The phosphene "bubbles," "blobs," and "curtains" all exhibit features similar to the amorphous, expanding clouds that we examined earlier in this chapter. Those shared features suggest the likelihood of a common etiology, even though the phosphene "bubbles" are green instead of dark blue or purple, and even though they appear much earlier in a meditation-induced sequence of light visions or in situations in which a meditative state has not yet been established.

In describing the consensus scenario that neuroscientists have proposed to explain the transition from waking to slow wave sleep, I mentioned that the first stage is that transition is the appearance of the cortical slow (<1 Hz) wave. During stage 1 NREMS, the cortical slow wave begins to oscillate, initiating the drowsiness that characterizes stage 1. During the stage 1 drowsy transitional state, some cortical neurons retain the ability to respond (i.e., to depolarize) in response to afferent sensory signals. Since the cortical slow wave is active, it will occasionally release eruptions of the "spontaneous, periodic, synchronized bursts in locally connected cortical neurons" described by Maeda et al. [1995], although at this stage of incomplete synchronization of cortical neurons the eruption of these spontaneous, periodic, synchronized bursts will be short-lived and limited in their expanse. Maeda et al. describe a phenomenon of this sort:

> When the probability of burst propagation is low . . . *there are abortive burst initiation events that fail to spread beyond their immediate locality*, the smallest of which are simply isolated action potentials. Such activity was often seen in immature cultures or in the presence of magnesium or APV [Maeda et al., Ibid., p. 6844].

This pattern of spontaneous, periodic, synchronized burst propagation through sheets of locally-connected cortical neurons, when intermixed with mirror-image waves of calcium spikes in the LGN, would be consistent with a person seeing faint, short-lived, and spatially-confined "bubbles" of phosphene. The findings by Maeda et al. allow for a lot of variability in the duration and propagation patterns of these expanding waves, so this mechanism can account for different types of short-lived phosphene phenomena—for the "bubbles," "blobs," and "curtains"—and also for the longer-lived, more powerful nebular waves that appear after the shrinking light-rings in a meditation-induced sequence of phosphene images.

5

IMAGES OF HYPERSYNCHRONY: DARK RINGS AND RADIATING SPARKS

PHENOMENOLOGY

The "Tunnel" Vision of Dark, Fast-Moving Rings

As I watched the bright twinkling "star" at the center of the visual field, feeling it pull all my attention into its vortex, I saw it suddenly disappear and, in the same instant, the visual field was inundated with a stream of thin, black rings that had the same shapes and followed the same trajectories as the earlier images of green light-rings, but these dark rings did not generate any phosphene sensations and they flowed into the visual field at a rate much faster than the green light-rings—I think as many as 2 to 3 dark rings streamed into the visual field with each passing second (≥ 2.0 Hz), a rate *ten times faster* than the green light-rings associated with the sleep spindles that normally become active during stage 2 NREMS that flow at a rate of one every five seconds (0.2 Hz). This influx of black rings shrinking in tandem, silhouetted against an already dark eigengrau, as shown in Figure 17B, saturated the visual field, creating the illusion that the rings were "receding" away in 3-dimensional space and that I was being moved through a dark tunnel of concentric rings which was itself in motion. This sensation of movement had a strange, paradoxical quality: it felt like I was being pulled forward into an irresistible vortex, but at the same time it felt like I was falling backward. I remember pressing my head back against the pillow, as if I were resisting a fall. An illusion of motion is a common reaction when a person is exposed to a visual scene in which there is "optic flow:"

Motion in the visual periphery elicits in the stationary observer an illusion of self-motion (vection) indistinguishable from real motion. . . . The illusion of vection is compelling, for it dominates contradictory proprioceptive signals. For example, subjects presented with optic flow consistent with backward self-motion perceive backward motion even if they are actually walking forward . . . . [Steinmetz et al., 1987, p. 189].

I was so surprised by the sudden shift from the bright star to the "tunnel" of dark, fast-moving rings that I forgot to count the passing seconds, but I'm sure that

Figure 17. Schematic drawings of the sequence of phosphene images that accompanied the shift from a tranquil meditative state to a paroxysmal episode. A. The phosphene image that appears just before the onset of paroxysmal phosphenes—the tiny star-like image formed by a densely-packed cluster of very small and very thin filaments of white and blue phosphene that flash into view and instantly disappear to generate a "twinkling" effect. B. The sudden and rapid influx of a stream of rings so dark that the individual rings are barely-perceptible. These rings shrink steadily in diameter and do not effloresce as phosphene sensations. They flood into the visual field at a rate of 2 or more per second (≥ 2 Hz), 10 times faster than the phosphene image of green rings that arrive at a rate of 1 every 5 seconds (0.2 Hz), generating a sensation of "optic flow" that produces the illusion of movement through a dark, tunnel-like space. C. A sudden, dramatic shift in which the dark, fast-moving rings disappeared and an instant later the middle and peripheral regions of the visual field were filled with innumerable tiny flecks of phosphene with a beige or yellow color that flowed out toward my forehead in a conical, radiating pattern. Because of this trajectory, the tiny sparks seemed to be emanating from a single source, but, if so, I could not see that source and indeed the central region of the visual field did not have any light-flecks and thus did not attract any attention, given the spray of sparks illuminating the middle and peripheral regions of the visual field. The visual effect of watching countless points of light radiating toward one's forehead presents a mezmerizing image that cannot be adequately communicated in a 2-dimensional drawing, so the drawings here can only suggest the general nature of the experience. It is important to note that a number of paroxysmal sensorimotor symptoms began with the advent of the spray image: the flecks of light almost seemed to strike perceptibly against the forehead (although clearly this did not actually take place); I felt microtremors in the small muscles of the face and hands; I felt some obscure compulsion to pull my head back against the pillow, to arch my back, to let my mouth fall slack while pulling down the upper lip, thereby drawing tight the skin of my nose—a constellation of odd movements which is often used by artists to depict subjects in a state of inner ecstasy and which is often cited in Hindu meditation texts as the distinctive movements (mudras) of ecstasy. D. The gradual brightening and bluing of the visual field begins to obscure the vision of the radiating spray in the same way that dawn gradually obscures the stars. E. The uniform brightening of the visual field eventually eclipses totally the vision of the radiating spray. (This does necessarily not mean that the neural mechanisms generating the spray image stopped operating once the spray was obscured by a brighter light, a point developed in the text.) Once the new phosphene effect took effect, the visual field looked exactly like a bright blue summer sky devoid of cloud formations or haze. The precise shade of blue that most closely resembles what I saw, based on comparisons with a CMYK Process Color Chart, is 40% Cyan without any contribution from Magenta, Yellow, or Black.

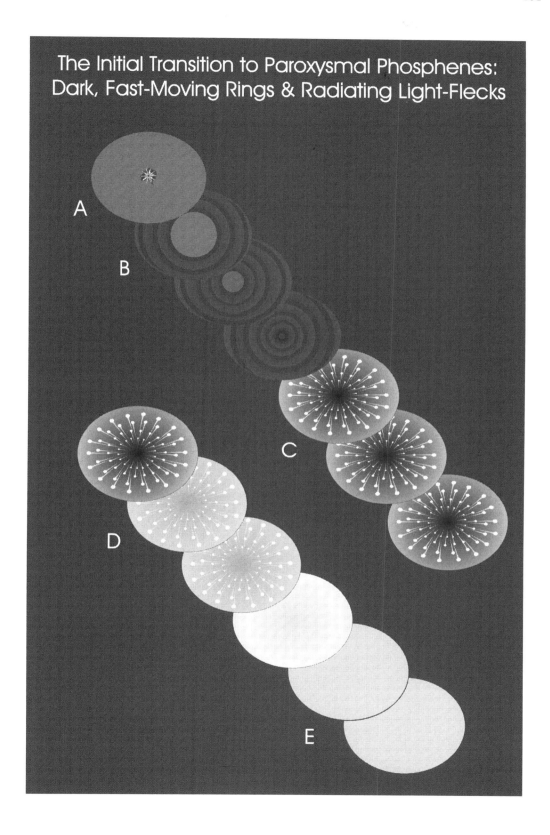

The Initial Transition to Paroxysmal Phosphenes:
Dark, Fast-Moving Rings & Radiating Light-Flecks

this influx did not last very long—probably no more than a few seconds—because I no sooner recognized what was happening than everything changed.

The Vision of a Radiating Spray

Once again, the change in phosphene imagery appeared to be instantaneous: instead of the "tunnel" of dark rings moving away from me, I was suddenly barraged by a spray of tiny, spark-like flecks of phosphene light that flowed straight towards me in a radiating pattern, as shown in Figure 17C. The flecks seemed to originate in the mid-region of the visual field, not from the center itself, but the effect of being pelleted by this radiating stream of light flecks was very much like being sprayed with water shooting out of a jet nozzle. The flecks had were very tiny with a beige or dull yellow color.

It seemed as if the flecks were "striking" against my forehead, even though clearly this could not be so, but in reaction I felt compelled to push my head back against against the pillow, as if anticipating a strike and recoiling to protect myself. I also felt compelled to arch my back and to let my mouth fall slack in a distinctive posture where the upper lip is stretched down so that the skin of the nose is pulled tight against the nasal cartilage, and it felt as if I were being "lifted up" by some unknown force. Meanwhile, the muscles in my face, fingers, and arms were twitching spasmodically. This combination of behaviors definitely felt like a "rapturous transport," and I have no doubt that any observers, had they been present, would have agreed that this was an appropriate description.

This cluster of paroxysmal sensorimotor symptoms alerted me that I might have inadvertently triggered some kind of seizure. This thought alarmed me. I quickly stopped converging my eyes and fixating my attention and felt relieved when the radiating spray and the paroxysmal sensorimotor symptoms also stopped. Thus reassured of my ability to exert control over this strange sequence of events, and mindful of the fact that my consciousness seemed to be relatively unimpaired, I decided that this must not actually be a *seizure*. At the time I knew next to nothing about epileptic seizures, because even though I am a medical writer, I'd never been given an assignment to write video scripts dealing with epilepsy or epileptic seizures; I shared the common impression that seizures are always involuntary, that they usually involve some loss of consciousness and may progress to physical collapse with convulsions. Since my consciousness seemed unimpaired, and since events had not escalated out of control, I concluded that this experience must not *really* be a seizure, that it was more likely some kind of mystical rapture and thus a rare and deeply moving experience that one should not miss. Having suppressed the residual concerns about where this all might lead, I determined to keep on meditating to see what would come of it—to see if I'd been chosen by some divine entity to experience some kind of mystical communication. I was familiar with accounts of religious mystics who told of seeing a sequence of light visions that, like these visions, kept evolving into new forms until they eventually culminated in an ecstatic rapture; if this was about to happen to me, however unlikely given my lack of any spiritual preparation, I didn't want to miss out.

When I refocused my attention, the spray of phosphene flecks reappeared and, with it, the paroxysmal sensorimotor symptoms—the arched back, stretched skin, and trembling muscles. This same constellation of visual and non-visual experiences continued for a while; it seemed to me like a relatively long time, but I was too preoccupied to count the passing seconds, so I can't be more specific about duration—in retrospect, given the fact that the entire experience lasted only one hour, I would guess that the spray phosphene lasted longer than 30 seconds but less than 2 minutes. As the spray continued to radiate out toward me, I noticed that the light-flecks seemed to be slowly fading in brightness. It was then that I realized that the entire visual field was gradually brightening with a sky-blue color and that this process of brightening and bluing was slowly obscuring the radiating spray, much in the same way that the growing light of dawn gradually dissipates the dark of night and, by so doing, obscures the lights of the stars. The gradual change from the radiating spray to the uniform brightness is illustrated by the schematic drawings in Figure 17D, and a color image of this transformation is included in the panel of color images on the back cover of this book.

NEUROLOGICAL ANALYSIS

Sleep-Onset Seizures: A Review of Current Research

The incidence of epileptic seizures reaches peak levels during the transition between waking and slow wave sleep, especially when the RTN begins firing synchronous spindles bursts at the onset of stage 2 NREMS. In studies of the neural mechanisms involved in the shift to paroxysmal events, researchers often use cats as an animal model of human sleep. In studies that implanted extracellular electrodes in the brains of cats, researchers found that a series of small, incremental changes can destabilize the sleep rhythm oscillators that govern a normal transition to NREMS, triggering an outbreak of hypersynchronous discharges that reverberate in the reciprocal circuits of the thalamus and neocortex [Steriade and Contreras, 1995; Contreras and Steriade, 1995; Lytton et al., 1997; Steriade and Contreras, 1998; Steriade et al., 1998; Neckelmann et al., 1998; Timofeev et al., 1998]. Destabilization of sleep rhythm oscillators is more likely to occur will occur if cortical neurons are already in a hyperexcitable condition when the transition from waking to slow wave sleep begins [Steriade et al., 1998]. On the one occasion when I saw the familiar sequence of tranquil phosphene images suddenly eclipsed by explosive imagery accompanied by paroxysmal sensorimotor symptoms, I had begun meditating in the early morning hours (4:00 a.m.) and had already accumulated a substantial sleep deficit, having slept only 4 out of the preceding 48 hours. Sleep loss is known to a increases the excitability of cortical neurons.

When destabilization occurs, it triggers an alternation between two types of hypersynchronous activity: spike-wave complexes with frequencies of 1.5 to 2 Hz which are generated as the RTN fires spindle bursts at an accelerated rate, or as cortical "fast-runs" where large number of neurons in locally-connected circuits discharge spikes at frequencies of 10 to 15 Hz. When the fast-run spikes get referred back to the thalamus, the sensory-relay neurons—and of course here we're most interested in the vision-relay neurons of the LGN—discharge calcium spikes, just as they did in response to the cortical slow wave, but now the waves of calcium spikes reflect the spatial propagation patterns of the hypersynchronous fast-runs rather than the oscillations of the cortical slow wave. If these two types of hypersynchronous activity were to generate phosphene images, what spatial and temporal features might we expect to see—and do these features match with the spatial and temporal characteristics of the phosphene images that I've described?

Spike-Wave Complexes and the Dark Rings

The dark rings that suddenly eclipse the twinkling star image have the same annular shape and the same "receding" trajectories as the green light-rings that appear as the threshold image of a meditation-induced series, but the dark rings do not effloresce as a phosphene sensation and they flow into the visual field at a rate almost ten times as fast as the green rings (≥ 2.0 Hz and 0.2 Hz, respectively). The spatial analogies suggest that both types of shrinking rings are likely generated by the same mechanisms, and since we already have concluded that the green rings are generated by RTN spindle bursts of the sort normally associated with stage 2 NREMS, it would seem likely that RTN spindle bursts might also generate the perception of dark, fast-moving rings. But then why does one set of RTN-generated ring images illuminate while the other set does not?

In Chapter 3 I explained how the green light-ring is generated when the RTN fires spindle bursts at intervals of one every five seconds (0.2 Hz), a relatively long interval that allows each spindle wave to move up through the RTN matrix, imposing a wave of inhibition that triggers vision-relay cells to fire rebound spikes once the inhibition passes. When sleep rhythm oscillators become destabilized, the RTN fires two or more bursts every second (≥ 2.0 Hz), which means there is not enough time between successive waves of inhibition for vision-relay cells in the LGN to recover and fire their rebound spikes. If there are no waves of rebound spikes, no signals encoding luminance and wavelength information are received by neurons in the primary visual cortices and thus no cortical lightness record results. Even the visual signals generated by random metabolic discharges in the retinae—the signals that would normally produce the background eigengrau—are suppressed by the passing of the fast-moving spindle bursts, and this momentary interruption of retinal "noise" signals generates the perception of a faint black ring that is barely perceptible because it is moving against a background that is only slightly less black. The drawing in Figure 18A illustrates my hypothesis about the generation of the "tunnel" of dark, fast-moving rings: a stream of thin black rings flowing into the visual field at a hypersynchronous rate of two or more per second (≥ 2 Hz) and shrinking rapidly in diameter creates a sensation of optic flow that generates an illusory sense of motion, in this instance, a sense that the viewer is moving through a dark, tunnel-like space which is itself in motion. Even if the influx of rings generates only a subliminal sensation, the meditator would experience this illusion of motion through a dark tunnel.

Cortical Fast-Runs and the Radiating Spray

A second type of hypersynchronous activity triggered by the destabilizion of sleep rhythm oscillators is the cortical "fast-run." In computer simulations of these hypersynchronous fast-runs, Lytton et al. [1996] found (1) that *cell discharges in the cortex radiate outward from a central focus in "an expanding epileptic penumbra,"* (2) that when the excitatory signals are referred back to the sensory-relay nuclei of the thalamus, *only 40% of sensory-relay cells respond by discharging spikes*, and (3) those relay cells that did discharge spikes in response to cortical fast-runs were *distributed in an annulus (ring-shaped band) around a central space in which no cells discharged*. The reason why the sensory-relay cells in the central region do *not* respond is that they are strongly inhibited by the receipt of signals sent from the epicenter of the cortical seizure:

> At the focus, intense cortical and [RTN] neuron activity would produce relative neuron quiescence, ... In the penumbra, neuron divergence would produce less intense hyperpolarization in [thalamocortical] neurons, allowing [low-threshold spikes] and the appearance of the mutual oscillation. . . . Such inhomogeneities might be transiently present on seizure initiation as one or more foci quickly coalesce and synchronize in a process of generalization. The rapidity of this process would make it hard to detect [Lytton et al., 1996, p. 1694].

In a follow-up study using animal models Timofeev et al. [1998] found the same pattern: an expanding epileptic penumbra in cortical networks that triggered less than half of the sensory-relay cells in the thalamus to discharge spikes. These researchers also noted that *each individual sensory-relay cell discharges its spike independently of other sensory-relay cells* [Timofeev et al., 1998]. They do not specify the distribution of the independent spiking other than to confirm that fewer than half of the sensory-relay cells participate. Given these findings, what can we infer about the likely impact of an "expanding epileptic penumbra" in the primary visual cortices on vision-relay neurons in the LGN laminae?

The drawings in Figure 19 illustrate how an expanding wave of excitatory signals generated in the primary visual cortices will likely affect vision-relay cells in the LGN, assuming (1) that only 40% of vision-relay cells respond by discharging spikes, (2) that the participating cells are located within an annular (ring-shaped) band, (3) that participating cells fire their spikes independently of adjacent cells, and (4) that there is a central region where no spikes are discharged. Figure 19 includes a reproduction of the visuotopic map of LGN lamina #6 developed by Connolly and Van Essen [1984] (Figure 11, Chapter 3). It shows that a wave of cell discharges expanding outward in all directions in the primary visual cortices will transmit a wave of excitatory signals through backprojections to lamina #6, a *wave that then flows dorsoventrally down the surface of the lamina, that is, the cortical stimulation first affects vision-relay cells in more dorsal regions and then affects cells in more peripheral regions.* If vision-relay cells in the most dorsal regions—the cells that represent central vision, which occupy about a quarter of the surface of the lamina—are too strongly inhibited to discharge, the descending wave of excitatory signals will not begin to discharge vision-relay cells until it reaches, say,

---

Figure 18. Neural correlates of the green phosphene rings and the dark, non-illuminating rings. The same neural mechanism operating at different speeds can generate both images. A. The neural mechanisms that generate the phosphene rings with shrinking diameters. This schematic drawing, which was originally introduced in Figure 12 (Chapter 3), is replicated here to review the conclusion that we reached in that earlier discussion, namely, how the shape, trajectory, and timing of the phosphene images of shrinking green rings can be attributed to synchronous spindle bursts discharged by the RTN during stage 2 NREMS. As spindle waves ascend ventrodorsally through the RTN matrix of inhibitory cells, spindle wave inhibits the efferent axons of vision-relay cells that fall within the wave's bandwidth. Because the inhibiting wave temporarily blocks the thalamic relay of all visual signals (including the random metabolic discharge of the retinal receptors that generates the background eigengrau), the subject either sees a barely-perceptible image of a dark wave sweeping into the visual field from all sides, or, alternative, the subject is subliminally aware of that image without being consciously aware of perceiving it. Once the spindle wave moves on, the group of vision-relay cells that are released from inhibition then fire rebound spikes, and this wave of rebound spikes registers in consciousness as a phosphene half-ring in one side of the visual field that is fused with the mirror-image half-ring in the other side of the visual field to form one integrated ring-image. B. The origin of the dark rings. If the RTN fires spindle waves at a rate of two or more per second (≥ 2.0 Hz), this is much, much faster than the RTN fires normal sleep spindles, which fires only 1 burst every 3 to 10 seconds. This accelerated firing rate means that the successive waves of inhibition that the spindle waves impose on vision-relay cells flow so fast that the vision-relay cells do not have enough time in between inhibitions to recover their capacity to fire rebound spikes. The fast-moving spindle waves block the thalamic relay of visual signals caused by the random metabolic discharges taking place in the retina, the signals that generate the charcoal gray color of the visual field, and this subtraction of all vision-related signals produces the dark waves. As the stream of black waves pour into the visual field and shrink in diameter, seeming to "recede" toward a distant point in 3-dimensional space, this evokes a sensation of optic flow which creates the illusion of moving through a dark "tunnel" which is itself in motion. This sensation of moving through this "tunnel" could vary between moving forward and moving backward, the sort of ambiguity in perception that arises in the figure-and-ground experiments in psychophysics where the attention shifts back and forth, first emphasizing the figure, then the ground.

How Spindle Waves Produce Dark Rings

A Origins of the Green Phosphene Rings

LGN Cells Fire Rebound Spikes After Spindle Wave Inhibition

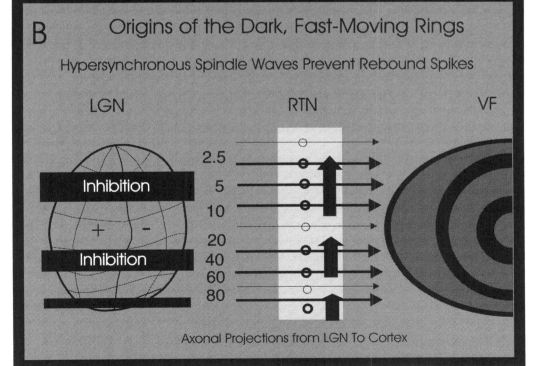

B Origins of the Dark, Fast-Moving Rings

Hypersynchronous Spindle Waves Prevent Rebound Spikes

at least 10° of isoeccentricity in the visual field, and from then on the descending wave will trigger discharges in cells that represent ever more peripheral regions of

Figure 19. Origins of the radiating spray image. If cortical cells happen to be abnormally excitable at the time that a normal transition to NREMS begins, the sleep rhythm oscillators can be destabilized, giving rise to a hypersynchronous seizure. In this event, two types of hypersynchronous activity can appear: (1) spike-wave complexes generated when the RTN begins firing spindle bursts at an abnormally accelerated rate, and (2) "fast-runs" of cell discharges spreading through locally-connected cortical networks. I've already demonstrated how spike-wave complexes generate the "tunnel" image composed of dark, fast-moving rings. The neural mechanism responsible for generating the phosphene image of a radiating spray is the alternative form of hypersynchronous activity, the onset of fast-runs in cortical cells. Researchers have discovered that the initial shift to fast-run activity generates an "expanding epileptic penumbra" of cell discharges in cortical networks [Lytton et al., 1996; Timofeev et al., 1998]. The expanding epileptic penumbra spreads out from the seizure focus like ripples from a stone thrown into a pond, as shown in this drawing where a wave of hypersynchronous discharges propagates out in all directions from a seizure focus in the primary visual cortices. Notice that the epileptic focus—the epicenter of the expanding penumbra—occurs in this illustration among those visual neurons in the primary visual cortices that represent the very center of the visual field where the star-like image had once appeared. The expanding penumbra of hypersynchronous discharges in cortical circuits is transmitted through back-projections to the LGN where it triggers vision-relay cells to discharge. The pattern of discharges in those vision-relay cells is determined by the direction of the wave of excitatory signals referred back to the LGN: to generate a phosphene image of a spray radiating out from more central to more peripheral regions in the visual field, the wave of cell discharges in the LGN (e.g., in lamina #6, which is shown here) would have to flow across the laminar sheets in a dorsoventral direction (i.e., from the uppermost regions to more ventral regions). A wave of excitation moving in this direction would causes vision-relay cells that represent more central regions of the visual field to discharge calcium spikes before the wave triggers discharges in vision-relay cells that represent more peripheral regions of the visual field. This pattern of neuronal discharges in the LGN laminae, which generates the phosphene image of radiating sparks, involves a wave of excitation moving in exactly the opposite direction from the ascending, ventrodorsal movement of the RTN spindle waves that generate the image of rings that shrink in diameter. In addition to explaining the directionality of the radiating spray, we need to account for the shape of the tiny, pixel-like, phosphene flecks. The same researchers cited above also found that when the waves of the expanding epileptic penumbra are referred back to the LGN, they trigger discharges in *only about 40% of the vision-relay cells*. Moreover, those vision-relay cells that discharge calcium spikes do so *independently* of one another, not in a synchronous wave. Taken together, these findings show that an expanding epileptic penumbra of cortical fast-runs referred back to the LGN (1) will flow in a dorsoventral direction, (2) will not activate the neurons representing the central vision, (3) will trigger discharges in less than half of vision-relay cells in peripheral regions, and (4) will trigger cells to discharge independently of neighboring cells. The flow of light flecks creates the illusion that individual light flecks retain their structural integrity as they move across the visual field from more central to more peripheral regions, whereas it seems more likely that different points of light are illuminated at different times in response to the wave descending through the LGN laminae.

Origins of the Radiating Spray

The "Expanding Epileptic Penumbra" Consists of Waves of Cortical "Fast Run" Discharges That Expand From the Epicenter of the Seizure & Drive the Discharge of LGN Vision-Relay Neurons

Axonal Projections from the Cortex to the LGN

Vision-Relay Neurons in the LGN Discharge in Response to the Dorso--Ventral Flow of Cortical Stimuli. This Generates Phosphene Flecks That Move Toward Peripheral Regions of the Visual Field

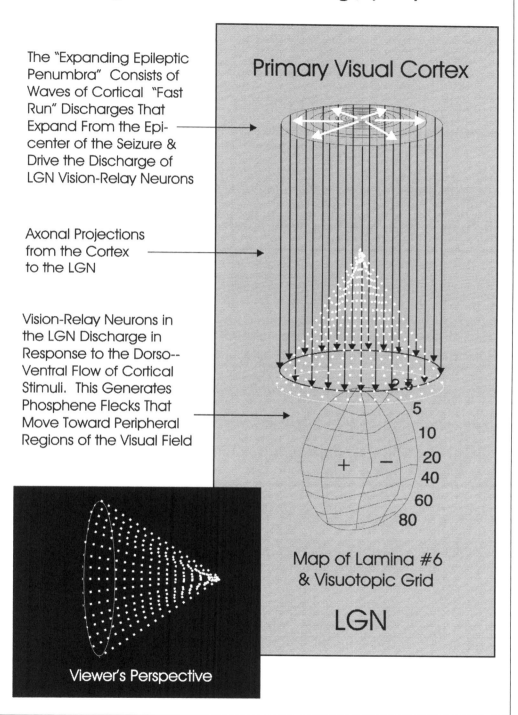

Primary Visual Cortex

2 5
5
10
20
40
60
80

Map of Lamina #6 & Visuotopic Grid

LGN

Viewer's Perspective

110

the visual field. Only about half of the cells will respond to the stimulation, and the distribution of cell responses is likely to be random since each cell fires its spike independent of adjacent cells. Since the epicenter of the hypersynchronous seizure in the primary visual cortices that generates the expanding epileptic penumbra will keep on producing these waves, so too will there be multiple waves of discharges by vision-relay cells in the LGN. The drawings in Figure 19 show how these progression of neuronal events is consistent with a phosphene sensation in which the viewer sees "points of light" appearing everywhere in the visual field except in the central region and where those points of light seem to be randomly distributed and seem to be flowing outward in all directions toward the rim of vision. If fewer than half of the vision-relay cell participate, and if each of them fires its spike independently of adjacent cells, then it is reasonable to expect that the phosphene sensation would consist of innumerable tiny sparks of light, and, indeed, the image of the radiating spray manifests a variegated or "grainy" texture.

The Paroxysmal Sensorimotor Symptoms

As I watched the spray of phosphene flecks, I felt compelled to arch my back, to pull my head back against the pillow, and to let my mouth fall slack, and I felt the muscles of my face and fingers jerking spasmodically. These symptoms are consistent with cortical reflex myoclonus, a symptom cluster typically associated with epileptic seizures [Hallet, 1997]. The onset of these sensorimotor symptoms at the same time as the onset of the "explosive" phosphene image of a spray of "sparks" radiating toward the viewer supports an inference that there was a meditation-induced shift from hypnagogic consciousness (i.e., stage 1 NREMS) to a sleep-onset hypersynchronous seizure in the corticothalamic circuits linking the primary visual cortices and the LGN.

The Eclipse of the Radiating Spray

The radiating spray of tiny, bright sparks lasted for a relatively long time—I can't give a specific estimate because I was wholly absorbed in the ecstatic qualities of the experience and didn't think about counting the passing seconds. The transition to the next phosphene display occurred very slowly: it involved a gradual brightening and bluing of the entire visual field, a change so subtle in its initial stages that it wasn't noticeable. But like early light of dawn that precedes the rise of the sun, the brightening and bluing effect eventually reached a threshold level where it was impossible to ignore, and then, shortly after that, it become strong enough that the light-flecks in the radiating spray began to fade in comparison to the blue background until they were completely obscured, leaving the visual field a bright, empty, sky-blue expanse. The dawn-like brightening and bluing effect is generated by a different set of neural mechanisms than the hypersynchronous spike-waves and fast-runs we've discussed in this chapter—the brightening and bluing are generated by more centrally-located mechanisms—but it's important, when we begin to analyze these central mechanisms in the next chapter, to remember that while the image of the radiating spray was obscured by the brightening and bluing effect, it is not clear that the hypersynchronous activity that generated the radiating spray vanished at the same time as its phosphene epiphenomenon; it's possible, although we have no reason given our present state of knowledge to decide one way or the other, that the hypersynchrony in corticothalamic circuits may have continued to oscillate despite the disappearance of the spray, and, indeed, that it may have been an important force driving the emergence of the bright blue visual field.

Finally, it is important to point out that the destabilization of corticothalamic sleep rhythm oscillators that we've discussed is likely to be much a more prevalent phenomenon than the medical profession currently recognizes. The researchers who first identified the mechanisms involved in animal models write that they were "surprised by the high incidence of seizures that occurred spontaneously," an observation that suggested to them "the possibility that many spontaneous electrographic seizures in 'normal' subjects are unrecognized, and that those sleeping individuals pass in and out of seizures during their slow sleep oscillation, as we showed here for cats [Steriade et al. 1998, p. 1476]." Applying this same observation to meditators who cultivate phosphene images, one might suspect that here too the transition in and out of hypersynchronous seizures may occur spontaneously with a much higher frequency than anyone has hitherto supposed and may not be recognized as seizures. Furthermore, it is reasonable to expect a meditator who repeatedly induces this shift to hypersynchronous activity might create a conditioned response that could induce this response with relative ease. I can't cite any case studies that document the phenomenon of slipping easily in and out of hypersynchronous seizures in the context of meditation, but there is a very interesting and potentially relevant EEG study by Persinger [1984]: in a subject who was adept at glossolalia (and who reported feeling a sense of unity with the cosmos while engaged in glossolalia), Persinger recorded spike-wave complexes of the sort that we've just discussed during a glossolalia performance. Later in this book when we examine EEG studies of expert meditators in the medical literature, we'll encounter a number of cases where the subjects have acquired the ability to move in and out of hypersynchronous trance states with apparent ease, even though none of the authors mentions this as a possibility.

The Dark, Moving "Tunnel" in Near-Death Visions

Accounts of near-death experiences (NDEs) often include references to "moving through a dark tunnel toward a bright light," a description that bears a striking resemblance to the phenomenon we've just discussed—a sudden influx of dark, fast-moving rings that creates an illusion of moving forward (or falling backward) through a dark "tunnel," which is superceded by a gradual brightening and bluing of the entire visual field which gives the viewer a sense of being immersed in a beautiful, blissful light. These striking parallels in visual imagery suggest the hypothesis that, as a result of traumatic injuries (or as a result of some acute but internally generated medical condition), these victims experience a sudden onset of hypersynchronous spike-wave complexes, and that it is the onset of this hypersynchronous seizure that generates the subliminal image of moving through a dark tunnel. In these NDE cases, there must not be the same shift to from spike-wave complexes to cortical fast-runs that I've described, because NDE victims do not mention seeing a radiating spray; in these cases, perhaps because the intensity of the spike-wave complexes may be sufficient to drive the rapid emergence of a hippocampal seizure that generates the bright light. This is the subject to which we now turn.

6

HIPPOCAMPAL IMAGES, I: BLUE SKY, WHITE MOON

PHENOMENOLOGY

The Vision of a Diffuse Brightening and Bluing

As I continued to watch the spray of tiny phosphene flecks radiating toward me, I noticed that the whole visual field was gradually becoming brighter and brighter and that the normal charcoal color was changing to a light blue. The effect was very much like watching a natural dawn. The schematic drawings in Figure 20 illustrate this transformation, and a color version can be found on the back cover. As the visual field brightened, the radiating spray of phosphene sparks continued to flow but to become ever-dimmer until the spray was totally obscured and I was staring at what looked like a bright summer sky devoid of clouds and haze. The eclipse of the radiating spray does not, in itself, establish that the neural mechanisms responsible for generating that image—the hypersynchronous activity in corticothalamic circuits—had ceased, since the installation of the bright blue visual field may have masked the receipt of visual signals from corticothalamic circuits. Once the bright blue visual field was installed, the paroxysmal sensorimotor symptoms that accompanied the radiating spray disappeared, and I felt a deep sense of calm and well-being. The shade of blue was beautiful; later, when I had a chance to search for the precise shade of blue using a "CMYK Process Color Chart," a book published for photographers who want to control what a color will look in when it appears in print format, I found the same shade of blue that had appeared in the visual field, and it was 40% cyan with no magenta, yellow, or black.

I stared at the cyan sky for a relatively long time—I didn't count the passing seconds, so I can't be more specific—but I do know that this vision lasted long enough that I began to feel bored. I was just about to stop meditating and to

114

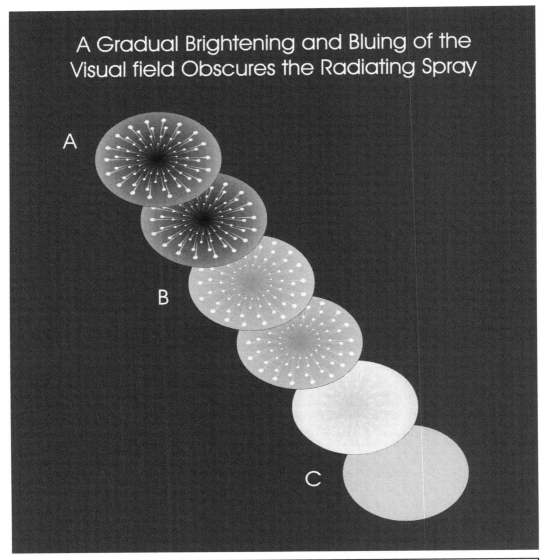

Figure 20. The brightening and bluing of the entire visual field. A. The image of a radiating spray of tiny light-flecks generated by cortical "fast-runs." B. The radiating spray becomes more and more obscured as the entire visual field gradually brightened with a light blue phosphene, a transformation that resembled the brightening and bluing of the sky at dawn. C. The radiating spray was totally obscured (although the underlying processes that generated it may still have been active) and the entire visual field was filled exclusively with a diffuse, undifferentiated, sky-blue phosphene display. The approximate hue of this light blue color, based on a comparison with printed color swatches in a CMYK Process Color Chart, is 40% Cyan without any Magenta, Yellow, or Black. This is a color comparable to the color of the sky on a clear, dry, summer day or to the color of a robin's egg. Once installed, the bright sky-blue phosphene remained unchanged for what seemed like a relatively long time. This light vision was not accompanied by paroxysmal sensorimotor symptoms.

abandon the attempt to force myself into sleep when I caught a glimpse of a faint smudge of white phosphene in the upper right quadrant of the visual field. At first this white smudge seemed to be partially obscured, but as I focused my attention on it, it became brighter and, with the brightening, its surfaces were more defined. I was staring at a hollow, "thimble-like" bulb with surfaces formed of translucent white phosphene. It looked very much like the pale white moon that sometimes appears in the sky during the daytime. The drawings in Figure 21 illustrate the basic shape of the bulbous phosphene. When I fixed my attention on it, the surfaces of this image glowed more brightly. This increase in brightness gave the figure more posterior extension, creating the illusion that it had somehow "moved" forward to "protrude" out from the sky-blue background; conversely, when I relaxed my attention ever so slightly, the bulbous figure dimmed and its more posterior, cylindrical walls disappeared altogether, creating the illusion that the figure had "receded" back into the blue background. I watched this apparent "movement" occur many times on this occasion. One distinctive feature of this bulbous phosphene, shown in the inset in Figure 21, is that when it shined with its brightest intensity, I could make out a thin, dark, curve line inverted just beneath the anterior pole like a frowning mouth with its tips pointing downward.

NEUROLOGICAL ANALYSIS, PART I. THE BRIGHTENING & BLUING

Clues About Causation

In the progression of meditation-induced phosphenes, the appearances of the diffuse brightening and bluing effect and the white, moon-like image are sandwiched in between phosphenes which have paroxysmal characteristics. The image of the radiating light-flecks that precedes the diffuse brightening is generated by the emergence of hypersynchronous activity in corticothalamic circuits, and after images of the blue-sky and white moon that we're examining in this chapter I'll describe the advent of lightning-like phosphenes and sensorimotor symptoms that are clearly paroxysmal. If the phenomenon that we're focusing on in this chapter is sandwiched between processes that clearly involve seizures (albeit different types of seizures), then it is reasonable to infer that the neural mechanisms responsible for generating the bright, blue "sky" and the white "moon" are also generated by paroxysmal processes.

Another clue worth noting at the outset is that a phosphene effect like the diffuse brightening which is capable of masking a phosphene effect generated in corticothalamic circuits, like the radiating spray, must itself be generated at some site located in more central regions of the brain. In theory those neural mechanisms could be located anywhere in the visual pathways between the primary visual cortices (where hypersynchronous activity is underway) and the hippocampus (which is the terminus for all visual pathways), but research in epileptology suggests that the most likely site by far is the hippocampus. This structure is notorious for being especially vulnerable to seizures, especially in temporal lobe epilepsy where *the most frequent cause of seizure is a gradual build-up of rhythmical firing in the hippocampus* [Paré et al., 1992; Barbarosie and Avoli, 1997; Engel et al., 1997; Williamson and Engel, 1997; Bragin et al., 1999; Velasco et al., 2000]. Accordingly, we'll begin our analysis by focusing on the hippocampal formation and its possible role in the generation of these phosphenes, both the diffuse brightening and bluing and also the bulbous figure.

A third clue that helps us focus our inquiry from the outset is that the white bulbous image appeared in the upper right quadrant of the visual field. Because the two optic tracks cross to the opposite hemisphere while en route to the LGNs, visual signals generated in the *right* retina, which are the signals triggered by external stimuli located in the right half of the visual field, are sent to the contralateral *left* LGN and then forwarded through the vision-processing centers in the left hemisphere until they reach the left hippocampus. This is the terminus of the visual system, the structure in which visual signals receive their highest level of representation prior to being sent on to the limbic region where emotional and mnemonic associations are added. The significance of these details is that we can use them to identify which hippocampus is responsible for generating the spatially-diffuse brightness and which is responsible for generating the spatially-specific phosphene of a bulbous figure. For a visual image with spatially specific characteristics to

Figure 21. The waxing and waning of a hollow, white, bulbous phosphene. This image first manifested as a faint whitish glow in the upper right quadrant of the sky-blue visual field. When I focused my attention on it, the glow brightened and coalesced as a phosphene figure shaped like the thimble a seamstress wears over her thumb. Its surfaces were formed by translucent white light and the anterior pole had a bulbous shape while more posterior regions looked cylindrical and hollow. The figure seemed to move forward when I stared at it. This caused the bulb to shine more brightly and, as a consequence of the brightening, to reveal more of its posterior extension; conversely, the figure seemed to recede back into the sky-blue background whenever my attention wavered, even for only a moment, but this too was an artifact of the figure's brightness—as the white phosphene dimmed, the more posterior regions evaporated so that the bulbous figure became shorter. Silhouetted against the sky-blue background, the bulbous figure looked very much like seeing the moon when it continues to shine in a sunlit sky. The schematic drawing in the inset provides a closer view of the white bulbous image at its peak brightness and extension; note, however, that this drawing is misleading in two respects: first, because it cannot convey the sense of a hollow, 3-dimensional form, and, second, because the exigencies of the computer drawing program made it necessary to construct the image in bands of different color, whereas the actual phosphene was a uniform white color. The inset also highlights one feature that attracted my attention when the bulbous figure reached its peak brightness: positioned beneath the anterior pole was a thin shadow-like line shaped like an inverted crescent.

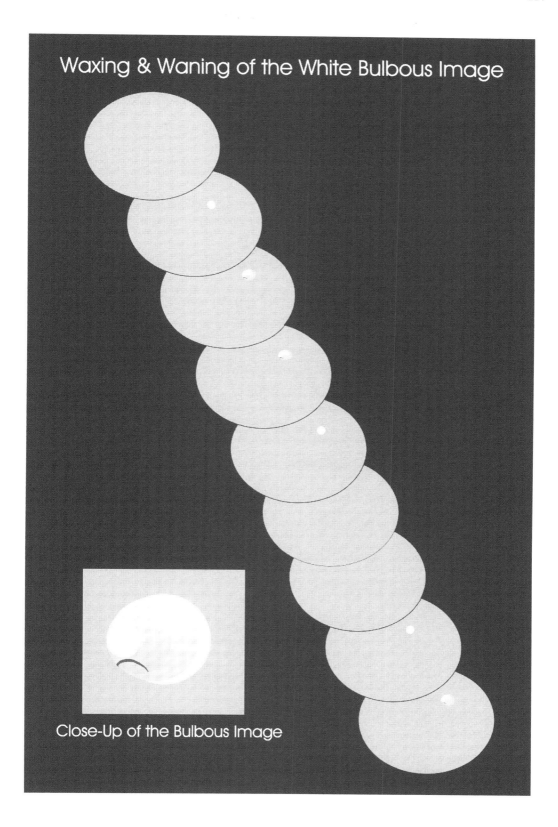

Waxing & Waning of the White Bulbous Image

Close-Up of the Bulbous Image

appear in the upper right quadrant of the visual field, we can infer that the left hippocampus must be able to function normally, and since there is only one such image visible in the circumstances that I've described, it is clear that the neuronal signals that generate the bulbous image must be processed in the left hippocampus, not the right. This suggests that the spatially-diffuse brightening and bluing of the visual field is most likely generated in the right hippocampus, but to be more precise about which hippocampus generates which phosphene effect and by what means, we need to know more about the functional anatomy of the entorhinal-hippocampal complexes (EC-H) that receive and process incoming sensory signals. In particularly, we need to know how the internal functions of these structures are affected when slow wave sleep rhythms become active—and how the internal operations change when sleep rhythm oscillators destabilize.

Signal-Processing in the Hippocampal Formations

Functional Anatomy of the Entorhinal-Hippocampal Complex

Afferent signals from the visual cortices are funneled into the hippocampus via the entorhinal cortex (EC). There are two of these entorhinal-hippocampal complexes (EC-H), one in each hemisphere [Buzsáki, 1986; Chrobak and Buzsáki, 1994]. The constituent structures and functional relationships of the EC-H complex are illustrated in the schematic diagram in Figure 22 (adapted from drawings by Duvernoy [1988, Fig. 37] with additions based on functional analyses in Gloor [1997, pp. 327, 350]).

Each EC sends visual signals into two intra-hippocampal circuits: one complete set of afferent visual signals is sent into the *trisynaptic perforant path* at the same time that an identical set is sent into the *monosynaptic temporo-ammonic path*. The two pathways perform different functions that complement one another and the products of their processing merge when these two sets of signals converge in hippocampal subfield CA1, the last signal-processing region located inside the hippocampus proper. The temporo-ammonic path consists of a direct, monosynaptic projection from EC to CA1 that is reciprocated by a direct, monosynaptic back-projection from CA1 to EC. This reciprocal, monosynaptic circuitry makes it possible to preserve a one-to-one registration as signals are transmitted back and forth. By contrast, visual signals sent into the perforant path pass through two processing centers before reaching subfield CA1: the EC sends signals into the dentate gyrus (DG) for processing by its constituent granule cells, then the granule cells send action potentials along their mossy fiber axons to target neurons in subfield CA3 where additional processing takes place. Neurons in CA3 send action potentials along their Schaffer collateral axons to target neurons in subfield CA1, so the results of signal-processing in the DG and CA3 subfields will eventually interact with the copy of the original signal-patterns preserved by the ongoing oscillations of neurons in the direct, reciprocal circuits that link the EC and CA1. From subfield

CA1, the final product of intra-hippocampal processing is fed back to the EC and also forwarded to retro-hippocampal cortices—the subiculum (S), the presubiculum (PRES), the parasubiculum (PAS), and the parahippocampus (PHG). The two EC-H complexes (and some pairs of retro-hippocampal cortices) are connected by projections that form a dorsal hippocampal commissure (DHC), as shown in Figure 22. The DHC connection makes it possible for excitation received in one EC to influence neuron activity in the contralateral EC. There may also be another inter-hippocampal projection, the *ventral* hippocampal commissure (VHC), but it is a matter of debate whether this structure, which is sizable in rats but miniscule in monkeys, continues to exist as a functional remnant in humans; if so, the VHC would be positioned to play a critical role in the propagation of seizures, because it would provide a direct, monosynaptic link between the right and left hippocampus in addition to the indirect link provided by the DHC. Given the controversy about the existence of the VHC, I will put off the discussion of the relevant research until we arrive at a point in the exposition where the subject can no longer be avoided. For that reason, I did not include an arrow representing the VHC in Figure 22.

Theories of Hippocampal Signal-Processing

There are two theories of hippocampal function that are particularly helpful in explaining how the EC interacts with the the various subfields inside the hippocampus proper (DG, CA3 & CA1) [Buzsáki, 1995, 1996; Vinogradova, 2001]. Both theories envision the EC-H complex as a mechanism that splits afferent signals into two sets and that processes them separately to extract different kinds of information before bringing the two sets of signals back together for comparison and synthesis into a single product. Vinogradova calls this interaction the "comparator" function of the EC-H complex. In this section we'll spend some time examining Vinogradova's comparator theory about the operation of the EC-H complex, because many of the operations that she describes are relevant for explaining how neuron discharges in the right hippocampus might generate the phosphene effect of a diffuse brightening and bluing of the visual field.

In the temporo-ammonic circuits of the EC-H complex, neurons in the EC are linked neurons in hippocampal subfield CA1 by one-to-one axonal connections. Also, the neurons in CA1 have the capacity to abruptly turn on or off in response to the receipt of signals sent from the EC. These characteristics make it possible for neurons in subfield CA1 to oscillate in such a way as to preserve an ongoing record of the signal-patterns they originally received from the EC. This means that the temporo-ammonic circuit can function as a "spatially-specific" circuit [Buzsáki, Ibid.] or, to use Vinogradova's terminology, as an "informational" circuit. By contrast, the trisynaptic perforant path does *not* preserve spatially-specific information. The reason why it does not—and cannot—is because neurons in subfield CA3 are locally connected in dense networks, a pattern of connectivity that makes it possible to amplify, attentuate, or otherwise transform afferent signals, but this kind of processing does not preserve a record of the same signal-patterns that were present when the EC sent the original signal-set into the perforant path. In this view, signal-processing in the perforant path produces a product that is "spatially-diffuse" [Buzsáki, Ibid.].

To explain how the spatially diffuse signals (that have been processed in the perforant path) interact with spatially-specific signals (that are preserved by oscillations in the reciprocal circuits of the temporo-ammonic path) to synthesize a single product, Vinogradova proposes the following scenario: granule cells in the dentate gyrus (DG) extract simplified, abstract patterns from the barrage of signals they receive from the EC, and they then forward these filtered signals to neurons in subfield CA3. In CA3, the networks of locally-connected neurons perform a

Figure 22. **The functional anatomy of the right and left entorhinal-hippocampal (EC-H) complexes. The schematic drawing, adapted from Duvernoy [1988, Fig. 37] and from analyses presented in Gloor [1997, pp. 327, 350], "unfolds" the complex anatomy of the hippocampus in relation to adjacent temporal cortices. Signals generated in the visual cortices of each hemisphere of the brain converge on the ipsalateral parahippocampal cortex and are directed into the entorhinal cortex (EC). The EC processes these afferent signals and sends them into the hippocampus proper which is where visual signals receive their highest level of representation. According to current theoretical analyses of hippocampal function, the EC sends identical signal-sets into two distinct intra-hippocampal circuits that eventually converge in the last of the signal-processing regions located within the hippocampus proper—subfield CA1 (CA for Cornu Ammonis). The EC sends one complete set of visual signals into *temporo-ammonic pathway* which consists of a direct, monosynaptic projection from EC to CA1 that is reciprocated by a direct, monosynaptic back-projection from CA1 to EC. This reciprocal, monosynaptic circuitry makes it possible to preserve a one-to-one registration as signals are transmitted back and forth. The EC also sends a complete set of visual signals into the *perforant path* where they are relayed through three separate synapses: (1) from the EC to the dentate gyrus (DG); (2) from the DG to subfield CA3; and (3) from CA3 to subfield CA1. When visual signals processed in the perforant path arrive in CA1, the last processing area located in the hippocampus proper, they interact with the original set of signals that the EC sent directly to CA1, and the product of this interaction is then relayed back to the EC and also sent on to retro-hippocampal cortices (i.e., to the subiculum [SUB], the presubiculum [PRES], the parasubiculum [PAS], and the parahippocampal cortices [PHG]). There is, in addition, some transmission of signals between the EC-H complexes in the right and left hemispheres. Contralateral projections that extend between the two ECs, the two presubiculums, and the two parahippocampal cortices are bundled into a structure called the dorsal hippocampal commissure (DHC). In most primates there is also a direct, monosynaptic projection that extends from the uncal extension of subfield CA1 to the contralateral uncus called the ventral hippocampal commissure (VHC), but given that there is an ongoing debate about whether or not this structure exists in humans, I have elected to omit the VHC from this diagram and to address this issue in the next chapter which deals with the origins of the phosphene rays.**

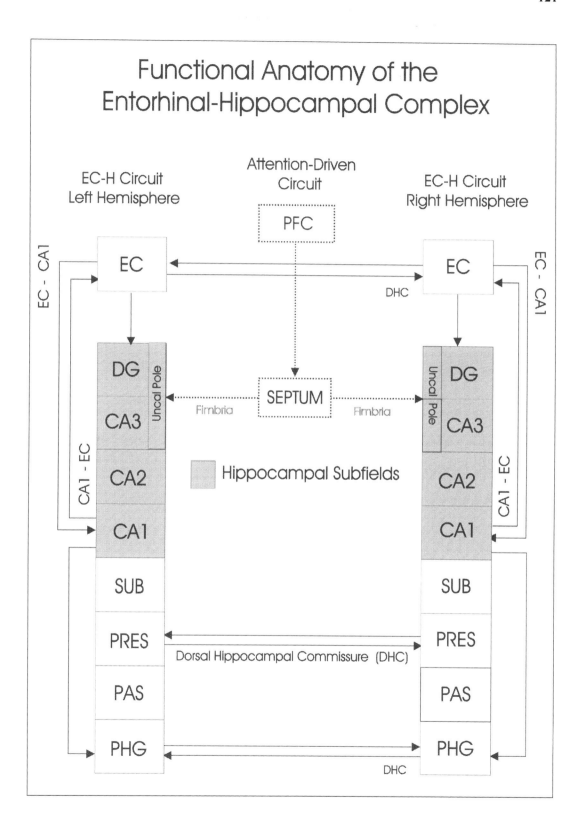

"differencing" function designed to determine which of the patterns encoded in the visual signals abstracted in the DG should receive amplification, attentuation, or some other transformation. The goal of the differencing function is to amplify those signal-patterns that are novel or otherwise worthy of attention. This differencing function is carried out by the neuronal networks forged by the organism's past experience: the connections linking those neurons that often fire in concert during an organism's lifetime are strengthened by longterm potentiation (LTP), the cellular basis for the familiar behavioral phenomenon of habituation. Once LTP induces a reorganization of neuronal connections in response to repeated exposure to similar stimuli and habituation is established, from then on those reorganized neuron networks in CA3 mute their reaction to incoming signals unless those signals encode some new feature or some dramatic increase in the intensity of a stimulus that has already produced habituation. It is these pre-existing neuronal networks embedded in subfield CA3 by LPT that perform the differencing process: if the abstract patterns embodied in the signals received from the DG do *not* match those the patterns already embodied in the pre-existing networks, then those signal-patterns are identified as being novel or otherwise attention-worthy when they signals are passed on to subfield CA1.

When the differencing process in the pre-existing neuronal networks of subfield CA3 marks a signal-pattern as new or attention-worthy, there is a change in the firing rate of the CA3 neurons involved in processing those signals, a change that amplifies that signal-pattern when the signals are received in CA1. The mechanism works as follows: neurons in CA3 normally fire at high rates and impose a tonic inhibition on target neurons in CA1. When CA3 neurons receive abstract signal patterns from the DG, their normally high firing rates are initially suppressed, but the duration of this suppression varies—and that turns out to be the determining factor as to whether or not afferent signals get amplified. If the signals received from the DG have patterns that *match* what has already been embodied in the neuronal networks of subfield CA3 by LTP, then the CA3 neurons quickly return to their normally high firing rates, and this inhibits the target neurons in CA1. If there is *no match* between the incoming signals and the pre-existing networks, then the suppression of the high firing rates in CA3 neurons is sustained for a longer interval. The sustained suppression of CA3 neuron firing rates inhibits the inhibition normally imposed on CA1 neurons, freeing them to discharge more frequently than other neurons in CA1 which have not been similarly released from CA3-imposed inhibition. The differences in the firing rates of CA1 neurons amplifies some afferent signals while attenuating other afferent signals. In CA1 these CA3-driven differences in CA1 firing rates interact with the original signal-patterns sent by the EC, signal-patterns that have been preserved in CA1 by excitation oscillating back and forth in the reciprocal circuits of the temporo-ammonic pathway that links CA1 directly with the EC. This means that intra-hippocampal processing can amplify those patterns encoded in the original sensory signals that were generated when the organism perceived that some object or event was novel or otherwise attention-worthy.

There is an important qualification that Vinogradova emphasized: in order to perform this differencing operation that amplifies some visual signals relative to others, neuron networks in CA3 must receive inputs from other parts of the brain, for example, from the brainstem reticular formation (which modulates the level of physiological arousal), and, most important for our purposes, there must be input from the anterior attentional networks. Later we'll see how the meditator's intense inward concentration activates the prefrontal cortices which then stimulate the medial septal nucleus and the vertical limb of the nucleus of the diagonal band to send excitatory signals to the anterior "uncal" third of the hippocampus. This attention-driven input produces a major impact and is the likely source of the bulbous image. But that's a subject that we'll take up later in the chapter; for now it's important to continue our analysis of the brightening effect.

Vinogradova's comparator theory of EC-H function has important implications for tracing the origins of the spatially-diffuse brightening of the visual field. It suggests that this brightening was most likely generated by a sustained suppression of the normally high firing rates of neurons in subfield CA3 in the right hippocampus, a suppression that lifted the normal inhibition on target cells in CA1, and, because the brightening is generalized across the entire visual field, the suppression must have affected virtually all of the CA3 neurons in the right hippocampus. This generalized increase in neuronal activity must have also spread to the contralateral EC-H complex via the dorsal hippocampal commissure. The CA3 neurons in the left hemisphere would likely respond to this generalized increase in excitatory signals as if it were a new signal-pattern that did not match patterns embodied in the pre-existing neuron networks, which would cause them to prolong the suppression of their normally high firing rates, thereby lifting the inhibition on CA1 neurons. But it is important to note that the prolonged suppression of the firing rates of CA3 neurons and the consequent increase in the firing rates of CA1 neurons must not have reached *maximal* levels at this point in time; we can make that inference because we know that it remained possible for a brighter, whiter image—the bulbous moon-like figure—to appear in the bright blue visual field, a phenomenon that would presumably require more intense neuronal activity than that required to produce the blue visual field itself.

Having identified differences in the firing rates of CA3 and CA1 neurons as the mechanism that most likely generates the phosphene effect of a diffuse brightening, the next question that needs to be addressed is what events caused the prolonged suppression in the firing rates of CA3 neurons. There is, of course, an obvious candidate—the build-up of rhythmical discharges in subfield CA3 of the left hippocampus—so we need to find out what caused this build-up to occur. My analysis of the phosphene evidence in previous chapters shows that my meditation activated slow wave sleep rhythms normally associated with stage 2 and stage 3

NREMS. What effect, if any, does the activation of slow wave sleep rhythms have on the functioning of the hippocampi? I also demonstrated that the sleep rhythm oscillators destabilized, giving rise to a hypersynchronous seizure in corticothalamic circuits, so we need to consider how the hippocampi would be affected by the onset of a hypersynchronous seizure in corticothalamic circuits. Can the build-up of rhythmical discharges in the right hippocampus be traced to either or both of these processes? And will this concatenation of neuronal events explain why I saw a gradual brightening and bluing of the visual field? To pursue these questions, I'll begin with what's known about the effects of slow wave sleep on intra-hippocampal functioning, then move next to the issue of how intra-hippocampal processing might be affected when sleep rhythm oscillators destabilize and trigger a hypersynchronous seizure in corticothalamic circuits.

Slow Wave Sleep and the Hippocampus

During slow wave sleep, neurons in the hippocampus shift from firing patterns associated with waking states to firing synchronous spike-bursts called "sharp waves" (SPWs). The principle neurons in subfield CA3 fire these synchronous bursts at intermittent intervals that can range between three bursts per second (3 Hz), which is on the fast side, to only one burst every 50 seconds (0.02 Hz). *The sharp waves initiated in subfield CA3 propagate through the hippocampal circuits, enhancing the excitability of neurons in all of subregions of the EC-H complex except for that part of the entorhinal cortex where incoming sensory signals are received and then funneled into the hippocampus—the superficial layers of the EC* [Buzsáki, 1986; Chrobak and Buzsáki, 1994]. Even granule cells in the dentate gyrus are affected by sharp waves, because CA3 has back-projections to DG that convey sharp waves as CA3 feedback to the DG [Penttonen et al., 1997]. The reason why neurons in the superficial layers of the EC are not excited by synchronous sharp waves is that intra-entorhinal circuits prevent this from happening: neurons in the deep layers of the EC have ascending intra-entorhinal projections that inhibit activity in the superficial layers when the deep layers are stimulated by sharp waves [Penttonen et al., 1997]. If it were not for this barrier, synchronous SPWs that originated as bursts in subfield CA3 would be relayed through the entire entorhinal-hippocampal loop and would then re-enter CA3, thereby establishing a reverberating loop of positive feedforward excitation. *The onset of SPWs during slow wave sleep enhances the excitability of neurons throughout the EC-H complex (except in the superficial layers of the EC) by 200% to 500%. In addition, if the SPWs happen to be fired at a time when the EC-H circuits are still engaged in the processing of sensory signals, the excitability of neurons can increase by as much as 900%* [Buzsáki, 1986; Chrobak and Buzsáki, 1994]. Since I've demonstrated that slow wave sleep rhythms had become active on the night when I experienced the paroxysmal episode, and since I've also reported that I was watching sleep rhythm phosphenes at the time, it is reasonable to infer that the excitability of neurons throughout the EC-H complexes (except for those in the superficial layers of neurons in the ECs) would have been enhanced by at least 200% and more likely by as much as 900% (because afferent visual signals were arriving in the EC-H complex and generating phosphene effects). Hyperexcitable neurons would make the hippocampus more vulnerable on this particular occcasion than it would be in a normal episode of slow wave sleep. But that is not the only factor that might lower the barrier to a build-up of abnormal discharges: at the same time that hippocampal sharp waves were activated, neurons in the superficial layers of the EC—the only neurons that do not have their excitability enhanced by SPWs—were being bombarded by afferent visual signals generated by hypersynchronous activity in corticothalamic circuits. How would these signals interact with other influences impinging on the EC-H circuits?

The superficial layers of the EC would have been receiving visual signals arriving in rhythmical pulses, first the signals generated by spike-wave complexes and then the signals generated by cortical fast-runs radiating out in an "expanding epileptic penumbra." If the superficial layers of the EC receive rhythmically-pulsed visual signals and direct them into the hippocampus, this means that the sole barrier in the EC-H complex to the progress of synchronous sharp waves, the sole barrier that prevents the SPWs from establishing a reentrant circuit of positive feedforward excitation, will be exposed to rhythmical discharges generated by the hypersynchronous seizure in corticothalamic circuits. These rhythmical pulses impinging on the superficial layers of the EC have the potential to be epileptogenic: a study by Steriade et al.[1998] found that *the pattern of rhythmical firing that characterizes cortical fast runs during a hypersynchronous seizure in corticothalamic circuits is similar to the rhythmical pattern recorded in mesotemporal regions during partial seizures*: "*The seizure epoch characterized by fast runs . . . resembles the stereotyped fast rhythm (10 - 20 Hz) reported in human temporal lobe epilepsy that may spread to perihippocampal structures and cingulate cortex. . . . (Steriade et al., Ibid., p. 1477).*" Other studies have reported similar rhythms [Stringer et al., 1989; Pare et al., 1992; Bragin et al., 1995; Barbarosie and Avoli, 1997]. If the visual signals bombarding the superficial layers of the EC have a hypersynchronous pattern similar to mesotemporal seizures, and if those rhythmical signals sent into a hippocampus that is already in a hyperexcitable state SPWs are activated during slow wave sleep, then hippocampal neurons are likely to resonate in response to this rhythmical stimulation.

When rhythmical discharges emerge in the hippocampus, they usually begin in subfield CA3 with its networks of locally-connected neurons, but this hypersynchronous activity in subfield CA3 has a paradoxical effect: it *suppresses* the outbreak of *ictal* discharges in that EC-H complex [Barbarosie and Avoli, 1997; Avoli and Barbarosie, 1999; Avoli, 2001; Avoli and Barbarosie, 2001; Avoli et al., 2002]. If the build-up of hypersynchronous activity in CA3 continues to be augmented by local recruiting waves, it might eventually become strong enough to trigger an outbreak of paroxysmal discharges—but when this happens *the initial outbreak of paroxysmal activity occurs in the contralateral hippocampus, not in the hippocampus engulfed by hypersynchronous discharges* [Goto et al., 1994; Engel et al., 1997; Williamson and Engel, 1997]. But it's not enough to establish that hypersynchronous activity in corticothalamic circuits could potentially drive a build-up of rhythmical activity in hippocampal subfield CA3; we need to look for evidence that this sequence of events was in fact what happened in my case.

Cortical Driving of Hippocampal Hypersynchrony

The hypothesis that I've just presented—that cortical fast runs can drive a build-up of rhythmical activity in the hippocampus—appears to contradict a generally-accepted principle about the neurogenesis of epileptic seizures, which is that the neural mechanisms that generate hypersynchronous seizures in corticothalamic circuits are different from the neural mechanisms that cause mesotemporal seizures and that there is little interaction between the two different mechanisms [Engel et al., 1997; Williamson and Engel, 1998]. A study by Kandel et al. [1996] illustrates this conceptual framework in action: the researchers induced a hypersynchronous seizure in rats by injecting kainic acid into corticothalamic circuits. While the seizure was underway, the researchers were unable to detect any changes in the firing patterns of hippocampal neurons, and, after the experiment, they were unable to find plastic changes in hippocampal neurons (i.e., the sprouting of new neuronal connections). This finding confirms the generally-accepted principle that hypersynchronous seizures in corticothalamic circuits do not produce detectable changes in hippocampal neurons, a principle that would seem to undermine the hypothesis that I've just proposed to explain the diffuse brightening and bluing of the visual field. But there is a confounding variable involved here that renders this study irrelevant for our investigation: Kandel et al. induced the corticothalamic seizures at night when the rats were awake and very active, so there is a question as to whether these findings are generalizable to a case where slow wave sleep rhythms are underway. We've already noted the dramatic enhancement of neuron excitability that takes place in the hippocampus during slow wave sleep, so the concurrence of slow wave sleep and hypersynchronous activity in corticothalamic circuits might well have a very different outcome. And this is precisely what has been reported by a number of studies published *after* Kandel et al. [1996]: researchers have found that slow wave sleep produced dramatic changes in the interaction of the hippocampus and that other parts of the brain change dramatically . For example, Siapas and Wilson [1998] reported that during slow wave sleep (and even during the lesser state of relaxed immobility) they detected a *coupling of cortical and hippocampal activity*: they recorded high-frequency "ripples" in subfield CA1 of the hippocampus—normal ripples, not the fast ripples often detected in epileptic tissue—and these high-frequency ripples discharged in close temporal synchrony with the firing of NREMS stage 2 sleep spindles in thalamocortical circuits:

[R]ipples and spindle waves are characterized by different time scales and occur in very different brain areas. However, as we show in this report, these two types of brain oscillations occur in close temporal synchrony. Coordinated spindle-ripple arrivals occur not only at a time scale of minutes, but more importantly at a time scale of 1 - 2 [seconds] . . . . [S]pindle-ripple episodes may constitute a general mode of cortico-hippocampal communication during SWS [slow wave sleep] [Siapas and Wilson, Ibid., pp. 1123-1124].

Also relevant to the issue of state-specific coupling of hippocampal and cortical neurons is a finding by Sirota et al. [2002] that clarifies the timing: they found that sleep rhythms in the cortex fire shortly *before* the hippocampal neurons discharge their synchronous sharp waves or high-frequency ripples. These researchers conclude that, during slow wave sleep, this timing sequence occurs with such reliability that *it is reasonable to infer that the cortical sleep rhythms determine the timing of the hippocampal discharges.* After the cortical neurons discharge their synchronous sleep rhythms, a "rhythmical sink" can be detected in hippocampal subfield CA3, a finding that leads Sirota et al. to conclude that the superficial layers of the entorhinal cortex (layers II and III) must transmit this rhythmical activity into the perforant path:

[I]t is reasonable to assume that neocortical events activated layer II and III entorhinal neurons, which, in turn, *induced an excitability bias within the hippocampal networks.* Although the emergence of sharp wave bursts does not require extra-hippocampal inputs, the present findings show that *the exact timing of sharp wave bursts can be influenced by neocortical events during sleep. . . . / . . .* The excitability fluctuations of neocortical neurons within the spindle effectively timed ripple occurence in the hippocampus. . . . / . . . . The functional importance of the demonstrated coupling between neocortical and hippocampal network activity is that it provides the temporal framework for coordinated information transfer between the two structures. *Particularly, we hypothesize that neocortical neuron discharges, associated with delta wave and spindle events, "select" via the entorhinal input which hippocampal neurons will participate in the triggered ripple events* [Sirota et al., Ibid., p. 2068; emphasis added].

The importance of this research for our investigation is that it identifies a mechanism—cortical influence on the timing of hippocampal activity during slow wave sleep—that can explain how a hypersynchronous seizure in corticothalamic circuits (which we've implicated as the origin of the phosphene image of a radiating spray) could drive the emergence of rhythmical firing in one or both of the EC-H complexes.

The prospect that this state-specific coupling of hippocampal and cortical activity (which would normally consolidate new memories by stimulating a reorganization of neuronal connections) could sometimes be mobilized to serve as a conduit for the transfer of paroxysmal excitation is a question that is specifically addressed by Steriade and Timofeev [2003]:

Potentials with progressively enhanced amplitudes evoked by rhythmical stimuli *may lead to self-sustained activities, similar to those seen in paroxysmal (epilep-tiform) afterdischarges (ADs).* This was observed in corticothalamic networks as well as in the hippocampus .... / .... It is fair to state the behavioral significance of development from neuronal plasticity, which is beneficial for normal mnemonic functions, to paroxysmal states, in those instances in which repetitive stimulation are prolonged beyond a certain limit, is not yet clearly understood [Steriade and Timofeev, Ibid., p. 573; emphasis added].

There is, in addition to what we've already discussed, another circuit which might serve as a conduit for the transfer of hypersynchronous activity in cortico-thalamic circuits into the hippocampus. Recent research by McKenna and Vertes [2004] shows that the nucleus reuniens (RE), which is located in the midline thala-mus, is a major source of thalamic input to the hippocampal complex. Signals forwarded from the RE excite neurons in the EC, in hippocampal subfield CA1, and in the presubiculum (PRES). Discussing the significance of their findings that the RE sends excitatory signals to the EC-H complex, McKenna and Vertes comment that:

Two recent reports have shown . . . that the RE exerts significant effects on neural activity at CA1 of HF [hippocampal formation]. . . . Dollemann-Van der Weel et al. (1997) proposed that *RE might "exert a persistent influence on the state of pyramidal cell excitability," depolarizing cells close to threshold for activation by other excitatory inputs.* / Along similar lines, Bertram and Zhang (1999) recently compared the effects of RE (midline thalamic) and CA3 stimulation on various population measures at CA1 and showed that *RE actions on CA1 were equivalent to, and in some cases considerably greater than, those of CA3 on CA1. They concluded that the thalamic-HF [hippocampal formation] connection exerts "a direct and powerful excitation of the CA1 region"* [McKenna and Vertes, Ibid., p. 18, emphasis added; see also Vertes et al., 2007].

A similar conclusion was reached by Zhang and Bertram [2002] in an earli-er study where they applied high-frequency stimulation to the midline thalamus and found that this induced long-term potentiation of neuronal connections in the mid-line thalamus and also in hippocampal subfield CA1. The RE receives projections from the LGN. Therefore, if vision-relay cells in the LGN are participants in the hypersynchronous activity reverberating back and forth in corticothalamic circuits (which gives rise to the phosphene images of dark, fast-moving rings and to the ra-diating spray), then it is likely that there will be a significant increase in the signals the LGN sends to the midline RE and which the RE then sends on to hippocampal subfield CA1, the subfield where the final product of intra-hippocampal processing is assembled. The excitation produced in CA1 by the RE signals will likely in-crease the firing rate of those neurons—and the increased activity in CA1 will then recirculate through the ipsalateral perforant path (CA1-EC-DG-CA3-CA1) and also be referred contralaterally from the right EC to the left EC via the dorsal hippocampal commissure. This analysis adds a second mechanism that could account for the diffuse brightening of the visual field, most likely by virtue of its interacting with the first mechanism (i.e., the rhythmical pulses bombarding the EC).

Having established the *likelihood* that a hypersynchronous seizure activated in corticothalamic circuits can drive the emergence of hypersynchronous activity in the hippocampus, I propose to move on to the question of whether hypersynchronous activity building up inside subfield CA3 in one hippocampus can generate a diffuse brightening and bluing of the visual field.

Hippocampal Hypersynchrony Generates Diffuse Brightening

In Figure 23 I've replicated the schematic diagram of anatomical and functional relationships in the EC-H complex, the same diagram introduced earlier in this chapter as Figure 22, but here I've made additions that illustrate the effects that a build-up of hypersynchronous activity in subfield CA3 of the right hippocampus would likely have on other structures in the EC-H complexes. The build-up of rhythmical discharges in subfield CA3 is indicated by a black color while various shades of gray are used to indicate the extent to which other subfields in the EC-H complex (and retro-hippocampal cortices) are likely to be impacted by the increase of neuronal activity flowing out of CA3. In addition to the obvious "downstream" effects of the hypersynchronous discharges (i.e., from CA3 to CA1 and back to the EC via the temporo-ammonic circuit), excitatory signals will be relayed contralaterally via the dorsal hippocampal commissure (DHC) and will also enter the perforant path of the ipsilateral hippocampus (CA1 to EC to DG to CA3)—hence the various shades of gray inserted in the appropriate blocks of the diagram. In Figure 23 I've also included an arrow representing the ventral hippocampal commissure (VHC), although I've added a question mark to indicate that the existence of such a structure in humans remains controversial—we'll deal with that issue in the next chapter where that issue becomes important. Here is it enough to show that, if there is a human VHC comparable to the monkey VHC, it would originate in subfield CA3 and terminate in the anterior portion of the contralateral hippocampus near the border between the DG and subfield CA3. The significance of these details will become evident in the next chapter when we analyze the origins of the phosphene image of trident rays.

Figure 23 illustrates my hypothesis describing a sequence of events that generates a gradual build-up of a diffuse brightening and bluing effect. In the right hemisphere, the EC is affected by two different kinds of hypersynchronous signals: it receives feedback from subfield CA1 via the temporo-ammonic connection that signals a dramatic increase in neuron discharges across the entire CA1 neuron sheet, an increase driven by the hypersynchronous activity that is building up in subfield CA3, and, at the same time, the EC is receiving signals from the hypersynchronous activity in the corticothalamic visual cortices, signals that arrive in pulses timed to the same rhythms that often appear during mesotemporal seizures. To make

Figure 23. Origins of the diffuse brightening and bluing of the visual field. This schematic diagram of the two EC-H complexes replicates Figure 22 but with new elements added to illustrate my hypothesis about how a build-up of rhythmical discharges in the right hippocampus would likely affect other structures located within the two EC-H complexes. Based on theories of intra-hippocampal function proposed by Buzsáki [1995; 1996] and Vinogradova [2001], we can infer that hypersynchronous activity in subfield CA3 of the right hippocampus will forward visual signals to CA1 that are "spatially-diffuse," i.e., that do not encode the kinds of "spatially-specific" patterns that would have been present in the original signal-set forwarded by the EC. In Vinogradova's theory, subfield CA3 detects novel signal patterns by performing a "comparator function:" visual signals from EC are converted into abstract patterns in the DG, then sent to subfield CA3 which detects signal-patterns that are novel or otherwise attention-worthy. Attention-worthiness is determined by a "differencing" process: neurons in CA3 normally fire at high rates and their action potentials impose a tonic inhibition on target cells in CA1. When the DG processes afferent visual signals and filters out the abstract patterns, it sends its product into CA3. The receipt of signals from the DG initially causes a suppression of the normally high firing rates of CA3 neurons, but this suppression is only *temporary*. If the abstract patterns in the incoming signals *match* the patterns that have been embodied in pre-existing neuron networks, networks forged over time by a process of longterm potentiation, then the firing rates of CA3 neurons quickly return to their normally high levels and their target neurons in CA1 are inhibited. By contrast, if there is *no match* between the incoming patterns and pre-existing neuron networks in CA3, then the firing rates of CA3 neurons remain suppressed for a longer time interval. *When the initial suppression of neuron firing rates in CA3 is sustained, the action potentials forwarded through Schaffer collateral axons to target neurons in CA1 inhibit the inhibition normally imposed on CA1 neurons, freeing those CA1 neurons to discharge more frequently, a change that constitutes, in effect, an amplification of those particular signals.* If we assume that a build-up of hypersynchronous activity will engulf all of the principal neurons in subfield CA3, this would suppress the firing rates of neurons distributed across the CA3 subfield, and this prolonged suppression will inhibit the inhibition normally imposed on CA1 neurons, affecting CA1 neurons distributed across the CA1 subfield. This will produce a spatially-diffuse increase in neuron activity in CA1 that does not preserve any of the spatially-specific information that might have been encoded in the original signal-set that the EC sent directly into CA1. There are two other important elements in this diagram. First, I've added a representation of the attention-driven, septo-hippocampal circuits that are activated by a meditator's fixation of attention: the anterior attention networks in the prefrontal cortices (PFC) send signals to the septum and related structures, and they send an integrated, stimulatory signal via septo-hippocampal projections to the anterior (uncal) pole of the hippocampus. These signals selectively activate the release of acetylcholine in the neurons sheets located in the uncal pole; the dramatic effects of this attention-driven stimulation of the uncal pole will be examined in detail in the next section. A second important addition to this diagram is the arrow representing the hypothetical trajectory that the ventral hippocampal commissure (VHC) would take if humans do have such a structure and if it follows the same trajectory as in the monkey. The VHC fibers project from subfield CA3 in the right hippocampus (where hypersynchronous activity is underway) to the contralateral uncus, terminating alongside the uncal extension of the DG. Evidence suggesting the likelihood of VHC input in this case will be discussed in the next chapter in the analysis of the trident ray image. Abbreviations: CA, Cornu Ammonis; DG, dentate gyrus; DHC, dorsal hippocampal commissure; EC, entorhinal cortex; PFC, prefrontal cortex; SUB, subiculum; PRES, presubiculum; PAS, parasubiculum; PHG, parahippocampal cortex; PFC, prefrontal cortex; VHC, ventral hippocampal commissure.

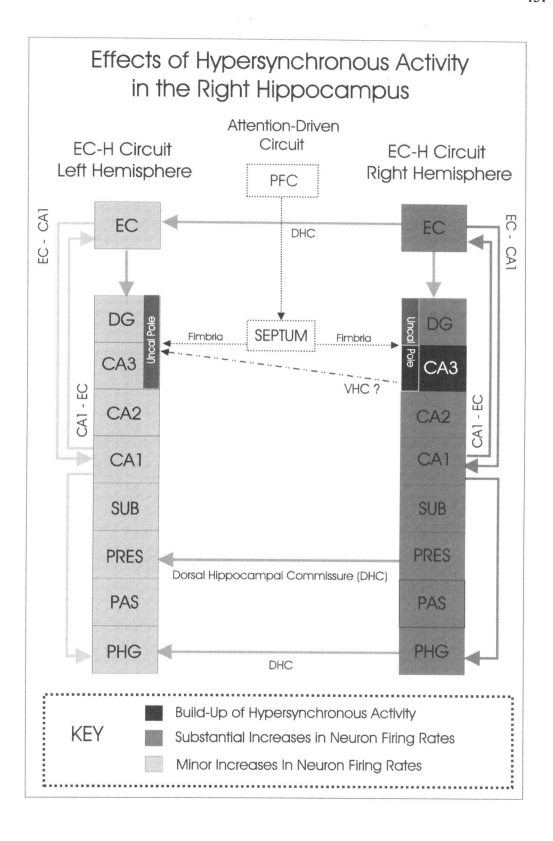

matters worse, neurons in the hippocampal subfields have already been rendered hyperexcitable as a result of synchronous sharp waves (SPWs) that are activated when slow wave sleep rhythms begin—and the discharge of these SPWs is coupled with the discharge of neurons in corticothalamic circuits, occurring shortly after the corticothalamic discharges. The interactions of these three variables (perhaps augmented by excitatory signals sent from the LGN to the RE to subfield CA1) might well drive a gradual build-up of rhythmical discharges and recruiting waves in subfield CA3 in the right hippocampus, converting it into an epileptogenic focus.

As the rhythmical firing intensifies in CA3, the dramatic increases in neuronal activity will be relayed through the ipsalateral EC-H complex and retro-hippocampal cortices, and it will affect the left EC-H complex as some increase in neuronal activity is stimulated by signals relayed contralaterally through the dorsal hippocampal commissure. If this scenario is correct, it means that neurons representing both the right and left sides of the visual field will be stimulated by excitatory signals which, having originated in the hypersynchronous activity of CA3 neurons, will not contain spatially-specific information. As a result of these processes, the visual field will gradually become brighter as the build-up of hypersynchronous activity in the right hippocampus becomes more intense. As the brightening continues, it begins to interfere more and more with the ability of the hippocampus to process the signals it receives from the visual cortices. These afferent visual signals generated by the hypersynchronous seizure in corticothalamic circuits, which would have formerly been included in the composition of the cortical lightness record (and in the meditator's consciousness as a radiating spray of tiny light-flecks) are now excluded from participating in the composition of the cortical lightness record, even though they might continue to bombard the EC, because the intra-hippocampal circuits in both hemispheres are already engaged in processing their own internally-generated signals.

If this scenario is correct, it explains (1) why I saw a gradual brightening of the visual field, (2) why the brightening was spatially-diffuse, (3) why it occurred when it did in the evolution of the meditation-induced phosphene sequence, and (4) why the brightening gradually obscured the competing image of the radiating spray. To explain why the brightening had a light blue color, we'll have to probe further; I'll address that issue at the of this chapter.

NEUROLOGICAL ANALYSIS, PART II: THE BULBOUS PHOSPHENE

Attention-Driven Excitation in the Anterior Hippocampus

To explain why a bulbous white figure appeared in the upper right quadrant of the bright blue visual field, I need add only one new factor to what we've already discussed. We've already determined that any figure that appears in the right visual field has to have been generated by neuronal activity in the left hippocampus. Also, I've proposed that a diffuse brightening is consistent with the cortical lightness record being determined by signals generated within intra-hippocampal circuits, signals driven by hypersynchronous activity in subfield CA3 of the right hippocampus. Now if we bring into the analysis Vinogradova's "comparator" theory of hippocampal function, we can ask what kind of signal-processing has to take place in the left hippocampus in order for a small, hollow, white bulbous phosphene to appear in the upper right quadrant of the visual field. Vinogradova's theory envisions a "differencing" process taking place in subfield CA3, a process that sorts out those incoming signal-patterns that do *not* match the pre-existing patterns already embodied in the circuitry of CA3 by longterm potentiation and then stimulates CA1 neurons in such a way as to insure that those non-matching signals are amplified in the final product of hippocampal processing. Applying these concepts to the generation of a bulbous image, we can infer that a subgroup of neurons somewhere in subfield CA3 must discharge at maximal rates and that the action potentials they send forward into subfield CA1 must impose a very strong inhibitory pressure on the normal inhibition circuits in CA1, thereby releasing a subgroup of CA1 cells to fire at maximal rates. This would produce a white phosphene sensation capable of overriding other signals already oscillating in the CA3-CA1 circuits, including that stream of spatially-diffuse signals that CA3 sends into CA1 (which will have already lifted the inhibition on CA1 cells to some extent before the arrival of the signal-set that generates the maximal responses). So we can explain why the phosphene figure is white in color and why the white figure stands out against the light blue background, but why does this figure have the distinctive spatial features that I've described? How could it acquire a bulbous shape given that the image is generated by neuronal activity taking place *inside* the left hippocampus?

Is there a structure located within the hippocampus where the neurons can be selectively stimulated to fire at much higher rates than neurons in the rest of the hippocampus? Indeed there is—the uncal pole—because the CA3 neuron sheets that wrap around the anterior pole of the hippocampus can be selectively driven by the exercise of sustained attention. Since sustained inward attention is the core of meditation practice, it is reasonable to assume that neurons in the anterior pole of my left hippocampus would be strongly facilitated in the circumstances that I've described. To explain how that would happen, I'll begin with a description of the "uncus," the Latin name for the anterior third of the primate hippocampus. The uncus begins at the "genu" where the anterior third of the hippocampus bends medially (i.e., away from the skull) and then points back in the opposite direction from the main body of the hippocampus, as shown in Figure 24. This drawing, adapted from illustrations and analyses in several sources [Duvernoy, 1988; Engel et al., 1997; Gloor, 1997; Williamson and Engel, 1998], shows how each of the three hippocampal subfields we've discussed—the dentate gyrus (DG), CA3, and CA1—have extensions that project into the uncal region. The uncal extension of subfield CA3, called the "gyrus intralimbicus" (GI), is a sheet of neurons—the stratum oriens—that wraps around the uncal pole, acquiring the pole's bulb-shaped geometry. An important characteristic of these CA3 neurons wrapped around the surface of the uncal pole is that they can be selectively stimulated by excitatory signals that originate in the anterior attention centers. The dentate gyrus (DG) also has an uncal extension, the "Ligature of Giacomini" [Duvernoy, 1988; Engel et al., 1997; Gloor, 1997; Williamson and Engel, 1998], and it is also selectively stimulated by the exercise of attention. The uncal extension for subfield CA1, the "gyrus uncinatus" (GU) is situated between the backward bend of the anterior hippocampus and the uncal extension of the DG. There is, in addition, a small but important

Figure 24. Origins of the white bulbous figure. This schematic drawing of the human hippocampus, adapted from Duvernoy [1988] and Gloor [1997], shows how the anterior region bends medially at the "genu" and points backward against the main body of the posterior hippocampus, forming the thumb-like "uncus." The anterior pole, called the *gyrus intralimbicus* (GI) [Buzsáki, 1995; Duvernoy , 1988], is formed by the uncal extension of subfield CA3 (CA3'). Bordering CA3' is the uncal extension of the dentate gyrus, called the *Ligature of Giacomini* (LG), which I'll designate as DG' in my analysis to distinguish it from the DG subfield in the main body—and to simplify the number of technical terms needed to understand the exposition. The uncal extension of the CA1 subfield, called the *gyrus uncinatus* (GU), is pulled out of its normal alignment with CA3 by having been stretched around the genu. I'll refer to the uncal extension of CA1 as CA1'. There is also a small "hilar" region that contains CA3/CA4 neurons. Meditation selectively enhances neuron activity at the uncal pole: it activates the prefrontal cortices which then stimulate the septum and related structures to send excitatory signals via septo-hippocampal projections that selectively stimulate neurons in the uncal pole. This stimulation occurs because of the release of acetylcholine in the CA3' neuron sheets wrapped around the outer layers of the uncal pole and also in the DG' and in the hilar neurons [Gloor, 1997]. The effect of the differential release of acetylcholine in the subfields at the uncal pole is to strongly enhance the firing rates of those neurons: as described by Vinogradova [2001] in her comparator theory of intrahippocampal processing, the attention-driven signals produce "cholinergic influences that prolong the period of stimulus processing," a prolongation that keeps the normally high firing rates of CA3 neurons suppressed. This kind of suppression of neuron firing rates in CA3 is the same mechanism that "differentiates" between afferent signal patterns that are novel and those that are not; therefore, the result of the acetylcholine release within the uncal pole will trigger significant increases in the firing rates of CA1' neurons. Since this attention-driven release of acetylcholine is selective and limited to the uncal pole, there will not be the same maximal enhancement of neuron activity in those portion sof subfields DG, CA3, and CA1 that are located in main body of the hippocampus. Therefore, in CA1' will fire at maximal rates while neurons in the rest of CA1 are firing at less elevated rates. These differences in neurons firing rates within the CA1 subfield will eventually register in consciousness as a brighter patch of phosphene in the right side of the visual field. While there is no research available that could be used to predict what that brighter patch might look like, we know from the phosphene observations that it manifests as a mirror-image of the uncal pole, that is, as a phosphene image with the same bulbous shape as the outer surface of the uncal pole, and, to be more specific, the shape of the stratum oriens sheet of CA3' neurons that wraps around the uncal pole.

region located immediately adjacent to the DG on the CA3 side which contains neurons of a different type which we have not yet discussed: the CA3/CA4 "hilar" neurons. These neurons are potentially important for our analysis because if the VHC still exists in humans, its fibers will originate in the hilar region.

The technical names for these several anatomical regions located inside the uncal hippocampus are difficult to remember (and seldom used even in scientific articles); for that reason, in what follows I'll identify the uncal extensions of the hippocampal subfields by appending an apostrophe, referring to the DG' instead of the Ligature of Giacomini, to CA3' instead of the gyrus intralimbicus, and to CA1' instead of the gyrus uncinatus.

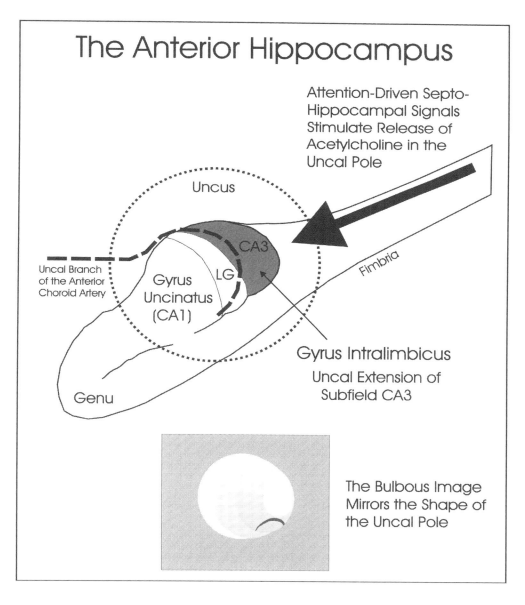

Apart from the superficial resemblance between the uncal pole and the bulbous phosphene, is there reason to believe that changes in firing rates of neurons in subfield CA3' at the uncal pole might somehow generate a distinct set of visual signals that register in consciousness as a bulbous white phosphene? I mentioned earlier that one important characteristic of CA3' neurons is that *they can be selectively stimulated by excitatory signals that originate in the anterior attention centers.* When meditators close their eyes and fixate attention on the "empty" visual field, this activates neuron assemblies in the prefrontal cortices (PFC) that then stimulate increased neuronal activity in the two structures—the medial septum (MS) and the vertical limb of the nucleus of the diagonal band (DB)—that pool their input before sending it on to the hippocampus via septo-hippocampal projections. *When the MS-DB signals are received in subfield CA3 of the hippocampus, they facilitate the intra-hippocampal processing of those signal-patterns that are novel or otherwise attention-worthy, or, put another way, they participate in the "differencing" function described by Vinogradova [2001]—to use her words, the attention-driven MS-DB signals produce "cholinergic influences that prolong the period of stimulus processing," a prolongation that keeps the normally high firing rates of CA3 neurons suppressed.* This attention-driven release of the inhibition that CA3' neurons would normally impose on CA1' neurons was sustained, in my case, for a relative long period of time. The effects of this prolonged suppression would be the same as if subfield CA3 were reacting to the receipt of afferent signals that did not match the pre-existing neuronal networks, i.e., an amplification of all CA1' discharges along with an attentuation of all other CA1 discharges:

> Theta-producing septo-hippocampal projection neurons participate in the organization of hippocampal tonic sensory responses. GABAergic components of this input are responsible for initial reset and synchronization of neuronal activity, while slower cholinergic influences prolong the period of stimulus processing. Once the theta-rhythm is triggered by a natural stimulus or experimental means, all other signals appearing in its background cannot reset the ongoing rhythmic process; they are filtered out and do not receive access to the processing mechanisms of the hippocampus. / Thus, reticulo-septal input may be regarded as a mechanism improving processing of novel information in the hippocampus and simultaneously protecting it from interference, i.e., as a part of attention mechanism [Vinogradova, Ibid., p. 585].

The terminals of the attention-driven, septo-hippocampal (MS-DB) projections are most densely packed in the *uncal hippocampus,* not only in the sheets of CA3' neurons in the stratum oriens layer that wraps around the uncal pole but also in the DG' and in the small colony of hilar neurons (CA3/4) situated immediately adjacent to the DG' [Engel et al., 1997; Williamson and Engel, 1998; Gloor, 1997]. An attention-driven stimulation of the CA3' neurons surrounding the GI pole will trigger release of acetylcholine (ACh) in the DG', exciting the muscarinic receptors of GABAergic interneurons in DG', thereby increasing the excitability of granule cells in DG' that are wired to feed signals into CA3' [Amaral and J. Kutz , 1985; Gulyás et al., 1991; Reece and P. A. Schwartzkroin, 1991; Buhusi and Schmajuk, 1996; Hájos et al., 1998]. Since virtually all of the granule cells in the DG' will be affected as well as the neurons in CA3', the abstract signal-pattern that the DG' sends into CA3' will be a spatially-diffuse pattern that activates all of the CA3' neurons, a pattern that presumably would *not* match patterns already embodied in the pre-existing neuron networks in CA3' and would release the inhibition that CA3' neurons normally impose on their target cells in CA1'. But in this case the firing rates of those CA3' neurons are also enhanced by the attention-driven release of acetylcholine at the uncal pole, and the effect of this release of acetylcholine, according to Vinogradova, is to "prolong the period of stimulus-processing" by CA3' neurons. *Therefore, the combined effect on CA3' neurons of their receiving novel patterns from the DG' while at the same time they are being subjected to a prolonged suppression of firing rates because of the high levels of ambient ACh will be a sustained inhibition of the normal inhibition imposed on target neurons in CA1', freeing those CA1' neurons to fire at maximal levels over a prolonged period of time.* By contrast, neurons located in the main body of the hippocampus are not stimulated by the attention-driven MS-DB signals and are not exposed to a similar release of acetycholine; therefore, they continue to discharge at the rates determined by the stream of excitatory signals generated by the hypersynchronous seizure in the right hippocampus. In sum, the final product of intra-hippocampal processing in subfield CA1 of the left hippocampus—the product that is relayed back to the ipsilateral EC, sent on the retro-hippocampal cortices, and transferred contralaterally via the dorsal hippocampal commissure—is a generalized increase in neuronal activity (driven by the processing of signals from the hypersynchronous activity in the right hippocampus) plus a small, spatially-constrained region of much more intense neuronal activity representing the ACh-activated uncal pole. As the product sent out of the left hippocampus gets circulated and recirculated through the circuits of the right and left EC-H complexes, these differences in the intensity of neuron activity in the CA1' subregion versus the rest of CA1 will be repeatedly reinforced as if the different intensity levels actually represent patterns that were encoded in visual signals generated in the retinae. When these signals participate in the composition of the cortical lightness record, it is reasonable to expect that the meditator will see a bright but spatially-diffuse background (generated by the hypersynchronous seizures) that contains a spatially-defined patch of brighter phosphene in the right side of the visual field. While there is no scientific research that addresses the issue of precisely what this brighter light would look like, we know from the descriptions of meditation-induced phosphene images—not only my own descriptions but also those in the traditional texts—that the image manifests as a bright, white, bulb-shaped phosphene, an image shaped exactly the same as the stratum oriens layer of CA3' neurons that surrounds the surface of the uncal pole. Paradoxical and counterintuitive as it may seem—even to me—this analysis suggests that a meditator in this situation sees a "ghost" image of the uncal pole of whichever hippocampus is not engulfed by hypersynchronous activity. This phosphene epiphenomenon is attention-driven, so the brightness of the bulbous figure would be expected to wax and wane in response to fluctuations in the intensity of attention, a waxing and waning that would make the figure seem to move forward and back.

It is important to emphasize that, in the explanatory hypothesis that I'm proposing here, the bulbous image is generated by *an intra-hippocampal modification—by an overriding of vision-related signals that are already being processed in the left EC-H complex.* Those signals already being processed in the left hippocampus are those generated by the hypersynchronous seizure in the right hippocampus and the afferent visual signals arriving in rhythmic pulses that are generated by the hypersynchronous seizure in corticothalamic circuits. It is not necessary, in this view, for the product of hippocampal processing to be referred back to the visual cortices in order for the unusual activity to register in consciousness as a visual image.

NEUROLOGICAL ANALYSIS, PART III: PHOSPHENE COLORS

Why is the Brightening Blue?

There are two color sensations I've described in this chapter without accounting for why they appear—the 40% cyan blue that characterizes the diffuse brightening, and the translucent white color of the bulbous image. The appearance of a white color is easiest to explain. In a study of the neurophysiological correlates of color induction, Creutzfeldt [1993] explains that "the neuronal signal for white consists of a balanced excitation of the M-cone excited, green-blue-sensitive WS-cells and the L-cone excited, yellow-red-sensitive WL-cells (p. 45)." I interpret this to mean that if all of the hippocampal neurons that represent a spatially-specific region in the visual field were driven to discharge at the same rates, these signals would be equivalent to hippocampal signals that would be activated by the normal process of perception in which the subject looks at a white object with spatially-specific dimensions. Similarly, if all of the hippocampal neurons within a spatially-defined area—in this case, all the relevant neurons in the stratum oriens layer that wraps around the uncal pole of the left hippocampus—are firing at maximal levels, then all the wavelength signals represented by neurons in CA3' and CA1' would be activated, generating a "balanced excitation" that would generate a white phosphene.

To explain why the gradual and spatially-diffuse brightening had a sky-blue color is more difficult. It seems unlikely that the blue phosphene could be generated

by wholly intra-hippocampal processes, that is, by the build-up of hypersynchronous activity in one hippocampus and its dispersion via the dorsal hippocampal
commissure into the contralateral EC-H complex. I've already suggested that the
result of that activity would be a "balanced" array of wavelength signals, and that,
based on the Creutzfield principle, that activity would most likely generate a uni-
formly white visual field. But if it were the case that the hypersynchronous activity
in corticothalamic circuits continued to bombard the EC-H complexes in both
hemispheres with rhythmical pulses even after the image of the radiating spray was
masked by the gradual brightening of the visual field, then perhaps it possible that
the blue hue of the brightening was already encoded in those afferent visual signals.
How might this happen?

In an earlier chapter I described how the S-cone "blue-on" signals from
the LGN get amplified in locally-connected neuron circuits in the primary visual
cortices, but recent research findings indicate that the "blue-on" signals continue be
enhanced as these signals move through higher-level vision-processing centers. In
a recent fMRI study, Mullen et al. [2007] compared the quantitative responses of
different processing centers in the visual cortices. They found that "the early visual
areas (V1, V2, V3, VP and hV4) all have a robust response to colour. . . . [and] *all
of these areas have a surprisingly strong response to S-cone stimuli, . . . suggesting
a relative enhancement of the S-cone cortical signal* (p. 491, emphasis added)."
Also of interest is another recent fMRI study by Rich et al.[2006] which found that
merely *imagining* color sensations produced patterns of activation in the visual cortices that were similar to those evoked by retinal responses to external light sources.
The findings in these two studies suggest that, even if all of the neurons in the LGN
that encode wavelength signals equally represented in the hypersynchronous activity oscillating back and forth in the reciprocal cortico-thalamo-cortical circuits, this
would not necessarily produce the kind of "balanced excitation" that Creutzfield
associates with a white color. The S-cone "blue-on" signals would be enhanced
relative to other wavelength signals, not only in the primary visual cortices but also
in the higher-level vision-processing centers and, as a result, the afferent visual
signals arriving in the EC-H complexes would encode a disproportionate weighting
for S-cone "blue-on" wavelengths. When these afferent visual signals with their
blue bias mix with white signals generated by intra-hippocampal processes, this
would produce a phosphene sensation of a white-brightened blue.

This analysis assumes that color perception in the human brain is an "additive" and not a "subtractive" process. When I specified that the blue color I
saw covering the visual field matched the color of a printed sample that was 40%
cyan with no magenta, yellow, or black, I was referring to color composition in the
CMYK format where color perception occurs when some the printed page absorbs
some wavelengths while reflecting others, so that the absorbed wavelengths are
subtracted from the composition of the cortical lightness record. By contrast, when
color is composed in the RGB format, which involves an *addition* of all component

wavelengths, as happens in film or slide projection and also in color generation on digital screens, then all of the wavelength signals contribute to the outgoing signal that is perceived by the viewer. Clearly the composition of color in the brain does not involve the kind of reflective process that generates CMYK colors, so it must involve some kind of additive process. Given that a mix of white signals and signals with a blue bias would produce a light, sky-blue color if composed by additive processes, I suggest that this is what happened to generate the light blue color during the gradual brightening of the visual field.

7

HIPPOCAMPAL PHOSPHENES, II: THE TRIDENT RAYS

PHENOMENOLOGY

The Vision of White Rays

The phosphene image of a white moon silhouetted against light blue visual field ended abruptly: the bulbous moon suddenly shined more brightly and became bigger than it ever had before, making it seem that the bulb had just jerked forward, but in the same instant the bulb disappeared and, along with it, the bright blue color. The visual field was once again its normal charcoal gray. In the upper right quadrant, in the exact same position just vacated by the bulbous moon, there were now three thin rays of white phosphene joined at the base to form a trident-like image, as shown in Figure 25. These rays extended only about halfway to the outer rim of the visual field, and the ray on the right had a distinctive feature that made an immediate impression—the tip of the right ray was bent to the left so that it looked like a jet of water that had been blown sideward by a strong wind. It also reminded me of a cobra rearing up above its coils and pointing its puffy head forward in an aggressive, warning gesture. I did not see the trident rays move into position; one moment I saw the bulb jerk forward in a blue sky, and the next moment I saw the three rays silhouetted against the charcoal gray visual field.

This vision of a trident of white rays remained in the visual field just long enough for me to consciously register its presence—probably no longer than a second—and then there was another sudden change in which the first ray image was replaced instantaneously by the next: where the three trident rays had once been, there were now *six* rays, and all six rays extended all the way to the perimeter of vision, as shown in Figure 25D. This second ray vision also lasted only a second. In the third transformation, I was able to watch the change unfold: the six white

142

rays fanned farther apart in a slow, smooth "wilting" movement. It reminded me of watching a time-lapse film of flower petals as they open wider and wider in response to the heat of an early morning sun. I've seen lotus petals blossom like this in a pond not far from my house. The third iteration of the ray-image continued to shine in its "wilted" position for a few seconds before I recognized that this image was not going to change as rapidly as the ray-images that had proceeded it. Realizing that it might prove useful to time how long the image lasted, I started to count silently; when I'd counted to twelve, the rays were overwhelmed by "explosive" flashes of lightning-like phosphene. Adding a few seconds to compensate for the time when I was not counting, I'd estimate that the "wilted" rays lasted longer than 15 seconds but less than 20 seconds. During the time when I was able to stare at the vision of "wilted" rays, I noticed an interesting detail that I didn't see in the two earlier version of the rays: all of the "wilted" rays had a small, triangular shard of very bright and opaque white phosphene covering their bases, as shown in Figure 25E. I also thought I could make out a very faint and translucent white haze illuminating the area where the rays touched the perimeter of the visual field, although I'm not sure about that.

Figure 25. The vision of trident rays and its transformations. A. A faint image of the white, bulb-shaped phosphene showing how it would become brighter and thus seem bigger. **B.** In the moment of its disappearance, the bulbous image suddenly shined much brighter than it ever had before, creating the illusion that it had just jerked forward toward the central meridian. **C. Ray image #1.** In the same instant, the bulbous image vanished and, along with it, the bright blue background; the visual field was once again its normal charcoal color, and where the bulbous image had been only moments before there were now three thin white rays joined at the base to form a trident image. The trident rays extended only about halfway to the perimeter of vision. The tip of the ray on the right side was bent 90° to the left, as shown in inset F. It reminded me of a cobra snake rearing up above its coils, puffing out its hood, and pointing its head in an aggressive, warning gesture. This initial trident image remained in the visual field for only about one second. **D. Ray image #2.** The trident rays suddenly disappeared, leaving in their place a cluster of six rays. This image, like the first, was already fixed in position when it appeared. The rays, in addition to having doubled in number, were now extended all the way to the perimeter of vision. This image of the six rays also remained in the visual field for about one second. **E. Ray image #3.** This transformation, unlike those that preceded it, did not occur instantaneously. As I was watching the six rays of the former image, I saw them fan farther apart in a single, smooth movement, like in a time-lapse film in which flower petals "wilt" or "droop" in the heat of midday. Also, I now noticed two details that I did not recall having seen before: first, behind the rays the dark visual field seemed to acquire a faint whitish haze, and, second, over the bases of all six rays I now saw triangular shards of a much brighter and more opaque white phosphene (see inset G). Once the rays "wilted," this third version of the ray image remained unchanged long enough that I realized it might be useful to count the passing seconds. I started to count silently and had counted to twelve seconds when the rays were suddenly overwhelmed by an eruption of lightning flashes and paroxysmal sensorimotor symptoms.

Transformations of the White Rays

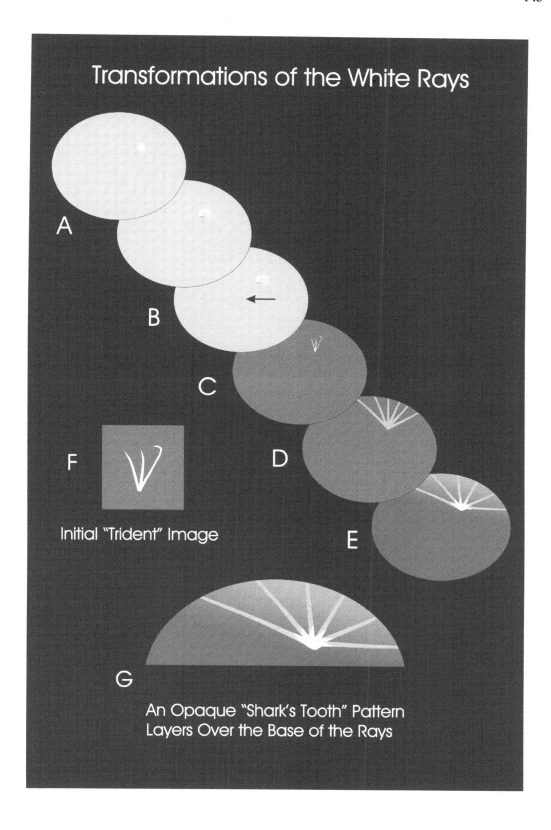

A

B

C

D

E

F

Initial "Trident" Image

G

An Opaque "Shark's Tooth" Pattern
Layers Over the Base of the Rays

NEUROLOGICAL ANALYSIS

Clues About Causation

The spatially-specific image of trident rays appeared in the upper right quadrant of the visual field in precisely the same location as the bulbous image that preceded it. From this we can draw several conclusions about causation. We can be confident that this image was generated by neuronal activity taking place in the left hippocampus which subserves the right half of the visual field. We can also assume as a working hypothesis that the neuronal activity that generated the rays began in the uncal region where attention-driven release of acetylcholine had enhanced neuron excitability to the extent that it generated the phosphene epiphenomenon of a bulbous white phosphene. Two other observations provide additional clues about what must have happened at the uncal pole of the left hippocampus. The bulbous figure shined very brightly just before it disappeared and was replaced by the ray image; this suggests that there must have been a sudden intensification of neuronal activity in the DG' and in the superficial layers of the CA3' sheets surrounding the uncal pole—hence the sudden brightening—but then the sudden disappearance of the bulb suggests that the intensification of neuronal activity that caused the sudden, intense brightening of the bulb must have been followed immediately by a sudden collapse of the underlying neuronal activity and its replacement by a different pattern of neuronal discharge. The same can be said about the sudden disappearance of the bright blue phosphene; there must have been a sudden collapse of the neuronal activity that was responsible for generating that phosphene display, which means a sudden cessation of the hypersynchronous activity in the right hippocampus. How can we account for these abrupt changes?

There is general agreement among epileptologists about the progression of events that culminates in mesotemporal (partial) seizure: the process begins with a gradual build-up of rhythmical (interictal) discharges in at least one of the hippocampi which gets augmented by local recruiting waves [Engel et al., 1997; Williamson and Engel, 1997]. But as the interictal activity builds, it has a paradoxical effect of suppressing the outbreak of paroxysmal (ictal) activity in the hippocampus where it occurs [Barbarosie and Avoli, 1997; Avoli and Barbarosie, 1999; Avoli, 2001; Avoli and Barbarosie, 2001; Avoli et al., 2002]. *If paroxysmal discharges break out, they usually break out in the contralateral hippocampus* [Goto et al., 1994; Engel et al., 1997; Williamson and Engel, 1997]. This scenario is consistent with the phosphene sequence that I've described: a build-up of hypersynchronous activity in the right hippocampus generated a diffuse brightening of the visual field. It also contributed the stream of excitatory signals converging on the uncal pole of the left hippocampus, so that, along with attention-driven, septo-hippcampal stimulation, it also participated in the generation of a bulbous white "ghost" image of the left uncal pole. If paroxysmal discharges were to break out in the left uncal pole contralateral to where the hypersynchronous activity was occurring, this would be a likely outcome. But did this actually occur? And, if so, what happened next?

The Initial Outbreak of Ictal Discharges

Studies of mesotemporal seizures by Paré et al. [1992] and Avoli et al. [2002] report that *paroxysmal discharges erupt only if neurons in the entorhinal cortex (EC) discharge in conjunction with granule cells in the dentate gyrus (DG)*. Since we know that the bulbous image continued to appear in the visual field for a relatively long time, waxing and waning in response to the intensity of my attentive fixation, and there was no outbreak of paroxysmal discharges during that time, something must have changed to push the system past a tipping point, and those changes would have to involve both the EC and the uncal extension of the DG (DG').

It is highly unlikely that the source of that extra stimulation that triggered the shift to paroxysmal activity was the result of EC input to the DG'. We can assume that because a study by Buzsáki [1996] found that *axonal projections from the EC to the DG diverge spatially so that terminals are widely distributed along the longitudinal axis of the dentate gyrus*. A study by Yeckel and Berger [1998] reports a similar finding: when granule cells discharge in response to excitatory signals relayed by the EC, there is a "frequency facilitation" which involves "a progressive increase in the number of active granule cells distributed over a wider spatial extent of the dentate gyrus." This means that *granule cell discharges in response to input from the EC occur in a spreading out pattern*. A similar spatial dispersion occurs when granule cells are discharged antidromically by feedback from CA3 cells [Wu et al., 1998]. So it seems unlikely that signals the EC sent into the DG' triggered the discharge of no more than three granule cells that would be required to generate the phosphene image of three thin white rays that I've described, images which don't conform to a "spreading out" pattern. It is more likely, I suggest, that there was some additional input, an input that would have to have been confined to a very narrow region of the DG' so that only three granule cells participated in the paroxysmal discharge.

There is a simple, elegant, and persuasive hypothesis that can account for this sequence of events, and I'd like to discuss it here, but I must acknowledge at the outset that there's a big problem with this hypothesis: it requires me to take a position in the ongoing debate about whether or not humans still have a functioning remnant of the ventral hippocampal commissure (VHC). The VHC in many mammals constitutes a direct, monosynaptic projection that is capable of conveying excitatory signals from one hippocampus to the other. At present the weight of the evidence seems to be clearly against the existence of a human VHC, but the issue has never been definitely resolved. Even those researchers who have provisionally concluded that there is no human VHC acknowledge that there are a number of contingencies that might have prevented them from detecting the impact of VHC-mediated signals or from finding anatomical evidence of a VHC fiber. The issue is seldom mentioned in the current literature: the last article on this subject (in which the authors emphasized that the issue was still open and still very important for epileptology) was published in 1992. But since a VHC input would provide the "best fit" hypothesis to explain why I saw the ray images, I can't avoid discussing the issue and reviewing the research with the hope that this new phosphene evidence of a VHC contribution will revitalize the debate about the existence of this commissure.

The VHC in Humans: A Review of the Research

Trajectory of the VHC Projection in Primates

Most of the research about VHC fibers is performed in rats where there is a massive VHC projection that extends along the entire body of the hippocampus; by contrast, monkeys have a relatively small and circumscribed VHC that extends only from the uncal region of one hippocampus to the contralateral uncus [Deadwyler et al., 1975b; Rosene and G. W. Van Hoesen, 1987; Stringer et al., 1989; Amaral et al., 1984; Demeter et al., 1985; Lothman et al., 1991]. Researchers have concluded that, despite these differences in size, the basic circuitry of the VHC fibers is the same in both monkeys and rats, so I will not make a point of distinguishing which type of animal was used for a particular study unless that fact becomes relevant.

The schematic drawings in Figure 26 illustrate the path of the VHC projec-

Figure 26. The inter-hemispheric trajectory of the ventral hippocampal commissure (VHC) in the monkey. A. The VHC in monkeys connects the uncal regions of the two hippocampi. Based on anatomical studies discussed in the main text, VHC fibers arise (1) from pyramidal cells in the proximal region of CA3c' (i.e., that portion of subfield CA3' located closest to the DG', designated from here on as CA3c) and (2) from CA3/4 hilar cells located immediately adjacent to the DG'. The fibers then cross the midline and enter the contralateral hippocampus via the fimbria where they divide into two branches, both of which terminate in the uncal region. B. The terminals of the VHC projection. In anatomical studies (see the main text), the VHC projection enters the hippocampus via that part of the fimbria that extends to the uncal region, and from there the VHC fibers pass through the most superficial layer of CA3' neurons covering the outer surfaces of the uncal pole, the *stratum oriens*, and push down toward the Ligature of Giacomini, the uncal extension of the dentate gyrus (DG'). Having entered the uncal pole, the VHC projection divides into two branches. One branch—the one with the highest density of VHC terminals—passes through the granule cell layer of the ventral blade of the DG' and terminates in the inner third of the molecular layer in a position that is both medial and also beneath the ventral blade of the DG'. The other branch courses around the outside of the ventral and dorsal blades of the DG' to terminate in the inner third of the molecular layer situated more laterally and above the dorsal blade. While these findings are based on an anatomical study of the VHC in rats performed by Deadwyler et. al. [1975a, b], the specific findings about the origins and terminals of the VHC fibers apply to monkeys as well. If humans have a functioning remnant of the VHC that follows the same trajectory as in the monkey, the findings just cited should apply to humans as well. *When the CA3c cells that give rise to the VHC projection are stimulated, this produces excitatory postsynaptic potentials in the contralateral hippocampus, a response that is confined to those apical granule cell dendrites that extend into the inner third of the molecular layer. The excitation only occurs in a very narrow zone (50 μm) adjacent to the afferent VHC terminals.

The Ventral Hippocampal Commissure

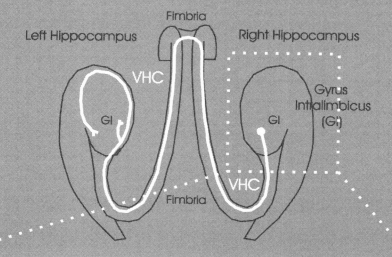

A Trajectory of VHC Projection from Right H in the Monkey

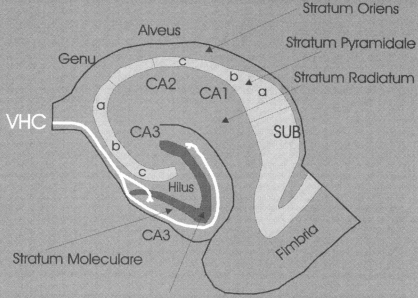

B Termination of a VHC Projection in the Hilar Region of CA 3 Near the Dentate Gyrus (LG) in the Monkey

tion in monkeys (Panel A) and the approximate location of the VHC terminals in the contralateral uncus (Panel B). To supplement this diagram, we can add what has been discovered about the circuitry of VHC fibers in studies with rats. The VHC fibers project from two types of neurons: (1) from pyramidal cells located in that part of CA3' situated closest to the DG' which is called the most "proximal" region of CA3 and designated by the label, CA3c, and (2) from the CA3/4 "hilar" neurons, a small, hybrid subgroup of neurons located immediately adjacent to the DG'. The VHC axons cross the midline and extend into the opposite hemisphere where they eventually terminate in the inner third of the molecular layer of the contralateral DG. *When excitatory signals generated in one hippocampus arrive at the VHC terminals in the contralateral hippocampus, they trigger excitatory post-synaptic potentials in the apical dendrites of granule cells, dendrites that extend into the inner third of the molecular layer* [Deadwyler et al., 1975a; Deadwyler et al., 1975b; Jung et al., 1994; Lothman, 1997]. The VHC terminals innervate only a very narrow zone of granule cells, a zone that extends no more than 50 microns (μm) into the inner molecular layer of the DG and another 50 μm in the subgranular layer [Deadwyler et al., 1975b], so the excitatory effect of afferent VHC signals is severely confined. It is important to keep this detail in mind, because it will clearly be relevant for explaining why so few granule cells participated in the first outbreak of paroxysmal discharges.

Stimulation experiments in rats demonstrate that when an electrode is applied to the fibers of the VHC, this stimulus *never discharges more than three granule cells, no matter how strong the stimulus applied* [Deadwyler et al., 1975a; Stringer et al., 1989; Jung et al., 1994; Lothman, 1997]. They also demonstrate that the discharge of a single granule cell will only trigger the discharge of a single pyramidal cell in CA3 [Acsády et al., 1998; Henze et al., 2002]; this is because the granule cell mossy fiber axons impose a strong feed-forward inhibition on the pyramidal cells in CA3 that can "efficiently suppress recurrent excitation in the CA3 collaterals but allow for the selective discharge of a few CA3 pyramidal cells [Acsády et al., Ibid., p. 3399]." Another important finding is that that once a granule cell fires a paroxysmal discharge, it needs *at least 30 seconds to recover* from the after-hyperpolarization before it can fire a second spike [Stringer and Lothman, 1992].

Taken together, these findings could have important implications for our "reverse-engineering" analysis of the phosphene rays and their rapid transformations. The narrowly-circumscribed input of a VHC fiber would be capable of adding just enough extra stimulation to the apical dendrites of a few granule cells to trigger paroxysmal discharges. The utility of assuming that there is a functioning remnant of the VHC is that it would support the following inferences: (1) that the hypersynchronous activity in subfield CA3' of the right hippocampus could send excitatory signals directly to a few granule cells in the contralateral DG' via a VHC projection; (2) that at most only three granule cells could have been discharged by

VHC input in my case since there were only three white columns in the initial ray image; and, (3) that each granule cell would only be able to fire one paroxysmal discharge during the time frame in which I observed the changes in the ray images, which I've set at 17 to 20 seconds. These observations would provide a very useful platform on which to build an explanation of why the ray image appeared and why it manifested the specific characteristics that I've described, but of course that's all futile if there is in fact no VHC projection in humans. We need to review the evidence for and against the human VHC and to weigh whether the phosphene rays provide convincing new evidence that the VHC is indeed a factor to be considered.

Conflicts in the VHC Research Data

The debate about VHC fibers in human began with an anomalous finding in a depth-electrode study of epileptic patients awaiting surgery: Spencer et. al. [1987] found that 20% of the spontaneous seizures that originated in one hippo-campus *propagated to the contralateral hippocampus even before those seizures spread into the temporal cortices that were immediately adjacent.* The authors proposed that the existence of a functioning VHC in humans would explain why this paroxysmal activity was transferred more rapidly to the contralateral hippocampus than to ipsalateral structures.

In the wake of this report, other researchers performed a number of experiments to test the hypothesis that Spencer et al. proposed. Some of these researchers recorded EEG coherence patterns and phase relationships during seizure onsets in epileptic patients to see if there were any linear patterns in the data that would be consistent with onset of seizure activity in the one mesotemporal region propagating directly to the left hemisphere [Mars and Lopes da Silva, 1983; Mars et al., 1985; Gotman, 1983, 1987; Lieb et al., 1986; Lieb and Babb, 1986; Lieb et al., 1997]. None of these EEG coherence studies found any evidence of linear relationships. Another group of researchers performed depth-electrode studies in epileptic patients awaiting surgery [Wilson et al., 1987, 1990, 1991]. These researchers administered a *single* shock to neurons in the CA3' subfield of the uncal hippocampus where VHC fibers would originate, but their single stimulus did not evoke any ictal discharges in the contralateral hippocampus. Because of ethical constraints, the researchers were unable to administer repeated shocks to their human subjects, so it remains uncertain what would have happened had that been possible. In discussing the last study in their series, Wilson et al. [1991] concluded that humans *probably* do not have a functioning remnant of the VHC, but they also added this important qualification: *if there is indeed a functioning VHC fiber in humans, then those VHC fibers would have to be very long, so long that an action potential moving along the VHC axon might well become so attenuated by the time it reached the contralateral hippocampus that it would be too weak to trigger a discharge in the target neuron.* This is a critically-important point for our investigation, so it bears repeating in the researchers' own words:

> . . . [T]he resulting field potential would be of such a long duration and such low amplitude that it could not be detected. Indeed, such an input might be below the threshold for local synaptic activation of a response, *unless other factors intervened such as temporal summation occurring with repetitive stimulation* [Wilson et al., 1991, p. 185; emphasis added].

In the circumstances that I've described, where hypersynchronous activity engulfs the uncal region of the right hippocampus for a relatively long period of time, there would clearly be a potential for precisely this kind of repetitive stimulation of the VHC fibers. And this repetitive stimulation, if it were to occur, would produce precisely the kind of temporal summation that is mentioned by Wilson et al.. In sum, the finding that a single shock applied to CA3' neurons in one hippocampus did not evoke paroxysmal discharges in the contralateral hippocampus does not preclude the possibility that multiple shocks would have been effective. But there is another confounding variable, one that is equally important in assessing to what extent the findings of the EEG coherence studies and the hippocampal stimulations studies can be generalized: all of these studies were performed in patients who had already experienced multiple, intractible seizures and who were awaiting imminent surgery when the experiments were performed. To determine if selecting patients with histories of prior seizures would confound the search for a human VHC, Spencer et al. [1992]—the same researchers who'd first proposed that hippocampal seizures might spread contralaterally through a VHC projection—decided to conduct a follow-on experiment to determine the extent of neuronal damage in the hilar region of the DG' in patients who'd already experienced multiple seizures. They found that *the interhippocampal propagation time in patients with chronic epilepsy was inversely correlated with the amount of cell loss in the dentate hilar region of the hippocampus, i.e., the more cell loss the researchers detected, the longer the time interval that was required for a seizure in one hippocampus to spread to the contralateral hippocampus.* Spencer et al. concluded that experimental studies using patients with chronic epilepsy as subjects are likely to produce results that are misleading and that underestimate the probability that there is a functioning remnant of the VHC in humans:

> These observations suggest that *anatomic changes associated with chronic epilepsy alter propagation patterns.* Because CA4 is believed to modulate the output of dentate granule cells and also has commissural connections to the contralateral homotopic area, the association of decreased CA4 cells with prolongation of ITSPT [interhippocampal seizure propagation time] suggests that the observed anatomic alterations may actively (through increased inhibition) or passively (through decreased recruitment) interfere with various routes of seizure propagation [Spencer et al., 1992, p. 862; emphasis added].

The hypothesis that a history of prior seizures is likely to damage the delicate neuronal circuits of the VHC was also demonstrated in a study using rats.

Here the VHC projection is massive, extending along the entire length of the hippocampus, so it would be expected that the rat VHC would continue to function despite an exposure to prior seizures, but this turned out not to be the case. In this study, Bragin et al. [1999] injected kainic acid into one hippocampus to initiate a build-up of hypersynchronous activity in that hemisphere of the brain, then, in a second stage of the experiment, the researchers triggered paroxysmal discharges in that hippocampus and watched to see if the paroxysmal activity would propagate to the contralateral hippocampus via the VHC fibers in the hippocampus that had been consumed by the hypersynchronous activity. Despite the robust nature of the VHC projection in rats, the hypersynchronous activity in the first stage of the experiment *prevented* the direct interhippocampal propagation of the seizures in the second stage of the experiment. This outcome surprised the researchers who had predicted that there would be VHC propagation, but given the outcome of the experiment they concluded that the failure to spread as expected was probably a result of the hypersynchronous activity having damaged the neurons that give rise to VHC fibers:

> Functional interhippocampal connections in the human are known to be weak to nonexistent, and this has been assumed to be the reason that hippocampal seizures in patients with TLE [temporal lobe epilepsy] remain localized to one side and may not propagate contralaterally at all. It is of great interest, therefore, to see the same phenomenon in unilaterally KA-treated rats where the hypersynchronous discharges often do not propagate contralaterally at all although these animals have very large hippocampal commissures. In the rat, therefore, *there must be intrinsic properties of the sclerotic hippocampus that prevent escape of the epileptiform discharges.* Clinical studies have shown a relation between prolonged propagation times and increased hippocampal cell loss, suggesting that some aspects of [seizure-induced] neuronal organization may provide a protective mechanism [Bragin et al., 1999, pp., 1219 - 1220; emphasis added].

Based on these findings reported by Spencer et al. [1992] and by Bragin et al. [1999], it is reasonable to conclude that the existence of a functioning remnant of the VHC in humans is a question that has not yet been definitely unresolved, that the EEG coherence studies and the single shock stimulation studies may have failed to find evidence of direct inter-hippocampal transmission of ictal activity because they studied human patients whose history of intractable mesotemporal seizures damaged any VHC circuits that might exist in humans.

Another attempt to resolve the issue of whether humans have VHC fibers was an anatomical study of the preserved brains of deceased humans by Gloor et al. [1993]. The researchers looked for hitherto unrecognized fibers that crossed the midline of the brain at the same place where VHC fibers were known to cross the midline in monkey brains. They did find a few unidentified fibers with thin myelination crossing the midline, but they were unable to trace those fibers to either their sites of origin or their sites of termination, so it was not possible to identify the fibers. The researchers concluded that the oblique trajectory of the fibers made it more likely that they were part of the hippocampal discussion, not VHC fibers, and that it was more likely than not that humans do not have a functioning VHC projection. Nevertheless, they hedged their bets by acknowledging that "It remains possible . . . that a small remnant of a ventral hippocampal commissure exists at this level in the human brain (p. 1253)."

Given the contradictory findings produced by the search for evidence of a human VHC, and given the difficulties involved in finding subjects for VHC-related experiments, it is easy to understand why the research community might decide that it is no longer worth spending time and resources in the quest to find a definitive answer. A cursory review of the recent research literature will show that the search has been largely abandoned, but this temporary stalemate does not mean that the debate about the existence of the human VHC should be allowed to languish. That's why I think it's important to point out that the meditation-induced phosphene image of three thin white rays provides new evidence of the existence of a VHC projection in humans. The presence of a VHC input would explain the fact that, in the circumstances that I've described, the uncal extension of the dentate gyrus (DG') in the left hippocampus shifted from processing the signals sent by the EC according to the normal "spreading out" pattern—a pattern that fits well with processing spatially-diffuse signals that originated in the hypersynchronous seizure in the right hippocampus but not with the discharge of only three granule cells—to a pattern in which there was a narrowly-target input of repetitive stimulation to a few granule cells and a temporal summation that pushed those few granule cells into paroxysmal activity. The alternative hypothesis can only be that it was just *fortuitous* which granule cells eventually discharged paroxysmally, that the inhibitory forces constraining these granule cells were simply the "weakest link" in the system, so they were first to succumb to the stream of excitation received from the EC. I find this theory to be unsatisfying, and I hope others will agree with me that the precision of the VHC-mediated hypothesis provides new evidence of a functioning VHC in humans.

We can't resolve that question, but we can ask what happens once the granule cells fire paroxysmal discharges. What is known about how granule cell discharges propagate through the intra-hippocampal circuits? How can we explain the transformations of the phosphene rays by reference to the intra-hippocampal propagation of paroxysmal discharges?

The Intra-Hippocampal Progression of Ictal Discharges

Columnar Phosphenes and Longitudinal Association Strips

How is it possible that the discharge of a few granule cells could generate a phosphene image of thin, columnar rays? And why would the rays change over time, doubling in number, becoming longer, and fanning farther apart? Is there any information available in the research literature on intra-hippocampal circuits that can be used to explain the origins and transformations of the phosphene rays? The discussion that follows is based on anatomical studies of intra-hippocampal circuits [Ishizuka et al., 1990; Tamamaki and Nojyo, 1991; Li et al., 1994] and theoretical studies analyzing how those circuits function [Deadwyler and Hampson, 1999; Andersen et al., 2000].

      Neurons in subfield CA3 have many local connections, and these interconnected neuron networks have a distinctive shape: they are arrayed in thin diagonal columns that are called "longitudinal association strips." If one CA3 neuron embedded in a longitudinal association strip discharges, all of the other locally-connected neurons in that strip also discharge, sending a stream of action potentials into subfield CA1. By contrast, neurons in CA1 are not locally-connected, but when they discharge on receipt of action potentials via the Schaffer collateral axons from CA3 neurons, the spatial distribution of the CA1 discharges also forms a diagonal strip. If the contiguous sheets of CA3 and CA1 neurons are visualized as being two rectangles that share a common border, then the paired responses of the CA3 neurons in a longitudinal association strip and the CA1 neurons linked to them, which will mirror the same diagonal pattern, can be envisioned as chevron-like pattern in which two diagonal strips, one in CA3 and one in CA1, slant toward each other and converge at the tops of the strips [Ishizuka et al., 1990; Deadwyler and Hampson, 1999]. The diagonal strip of discharges that CA3 neurons trigger in CA1 intermixes with the original set of signal-patterns that the EC refers directly to CA1 via the temporo-ammonic path, signals that are maintained because neurons in subfield CA1 maintain a one-to-one, reciprocal interaction with the EC, and it is the outcome of this interaction that constitutes the final product of hippocampal processing. This suggests the possibility that the phosphene image of three thin white rays might represent the paroxysmal discharge of three longitudinal association strips in subfield CA3 which then triggers the paroxysmal discharge of CA1 neurons that are aligned in three diagonal columns. Of course this inference is highly speculative, as was my earlier proposal that VHC input was involved in generating the image of trident rays, but as the analogies between what I saw and what is reported in the research literature keep on accumulating, the inference that there is indeed a causal connection becomes more difficult to avoid. But of all the parallels between phosphene characteristics and experimental results, the most amazing coincidence is the similarity between the transformations of the phosphene rays and the outcome of a computer simulation of the intra-hippocampal propagation of granule cell discharges.

A Computer Model of Intra-Hippocampal Discharges

      Undeterred by the complexities involved in tracing how hippocampal circuits actually function, Bernard et al. [1997] designed a computer software program that incorporated what was known about intra-hippocampal circuits at the time, and they then conducted a series of simulations to find out what kinds of outcomes were associated with different kinds of initial events. One of the initial events they modeled was the discharge of a single granule cell and the effects evoked by its mossy fiber action potential as it moved across subfield CA3, triggering the discharges of neurons located in different subregions within CA3 that then sent their action potentials into subfield CA1, triggering target neurons located in different subregions of that terminal field. The results of this computer simulation are illustrated in the schematic drawings of Figures 27 and 28 (both adapted from illustrations in Bernard et al.). In Figure 27, the two hippocampal subfields, CA3 and CA1, are represented as 2-dimensional rectangles with a grid of 50 μm squares superimposed. The clusters of neuron discharges evoked in subfield CA1 are represented as "spike-peaks," but this conical shape does *not* reflect the *actual* distribution of those discharges; rather, the authors arbitrarily assigned a conical shape because they concluded there was not have enough research data available at the time to warrant their specifying the actual geometric distributions of the discharges evoked in CA1.

The results of the simulation surprised even the researchers themselves. As shown in Figure 27, the first effect evoked in subfield CA1 by the discharge of a single granule cell was the appearance of a single spike-peak of neuron discharges in the lower (temporal) third of the CA1 rectangle at 4.4 milliseconds. The basal skirt of this first spike-peak was truncated on one side because it pushed up against the border of CA1 and CA3. At 5.8 milliseconds, *the first spike-peak disap-*

Figure 27. Origins of the phosphene rays, part I: The results of computer simulations performed by Bernard et al. [1997]. These schematic drawings, all adapted from Bernard et al. (pp. 62-63), represent hippocampal subfields CA3 and CA1 as rectangular boxes with a grid of 50 μm squares superimposed . This grid allowed the researchers to plot the relative positions of the clusters of neuron spikes ("spike-peaks") that are generated in CA1 by the simulated discharge of a single granule cell. Note that the conical shape used to represent the spike-clusters is a shape that was arbitrarily assigned and thus does not reflect the actual distribution of discharges. A. The first effect generated in CA1 by the discharge of a single granule cell in the DG was the appearance of a single spike-peak after 4.4 milliseconds. The apron of this first spike-peak was truncated on the side closest to the DG granule cell (i.e., on the *proximal* side of CA1) where the spike-peak pushes up against the CA1 border with CA3. B. At 5.8 milliseconds, a second effect was observed: the single spike-peak in the first display was abruptly replaced by two spike-peaks, both located at a more central position in CA1. The two spike-peaks began to move apart, one moving toward the septal border (the upper side of the rectangle) and the other toward the temporal border (the lower side). C. At 9.6 milliseconds, a third effect was observed: the two spike-peaks were now replaced by a single spike-peak. This third spike-peak, like the first, had its apron truncated on one side; in this case, the spike-peak pushed up against the distal border of CA1 (i.e., on the side located farthest away from the DG). Note that none of these changes involved any additional discharge by the granule cell.

Computer Modeling of Spike-Peaks in CA 1 Generated by a Single Granule Cell Discharge

A

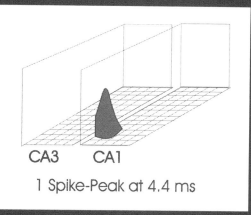

1 Spike-Peak at 4.4 ms

The first effect of the simulated granule cell discharge is the appearance of a single "spike-peak" in subfield CA 1 that is truncated by its proximity to the CA 3-CA 1 border.

B

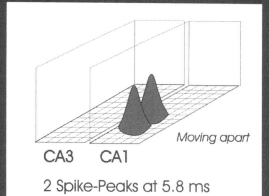

2 Spike-Peaks at 5.8 ms

The second effect, which occurs only milliseconds later, is the appearance of *two* spike-peaks that move apart.

C

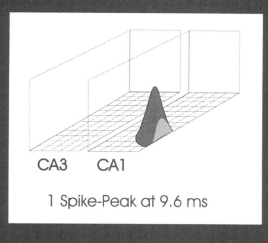

1 Spike-Peak at 9.6 ms

The third effect is a shift back to a single spike-peak, one that is again truncated, this time by its promixity to the distal border of CA 1.

Adapted from Bernard et al. [1997]

peared and was abruptly replaced by two separate spike-peaks situated in a more central position in the CA1 subfield than the first spike-peak. As soon as the two spike-peaks appeared, they began moving apart. This doubling in the number of spike-peaks did not require any additional input from the granule cell that fired the original discharge. At 9.6 milliseconds a third and final change occurred: the two moving spike-peaks were replaced by a single spike-peak which pushed up against the distal border of CA1 (i.e., the border farthest away from the dentate gyrus), and this proximity caused its basal skirt to be truncated in the same manner as the first spike-peak but now on the opposite (distal) side of the spike-peak.

The outcomes of the computer simulation resemble the transformations of the phosphene image of thin white rays in three respects: (1) there was a truncation of the first spike-peak because it pushed up against the proximal border of CA1, and, similarly, the first phosphene rays were truncated, extending only halfway to the perimeter of vision, and one of the three rays in the first ray image had its tip bent sidewards as if it had encountered some barrier; (2) there was an unexpected doubling in the number of spike-peaks evoked in CA1 in the second stage of events triggered by the discharge of a single granule cell, just as there was a doubling of the phosphene rays in the second version of that image; and (3) the two spike-peaks moved apart, just as the phosphene rays were seen to move apart at the same time that they doubled in number. These three parallels are striking because they are so unexpected and counter-intuitive. But are these parallels merely coincidental, or does the simulation reveal important clues about the neural mechanisms that underlie the phosphene phenomena: are the transformations of the ray image generated by the paroxysmal discharge of granule cells propagating through intra-hippocampal circuits?

Bernard et al. [1997] propose a hypothetical explanation for their findings, and I've adapted one of their illustrations for use in Figure 28. In this illustration, they converted the conical spike-peaks from Figure 27—a shape which they assigned arbitrarily—into 2-dimensional disks that represent the same clusters of neuron discharges and occupy the same positions. In Figure 28 the rectangles representing subfields CA3 and CA1 do not have the old grid superimposed, and here the orientation of the subfields is more clearly marked: there are labels indicating which side of the subfield is proximal (i.e., situated closest to the dentate gyrus) and which is distal (located farthest from the DG), and labels indicating which end of each subfield is closest to the temporal region and which is closest to the septal region. There are also markers that designate subregions within CA3 and CA1.

It is important to note that the neuron located in the proximal region of CA3 (i.e., closest to the dentate gyrus), or CA3c, has a Schaffer collateral axon that is very long because it has to project all the way across the CA3 subfield and across most of CA1 before establishing a synapse with its target neuron, CA1c; by contrast, the neuron located in the most distal region of CA3, CA3a, has a relatively short Schaffer collateral that reaches its target neuron in CA1a soon after crossing the CA3-CA1 border. Figure 28 also includes one item that was not present in the original illustrations by Bernard et al.: after the publication of their simulation, an anatomical study of hippocampal circuits by Deadwyler and Hampson [1999] showed that when neurons in subfield CA3 discharge, they activate other CA3 neurons connected with them in a thin, columnar "longitudinal association strip" that stretches across CA3 at an oblique angle, and when the cluster of neurons connected in a longitudinal association strip discharges, that triggers discharges in CA1 cells that form a mirror-image diagonal. Taken together, the discharges of neurons in the longitudinal association strip in CA3 combined with the discharges of neurons in the mirror-image diagonal strip in CA1 form a chevron-like pattern. In Figure 28 I've inserted representations of these two strip patterns into the original drawings from Bernard et al., because this additional information, which was not available at the time the computer simulations were performed, reveals that the spike clusters do not form a cone or a disk, as in the original illustrations by Bernard et al., but instead form oblique columns. Given that the neuronal events that are the subject of our investigation all occurred in the uncal region which constitutes the anterior (temporal) third of the hippocampal body, I've inserted diagonal strips in the lower (temporal) third of the hippocampal subfields in Figure 28. Now we're ready to see how Bernard et al. explain the results of their computer simulation—and to see if these hypotheses can account for the image of the phosphene rays and its transformations.

The explanation proposed by Bernard et al. [1997] to account for their results is based on the interaction of two variables: (1) differences in axon conduction velocities which are much faster in granule cell mossy fibers than in Schaffer collaterals, and (2) differences in the lengths of the Schaffer collateral axons that project from CA3 to CA1. Panel A shows an action potential moving along the granule cell's mossy fiber following a propagation pattern documented by other researchers [Ishizuka et al., 1990; Demeter et al., 1985; Tamamaki and Nojyo,1991]. The action potential discharges three neurons in the order it encounters them: first CA3c, then CA3b, then CA3a. Because the conduction velocity of the mossy fibers is so much faster than the conduction velocity of the Schaffer collateral axons, and because the Schaffer collaterals in different positions along the proximo-distal axis of CA3 have different lengths, the *first* neuron to discharge in CA3 (at CA3c) is the *last* to discharge its target neuron in CA1 (at CA1c), and, conversely, the *last* neuron to discharge in CA3 (at CA3a) triggers the *first* discharge in CA1 (at CA1a).

The discharge of each of the CA3 neurons initiates the discharge of the other neurons in its longitudinal association strip, and that strip of discharges produces a mirror-image diagonal strip of discharges in CA1, shown here in Figure 28 as oblique columns forming a chevron-like pattern that I've inserted over the disk shapes used by Bernard et al. Notice that the diagonal strip and the oval disk beneath it are both truncated on one side because they push up against the CA1-CA3 border. This truncation of the CA1a diagonal might explain why the first

Figure 28. Origins of the Phosphene Rays, Part II: Analysis of the findings of the computer simulations by Bernard et al. [1997]. These schematic drawings, adapted from illustrations published by the authors of the computer modeling study, present the hypotheses they proposed to explain their findings. I've added representations of longitudinal association strips in subfield CA3 based on studies of intra-hippocampal circuits by Deadwyler and Hampson [1999]. Longitudinal association strips are networks of locally-connected neurons in CA3 shaped in long, thin diagonal column that discharge in unison when one constituent neuron discharges. When neurons in a longitudinal association strip discharge, they trigger discharges in CA1 that mirror the diagonal pattern in CA3, so that, together, the paired diagonal discharges form a chevron-like pattern. Given that the neuronal events that we're investigating took place in the uncal hippocampus, that is, in the anterior (temporal) third, I've kept the chevron discharge patterns within that region. **A. Origins of the first spike-cluster.** As described by Bernard et al., the discharge of a single granule cell in the DG triggers an action potential that speeds along its efferent mossy fiber axon, crossing the transverse axis of CA3 in a proximodistal direction (i.e., moving away from the DG granule cell), and discharging en route a series of CA3 neurons. The first neuron to be discharged, as shown here, is in that part of CA3 located closest to the DG (CA3c). I've added a diagonal column here to indicate that all of the CA3 neurons linked with it in a longitudinal association strip will also discharge. The discharge of the CA3c neuron (and the rest of the neurons in its longitudinal association strip) sends an action potential moving toward a target neuron in CA1c, which is located, as shown here, in distal CA1c, on the far side of that subfield. The Schaffer collateral axon that links the CA3c neuron with its target cell in CA1c is very long, so long that its action potential does not reach its target neuron in CA1c until after the granule cell's mossy fiber discharges both of the other neurons it encounters in its trajectory across the tranverse axis of subfield CA3. The second CA3 neuron discharged by the mossy fiber is CA3b (and its associated diagonal strip), but its action potential also has to move through a very long Schaffer collateral axon to reach its target cell in CA1b. The *last* cell to be discharged by the granule cell's mossy fiber—the neuron in distal CA3a—is the *first* to have its action potential reach its target neuron in CA1a. Therefore, the first cluster of spikes will be triggered in subfield CA1a, as shown in Panel A. These CA1a spikes will be distributed in a diagonal strip that mirrors the diagonal of the longitudinal association strip in CA3a that triggered it. Beneath the diagonal strips that I've inserted in CA1a is an oval disk that occupies the same spot in the CA1 subfield as the single "spike-peak" that was the first outcome recorded by Bernard et al. (see Figure 27, supra). **B. Origins of the 2nd spike-cluster.** When action potentials from the mossy fiber's discharge of the CA3b neuron reaches CA1b, it activates not one but two diagonal clusters of discharges, which means there must have also been two longitudinal association strips activated in CA3b. In the computer simulation, the two spike-peaks begin moving apart in an undetermined direction, so here I've indicated movement of the diagonal strips without specifying direction. **C. Origins of the 3rd spike-cluster.** The action potentials from CA3c (and its longitudinal association strip) finally reach target cells in CA1c, triggering the discharge of a mirror-image diagonal strip. If my speculations about the positions of the mirror-image diagonal strips in CA1 are correct, these drawings show how the diagonal strips in CA1 will get longer in each iteration, so that where the tips of the diagonals touch the temporal border of subfield CA1, the tips will have to move along the proximodistal axis, i.e., a fanning farther apart with each successive set of discharges. This progression is analogous, at least in some respects, to the lengthening and fanning apart of the phosphene rays.

Hypothetical Explanation of Spike-Peak Sequences

A
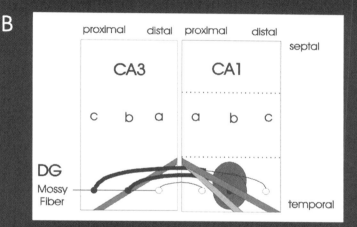

The mossy fiber's fast-moving action potential discharges all target neurons in CA 3 before there is any effect in CA 1.

Because the Schaffer collateral from CA 3a to CA 1a is shorter, the CA 1a cell discharges first, activating other cells in its longitudinal association strip.

B

Next to discharge is the CA 1b cell and its diagonal strip. In the simulation, there are *two* spike-peaks that are moving apart. A possible explanation for the doubling is that the diagonal of the initial CA 1a discharge may persist and be "pulled" toward CA 1b.

C
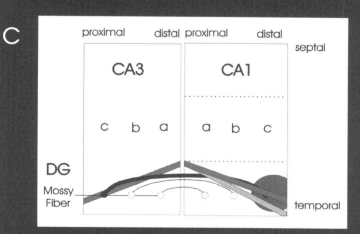

Because of the length of its Schaffer collateral, the CA 1c cell is last to discharge, activating a new diagonal that pushes up against the distal border of CA 1. Here the diagonal of the CA 1b discharge has been "pulled" toward CA 1c & the CA 1a diagonal has disappeared.

phosphene image of trident rays reached only halfway to the perimeter of vision.

The second event in the computer simulations is depicted in Panel B: when the action potential initiated by the discharge of the second CA3 neuron (at CA3b) reaches its target cell at CA1b, it triggers not one but two clusters of neuron discharges, represented here by two oval disks (in the same position as the original spike-peaks) and by two diagonal strips. This doubling in the number of spike clusters (that occurs without any additional discharges of the granule cell) is analogous to the doubling in the number of phosphene rays that appeared in the second version of that image. Panel B shows that the diagonal strips in CA1b do not encounter any anatomical constraints, so the two new diagonals stretch longer and their tips move closer to the distal border of CA1, generating diagonal strips that are significantly longer than the first strip at CA1a. This doubling in the number of strips at CA1b along with their lengthening as they move along the proximo-distal axis of CA1 might explain why the second transformation of the phosphene rays showed those rays doubling in number (from three to six) and extending all the way to the perimeter of vision.

Some of the explanations that Bernard et al. propose to explain the strange and counter-intuitive outcomes of their computer simulations have been corroborated by in vitro and in vivo experiments. Andersen et al. [2000] prepared an intact slice of hippocampal tissue, preserving the CA3-CA1 connections, and then stimulated the Schaffer collateral axons of CA3 neurons to find out what effects this stimulation would evoke in CA1. They found that the spikes triggered in CA1 were distributed over a long columnar base, which is consistent with a diagonal strip. They also found that the spikes evoked in CA1 had a peak-like distribution with "ridges" that sloped down on either side as the amplitude of the response fell off; however, in some cases, the ridges did not slope down gradually but rather dropped off with almost perpendicular abruptness, and these precipitous borders occurred more frequently "towards the subiculum." Andersen et al. also performed an in vivo experiment in which they placed electrodes in the hippocampus of an anesthetized rabbit. Here too they observed that their stimulation of a single Schaffer collateral evoked a long, thin column of activation in CA1 with peak down the central spine, consistent with the findings in their other experiment. Finally, the researchers also found that when they stimulated the simultaneous activation of two Schaffer collaterals that were "neighbors," this generated a single column of discharges in CA1, and that single column occupied a position located midway between the diagonal discharges that had been produced when each Schaffer collateral had been stimulated separately: "Stimulation of two neighboring sites of the CA3 region caused a summation of signals with the largest amplitudes along a line between the ridges of maximal responses to each stimulated site alone (p. 169; emphasis added)." This finding suggests a possible explanation for why the initial effect of a single spike-peak at CA1a was transformed into the second effect in which two spike-peaks appeared: if the discharge of the first diagonal strip at CA1a persists for a few milliseconds, and then, before the strip associated with CA1a disappears, the discharge of a second diagonal strip at CA1b occurs, then, based on the findings of the Andersen team, there might be a summation of these two sets of signals that generated a diagonal situated between the CA1a and CA1b diagonals, so that, in effect, the CA1a diagonal gets "pulled" away from its former position and toward the second diagonal at CA1b. The intra-hippocampal discharges happen over a time scale of milliseconds, but it will inevitably take time for those changes to register in the cortical lightness record and thus become present in the conscious awareness of the subject; a delay in the conscious perception of a series of changes taking place in a few milliseconds might explain why the transformations of the phosphene ray images occurred at one-second intervals, a timing that seems very rapid to the perceiving subject even though it is very slow in relation to the progression of the underlying neuronal events. These delays might also explain why each of the ray images appeared to me to be a discrete event rather than a continuously evolving sequence.

In the third and final event, shown in Panel C, the action potential set in motion by the first neuron to be discharged by the granule cell mossy fiber—the neuron in CA3c—finally reaches its target cell on the far (distal) side of CA1 (at CA1c); this triggers discharges aligned, once again, in a single oval (or single diagonal strip), and this oval (or strip), like the first, pushes up against the distal border of subfield CA1. There should be some distortion in the shape of the diagonal caused by its having been blocked by the far border, and some distortion does indeed incur, but it is quite different than the truncation that limited the expansion of the first diagonal (at CA1a). The strip formed by the discharge of CA1c has no more room to move out along the proximo-distal axis and must move along the temporoseptal axis: that means the strip does not get longer but rather changes the angle of its slope—the slope "flattens," becoming a more shallow than any of the strips that occurred earlier. This flattening out of the diagonal strips suggests a possible explanation for the phosphene observation that in the third and final transformation all six rays spread farther apart with more shallow angles, a change that looked like they were "wilting" or "drooping."

My application of the computer simulations by Bernard et al. [1997] will appear wildly speculative to any fair-minded, scientifically-informed reader, and so they seem to me, but, while retaining a prudent scepticism, one cannot but be impressed and intrigued by the parallels between the characteristics and transformations of the simulation spike-peaks, on one hand, and the characteristics and transformations of the phosphene ray images, on the other. If there is in fact a causal connection underlying these similarities, it would mean that meditators who induce this penultimate image of the complete meditation-induced progression are able to "see" visual epiphenomena of ictal discharges propagating through intra-hippocampal circuits.

Why Are the Rays White?

The white color of the phosphene rays is probably generated by the same processes that produced the white color of the bulbous image. In the study of the neurophysiological correlates of color induction by Creutzfeldt [1993] that we discussed in the preceding chapter, I quoted his comment that "the neuronal signal for white consists of a balanced excitation of the M-cone excited, green-blue-sensitive WS-cells and the L-cone excited, yellow-red-sensitive WL-cells (p. 45)." If all neurons in one diagonal strip in hippocampal subfield CA1 were to discharge at maximal rates, as would happen at the outbreak of paroxysmal activity in the left uncal region, then those signals, consisting of a balanced excitation of all possible signals, would register in the cortical lightness record as a white diagonal strip.

8

ECSTASY & AFTERMATH

PHENOMENOLOGY

Visions of Lightning

The visual field suddenly "exploded" with flashes of dull white phosphene that seemed to alternate between the right or left side of the visual field, as shown in Figure 29. The individual flashes were separated by relatively short and unpredictable timing intervals, and the flashes in the right side of the visual field seemed to occur independently of flashes in the left side so that sometimes the two sets of flashes occurred with near simultaneity in both hemifields. It felt like I was caught up in the middle of a dark stormcloud as it was being illuminated by flashes of sheet lightning. I heard loud noises that were clearly internally generated: crackling, buzzing, sizzling sounds that reminded me of hearing electrical circuits shorting out. Most of my muscles were trembling, including the bulbospongiosus muscle (located just behind the scrotum in males) which would usually only attract attention during sexual orgasm when it clenches spasmodically .

The impression created by these wide-spread muscle tremors was that a "current of energy" was flowing up through the body: it seemed to originate in the tremors of the legs and perineal region (where the bulbospongiosus muscle is located) and then move into the muscles of the arms, hands, and face. I recognized that this "current" must be what I'd read about in Tantric accounts of "kundalini rising:" a spiritual energy that supposedly rests in a reservoir (*kunda*) at the base of the trunk, "coiled like a sleeping cobra," and that begins to rise. As it rises and that penetrates a hierarchy of energy centers (*cakras*) until suddenly the "serpent-piercing" occurs as the kundalini energy shoots out of the top of the head and reunites its small spark of spiritual light with the primordial radiance of Brahman, the Ultimate Reality. Now that I'd had this experience myself, I could see how someone might

164

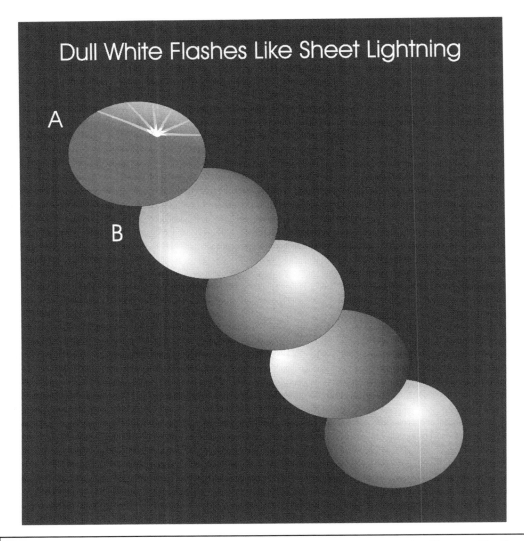

Figure 29. Lightning-like flashes. A. The predecessor image of six "wilted" rays. B. Onset of the dull white phosphene flashes against the dark charcoal-colored background that looked exactly like flashes of sheet lightning illuminating dark stormclouds from within. These "explosive" flashes seemed to alternate between the right or left hemifields, although because the timing of individual flashes was unpredictable, there were occasions in which flashes seemed to explode almost simultaneously in both hemifields. The lightning-like flashes were accompanied by sensorimotor and psychic symptoms that were clearly paroxysmal: loud, crackling, "short-circuit" sounds; tremors in many muscle groups, including the bulbospongiosus muscle at the back of the scrotum; the sensation of an "current" of energy flowing up from the lower extremities toward the crown of the head; a sensation resembling sexual orgasm which was not localized in the genital region but rather diffused throughout the body; and feelings of exhilaration and euphoria intermixed with fear and awe. If I diverted my attention from the visual field, the paroxysmal visual and sensorimotor symptoms stopped immediately; if I refocused my attention, the symptoms reappeared just as rapidly.

come up with the metaphor of a "current of energy" to explain what happened to them, but it would be more accurate to describe the "current" as simultaneous muscle tremors occurring throughout the body. I have my own metaphor, no less arbitrary than the Tantric offering, to describe the sensorimotor "current" (or what *felt* like a "current"): the metaphor of body-as-magnet. I imagined magnetic lines of force of the sort one sees in illustrations in physics texts, but I envisioned these force-fields emerging out of my head (at the positive pole) and then curving back in a great arc to re-enter the body in its nether regions (at the negative pole).

In addition to the flashing lights, electric sounds, and muscle tremors, there was an orgasmic sensation that was intensely pleasurable but also diffuse and thus quite unlike the sexual orgasm in males which is focused primarily in the genitals. The paroxysm also produced psychic symptoms—exhilaration, euphoria, and a mixture of awe and fear. The compulsion to arch my back and let my mouth fall slack that I'd experienced earlier (during the vision of the radiating spray) now returned. I yearned to surrender to the flow of events and to allow the blissful rapture to continue, but there was just enough fear to keep this from happening: however blissful the ecstatic rapture might be, however intense and compelling, and however easy it would have been to let one's defenses down and to lose oneself in the experience, I was afraid that if I did this I would not be able to come back, that I might cease being my normal self. That might be a consummation longed for by Tibetan lamas, Hindu sadhus, and Daoist masters, but not by me.

I did suppress my fears and surrender to the ecstasy for a while, but I soon recovered enough presence of mind to realize that paroxysmal symptoms like these were likely to be harmful, and that, even though this kind of paroxysmal experience might be highly-prized as a form of mystical transcendence, it also had to be a seizure—and any seizure, even an "ecstatic" one, would likely damage neurons I could ill afford to lose. Stirred to action, I diverted my attention from the flashing lights and was pleased to find that the lights and the paroxysmal symptoms ceased immediately. When I refocused attention, the flashes reappeared along with the tremors and the other paroxymal symptoms. I was reassured to find that I was still in control of whatever was happening to me. Feeling much too excited to have any hope of falling asleep, I got out of bed and went to the kitchen to make some toast and marvel at this extraordinary mystical experience. In the kitchen I noticed that it was only five o'clock in the morning. No more than an hour had elapsed from the time that I'd forced myself to get into bed to the end of the ecstasy.

I decided to take an early morning walk. Once outside, I was amazed to see that familiar neighborhood scenes were dramatically transformed. I was surrounded by a magical landscape. Particularly striking was the impression that my vision had become particularly acute: colors seemed more vivid and the empty spaces between objects seemed almost tangible. I stared, awestruck, in every direction, amused by the thoughts pouring into my mind, the very same thoughts which I'd formerly regarded as naïve and unimaginative clichés when I'd encountered them, as one so often does, in the autobiographies of religious mystics—"The world is perfect just as it is if only we looked at it afresh," or "After enlightenment, everything changes, but everything also stays the same." What once seemed simplistic now seemed profound.

As I hiked around the water reservoir located near my house, the euphoria began to fade. Suddenly I felt very tired, and when I looked at my watch, I realized that it would soon be time to wake the children for school, so I hurried home. Realizing that I wasn't up to the task of cooking breakfast and driving the children to school in morning traffic, I woke my wife and asked her to take over those chores for the day. Then I climbed into bed and fell fast asleep.

The Aftermath of Ecstatic Seizure

Residual Phosphene Effects

For several nights after the seizure, I experienced a resurgence of the white flashes and the paroxysmal sensorimotor symptoms. I would get in bed and close my eyes, waiting for sleep to come, and then I would glimpse a faint patch of white light hovering in the upper right quadrant of the visual field. The glow seemed to be obscured by something, but when I looked at it the glow would brighten and simultaneously begin to expand like the roiling white billows of an expanding cloud, as shown in the drawings in Figure 30. The first few times this residual phosphene appeared, its expanding surface displayed a variegated pattern that reminded me of the fractal surface of a cauliflower or a rising foam of soap bubbles. After two or three nights, this variegation disappeared, and from then on the expanding cloud was a soft white light that enveloped the visual field like a fog or a snowstorm. When the white glow expanded, I felt a stirring of a weaker version of the same sensorimotor and psychic symptoms that had accompanied the original seizure—the "electric" buzzing sounds, the muscle tremors creating the illusion of an ascending "current," the arched back, the diffuse orgasmic sensations, and the feelings of exhilaration, euphoria, awe, and fear; if I remained passive and acquiesced to the arrival of these stirrings, they quickly became stronger.

While it felt wonderful being caught up in the rapture of the white light, I didn't want to risk causing more excitotoxic damage. My solution to this dilemma was to delay going to bed until I was really tired, and then, once in bed with eyes closed, I made a point of keeping my attention dispersed and not looking in the direction where I knew the white smudge would be waiting. After a few nights the white glow stopped appearing spontaneously, even though it was easily rekindled by staring at where it had formerly appeared. With the passage of time, it became harder and harder to summon the white glow, and now, because long ago I stopped trying to induce the white fog, I've lost the ability to recall it. I would not be surprised, however, to find that it would appear once again if, contrary to my present

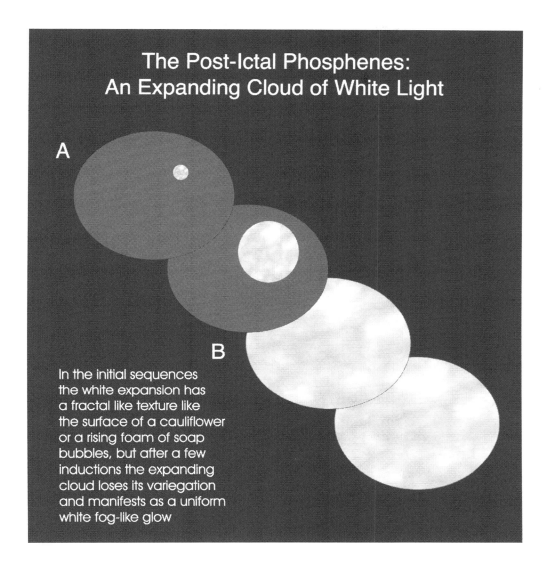

The Post-Ictal Phosphenes:
An Expanding Cloud of White Light

A

B

In the initial sequences
the white expansion has
a fractal like texture like
the surface of a cauliflower
or a rising foam of soap
bubbles, but after a few
inductions the expanding
cloud loses its variegation
and manifests as a uniform
white fog-like glow

Figure 30. Residual phosphene displays. For several nights after the ecstatic paroxysm, when I went to bed and closed my eyes I would see a faint smudge of white in the upper right quadrant of the visual field where the bulbous image and the ray images had once appeared. If I stared at this smudge, it would brighten and then suddenly begin to expand until it filled the entire visual field with a steady white light. As the white glow expanded, the paroxysmal sensorimotor and psychic symptoms reappeared. The surface of the expanding cloud of white phosphene changed over time: at first, the surface of the cloud was variegated—it looked like I was being engulfed by a fireball of the sort that boils out from the epicenter of an explosion, or like the fractal surface of a cauliflower, or like a rising foam of soap bubbles —but after several activations, the variegation disappeared and from then on the surface of the expanding cloud was an undifferentiated whiteness that looked like being overtaken and enveloped by a dense white fog or a snowstorm white-out.

practice, I were to take up cultivating meditation-induced light visions on a regular basis.

In addition to the residual phosphene glow, which was a relatively short-lived phenomenon, there were a number of other unusual experiences that first appeared after the ecstatic seizure: on a number of occasions I would feel stirrings of the same paroxysmal sensorimotor symptoms that had accompanied the seizure when I looked at visual scenes with certain specific characteristics that I'll describe in the next section. There were also some interesting changes in my emotional reactions to familiar events. I'll discuss these sequelae in more detail because they offer some unexpected clues about the precise location of the excitotoxic damage caused by the ecstatic paroxysm.

Residual Visual and Visuo-Vestibular Disturbances

I discovered that certain kinds of external stimuli could trigger a weaker version of the visual and sensorimotor symptoms associated with the ecstatic seizure. In May, about one month after the seizure, I was hiking on a trail high in the desert mountains of Arizona. The sun was setting behind a thick haze of dust which made it possible to stare directly at the red-orange orb. As I watched the sun set, I felt the familiar buzzing sounds, the muscle tremors, and the compulsion to let my mouth fall slack; I felt the bulbospongiosus muscle clenching which reintroduced the sensation of a "current" of energy ascending up through the body. This time I experienced an actual erection as well as the diffuse orgasmic sensations. It was all too bizarre—an erotic response to Nature itself. The resurgence of ecstatic symptoms in the context of a beautiful mountain environment was exhilarating and awe-inspiring, but I was shocked to learn that merely looking at the sun would produce such a strong reaction.

On another occasion I was riding in a car and looking out the window at a large snowfield as it reflected very bright sunlight. This broad expanse of reflected light evoked a weak version of the seizure-related stirrings. I would get the same reaction when I stared at sparkles of sunlight reflecting off the surface of a large lake. These experiences taught me that it was important to look away from scenes like these to keep from dissociating.

Another type of external visual stimulus that would reactivate the ecstatic symptoms was staring at a dark, towering stormcloud as it was being illuminated from within by flashes of sheet lightning. Here the post-paroxysmal symptoms were triggered not by external light stimuli but rather by my memories and emotional associations of having seen eerily similar lightning flashes reverberating inside my own mind.

Perhaps the most unexpected—and hence interesting—residual effect of having experienced the ecstatic seizure was the stirring of the seizure-like sensimotor symptoms in response to certain scenes that presented an unusually strong visuo-vestibular conflict. Visuo-vestibular conflict refers to environments in which a subject perceives the plane of the foreground to move in the opposite direction from the plane of the background. A scene of strong visuo-vestibular conflict that I often experience while I'm hiking on mountain trails is walking up to the edge of a cliff and peering down into the valley far below: here the plane of the foreground appears to receding under my feet at the same time that the plane of the background (valley) seems to be moving up and away as it drops down. I'd experienced this scene of strong visuo-vestibular conflict many times before the seizure without noticing anything out of the ordinary, but after the seizure this all changed: no sooner did I arrive at the edge of a cliff than I would begin to hear a tell-tale buzzing sound—the internally-generated sound I mentioned in earlier chapters as a sign of accelerating dissociation—and at the same time I would feel subtle tremors begin to flicker in the muscles of my arms and legs along with an unmistakable clenching of the bulbospongiosus muscle.

A similar reaction occurred when I indulged my hobby of climbing high up in tall trees. One tree I encountered on my morning walks was a particular favorite: it was a massive copper beech with branches sprouting out in all directions, some of them layered so low to the ground that it was easy to clamber on and then climb up limb after limb to an aerie about fifty feet off the ground. Sitting in this perch surrounded by the canopy of reddish leaves, I would sit quietly for a few minutes, admiring the view and marveling how quickly it was possible to slip out of the normal suburban routines. The first time I tried climbing in the copper beech after the ecstatic seizure I noticed right away that something was different: if I looked down at the ground from my elevated perspective, I felt a stirring of the same post-paroxysmal symptoms that I had experienced at the edge of mountain cliffs. High up in this tree with its dense canopy, the branches and leaves formed many different planes, both foreground and background planes, layered in such a way as to created a strong sense of depth, and when I looked down through these layers of leaves I could see the ground far below, which established another plane of reference. These multiple planes moving in different directions presented a scene with strong visuo-vestibular conflict, and my body responded in the same way that it responded at the edge of a cliff. Fascinated by the observation that by simply sitting at this great height and looking down I could evoke a weak version of the seizure-related symptoms, I decided to experiment with different body positions to determine how various changes would affect the intensity of the post-paroxysmal symptom complex. I discovered that there was one position in particular that provoked the strongest resurgence: if I stretched my hand out towards a nearby branch located just out of reach, and if I imagined that I was about to leap through space to grab that branch (even if actually I was planning no such thing), then as I imagined this action I would hear that tell-tale buzzing sound and feel a faint stirring of the sensorimotor "current" along with the clenching of the bulbiospongiosus muscle.

I became convinced that these post-paroxysmal symptoms were providing me with some useful proprioceptive feedback, that I was being alerted to the position of my body in 3-dimensional space and to its weight distribution in order to prepare me to leap safely toward that nearby branch. The sensorimotor "current" seemed designed to perform a balancing function, although in this case the proprioceptive feedback had become much too prominent so that what was meant to be a subliminal adjustment had now become a conscious experience due to the excessive excitability of the neuron networks involved. Given the recent advent of the ecstatic seizure, this excess excitability that intruded the "current" into conscious awareness was presumably due to excitotoxic damage caused by the outbreak of the paroxysmal discharges. What interested me most about these musings was the thought that the same neuronal networks that make it possible for arboreal primates to leap through physical space might be the same circuits that make it possible for human primates to throw themselves mentally into the dark, empty inner space conjured up by the practice of deep meditation or "empty-mind" prayer vigils. Perhaps the phrase, "leap of faith," has a literal biological meaning in addition to its metaphorical religious meaning.

Auto-Suggestion Provokes a Recurrence of Symptoms

About two months after my hiking trip in the Arizona mountains, the seizure-related symptoms were activated spontaneously by merely thinking about what had happened. This reaction struck me as particularly unsettling because it challenged my sense of still being in control of events. It was the Fourth of July holiday, but I had to stay at home and work to meet some writing deadlines. My wife had taken our children with her to visit her parents, so I was spending a lot of time alone. One morning on my customary walk this thought popped into my mind: "Nothing has happened with the light visions for some time now. I wonder if that's all over now?" It was nothing more than a fleeting thought immediately supplanted by other more practical concerns, but despite the brevity and apparent casualness, this thought must have continued to cause reverberations at some subliminal level of consciousness, because that night when I went to bed, the faint, barely-perceptible smudge of white phosphene that I'd seen for a few nights after the seizure now reappeared after weeks of having been absent. I looked at it out of surprise, and this was enough to trigger the expansion that immersed me once again in a white fog. The seizure-related symptoms also reappeared. Was it just a coincidence that this happened the same day that I had the fleeting thought? Was some kind of auto-suggestion involved? What was the significance of this resurgence of the seizure-related symptoms and their portent for the future? It was disconcerting to think that perhaps I was only fooling myself that these events were subject to my control and had been put aside long ago. I told my psychotherapist I was ready to see a neurologist.

The Neurological Exam

When I met the neurologist, I handed him a page of notes about my experiences. Not wishing to leave out any details that might turn out to be important, I'd included a description of the erotic response caused by staring at the setting sun. He read for a minute or so without comment, then began the clinical examination. The exam turned out to be uneventful, as I had expected it would be, but when it was over the neurologist returned to my notes and seemed quite interested in them. He asked me if I'd prepared other written materials about these experiences—diaries, notebooks, and the like—and indeed I had, knowing that someday I'd want to write up about these strange events, and of course that's what writers do, so my having brought in a set of notes didn't seem that unusual to me. I asked him why he was asking about my note-taking, and he told me that some researchers had proposed that there is a distinctive cluster of behavioral and emotional changes that occurs so often in patients diagnosed with temporal lobe epilepsy that the presence of those symptoms should be regarded as a sign that some kind of epileptiform process might be taking place in the temporal lobes even in patients who do not have overt seizures nor any EEG evidence of occult epileptic activity. One of the symptoms in this "interictal behavioral syndrome" is *hypergraphia*, an urge to write that is out-of-character, compulsive, and can't be explained by the patient's profession (or by some other obvious reason). Other symptoms in the interictal behavioral syndrome include *hyperreligiosity*, which refers to a dramatic deepening of interest in religious or philosophical issues; an *enhanced sense of personal destiny*, which refers to the person's belief that he or she has been entrusted with a important mission; a dramatic and unexplained change in sexual behavior which can manifest as a loss of libido (*hyposexuality*), an increase in libido (*hypersexuality*), or as a shift to some bizarre expression of sexuality; and, finally, the symptom of *circumstantiality*, which refers to a style of writing or talking that gets lost in details that a normal person would deem insignificant, as in the saying, "He can't see the forest for the trees." Often the symptoms of hypergraphia, hyperreligiosity, and circumstantiality are combined—for example, an illiterate taxi driver might feel called by destiny to teach himself to write a single phrase praising God and to record that single phrase over and over again, accumulating a large number of voluminous notebooks. Now I could see why the neurologist might be interested in my note-taking, and he would obviously consider the content of my notes to also be relevant.

The neurologist didn't say that an interictal behavior syndrome might be a factor in my case, but he didn't need to be explicit—clearly he was entertaining the possibility. His comments riveted my attention; I was fascinated, not only as a patient but also as a medical writer, and I wanted to find out everything I could about this so-called interictal behavior syndrome as fast as possible. As soon as I left the neurologist's office, I went to the regional medical library to begin tracking down whatever articles I could find on the subject.

What I learned was this: in the 1960s an eminent neurologist named Norman Geschwind proposed that physicians might assign patients a provisional diagnosis of temporal lobe epilepsy even in the absence of positive EEG findings if they (or their friends or family) reported the kinds of behavioral changes that formed this syndrome [Geschwind, 1961, 1983; Waxman and Geschwind, 1975]. Tests were designed to help clinicians make this determination [Bear and Fideo, 1977; Bear, 1979, 1986]. Soon other researchers began to challenge this hypothesis, pointing out that while it was true that this cluster of symptoms often appeared in patients with temporolimbic epilepsy, it was also the case that many of the *same* symptoms appeared in patients with *other* kinds of psychiatric and neurological problems, a lack of specificity that ruled out using the concept of an interictal behavioral syndrome to justify a diagnosis of temporal lobe epilepsy in the absence of EEG documentation [Rodin and Schmaltz, 1984; Sorensen and Bolwig, 1987]. This debate about whether or not there is an interictal behavioral syndrome (sometimes called the "Geschwind syndrome") associated specifically with temporal lobe epilepsy still surfaces occasionally in the medical literature. In a survey of medical literature on the behavioral and emotional changes associated with temporal lobe epilepsy, Benson [1991] testifies that, based on his own clinical experiences as a neurologist, the concept of an interictal behavioral syndrome is useful in clinical practice:

> Use of this term offers a distinct advantage. The Geschwind syndrome correctly refers to a final, phenomenologically specific behavior pattern; by contrast, the term 'epileptic personality disorder' has a far more general connotation, suggesting that behavioral problems exist in many epileptic patients; this consideration is unacceptable (p. 412).

Similarly, Tisher et al. [1993] point out it is clinically useful to have a theoretical concept like the interictal behavior syndrome that links specific symptom-clusters with the malfunctions of specific temporal lobe mechanisms and helps physicians order the perplexing diversity of symptoms presented by patients with temporal lobe epilepsy:

> In contrast to the episodic, time-limited symptoms associated with simple partial seizures, a pervasive and persistent alteration in behavior . . . may result from chronic discharges within the temporolimbic structures. In seeking mechanisms to account for the interictal behavior syndrome of temporolimbic epilepsy, we draw on the well-documented role of the primate amygdaloid complex in associating sensory percepts with biological drives such as sexuality, aggression, defense, and social bonding. We have proposed that *chronic temporolimbic discharges produce adventitious sensory-limbic associations, resulting in a suffusion of experience with enhanced emotional coloration.* / The behavioral consequences of this progressive neuro-psychological process may reflect the location of the epileptic focus, its projection pathways, or mixed neurobiologic and psychosocial influences on personality. Such variables may determine whether deepening reli-

gious beliefs, moral deliberation, animated writing, or a craving for interpersonal attachment dominates the clinical picture (p. 227; emphasis added).

None of the commentators participating in the debate disputes the basic observation that this cluster of symptoms is often seen in patients who are diagnosed with temporal lobe epilepsy, even if some of those same symptoms are also presented by patients with other kinds of problems. Fortunately, it is not necessary to resolve this debate about the clinical specificity of the interictal behavior syndrome to figure out why the neurologist suspected that it might be relevant in his management of my case. I'd presented him with a set of notes that formed part of a larger corpus of writing (*hypergraphia*), but since I am a professional writer, it would have been the content of the writing and the experiences that would have attracted his attention: I had reported the ecstatic emotions accompanying the seizure and my awe at having been "visited" by mystical experiences similar to those described in religious texts. I couldn't help but wonder if there might be some special meaning hidden beneath the surface of these events. And then I said that I thought it was my obligation, as one of the few scientists to have experienced this kind of ecstatic seizure, to track down the causes of the event—once again, an enhanced sense of personal destiny. If I were the neurologist, I would have regarded these thoughts as bordering on *enhanced sense of personal destiny* with the potential to evolve over time into *hyperreligiosity*. I'd also described a bizarre episode in which I had a sexual response while seeing the sun set (*hypersexuality*). And then there were the observations that I did not tell the neurologist because I didn't notice them until after reading about the interictal behavioral syndrome. These symptoms might well be the product of my vulnerability to suggestion, but I think it's important to report them nonetheless.

One change I noticed after having read about the interictal behavioral syndrome and having combed through the autobiographies of several mystics who'd described their visionary experiences was that my emotional reactions to other people seemed to have undergone a paradoxical change: I'd become more interested in the aesthetic attributes of the individuals I encountered and their significance as examples of abstract philosophical qualifies—more interested in them as embodiments of the "Meaningfulness of All Life" and the "Beauty of All Humans" than in the normal social exchange. I first noticed this on my morning walks when I'd encounter one of the many attractive women who lived in our neighborhood: whereas before when we'd meet I would typically notice some faint stirrings of sexual attraction (which I naturally kept to myself), I now realized that I was no longer getting this reaction; instead, while we chatted amicably, I was preoccupied by some detail in the woman's face—by subtle fluctuations that were sweeping across the face like clouds swirling overhead in a high wind. I recognized that this de-sexualized reaction to women could qualify as *hyposexuality*, and once I recognized this, it was amusing to find myself distracted in this way. I remember thinking that, contrary to common supposition, it would not be all that difficult to be a chaste, celibate saint if you were able to induce temporal lobe seizures at will; the onset of hyposexuality would make it easy to avoid entanglement in the kinds of sexual improprieties that often enmesh those who put themselves forward as spiritual authorities. This experience of detachment did not last very long—probably no more than a few weeks. I would be inclined to regard what I've just said about having an abstract, aesthetic reaction to people as fanciful were it not for the fact that a similar abstracting and aestheticizing reaction intruded into my attitude toward my wife and my three daughters: for a few weeks after the seizure, I felt noticeably detached from the deep emotional bonds that I have always shared with these loved ones. Like the other people I met in the street, they'd become representatives of Beauty and The Meaningfulness of All Life. This odd sense of emotional detachment did not persist for very long, and I was relieved when I noticed that the special emotional attachment to my wife and children had returned.

Perhaps the most telling behavioral change in the wake of the ecstatic seizure was that I completely abandoned the research and writing project I had been working on at the time—a book on the cumulative psychological effects of working on computers and living in computer-driven environments—and from then on I devoted my efforts to discovering how it could be possible for an apparently normal human being to trigger mystical ecstasies by practicing meditation. Based on this change and the others that I've cited here, I conclude that I did experience a relatively weak and transient version of an interictal behavioral syndrome. If this is indeed the case, the evidence would support the hypothesis that my meditation-induced, phosphene-mediated seizure originated in the temporolimbic region.

The EEG Test

A week later after initial visit with the neurologist I returned to his office to take an EEG test. It had been almost four months since the seizure. I sat in a comfortable chair and the EEG technician attached the standard 10-20 array of electrodes to my scalp. He told me to sit quietly and relax for an hour. I would like to say that I followed his instructions for the entire session, but I confess that I had my own agenda—I wanted to know what happened when I engaged in my usual meditation behaviors, and I wanted to show the neurologist what happened so that he could assess if there was any reason for concern. I decided to comply with the technician's instructions for the first half-hour, then shift to meditation during the second half. In retrospect, I realize that this was not a wise decision, just as it had been unwise for me to prolong the paroxysmal ecstasy when it occurred, but I thought it was highly unlikely that there would be any evidence of epileptiform process in this test, and that, if I were to follow directions, I would not learn anything about what happened while I induced phosphene images. When I began to meditate about halfway through the test, I heard the EEG tracer pins registering brainwave amplitudes on the scroll of paper suddenly begin to scratch loudly, a sign that the pins had begun to oscillate back and forth much more vigorously than before. These loud scratching sounds continued as long as I kept fixating on the visual field and watching the green light-rings and blue nebulae float into consciousness. When the technician returned, he glanced at the EEG tracings and remarked that "there might be something here" but didn't elaborate. He moved me in front of another machine for the photostimulation test where the subject is forced to stare at a bright strobe light flashing at frequencies known to trigger paroxysmal discharges in most patients with photosensitive epilepsy. Watching this brilliant strobe immediately transported me back into the middle of the ecstatic seizure at its peak intensity: bright flashes filled my visual field and triggered the full comple-ment of paroxysmal sensorimotor symptoms. The main difference between the photostimulation and my ecstatic seizure was that the strobe used in the text evoked an unpleasant, "driven" quality, a feeling that I was being forcibly "turned on" by an external stimulus without regard to whether or not this was an experience I wanted. Also, the test did not evoke the psychic symptoms that had accompanied the ecstatic seizure—there was no sense of exhilaration, no euphoria, no awe, and no reason to fear losing oneself in the experience with the technician was observ-ing nearby. When the strobe was turned off, the visual flashes and sensorimotor symptoms ceased immediately, demonstrating that the paroxysmal responses were stimulus-bound and did not trigger the kind of after-discharges that often occur when a patient has photosensitive epilepsy.

I looked forward to hearing the neurologist's assessment of the test results, but I never got a chance to talk to him in person; instead, he sent his report to my psychotherapist who then told me that the test results were negative, that there was no indication of epileptiform activity. The psychotherapist didn't elaborate, and I didn't pursue the matter, although I suspected that there was more to the test than the physicians were sharing with me. I concluded that the two of them must have discussed my case and must have agreed that it would be better to be vague and non-committal about the outcome, given that I was already in a therapeutic relationship and could be closely watched. And then I had my own reasons for not wanting to press the matter—I didn't want to admit that I ignored the instructions during the last half of the EEG test, and I didn't want to seem disappointed at hav-ing received a favorable report, which, after all, was the best possible outcome.

Years later while I was researching this book I re-established contact with the neurologist and asked him if he would send me a copy of my original EEG re-cords. Unfortunately the original tracings were not available because they'd been committed long ago to storage boxes that had migrated from one storage site to another and that now were located in an unknown location. The neurologist had saved a series of computer-generated Polaroid photos that showed the basic topolo-gies of the brainwave patterns, and these he was willing to share. We'll inspect copies of those photos in the neurological analysis.

Neurological Analysis

Origins of the Ictal Symptoms

Lightning-Like Flashes and Short-Circuit Sounds

When the sheet-lightning flashes erupted, the flashes appeared at irregular, unpredictable intervals and they seemed to alternate between the right and left sides of the visual field. This bursting pattern is consistent with the onset of paroxysmal "population discharges" of dentate gyrus granule cells: discharges in the right and left dentate gyrus occur independently of one another, and there is always a hyperpolarization of granule cell membranes after each paroxysmal population discharge which requires at least a half-second before the discharged cells recover the capacity to fire again [Deadwyler et al., 1975, pp. 176-7]. The observation that the white flashes appeared in both sides of the visual field indicates that the paroxysmal discharges that were initiated by three granule cells in the uncal extension of the dentate gyrus in the left hippocampus must have propagated contralaterally and engulfed the dentate gyrus in the right hippocampus in ictal activity. In the previous chapter I noted that each of the three transformations of the ray images occurred at one-second intervals and that the third image of the "wilted" rays then remained in place for an additional 12 to 15 seconds. The entire sequence lasted no longer than 15 to 18 seconds, a duration is consistent with research showing that the mean time required for the paroxysmal discharge of hippocampal neurons to propagate to the contralateral hippocampus, triggering a bilateral mesotemporal seizure, is 8.7 seconds with a range that varies from 1 second to 51 seconds [Spencer and Spencer, 1994].

The vision of lightning-like flashes was accompanied by loud crackling and sizzling sounds reminiscent of an electrical circuit "shorting out." A similar combination of visual and auditory symptoms was reported in a study by Ketter et al. [1996] where the researchers injected procaine in the anterior limbic regions of 32 volunteer subjects to see what developed once the neuron assemblies became hyperexcitable. *More than a quarter of the subjects (9/32 = 28%) reported seeing "unformed visual hallucinations (lights or colors reported as intense or very intense)," and almost all of the subjects (29/32 = 90%) reported hearing auditory hallucinations described as "unformed buzzing, ringing, or electronic sounds."*

Paroxysmal Sensorimotor Symptoms

The ecstatic seizure caused muscle tremors in my toes, legs, arms, fingers, face, and in the bulbospongiosus muscle in the perineal region. These widely dispersed tremors are consistent with cortical reflex myoclonus, a symptom often associated with partial seizures [Hallet, 1997]. The spread of paroxysmal activity from the hippocampus to the amygdala could eventually trigger an outbreak of cortical reflex myoclonus if the paroxysmal activity spread from the amygdala to the anterior nuclei of the thalamus, then on to the cingulate cortex, then on to the sensorimotor cortices [Amaral et al., 1992].

I don't know how to explain the perception that a "current of energy" was flowing up from the lower extremities into the trunk toward the crown of the head, even though many Tantric teachers have described such an experience ("the rising of kundalini"). I can think of two possible explanations for this perception, both of which involve some degree of imaginative reconstruction of the actual physiological event: (1) there might be a veridical perception of a "current," but, if so, it is probably limited to the lower extremities, arms, and trunk, so that the perception of a continuous "current" rising all the way to the top of the head is a misreading of the actual situation; or, (2) there might be no directional "current" at all but only the subject's imaginative interpretation that so many tremors occurring contemporaneously must somehow be linked. My best guess is that this sensation of a "current of energy" is a proprioceptive awareness that waves of paroxysmal excitation generated in the hippocampus are coursing through the sensorimotor nuclei of the thalamus—the VPL and the VPM—where the relay-neurons are organized in somatotopic patterns [Kahle et al., 1978]. These thalamic neurons project to target cells in the sensory and motor cortices which are also organized in somatotopic patterns [Penfield and Jasper, 1954]. The somatotopic organizations of the sensorimotor nuclei of the thalamus and the sensorimotors cortices are often represented by drawings of an "homunculus" where small icons representing body parts are arrayed along a crescent arc that represents the curve of the anatomical structure. At first I thought it might be possible that a wave of seizure-driven excitation would flow through the sensorimotor nuclei in a continuous stream which would stimulate the neuronal circuits that subserve the toes and legs first and then the regions subserving the trunk, arms, fingers, and face. In this view, the signals relayed from the thalamic nuclei to the sensorimotor cortices would then activate a similar flow there, so that the subject would perceive some continuity underlying the myriad muscle tremors. Then I noticed that there is a major problem with this hypothesis: the somatotopic patterns in the sensorimotor cortices are not aligned in a continuous pattern beginning with the lowest extremities and ascending up the body to the crown of the head. The lower extremities are represented first, occupying the apex of the cortical mantle, and as one moves in a lateral direction along the crescent arc, the trunk, then the mid-body, then the shoulders are represented, *but this ascending progression stops at the shoulders*; as one continues to trace along the surface of the cortical mantle in a lateral direction, moving down toward the base of the brain, the body parts are aligned in *descending* order: the crown and forehead is represented next, then the eyes and face (which are situated farther down the curve), and the lips, tongue, and chin are located even lower down. Therefore, even if a wave of seizure-driven excitation were to move through the sensorimotor nuclei of the thalamus in a continuous direction, this flow could only generate the prioperception of an *ascending* "current" in the lower extremities, the trunk, and the arms and fingers, then, if the wave of excitation were to keep on moving in the same lateral direction, it would begin to generate the prioperception of a "current" *descending* from the top of the head to the eyes and face and on to the lips and tongue. This discontinuity suggests that the perception of a sensorimotor "current" ascending all the way from the toes to the crown of the head must involve some degree of confabulation by subjects who are trying to make sense of their having so many tremors occurring simultaneously.

The Psychic Symptoms of Ecstasy

The paroxysm produced feelings of exhilaration and of awe mixed with fear. The fear component, an experience often reported by patients with temporal lobe epilepsy, is consistent with paroxysmal activity having spread from the hippocampus to the amygdala [Buzsáki et al., 1995; Ketter et al., 1996; Rauch et al., 1996]. Another psychic symptom was the orgasmic sensation diffused throughout the body, not focused in the genitals. This sensation is consistent with the spread of high amplitude paroxysmal activity from the hippocampus to the septum which emits high-amplitude discharges during normal sexual orgasm [Stevens et al., 1969; Heath, 1972; Liporace and Sperling, 1997].

After the seizure, I felt euphoric for about an hour. Euphoria is only rarely reported as a symptom of epileptic seizures [Fish, 1997]; there are, however, a few accounts. In the procaine injection study by Ketter et al. [1996] that I mentioned earlier—the same study where subjects saw phosphenes and heard phantom sounds—a quarter of the volunteer subjects reported feelings of euphoria (9/32, or 28%). Endogenous opoids probably play an important role in generating post-seizure euphoria. Limbic seizures release endogenous opoids which can persist at enhanced levels for up to two weeks [Bausch and Chavkin, 1997; Engel and Rocha, 1992]. Endogenous opoids are intimately involved in neural transmission and synaptic reorganization in the hippocampus [Simmons and Chavkin, 1996]. When seizures interfere with the normal regulation of these opoids, this often causes an imbalance in the normal process of homeostasis and unpleasant rebound effects:

> The activity-induced plasticity associated with recurrent temporal lobe seizures, therefore, should result in changes in opoid function that predispose to withdrawal phenomena. Limbic seizures induce enhanced enkephalin synthesis lasting for up to 2 weeks. . . . Patients with temporal lobe epilepsy demonstrate enhanced mu [opiate] receptor binding in the neocortex of the epileptogenic temporal lobe on PET. . . . if animals or patients become dependent on enhanced endogenous opiate activity as a result of seizures, and also have up-regulation of mu receptors, then

severe withdrawal effects, such as . . . depression in humans, might be expected when seizures do not recur frequency [Engel and Rocha, 1992, p. 341].

Anyone familiar with the literature of religious mysticism will recognize the potential relevance of a rebound effect in the regulation of endogenous opoids for explaining the complaints one often reads in the autobiographies of religious mystics. John of the Cross, a famous Spanish mystic of the 16th Century, often complained that his ecstatic raptures of "fire-like light" were too few and too far between, and he described the long fallow periods that often occurred between ecstasies as his "dark night of the soul" [John of the Cross, 1973]. The modern Hindu mystic, Gopi Krishna, cited a similar complaint [Krishna, 1967].

The medical literature contains a number of case studies of patients who experience "ecstatic auras." In epileptology the word, "aura," is used to refer to simple partial seizures in which the patient retains conscious awareness of what's happening. Auras often occur as harbingers of more severe seizures in which consciousness is significantly impaired or lost altogether. The case studies of ecstatic auras are particularly important for our investigation and warrant an extended review, which I present in Chapter 10, "What Kind of Seizure Is It?"

The EEG Test Results

In the EEG test administered about four months after the ecstatic seizure, I was monitored for an hour by a routine 10-20 array of scalp electrodes and also given a photostimulation test. The EEG machine used in my test was not the most recent model even in 1989 when the test was administered, which means the topological maps of brainwave frequencies are not as legible as the more recent vintages used in the studies of experienced meditators that we'll examine in the next chapter. My test results are preserved in small (3x3) Polaroid photos with very low resolutions which makes them hard to read even in the originals, a problem exasercbated by my having to confine myself to grayscale images in this book. Given these constraints, I thought it best to convert the original photos into the digitalized drawings that are presented in Figure 31.

Panel A in Figure 31 compares the two brainmaps that summarize the "highest" and "second highest" brainwave frequency distributions that occurred during the EEG test. The highest and second highest brainwave distributions are virtually mirror-images of one another: when low-alpha and theta frequencies were predominant in one hemisphere, beta activity was predominant in the contralateral hemisphere. A predominance of low-alpha and theta frequencies is a pattern typically reported in EEG studies involving subjects who are still in the early stages of meditation (see Chapter 9, "Empirical Studies of Meditators"). There is significantly more beta activity in my EEG than one would normally expect to find while someone is meditating. I attribute this anomaly to the fact that I was not meditating during half of the session and also to my practice of engaging in "participant observation" where I split off a portion of conscious awareness in order to be able to critically examine and evaluate the fluctuations of mental phenomena at the same time that I'm observing them—a skill that obviously played an important role by enabling the observations I've described in this book.

Panel B shows the average power spectra (PS) for delta frequencies. Power spectra are displayed as Z-scores which indicate the number of standard deviations (SDs) above or below normal. My delta band Z-score was abnormally high: in the small white oval positioned over the right temporo-parietal region the delta activity reached 5 SDs above normal; in the jagged band surrounding that oval, the delta activity reached 7 SDs above normal; and over the rest of the cortical mantle the Z-score rose above the maximum recording range of the EEG machine to register as "more than 7 SDs above normal." Puzzled by this unexpected surge of delta activity, I wrote the manufacturers of the machine to ask their advice in interpreting these Z-scores. Dr. Pierre Le Bars, who was at that time the physician-advisor and executive vice president at the HZI Research Center, sent me this note:

Figure 31. The EEG test results. A. The highest and the second-highest distributions of brainwave frequencies recorded during my EEG test. This test was conducted about 4 months after the ecstatic seizure. The highest frequency distribution is a predominance of low-frequency theta and alpha waves over the *right* hemisphere with a preservation of beta activity (typical of waking consciousness) in the left hemisphere. The second-highest distribution of brainwave frequencies is a mirror-image of the highest: the alpha/theta activity predominates in the *left* hemisphere while the beta activity shifts to the right hemisphere. These brainwave frequency distributions are typical of those reported in studies of meditators who are in the earlier stages of meditation, except that beta activity is more prominent than would be expected. The beta activity is most likely the result of my having meditated for only half of the session and also may be an artifact of my ability to split off a portion of consciousness to engage in "participant observation." B. The EEG power spectra for delta band activity. The Z-score summarizes delta activity in terms of the number of standard deviations (SDs) above or below normal. In my reading, the delta band Z-score is highly abnormal: in the small, white oval shape positioned over the right temporo-parietal region there is a surge of delta activity rising to 5 SDs above normal; in the jagged band that surrounds the oval, delta activity soars 7 SDs above normal; and over the rest of the cortical mantle the delta activity rises above the maximum recording range of the EEG machine, registering at "over 7 SDs." Note the "earmuff-like" pattern of the small oval shape positioned over the temporo-parietal region where delta activity reaches 5 SDs above normal. This distinctive earmuff pattern appears frequency in the EEGs of expert meditators concurrent with their report of "peak experiences." The presence of high-amplitude activity centered around the vertex of the skull to form a "table-top" is another pattern frequently observed in expert meditators, but here the EEG topology is not detailed enough to reveal if this pattern is present or not. C. The original Polaroid photo presenting the computer-generated results of my EEG test compared with averages from an age-adjusted database. While the low-resolution image is barely legible, it is possible to make out that, in my case, there are abnormal surges in delta band activity in almost all electrodes.

A The Highest & 2nd-Highest EEG Frequencies

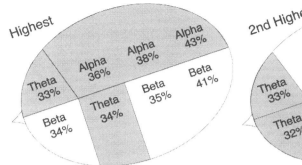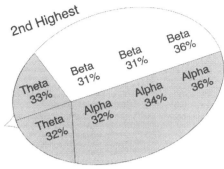

B EEG Power Spectra

Delta Activity Z-Score
(Number of Standard Deviations
Above Normal)

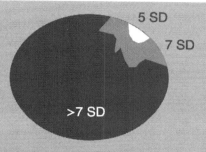

C Delta Activity Above Age-Adjusted Norms

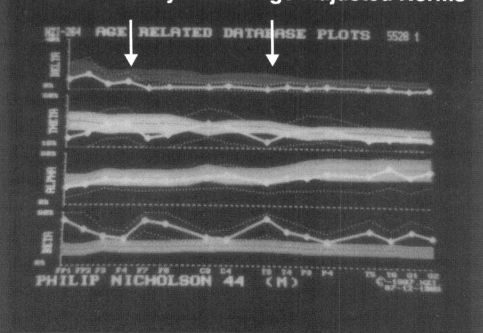

In this type of printout, the system used a Z-score scale where red [the color of the jagged band in the original photo - PN] and black [the color of rest of the cortical mantle] are standard deviations of 7 and above 7, respectively. In the case presented in your picture, the color scale needs explanation as follows: delta—deviation from age-matched norms is highly significant with more than a 7 standard deviation increase, while, on the other end, if we consider alpha, a statistically significant decrease (blue-white) is observed in almost all brain areas [Le Bars, 1996, personal communication].

What is the significance of having so much high-amplitude delta activity in the EEG? Is this a common occurrence? Does this same anomaly appear in the EEG studies of experienced meditators published in the medical literature? If so, why aren't there more comments that point out this phenomenon and assess its potential significance? As my investigation continued, the importance of this question became increasingly evident and the unanimous disregard of this subject by prominent researchers working in the field seemed more and more puzzling.

Excess Excitability and Compromised Inhibition

The observation that sensorimotor and emotional symptoms similar to those I experienced during the seizure could later be evoked by exposure to certain specific kinds of visual stimuli suggests that there must have been some excitotoxic damage to inhibitory circuits that would normally prevent or dampen these particular responses. It seems likely that the compromised inhibitory circuits would be located where the paroxysmal discharges first broke out—in the uncal region of the left hippocampus, and, to be more specific, in the neurons that inhibit the granule cells located in the uncal extension of the dentate gyrus, the Ligature of Giacomini. This points to hilar (CA3/CA4) neurons that are situated immediately adjacent to the uncal extension of the dentate gyrus (DG'), a site which is particularly interesting because it is where axons of the ventral hippocampal commissure projecting from the contralateral hippocampus would terminate if humans still have a functioning remnant of the VHC. Suppose, then, that a few inhibitory neurons were damaged in the initial outbreak of paroxysmal discharges—for example, assume that the inhibitory neurons controlling three contiguous granule cells were damaged, since this is the minimum number of granule cells needed to produce the phosphene image of the trident rays according to the computer modeling scenario we discussed earlier in this chapter. When these damaged neurons are unable to carry out their normal function of modulating the excitability of those three granule cells, this disinhibition will allow more exitatory signals to pass through the dentate gyrus than would formerly (and normally) have been allowed. Damage to inhibitory interneurons in the hippocampus is a common finding in patients who suffer from recurring mesotemporal seizures [Lothman, 1997; Williamson et al., 1999], and even a single epileptiform afterdischarge can cause some structural impairment to those circuits [Horvath et al., 1990; Mello and Covolan, 1996]. This disinhibition and the effects of the excess excitation thus released might explain why, after the seizure, I continued to see a residual glow of white phosphene in the upper right quadrant of the visual field where I saw the "explosive" phosphene events during the seizure onset. It might also explain why I experienced a recurrence of the seizure-related sensorimotor symptoms when I looking at a scene where bright sunlight was reflecting off the surface of a large lake or snowfield.

It is more difficult to explain why similar symptoms of excess excitability would appear when I looked at scenes where there was a strong element of visuo-vestibular conflict. Some studies in monkeys provide interesting clues about the effects of visuo-vestibular conflict not only in the vestibular nucleus but also in the hippocampus. Baloh and Honrubin [1990] implanted monkeys with depth-electrodes and placed them in situations where their visual cues about self-motion conflicted with their vestibular cues, a mismatch that caused neurons in the vestibular nucleus to fire at maximal rates, and, similarly, Vibert et al. [1997] found that other neurons in the monkey vestibular nucleus responded only when the visual and vestibular cues matched. These findings show that some aspects of visual and vestibular information get integrated in the vestibular nucleus, but other studies show that hippocampal neurons also respond to visuo-vestibular conflict. Horii et al. [1994] induced vestibular conflict in rats by inserting a heat stimulus in one ear only; this challenge produced a significant increase in the release of acetylcholine in the hippocampus. This finding is corroborated by Vitte et al. [1996] who found that *a mismatch in vestibular signals activates the septohippocampal cholinergic system, a stimulus which evokes the release of acetylcholine in the uncal pole* (see Chapters 6 & 7). Research on the processing of spatial information also documents the participation of hippocampal neurons in the processing of signals encoding visuo-vestibular conflict. In primates the processing of information about spatial location has long been thought to take place exclusively in the retro-hippocampal cortices, not in the hippocampus proper [Aguirre et al., 1996], but there appears to be an important exception to this general rule: a study by O'Mara et al. [1994] found that *the processing of integrated visuo-vestibular information is processed, not in the retro-hippocampal cortices like other types of spatial information but in subfield CA3 of the hippocampus proper:*

> Some of the neurons of the hippocampus in this study were influenced by visual stimuli, and in particular by the movement (rotation/translation) of the walls of the testing chamber . . . . This was shown by the smaller responses some whole-body motion neurons showed when the visual field was occluded (60% of the sample tested with occlusion), and by the finding that some of these neurons responded when the testing chamber moved but the monkey was still. *Some neurons had direction-sensitive responses that were consistent with the hypothesis that they received appropriate direction-selective inputs from both vestibular and visual inputs* (p. 6520; emphasis added).

If a significant proportion of the processing of integrated visuo-vestibular information in primates takes place in subfield CA3 of the hippocampus, and if exposure to visuo-vestibular conflict triggers septohippocampal stimulation of the entire hippocampal pole, then it is reasonable to infer that visuo-vestibular conflict enhances neuron excitability in the uncal extension of subfield CA3—in the stratum oriens layer wrapped around the surface of the uncal pole, in the Ligature of Giacomini (the uncal extension of the dentate gyrus), and in the hilar (CA3/CA4) neurons which are sandwiched between. Humans are often exposed to visuo-vestibular conflict with no ill effects and usually the subject is not aware of the proprioceptive processes are activated to support an appropriate behavioral response, but, in the circumstances I've described, where a simple partial seizure damaged a small number of inhibitory neurons in the uncal extension of the dentate gyrus, the exposure to visuo-vestibular conflict and the consequent enhancement of neuron excitability in the uncal pole might cause the disinhibited granule cells to send more excitatory signals through the perforant path of the hippocampus, and, from there, into the retro-hippocampal temporolimbic cortices.

This hypothesis about visuo-vestibular conflict and the selective enhancement of neuron excitability in the uncal pole fits well with the "comparator" model of hippocampal function proposed by Vinogradova [2001]. We can combine the two hypotheses to arrive at a possible explanation for why I experienced a weak resurgence of seizure-related sensorimotor symptoms in response to scenes presenting strong visuo-vestibular conflict. In Vinogradova's view, hippocampal subfield CA3 contains many pre-existing neuron networks that have been forged by long-term potentiation. The function of these pre-existing neuron networks is to determine which afferent signal patterns do not match the patterns already embodied in pre-existing networks, where a mismatch would mean that these afferent signals are either new or otherwise attention-worthy. Neurons in CA3 normally fire at very high rates, but there is a brief suppression of this high firing rate upon the arrival of afferent signals, then a rapid return to the normal rate. If the afferent signals do not match the pre-existing networks, the initial suppression of firing rates is maintained just long enough to amplify those signals, thereby encoding them as novel or otherwise attention-worthy. The amplification and encoding occurs when the prolonged suppression of CA3 neurons inhibits the inhibitory effect the CA3 neurons would normally impose on target cells in CA1. Where the CA3 inhibition is lifted, CA1 neurons discharge more frequently, a differential firing rate that reinforces the signal patterns in which those neuron participate—and those amplified signal patterns become salient in the reciprocal temporo-ammonic circuits that maintain a record of the signals that were initially received by the entorhinal cortices and referred into the hippocampus for further processing. But suppose that, by contrast with this normal course of events, the structural integrity of the uncal extension of the dentate gyrus is slightly compromised because a small number of inhibitory neurons were damaged as a result of a temporolimbic seizure: in this circumstance, an exposure to visuo-vestibular conflict such as I've described might alter the normal CA3 processing of signals received from the dentate gyrus. This would create three effects that compete with one another. Most CA3 neurons would respond in normal ways, that is, they would undergo an initial suppression that would be sustained if there was no match between the afferent signals and the pre-existing neuron networks. But at the same time there would be a diffuse increase in neuron excitability throughout the uncal pole triggered by the exposure to visuo-vestibular conflict (and by attentive fixation, if that behavior happened to also be involved); this general increase in neuron excitability would affect neurons in subfield CA3 and also granule cells in the uncal extension of the dentate gyrus— and the enhancement of neuron excitability in these regions is likely to compete with the prolonged suppressions imposed on CA3 neurons when incoming signals do not match pre-existing networks. Finally, the excitotoxic damage to inhibitory neurons would allow a few granule cells to discharge more frequently than normal, a process potentiated by septohippocampal stimulation of acetylcholine release, and the effect of this excess excitation leaking into subfield CA3 would further exascerbate the hyperexcitability already present. If we infer that this stream of excess excitation is relayed through the hippocampus into the adjacent temporal cortices, then referred back to the midline thalamus and the on into the sensorimotor nuclei, this small amount of abnormal excitation might be enough to initiate unidirectional waves in that structure that eventually register in consciousness as the sensation of a "current" triggering muscle tremors throughout the body. If this were to occur, then behaviorally-relevant perceptions that would normally be amplified by the CA3-CA1 interaction as being novel or attention-worthy would be disrupted to some extent by competition with abnormal signals that are generated by the compromise of certain inhibitory circuits, signals that increase neuron activity in sensorimotor circuits to the point of establishing conscious awareness of prioperceptive processes that would normally remain subliminal.

9

EMPIRICAL STUDIES OF MEDITATORS

DOES A SLEEP RHYTHM THEORY EXPLAIN THE EXISTING DATA?

ELECTROENCEPHALOGRAPHIC STUDIES

Different Patterns in Expert and Novice Meditators

In EEG studies of meditation and hypnosis that use novices or student volunteers as subjects, the changes in brainwave frequencies typically evolve in a continuous direction: the beta activity associated with waking consciousness (≥ 13 Hz) gives way to a dominant pattern of "resting occipital alpha" with brainwave frequencies of about 8 Hz and wave amplitudes of about 20 microvolts (μV). If the meditative trance deepens, the 8 Hz activity gradually becomes intermixed with slower theta frequencies (4.5 to 7 Hz) [Corby et al., 1978; Steriade et al., 1993; Broughton and Hasan, 1995; Maquet et al., 1996, 1999; Lou et al., 1999; Tanaka et al., 1996, 2000]. This EEG pattern of mixed alpha and theta activity is similar to what is recorded during the drowsy transition from waking to the first episode of non-rapid-eye-movement sleep, a state conventionally designated "stage 1" NREMS. During stage 1, while the subject experiences a relaxed, drowsy consciousness, the brain has already initiated the processes that will eventually induce EEG-synchronized slow wave sleep: large numbers of neurons in the cerebral cortex have already begun to oscillate with a synchronous slow rhythm of less than one pulse per second (< 1 Hz). The cortical slow wave is referred back to the thalamus where it lowers the polarization of cell membranes toward the threshold value that triggers the RTN to begin firing spindle bursts, inaugurating "stage 2" NREMS. During stage 1, a person is relaxed and drowsy but is still aware of sensory signals, mental images, or thoughts that intrude into consciousness. In processing these conscious mental events, cortical cells desynchronize and those intermittent desynchronizations impede the progress toward a complete synchronization of cortical and thalamic networks that is established at the onset of stage 2. In studies of novice meditators and hypnotized volunteers, the EEG pattern of mixed alpha and theta waves characteristic of stage 1 NREMS is usually sustained for the duration of the session. Figure 32A, which is presented later in this chapter, shows a typical pattern from the study by Maquet et al. [1999]. It is not unusual for a few novice meditators in a study to actually fall asleep, in which case their EEG is not included in the calculation of the study's findings.

Compared to EEG studies of novice meditators and hynotized volunteers, the EEG studies of experienced meditators report more variation over the course of a typical meditation session. Initially there is a sudden increase in alpha band frequencies from a baseline of resting occipital alpha (8 Hz) to frequencies in the high-alpha (12 Hz) or low-beta range (13 - 14 Hz) [Anand et al., 1961; Kasamatsu and Hirai, 1966; Das and Gastaut, 1955]. Ths sudden increase occurs within the first minute of meditation [Kasamatsu et al., 1957; Travis and Wallace, 1999; Arambula et al., 2001] and establishes a coherent pattern across the cortical mantle [Travis and Wallace, 1999]. The next major shift occurs when high-alpha/low-beta activity begins to fragment and is replaced by slower frequencies—by theta waves (4 to 8 Hz) and even slower delta waves (0.5 to 4 Hz). Finally, in a surprisingly high number of experienced meditators the slow, theta/delta pattern is suddenly and dramatically disrupted as wave amplitudes suddenly double from the 20 µV associated with the baseline state of "resting occipital alpha" to 40 to 50 µV or even as high as 100 or 150 µV [e.g., for 40 to 50 µV, see Das and Gastaut, 1955; Travis and Wallace, 1999; for 100 to 150 µV, see Kasamatsu et al., 1957; Anand et al., 1961; Corby et al., 1978; Fahrion et al., 1992; Wilson, 1994]. The high-amplitude

---

Figure 32. Comparisons of EEG changes in six studies of meditators. Chart A in the upper left corner shows the pattern of brainwave changes reported in an EEG study of novice meditators by Maquet et al. [1999], a pattern typical of the progression from a state of resting occipital alpha to a persistent mix of alpha and theta activity similar to that associated with stage 1 NREMS, the relaxed, drowsy, "hypnagogic" state. By contrast, all of the remaining charts show the patterns of brainwave changes reported in some studies of expert meditators that were among the earliest to be reported in the medical literature. These charts show the length of time that elapsed between the start of the meditation session and the sudden outbreak of high-amplitude surges, and they identify the frequency bands in which the surges occurred. Note that in two studies [Anand et al., 1961; Fahrion et al., 1992] the shift to high-amplitude surges occurs relatively soon after the meditation begins—at "Time 1" (T1)—while in three other studies [Das and Gastaut, 1955; Corby et al., 1978; Wilson, 1994] the surges erupt relatively late in the meditation session (T3).

Time to Onset of High-Amplitude Surges

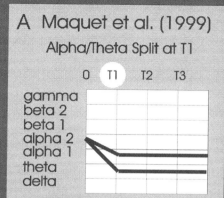

A   Maquet et al. (1999)
Alpha/Theta Split at T1

| | 0 | T1 | T2 | T3 |

gamma
beta 2
beta 1
alpha 2
alpha 1
theta
delta

D   Corby et al. (1978)
High-Alpha/Theta Split at T3

| | 0 | T1 | T2 | T3 |

gamma
beta 2
beta 1
alpha 2
alpha 1
theta
delta

B   Das & Gastaut (1955)
High-Amplitude Beta at T3

| | 0 | T1 | T2 | T3 |

beta 2
beta 1
alpha 2
alpha 1
theta
delta

E   Fahrion et al. (1992)
Alpha/Theta/Gamma Split at T1

| | 0 | T1 | T2 | T3 |

gamma
beta 2
beta 1
alpha 2
alpha 1
theta
delta

C   Anand et al. (1961)
High-Amplitude Alpha at T1

| | 0 | T1 | T2 | T3 |

beta 2
beta 1
alpha 2
alpha 1
theta
delta

F   Wilson (1994)
Theta/Gamma Split at T3

| | 0 | T1 | T2 | T3 |

gamma
beta 2
beta 1
alpha 2
alpha 1
theta
delta

KEY

━━━ Normal Amplitude (20 μV)   ■ High Amplitude (> 50 μV) surges can erupt simultaneously in more than one frequency band and the time of onset varies (see Figure 32B-F). Several studies report that once these high-amplitude surges begin the EEG pattern cannot be disrupted by challenging the meditators with strong sensory stimuli known to disrupt "resting occipital alpha," such as ordering them to open their eyes and look around, or setting off loud noises, or submerging their hands in freezing water [e.g., Katsumatsu et al., 1957; Anand et al., 1961; Kasamatsu and Hirai, 1966].

If meditative states are generated by an activation of slow wave sleep rhythms, as I've proposed, then we should be able to find evidence of slow wave sleep rhythms in the EEGs of experienced meditators. The first question, then, is can we explain the sudden increase of coherent alpha-band frequencies in the first minute of meditation as artifacts of the onset of RTN spindle bursts normally associated with stage 2 NREMS?

Stage 2 Sleep Rhythms and Cortical Alpha

At onset of stage 2 NREMS, the thalamic reticular nucleus (RTN) begins firing spindle-bursts at a rate of one every three to ten seconds (0.3 to 0.1 Hz). These spike-bursts wax and wane over an interval of 1.5 to 2 seconds [Steriade and McCarley, 1990, pp. 9, 208-209]. Only 3 to 7 spindle bursts are required, on average, to push the polarization of thalamic cell membranes down to a threshold level where the RTN stops firing spindle bursts, making the way for the onset of corticothalamic delta activity that characterizes stage 3 NREMS [Uchida et al., 1994].

In the scalp EEG, thalamic sleep spindles and cortical alpha waves generate patterns that are similar in two respects: the frequencies of thalamic spindle bursts range from 7 to 14 Hz while the frequencies of cortical alpha waves range from 8 to 12 Hz [Steriade and McCarley, 1990]. Also, cortical alpha waves wax and wane in a manner similar to sleep spindles. These similarities make it difficult to distinguish spindle waves and alpha waves when they appear in the scalp EEG [Corsi-Cabrera et al., 2000], but the importance of making that distinction is emphasized by Steriade and McCarley [1990] in their review of research on brainstem mechanisms and slow wave sleep:

> Although some authors regard [alpha] waves (8-12 Hz) as embryos or congeners of spindles, probably because of the overlapping frequencies of these two rhythms, [alpha] and spindle waves must be dissociated because of their quite different grouping, cortical distribution, but especially because of their quite different behavioral connotations. Indeed, spindles are characteristically associated with blockage of information transfer through the thalamus and unconsciousness . . . whereas the incidence and amplitude of occipital [alpha] waves may increase during some attentional tasks (Cruetzfeldt et al., 1969; Ray and Cole, 1985). Besides, *spindles are transmitted over the cortex by thalamocortical neurons, whereas [alpha] waves are thought to propagate mainly through surface-parallel intracortical connections* (Lopes da Silva et al., 1980; Lopes da Silva, 1987) [Steriade and McCarley, Ibid., p. 209-210; emphasis added].

If the alpha waves registering in the scalp EEGs of experienced meditators are generated by the reverberation of neuron discharges in the excitatory networks of locally-connected, surface-parallel neurons, as Steriade and McCarley suggest, then it would seem likely that these same locally-connected, surface-parallel neuron networks will also react to the receipt of spindle waves. In order for the spindle waves with frequencies ranging from 7 to 14 Hz to generate high-alpha (12 Hz) and low-beta (13 to 14 Hz) frequencies in the scalp EEG, as reported in the studies cited above, the initial frequencies of spindle waves would have to be amplified by 4 to 6 Hz before they register in the scalp EEG. Is it reasonable to suppose that this amount of intracortical amplification does occur? What neural mechanisms would be able to produce this effect?

An anatomical study that compared the number of excitatory circuits that project from the LGN to the primary visual cortex with the number of excitatory circuits embedded in networks of locally-connected cortical cells found that there are nine times as many excitatory circuits in the intracortical networks as there are in the LGN [Suarez et al.. 1995] The authors of that study conclude that "geniculate input provides only a minor fraction of the excitatory input, the majority originating in neighboring and recurrently connected cortical cells." When the excitability of the neurons in intracortical networks became "slightly higher" than normal, Suarez et al. observed a "hysteretic" firing mode in which the intracortical networks continued to amplify the signals it already received from the LGN even after the LGN stopped sending signals. The intracortical excitatory circuits are capable of amplifying relatively weak signals arriving from subcortical sources [Churchland et al., 1994], and recent studies have demonstrated that *RTN-generated spindle waves do in fact receive intracortical amplification and that, moreover, their receipt in the primary visual cortices often triggers an "hysteretic firing mode:"*

> Neuronal plasticity during and following natural sleep spindles or their experimental model, augmenting responses (Morrisey and Dempsey), has recently been studied . . . . the results show that augmenting responses are modulated by behavioral states of vigilance, *displaying the highest amplitudes during SWS* [slow wave sleep] and being disrupted upon natural arousal or during forebrain activation . . . . *thalamic and neocortical neurons increase their responsiveness during, as well as after, cessation of rhythmic responses in the frequency range of spindles, and they display self-sustained activities that strikingly resemble the patterns of responses during the prior period of stimulation, indicative of "memory" events due to resonant activities in reverberating corticothalamic loops* [Steriade and Timofeev, 2003, *Neuron*, Online Archive, p. 5; emphasis added].

The hypothesis that spindle waves receive intracortical amplification can also explain the other changes reported in the EEG studies of experienced meditators. The sudden appearance of high-alpha/low-beta activity is reported to occur within the first minute of beginning meditation. If we assume that spindle bursts are fired at intervals of 1 burst every 5 seconds (the timing of spindle-generated light-rings that I see myself), that an average volley consists of 3 to 7 bursts, and that each of these spindle bursts lasts no more than 1.5 to 2 seconds, then the total time required for the RTN to complete a full volley of spindle bursts will range from a minimum of 8 seconds (calculated as 3 bursts, each 2 seconds long, separated by two 1-second intervals) to maximum of 20 seconds (calculated as 7 bursts, each 2 seconds long, separated by six 1-second intervals). Whether we use the maximum and minimum calculation, the total elapsed time remains less than one minute. This sudden increase in alpha band frequencies is distributed across the cortical mantle because spindle bursts are transmitted first to the central and frontal cortices, so the posterior cortices "go to sleep last" [Wright et al., 1995; Tanaka et al., 1996, 2000]. Finally, the intracortical amplification of thalamic spindle bursts can explain reports that the EEGs of expert meditators are not disrupted by the administration of a strong sensory stimulus. If synchronous spindle bursts are monopolizing the reciprocal circuits that link relay nuclei in the thalamus with their cortical targets, those slow wave sleep rhythms will block or significantly impede the thalamic relay of signals from sensory receptors just as they do during a normal episode of stage 2 NREMS:

> During SWS [slow wave sleep] oscillations, signals from the outside world do not reliably reach the cerebral cortex, thus ensuring a safe sleep. The transfer of information is prevented throughout SWS because thalamocortical neurons are steadily hyperpolarized during this state (Hirsch et al., 1983), and afferent stimuli do not reliably produce an EPSP [excitatory postsynaptic potential] that reaches firing threshold. An additional role is played by the increased conductance of IPSPs [inhibitory postsynaptic potentials] in thalamocortical neurons during sleep spindles, which further diminishes the probability of faithful synaptic transmission through the thalamus (Timofeev et al., 1996). These data, from studies on experimental animals, are corroborated in humans by investigating event-related potentials and showing the role of spindles in gating information processing, to protect the sleeper from disturbing sounds (Elton et al., 1997) [Steriade and Timofeev, 2003, at *Neuron*, Online Archive, p.4].

This analysis supports the inference that amplification of RTN spindle bursts by intracortical, surface-parallel networks is indeed responsible for initiating the sudden, short-lived increase in alpha band frequencies (i.e., from low-alpha at 8 Hz to high-alpha/low-beta at 12 to 14 Hz) that spreads across the cortical mantle of expert meditators in the first minute of meditation.

The next change reported in the studies cited above is a shift from high-alpha/low-beta activity to slower frequencies—to a predominance of theta and delta activity. The next question, then, is can we explain this dramatic slowing as an artifact of sleep rhythms, to be more specific, as an artifact of the phasic shift from RTN spindle bursts normally associated with stage 2 NREMS to delta activity normally associated with stage 3 NREMS? And if the conventional criterion for stage

3 NREMS is the presence of delta waves globalized across the cortical mantle, how can we explain that in the case of a meditating subject the stage 3 sleep rhythms produce a mix of theta and delta activity?

Stage 3 Sleep Rhythms and Cortical Theta

When the RTN stops firing spindle bursts, initiating the shift from stage 2 to stage 3 NREMS, the cortical slow (<1 Hz) wave continues to oscillate. When the pulse of the cortical slow wave is referred back to the thalamus, it stimulates large numbers of vision-relay neurons in the LGN to fire calcium spikes that ascend in waves to the primary visual cortices. The *interaction* of the synchronous pulses of the cortical slow wave and the ascending waves of calcium spikes generates delta waves in the scalp EEG with frequencies ranging from 0.5 to 4.5 Hz. Delta band activity globalized across the cortical mantle is the conventional criterion for onset of stage 3 NREMS, but when a meditator activates sleep rhythms without losing consciousness, the brainwave patterns will not be the same as in a person who has actually fallen asleep: for a meditator to see phosphene images generated by stage 3 sleep rhythms, some networks of locally-connected, surface-parallel neurons in the primary visual cortices must retain their capacity to desynchronize in response to the waves of calcium spikes fired by vision-relay cells in the LGN, even though the cortical cells continue to participate in the synchronous oscillations of the cortical slow (<1 Hz) wave. Assume, for the moment, that the intracortical amplification of ascending calcium spikes during stage 3 NREMS receives the same 4 to 6 Hz boost that we proposed earlier for the spindle-driven rebound spikes: in a sleeping subject, the ascending calcium spikes that would interact with the cortical slow wave to generate delta band frequencies (0.5 Hz to 4.5 Hz) in the scalp EEG, but *if the intracortical excitatory networks amplify the calcium spikes by 4 to 6 Hz, as we've postulated for the spindle-driven spikes that preceded them, then the calcium spikes will register in the scalp EEG as theta waves (with frequencies ranging from 4.5 to 7.5 Hz) or even as low alpha waves (7.5 to 9.5 Hz).* This analysis fits well with a theory proposed by Corsi-Cabrera et al. [2000] that theta rhythms observed in the scalp EEG are not generated by independent oscillators but rather are artifacts of the interactions of brain rhythms generated by delta and alpha wave oscillators.

In addition to the theta and alpha waves generated by intracortical amplification of ascending calcium spikes, there is also abundant delta band activity intermixed with theta waves. This suggests that the cortical slow wave which oscillates at frequencies of less than 1 Hz, must produce its own, independent impact on brainwave activity in the scalp EEG, even as it interacts with the ascending calcium spikes while their intracortical ampification is taking place, and that this accounts for the presence of delta waves (0.5 to 4.5 Hz) intermixed with the theta waves.

The Neural Correlates of the High-Amplitude Surges

Early Meditation Studies Establish a Pattern

In the early EEG studies of experienced meditators, researchers often found a sudden, dramatic surge of brainwave amplitudes from the 20 µV amplitude typical of "resting occipital alpha" to 40 to 50 µV [Travis and Wallace, 1999]) or even higher to 100 or 150 µV [Kasamatsu et al., 1957; Anand et al., 1961; Fahrion et al., 1992; Wilson, 1994]. The meditating subjects typically report having a "peak experience" when the surges appear in the EEG [Das and Gastaut, 1955; Anand et al., 1961; Fahrion et al., 1992; Corby et al., 1978; Wilson, 1994]. In this section we'll review some of the earliest EEG studies of experienced meditators who reported high-amplitude surges, then look at an important depth-electrode study that reveals what is going on in the temporolimbic region during this high-amplitude surges, and then we'll apply what we've learned to the most recent EEG studies of experienced meditators, all of which report the same high-amplitude surges.

In the study of a Hindu yogi by Das and Gastaut [1955], meditation evoked a steady increase in brain wave frequencies from resting occipital alpha (8 Hz) to high alpha (12 Hz) to low-beta (13 to 17 Hz) and on up into high beta (20 to 25 Hz). At this point there was a sudden surge in wave amplitudes from 20 µV to 50 µV that erupted simultaneously in all electrodes (Figure 32C). Similarly, in the study of Zen monks by Kasamatsu and Hirai [1996], the EEG recordings of the older and more experienced subjects showed an initial increase in alpha band frequencies and then a slowing which was sustained for a prolonged period until suddenly there was a doubling of wave amplitudes in both the alpha and theta frequency bands. In a study by Corby et al. [1978] which used experienced Tantric yogis and compared their EEGs with those of a control group of volunteers, the researchers found that changes in brain wave patterns were significantly greater in 17 of the 20 experienced Tantric practitioners (85%) than in the volunteers. One of the most experienced meditators was a woman who reported having a "near-samadhi" experience; her EEG showed a surge to wave amplitudes of 100 µV in the alpha band and to 150 µV in the theta band (see Figure 32D).

This phenomenon of frequency-splitting and amplitude-doubling can be measured with greater precision in EEG studies which can use modern quantitative brain-mapping techniques. The advent of computer-enhanced EEG machines makes it feasible to measure higher brainwave frequencies than before—to measure frequency increases that soar into the gamma band (64 Hz to 128 Hz) that would formerly have been reported as high or "off-the-charts" beta waves—and these newer machines can also generate topographical "brainmaps" that make it easier to analyze how frequencies are distributed across the cortical mantle and how they change over time. In Fahrion et al. [1992], where the subject was a renowned "therapeutic touch healer," the researchers observed a sudden surge of wave amplitudes to 100 µV in the high-alpha and gamma bands. These surges were localized over the temporal lobes, forming a topological pattern that resembles an "earmuff." The significance of this distinctive "earmuff" topology will become evident as we proceed with our review of meditation studies in the medical literature.

In another EEG study of an experienced "therapeutic touch healer," Wilson [1994] observed an initial increase in EEG alpha-band activity, followed by a shift to theta and delta activity, but in this subject the brainwave frequencies kept slowing and slowing until a coherent pattern of "really low frequencies, like low delta" was established. Soon after wave amplitudes in the theta, delta, and gamma frequency bands nearly doubled—soaring from 20 to 39 μV. In this same article, Wilson included his findings in another study: he was allowed to perform before-and-after EEG tests on attendees at a well-known meditation training course that uses biofeedback techniques to deepen trance states. As part of that course, attendees listen to audiotapes with binaural beats embedded, beats timed to delta band frequencies. When the EEGs were administered after the course, Wilson found "a sudden shift from slow waves to temporal lobe activation occurred in 80% of these subjects." The EEG of one woman who said that she experienced an "out-of-the-body" experiences" during the test showed high-frequency (64 Hz), high-amplitude surges over the temporal regions—the distinctive "earmuff" pattern. Based on the results he obtained in these two EEG studies, Wilson concluded that the high-amplitude surges induced by experienced meditators could generate either of two different types of topological patterns, shown here in Figure 33A. In Panel A, adapted from Wilson's own illustration, there are three topological brainmaps: the map on the left shows the typical frequency distribution during the baseline condition of "resting occipital alpha;" the map in the middle shows a typical "table-top" distribution of high-amplitude surges clustered around the central vertex; the map on the right shows a typical "earmuff" distribution with high-amplitude surges localized over one or both temporal lobes. Wilson initially thought that these high-amplitude gamma surges must be caused by temporal lobe seizures:

> When people are really going up into ecstatic or transcendent experiences, I've seen them go up to 120 to 150 μV activity in the temporal lobe. . . . The first time I saw this evidence of temporal activation, I thought the person probably had a temporal lobe seizure, and I continued to think that for some time because of the intensity of that response (p. 181).

Later he would reconsidered this initial interpretation and favor instead a more spiritual interpretation—that these surges, whatever the mechanisms involved, should be regarded as "transits of consciousness" that facilitated the emergence of a new and more spiritually-elevated form of human consciousness. However, Wilson never explicitly rejected his initial finding that the high-amplitude surges with "table-top" and "earmuff" topologies were generated by simple partial seizures in the temporolimbic region. More recent studies of expert meditators suggest that Wilson's diagnosis of temporolimbic seizures is indeed warranted.

Which EEG Patterns Point to Temporolimbic Seizures?

In a study of temporolimbic seizures using depth-electrodes, Pacia and Ebersole [1997] compared brainwave activity in the temporolimbic region at seizure onset with activity recorded in the scalp EEG. They found that simple partial seizures confined within the hippocampus produced little or no change in the scalp EEG:

> In fact few, if any, epileptiform discharges confined to this structure had a scalp EEG coordinate. . . . Likely reasons for this lack of identifiable scalp potentials are a relatively small activated tissue volume, curved geometry (which encourages external field cancellation), plus the usual shielding effect of the skull and scalp (p. 650).

When the hippocampal-onset seizures spread outside the hippocampus to involve adjacent temporal cortex, two different patterns could appear in the scalp EEG. In the pattern they designate as "Type 1A," a synchronous rhythm appears in the EEG that is "regular, 5-9 Hz, and subtemporal and temporal in distribution

---

Figure 33. A comparison of topological patterns in EEG studies of expert meditators and patients with simple partial seizures of hippocampal origin. A. Topological brainmaps of high-amplitude surges in meditators reported by Wilson [1994]: from left to right, (1) the topological pattern associated with the baseline condition of "resting occipital alpha;" (2) high-amplitude surges clustered around the vertex to form a distinctive "table-top" pattern; and (3) high-amplitude surges localized over the temporal lobes to form a distinctive "earmuff" pattern. In a depth-electrodes study of epileptic patients with simple partial seizures (discussed in the text), Pacia and Ebersole [1997] found that the distinctive table-top pattern was generated by a simple partial seizure of hippocampal origin after it spread into adjacent temporal cortex—a type of seizure they classify as "Type 1B"—and they found that the distinctive "earmuff" distribution was also generated by a simple partial seizure in the temporolimbic region—a type of seizure they classify as "Type lA." B. This drawing, adapted from Bare et al. [1994], shows the distribution of maximal brainwave amplitudes recorded in the scalp EEG of a patient who was experiencing a simple partial seizure. These high-amplitude surges, which the authors describe as being typical of the patients in their study, have the "earmuff" distribution described by Pacia and Ebersole. Bare et al. point out that these maximum amplitudes were recorded in electrodes that had been added below the normal 10-20 array. The extra electrodes helped "clarify the presence and location of the ictal focus" and also "helped demonstrate that the episodes that did not progress to become CPS [complex parital seizures] or GTC [generalized tonic-clonic seizures] also were epileptic seizures (Bare et al., Ibid., p. 718-179; emphasis added)." Of the 77 simple partial seizures recorded during the course of this study, there were 8 seizures (10%) that did not register any changes except in the extra electrodes that had been added below the normal array. In the cases studies by Bare et al., the highest amplitudes registered in the frontotemporal electrodes (FT12). The second highest wave amplitudes registered in the temporoparietal electrodes (TP12) where they are in a position to record surges with the distinctive "earmuff" topology associated with simple partial seizures.

EEG Topologies in Simple Partial Seizure

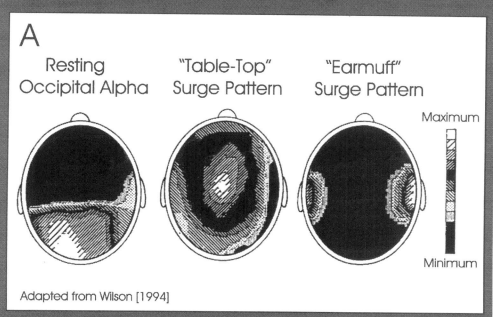

A

Resting Occipital Alpha   "Table-Top" Surge Pattern   "Earmuff" Surge Pattern

Maximum

Minimum

Adapted from Wilson [1994]

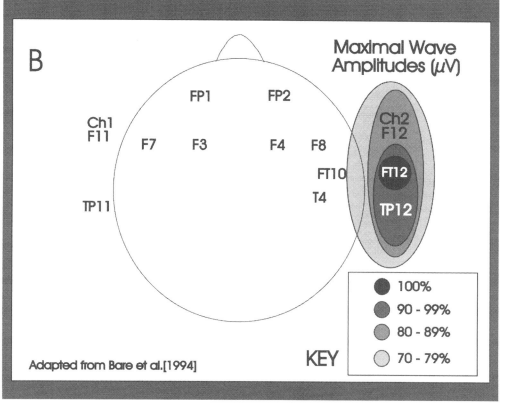

B

Maximal Wave Amplitudes (μV)

FP1   FP2

Ch1
F11   F7   F3   F4   F8   Ch2
F12

FT10

FT12

T4

TP11   TP12

Adapted from Bare et al.[1994]

KEY
100%
90 - 99%
80 - 89%
70 - 79%

(p. 650)," and the amplitudes of this wave are very high (100 μV). The reference here to "subtemporal and temporal distribution" indicates that the high-amplitude surges are localized over the temporal lobes, i.e., they form the same distinctive "earmuff" topology described in the earlier EEG studies by Fahrion et al. [1992] and Wilson [1994]. The second pattern associated with hippocampal-onset seizures that spread into adjacent temporal cortex, which Pacia and Ebersole designate as "Type 1B," there are high-amplitude surges clustered around the vertex of the skull, i.e., a pattern that matches the distinctive "table-top" distribution reported in the earlier EEG studies. The authors state that anatomical reasons explain why temporolimbic seizures generate these particular EEG patterns: "The base of the temporal lobe represents a large cortical generator area, and it is oriented to produce maximal voltage fields at the vertex and base of the skull (p. 652)." Finding either of these distinctive patterns in the scalp EEG is a reliable indicator that the subject has experienced a simple partial seizure of temporolimbic origins:

> Seizure activity confined to the mesotemporal area can produce an unusual scalp EEG seizure pattern . . . in which the predominant rhythm recorded from standard 10-20 placements is around the vertex. Although seemingly unlateralized, this type 1B pattern is in fact quite localizing, because a particular cortical orientation is necessary for its generation. Specifically, cortical EEG sources in basal temporal cortex produce a dipolar field with a net vertical orientation. This results in scalp EEG field maxima, positive and negative, being located at the vertex and base of the skull, respectively. Few electrodes record from the latter, except subtemporal and sphenoidal placements (p. 650; emphasis added).

Another type of simple partial seizure discussed by Pacia and Ebersole, which they designated as "Type 2," originates not in the hippocampus but rather in the temporal cortex. In these Type 2 seizures, high frequency, low-amplitude surges appear over the temporal lobes:

> Low-voltage, high-frequency discharges in the beta and "gamma" range that could be focal or regional were a consistent finding at the onset of these seizures. . . . Such focal gamma activity . . . could be missed easily with sparse cortical electrode coverage. A recent study reported frequencies as high as 120 Hz at the onset of neocortical seizures (Fisher et al., 1992). These authors believe that the cortical region demonstrating such gamma activity more likely represents the seizure-onset zone than adjacent cortical areas showing only attenuation of background rhythms (p. 652).

Pacia and Ebersole warn that the Type 1A and Type 2 topologies which present the distinctive "earmuff" pattern are easily missed if subtemporal electrodes have not been added to the standard 10-20 electrode array. Their warning corroborates the findings of another, earlier study by Bare et al. [1994] which compared electrographic activity in depth-electrodes with brainwave patterns appearing in scalp EEGs with extra electrodes inserted between and below the standard 10-20 array. The objective of this study was to see if adding the extra electrodes increased the chances of detecting onset of simple partial seizures in the temporolimbic region. During the study, the 13 patients experienced a total of 77 simple partial seizures. In 30 of the 77 seizures (39%), the researchers observed clinical signs that indicated a simple partial seizure was taking place, but the EEG did not register any changes in these cases. In 47 of the 77 seizures (61%), changes could be observed in the scalp EEG, but within this subgroup, 8 seizures (8/47 = 17%), those changes could only be detected in the extra electrodes added below the normal array. Adding the extra electrodes not only helped "clarify the presence and location of the ictal focus," the authors write, but this also "helped demonstrate that the episodes that did not progress to become CPS [complex partial seizure] or GTC [generalized tonic-clonic seizure] also were epileptic seizures (pp. 718-179; emphasis added)." An example of brainwave amplitudes observed in one patient who experienced simple partial seizures of temporolimbic origin is depicted in Figure 33B (adapted from an illustration in Bare et al., p. 718). The maximum wave amplitudes were recorded in two electrodes added below the normal array: the highest amplitudes registered in a frontotemporal electrode (FT12), and the second-highest amplitudes registered in a temporoparietal electrode (TP12).

These two studies by provide important insights about how to interpret the high-amplitude surges that often appear in the EEGs of experienced meditators, so it is reasonable to expect that more recent EEG studies—those published after Pacia and Ebersole [1997]—would take their findings into account, but in fact none of the researchers whose studies appeared after Pacia and Ebersole cite this study and none of them consider the potential relevance of their findings about the EEG patterns associated with simple partial seizures of temporolimbic origin. That oversight means many researchers do not have the key insights they need to engage in a discussion of the neural mechanisms underlying the EEG patterns they report, or, worse, missing the clues provided by Pacia and Ebersole can lead to serious misinterpretations of data, as we'll discover in the next section.

Recent Studies of Experienced Meditators

In Lehmann et al. [2001], the researchers used Low Resolution Electromagnetic Tomography (LORETA), a form of computer-enhanced analysis of EEG brainwaves, to study a Tibetan lama while he meditated in what the lama described as four different "modes," each having a different level of intensity. During the meditation that the monk described as the most intense and the most spiritually-elevated—the "self-dissolution" mode—the EEG registered *high levels of gamma band activity distributed around the vertex in the distinctive "table-top" pattern.* During the "self-reconstruction" mode, which the monk designated as second in intensity and in its degree of spiritual-elevation, the EEG registered *high-amplitude gamma surges in both the "table-top" and "earmuff" patterns* [see Lehmann et al.,

Ibid., Figures 2C & 2D, p. 116]. Both of these patterns match those identified by Pacia and Ebersole as correlates of simple partial seizures of temporolimbic origin. The authors of this LORETA study do not cite Pacia and Ebersole, nor do they attempt to discuss the issue of what neural mechanisms might have caused the EEG patterns they observed.

In another LORETA study of a Tibetan lama, DeLuca and Daly [2003] recorded a typical slowing of the EEG followed by an eruption of gamma surges with an "earmuff" distribution. When the surges occurred, the monk signaled the researchers that he was having a "peak experience" by pressing a button on a small, hand-held device. DeLuca and Daly do not cite Pacia and Ebersole, nor do they discuss possible etiologies.

In the most widely-publicized study of Tibetan lama meditators, Lutz et al. [2004] recorded *high-amplitude gamma surges over the vertex and over the temporal lobes—the distinctive "table-top" and "earmuff" patterns*. This unexpected outcome so surprised the researchers (who do not cite Pacia and Ebersole in their references) that they decided the surges must be some kind of "artifact" generated by unobserved muscle movements of unknown origin. They decided it would be appropriate to remove the effects of the muscle movements by *subtracting all of the gamma activity over 70 Hz and reanalyzing their data*. After that revision, the frequencies of the gamma waves in the brainwave maps of the lamas were significantly slower and appeared to be "balanced bilaterally" over the parieto-temporal and mid-frontal cortices. Based on their analysis of the reconstituted data, Lutz et al. concluded that Tibetan lamas who have spent most of their lives practicing meditation and who have achieved the highest level of skill (attested by the fact that these particular lamas were recommended by the Tibetan religious authorities) must be able to condition their brains to produce this kind of "balanced" pattern. The implication is that this "balanced" pattern is healthier than brainwave patterns observed in normal people.

There is a major problem with this study, which is this: to conclude that the high-amplitude, high-frequency surges were generated by muscle artifact, the researchers had to ignore a subset of their own original data that should have put them on notice that the surges were more likely generated by subcortical and temporal discharges. In the article published online, the authors include figures that display the results of their dipole source analysis of the original findings [see Lutz et al., "Online Supporting Figures 7-9," in *The Proceedings of the National Academy of Sciences of the United States,* November 8, 2004, 10.1073/pnas.0407401101], figures that are not included in the article published later in the hardcopy of *PNAS*. A dipole source analysis employs computer algorithms to calculate which regions of the brain are most likely responsible for generating a particular frequency patterns in the scalp EEG. In the online version of Lutz et al., *the dipole source analysis identifies the source of the activity registering in the scalp EEG as originating in "two deep central dipoles and two shallow dipoles over the temporal lobes."* The reference to "two deep central dipoles" implicates the mesotemporal region, and this, in turn, points to the hippocampus, first, because it is intimately interconnected with many of the structures in the mesotemporal region, and, second, because the hippocampus is the structure most vulnerable to seizures. This dipole is consistent with the Type 1A and Type 1B patterns identified by Pacia and Ebersole in which a hippocampal seizure spreads to the adjacent temporal cortices and then generates high-amplitude surges over the vertex and/or the temporal lobes. The reference to "two shallow dipoles over the temporal lobes" indicates the same etiology. Lutz et al. acknowledge that "*The high-amplitude gamma activity found in some of these practitioners is, to our knowledge, the highest reported in the literature in a non-pathological context* (p. 16372; emphasis added)," but this clue does not lead them to consider the possibility that pathological activity did occur during this study.

All of the recent EEG studies of experienced meditators that I've reviewed here observed sudden outbreaks of high-amplitude activity localized over the vertex or over the temporal lobes, but none of the studies cite Pacia and Ebersole, and apparently none of the authors suspects that temporolimbic seizures might be implicated. One reason why meditation researchers might not encounter the Pacia and Ebersole study is that the medical databases index it under headings related to epilepsy or simple partial seizure, so a literature search that focuses exclusively on meditation would be likely to miss this citation. But I suspect that there may be other reasons as well: I suspect that many researchers who undertake studies of expert meditators are motivated by their belief that meditation is good for one's health—that it is *always* good for one's health—and that, therefore, it is not possible for a person to become too proficient at meditation. And of course the corollary is that meditators who have practiced for the longest time, who have attained the highest level of recognition in their tradition, and who are able to demonstrate their prowess at will by producing the most unusual physiological effects, are the best subjects to recruit for a study designed to document the benefits of meditation. The strength of this belief in the inherent virtues of meditation might account for Wilson's shift from his initial opinion that high-amplitude surges in the EEGs of expert meditators were signs of temporolimbic seizures to his later opinion that the surges, because they are associated with peak experiences, must be not only less harmful than he originally thought but must also be inherently good—must be "transits of consciousness" that bring spiritual elevation.

The thesis of this book is that this assumption—that meditation is always benign and the more meditation the better—cannot be correct. There are some types of meditation which, despite being considered by some religious traditions as the epitome of spiritual attainment, also carry a real risk of self-injury—the risk of excitotoxic damage to hippocampal neurons that the meditator can ill afford to lose. In particular, if meditators are successful at inducing the full complement of light visions, it is inevitable that some kindling of new neuronal connections will take place—"Neurons that fire together, wire together"—and frequent inductions practiced over a long enough period of time are likely to reorganize neuron networks in ways that are potentially harmful. If a meditator succeeds in triggering the vision of inner lightning, the culminating event in a meditation-induced phosphene progression, this event alone signals a high risk that continuing to induce that ecstatic vision will forge a new "sensory-limbic hyperconnection" of the sort that neurologists regard as a basic mechanism in temporal lobe epilepsy [Bear,1979; Tisher et al. 1993]. The meditation-induced, phosphene-mediated, ecstatic seizure has the potential to forge a sensory-limbic hyperconnection linking the anterior attention centers, the septum, the sleep rhythm oscillators, the post-geniculate visual pathways, and the hippocampus. The very real risk involved in repeatedly inducing the lightning-like vision can be illustrated by reference to the mystical literature. Many of the traditional meditation texts advise Hindu yogins, Tibetan Buddhist lamas, and Daoist masters to attempt to establish just this sort of sensory-limbic hyperconnection: they are advised that, having once attained the vision of the fiery white light and its blissful sensations, they should attempt to make that vision permanent, to continue inducing it again and again until the bright inner light continues to appear in the visual field even when they've opened their eyes to look around them. The goal, in this view, is for meditators to spend as much time as possible wholly submerged in that consciousness which indistinguishable from the primordial radiance of Ultimate Reality called "Brahman" in the Hindu yoga meditation tradition, "The Final Realization" in Tibetan Buddhism, and "The One" in traditional Daoism.

It is important to emphasize here that I am *not* claiming *all* types of meditation warrant the same concerns: there are many variants that do not involve cultivation of phosphene visions—the Theravadan Buddhist "Insight" tradition, for example, teaches meditators to ignore phosphene images as a particularly seductive type of apparitional reality likely to distract them from the True Path, as I mentioned in Chapter 2. Zen Buddhist meditation follows a similar course. And there other types of meditation that rely primarily on guided imagination where frequent inductions of the same simple phosphene images are not required.

Certainly I know, based on my own personal experience, that moderate amounts of meditation can have positive benefits, both physiological and psychological, but now, having discovered how cultivation of phosphene images can trigger an ecstatic seizure, I make a point of not actively *trying* to induce phosphenes, and if sleep rhythm phosphenes begin to appear spontaneously, as they often do when I'm lying down and feeling very relaxed, I limit the amount of time I spend contemplating the beautiful inner lights.

The EEG studies of meditators that we have reviewed report findings that are consistent with an activation of slow wave sleep rhythms. Now it is time to examine the findings reported by radionucleide imaging studies of meditators to see if activation of slow wave sleep rhythms can account for those outcomes as well.

RADIONUCLEIDE IMAGING STUDIES

Predictions of the Sleep Rhythm Activation Theory

There are a number of studies of meditators that use positron emission tomography (PET), single photon emission computed tomography (SPECT), or functional magnetic resonance imaging (fMRI) to measure changes in cerebral blood flow that are associated with increases in neuronal activity in a particular region of the brain. If the sleep rhythm activation theory is correct, the PET, SPECT, and fMRI studies of experienced meditators should report significant increases in blood flow to those regions of the brain where sleep rhythm oscillators are located: (1) in the *thalamus* (where the RTN generates spindle bursts and vision-relay cells in the LGN fire waves of rebound spikes); (2) in the *primary visual cortices* (where the cortical slow wave oscillates and where waves of rebound spikes from vision-relay cells in the LGN are received and processed); and, finally, (3) in the *hippocamus* (where the visual pathways converge and terminate).

Blood Flow During "Empty-Mind" Meditation, Part I

The studies most relevant for this investigation are those that use expert meditators and permit them to use empty-mind meditation rather than prescribing some kind of mental imagery task. Several single positron emission tomography (SPECT) studies organized by radiologist Andrew Newberg meet this criterion [Newberg et al., 1997, 2000, 2001, 2003]. In a study of 8 experienced Tibetan Buddhist meditators [Newberg et al., 2001], the researchers observed significant increases of blood flow to the *anterior attention centers* (i.e., to the cingulate cortices and the dorsolateral prefrontal cortices [DLPFC]), to the *thalamus*, and to the *medial temporal lobe of the right hemisphere*. Since the medial temporal lobe surrounds the hippocampus and is densely interconnected with it, increased blood flow to that region would increase blood flow to the *hippocampus*. They also found that there was an inverse relationship between the *increase* in blood flow to the DLPFC and the *decrease* in blood flow to the left superior parietal lobe (PSPL) which "may reflect an altered sense of space experienced during the meditation (p. 113)."

In a review of meditation studies published in the medical literature, Newberg and Iversen [2003] discuss possible reasons why two of the SPECT studies by Newberg et al. [1997, 2001] found significant increases in blood flow to the thalamus.

> Several animal studies have shown that the PFC [prefrontal cortices], when activated, innervates the reticular nucleus of the thalamus, particularly as part of a more global attentional network. . . . / . . . . During meditation, due to the increased activity in the PFC, there should be a concomitant increase in the activity in the

reticular nucleus of the thalamus. *While brain imaging studies of meditation have not yet had the resolution to distinguish the reticular nuclei, our recent SPECT study did demonstrate a general increase in thalamic activity that was proportional to the activity levels in the PFC* [Newberg and Inversen, Ibid., p. 285].

The comments by Newberg and Iversen are particularly interesting for our investigation because they suggest that the reason for the increases of blood flow to the thalamus is that there must have been an activation of the thalamic recticular nucleus (RTN). The RTN is the anatomical structure that fires spindle bursts during stage 2 NREMS, so the sleep rhythm activation theory provides an explanation for why there is an increase in blood flow to the RTN and why this activation produces certain other effects, for example, why afferent sensory signals would be blocked and prevented from reaching the left PSPL:

> If the activation of the right PFC causes activity to increase in the reticular thalamus during meditation, the result may be a decrease in sensory input entering the PSPL [posterior superior parietal lobule]. . . . Several studies have demonstrated an increase in serum GABA during meditation. This functional deafferentation related to increased GABA would mean that fewer distracting outside stimuli would arrive at the visual cortex and PSPL enhancing a sense of focus [Ibid., p 285].

The sleep rhythm activation theory also explains why visual signals generated in the retinae will be blocked at the thalamic relay, but, at the same time, there will be activity (and hence increased blood flow) in the primary visual cortices, despite the thalamic blockage. Why? Because the primary visual cortices are engaged in the processing of signals that vision-relay cells in the LGN generate during stage 2 and stage 3 NREMS.

Some of the findings in Newberg et al. are consistent with findings reported by other studies. Increases of blood flow to the dorsolateral prefrontal cortices (DLPFC) are reported by other radionucleide imaging studies [Herzog et al., 1990-1991; Maquet et al., 1996; Lou et al., 1999; Lazar et al., 2000]. Increased blood flow to the hippocampus has also been documented by others: by Lou et al. [1999] in a PET study of experienced meditators, by Maquet et al.[1999] in a PET study of hypnotized volunteers, and by Lazar et al. [2000] in a fMRI study of experienced meditators.

Only one PET study proposes that trance states might be generated by slow wave sleep rhythms. In a study of hypnotized volunteers, Rainville et al. [1999] measured changes in cerebral blood flow during PET scans and compared that data with brainwave patterns in the scalp EEGs. The researchers report *significant increases in blood flow to the occipital cortices at a time when delta activity was prominent in the scalp EEG, "a pattern similar to the results obtained in slow wave sleep (p. 116)."* This leads Rainville et al. to propose "a state theory of hypnosis in which occipital increases in rCBF and delta activity reflect the alteration of consciousness associated with decreased arousal and possible facilitation of visual imagery (p. 110)." They do not elaborate about the kinds of "visual imagery" that might have been involved in this study, but the presence of delta band activity suggests that activation of the visual cortices in this study was not generated by having the subjects use their imagination to conjure up dream-like mental scenes. Why? Because the blood flow patterns in mental imagery experiments are very different from studies where the subjects engage in "empty-mind meditation."

Blood Flow During Meditation with Guided Imagery

If the findings I've just described were the only findings reported by radio-nucleide imaging studies of meditators, it would be reasonable to conclude that the imaging studies support the theory the sleep rhythm activation theory of meditation, but there are two radionucleide imaging studies which report findings that appear to contradict an important prediction of the sleep rhythm activation theory—that contradict the hypothesis that the RTN will start firing spindle bursts and this will produce a significant increase in blood flow to the primary visual cortices as they process the waves of rebound spikes arriving from the LGN.

In one of these PET studies, Lou et al. [1999] recruited experienced "Yoga Nidra" meditators as subjects, but they asked the meditators to practice their normal techniques *before* coming to the laboratory. During the experiment, the meditators were asked to perform visualizations and other imagination-based tasks. Lou et al. found *significant increases in cerebral blood flow to the extrastriate visual cortices but not to the primary visual cortices*. In the other PET study, Maquet et al. [1999] hypnotized volunteer subjects and instructed them to imagine pleasant autobiographical scenes from their past. Here too the researchers found increased blood flow to the extrastriate cortices and not to the primary visual cortices. The subjects in both of these studies were asked to imagine dream-like scenes "in the mind's eye," so it is not surprising that the pattern of cerebral blood flow would resemble the patterns commonly reported in studies that assign visualization tasks or other kinds of imagined events, as, for example, in a study where volunteers were asked to close their eyes and imagine the same objects that they had just been shown [Kosslyn et al., 1995], or a study which monitored schizophrenic patients while they experienced their typical auditory hallucinations [Szechtman et al.,1998], or in studies of dreaming during rapid-eye-movement sleep in normal subjects [Hofle et al., 1997; Maquet et al., 1992, 1995, 1996; Braun et al., 1998]. In all of these studies, the mental task requires the use of memory-related circuits which leads to a reactivation of some subset of the sensory and emotional circuits that participated in forming the original perceptions that were then implanted in memory. The reactivated memory circuits typically include the feature-extraction networks situated in higher-level processing centers of the brain. In the case of visual signals, the higher-level processing structures are located in the extrastriate cortices or in more centrally-located regions. Little, if any, participation by visual circuits located in the primary visual cortices is required during a reactivation of memory-related visual circuits. It should be no surprise, then, that cerebral blood flow patterns in studies of meditators who are assigned imagination-based tasks produce outcomes that resemble studies of mental imagery, auditory hallucinations, and dream-sleep.

I do not want to suggest that there is anything wrong with the research designs in the PET studies by Lou et al. and Maquet et al.; I recognize that their approaches are perfectly legitimate for studying certain kinds of meditation, especially for studying techniques used by novices who are often taught to rely on mental imagery. However, if subjects in an experimental study are assigned tasks that require the use of imagination or memory, the outcomes will be significantly different from what happens in the brains of experienced meditators who induce a state of "empty-mind consciousness." The importance of the distinction between meditation studies that assign mental imagery tasks and those that allow empty-mind meditation was revealed by a fortuitous observation in a PET study of mental imagery by Kosslyn et al. [1995].

Blood Flow During "Empty-Mind" Meditation, Part II

In Kosslyn et al. [1995], subjects were asked to imagine visual images of simple everyday objects immediately after looking an external object. After the experiment, when the researchers were analyzing their data, they found what they had predicted—increases of cerebral blood flow to the extrastriate cortices and in the limbic targets of the extrastriate projections and no significant increases of blood flow to the primary visual cortices—but they were surprised to find that the patterns of blood flow were different *before* the experiment began. When the researchers were recording baseline measurements for later comparison, they'd asked their subjects to lie down and rest comfortably, keep their eyes closed, and to "have it black in front of the mind's eye." There were no specific instructions to *fixate* attention on the dark, empty visual field, but, as readers can experiment and attest for themselves, this is the natural consequence of trying to follow the instructions: you find yourself staring straight ahead at the dark visual field with an attitude of expectancy—the same behaviors employed by experienced meditators as they begin their induction of empty-mind consciousness. *When the researchers looked at changes in blood flow that occurred while the baseline measurements were still being taken—at a time when their subjects were relaxing with eyes closed and "keeping it black in front of the mind's eye"—they found a significant increase in blood flow to the primary visual cortices, not to the extrastriate visual cortices, a pattern directly opposite of what the researchers recorded once the subjects began performing the assigned mental imagery tasks.* This fortuitous observation reported by Kosslyn et al. shows that "empty-mind" consciousness, even when practiced for a very short time by volunteers who are not trying to meditate, will produce changes in cerebral blood flow that are consistent with activation of slow wave wave sleep rhythms—in this case, with the early stirrings of the cortical slow rhythm that initiates a gradual installation of the drowsy state called stage 1 NREMS.

Does A Sleep Rhythm Theory Explain the Existing Data?

Radionucleide imaging studies of meditators report increased blood flow to the same anatomical structures that produce the slow wave sleep rhythms that generate phosphene images during empty-mind meditation: to the *thalamus*, to the *primary visual cortices*, and to the *hippocampus*. If we shift our point of view from asking how the radionucleide imaging studies support the sleep rhythm activation theory of meditation to asking instead if the sleep rhythm activation theory can explain why the imaging studies report the findings they do, we see that the explanatory power of the sleep rhythm activation theory is considerable: it specifies which particular neural mechanisms are responsible for generating the increased neuron activity measured by blood flow, providing a detailed account of processes taking place inside the RTN and LGN and inside the hippocampus that cannot be captured by the measuring instruments currently available. It can also track the evolution of neuronal activities in each structure as time elapses. It can even account for observations that would initially seem unrelated to sleep rhythms, as, for example, by explaining that the decrease in blood flow to the posterior superior parietal lobule reported by Newberg et al. [2001] as being a natural consequence of synchronous sleep rhythms blocking the thalamic relay of posture and position-related signals.

The results reported by EEG studies of meditators can also be explained by the sleep rhythm activation theory of meditation: the EEG patterns typical of novice meditators and hypnotized volunteers resemble the patterns associated with the drowsy stage 1 transition to slow wave sleep, and the EEG patterns of expert meditators are consistent with a further progression of sleep rhythms beyond stage 1 to stage 2 and then on to stage 3 NREMS. This progression can explain the sudden, short-lived, coherent increase in alpha band frequencies within the first minute of meditation, and also the subsequent shift to slower theta and delta frequencies. The sleep rhythm activation theory also provides insights into why there is often a sudden, dramatic onset of high-amplitude surges in the EEGs of experienced meditators when they have "peak experiences." In many of the EEG studies of expert meditators featured in this review, the subjects were able to trigger high-amplitude surges within a short time after beginning meditation; the rapidity of this response suggests that these individuals had used meditation-induced phosphenes to trigger temporolimbic seizures on many previous occasions, and that, as a consequence, they'd cultivated a reorganization of neuron networks and thereby forged a sensory-limbic hyperconnection that enabled them to induce temporolimbic seizures with alacrity.

If a scientific theory is comprehensive, if it can explain in detail how specific neural mechanisms interact and evolve to produce the full range of outcomes reported in the scientific and medical literature, and if the theory builds on the general body of knowledge already accepted by the scientific community—in this case, on what is known about the neural correlates of vision, sleep, and epilepsy—and if it does so with economy and elegance, then that theory deserves attention. Most important of all, it deserves to be subjected to rigorous testing by those researchers who have the skills, instruments, and funding to carry out that task. I believe the sleep rhythm activation theory of meditation (and self-hypnosis) has satisfied these criteria: that it will stand up to empirical tests and that it will help researchers probe ever deeper into the mysteries of the human brain.

10

WHAT KIND OF SEIZURE IS IT?

WHAT COUNTS AS A "SEIZURE?"

Epileptic versus Non-Epileptic Seizures

In clinical medicine patients who complain of seizure-like symptoms are diagnosed with "epileptic" seizures only if the neurological symptoms are *recurring* and *unprovoked*. Clearly these two criteria would exclude the meditation-induced, phosphene-mediated seizure I've described: it was an isolated incident, deliberately induced, which remained amenable to voluntary control for its duration. Unless a neurological work-up produced additional evidence of some occult epileptogenic potential—unless the EEG test detected epileptiform spiking or the CAT scan detected organic lesions—the meditation-induced, phosphene-mediated seizure would not qualify as being the product of epilepsy.

Seizures can be caused by conditions other than epilepsy. Sleep deprivation for a term of thirty-six hours or longer is associated with a lowered seizure threshold [Gunderson et al., 1972; Rajna and Veres, 1993; Lorenzo et al., 1995; Bettendorff et al., 1996; Brunner et al., 1997; Hesdorffer and Verity, 1997; Leproult et al., 1997; Wolf, 1997]. A sleep deficit was definitely a contributing factor in my case. The seizure-inducing effects of sleep loss can be aggravated by co-existing factors such as emotional stress or depression [Friis and Lund, 1974; Friis, 1990; Loiseau, 1997]. Even transient sadness can increase neuron excitability in the thalamus and mesotemporal cortices [George et al., 1995], and, as we discussed in previous chapters, abnormal neuron excitability present at the time the transition from waking to slow wave sleep begins can facilitate destabilization of sleep rhythm oscillators. This might also be a contributing factor in my case, since I was being treated for "atypical dysphoria" at the time.

When a person manipulates a psychological state in order to induce somatic symptoms, this suggests that a dissociative disorder might be involved. When the somatic symptom happens to be a seizure, the most relevant subtype among the Dissociative Disorders in the *Diagnostic and Statistical Manual of Mental Disorders, Fourth Edition* [DSM-IV, 1994] would be "Conversion Disorder," defined as "the presence of symptoms or deficits affecting voluntary motor or sensory function that suggest a neurological or other general medical condition (§300.11, pp. 452-457)." During the late 19th century when young neurologists like Sigmund Freud were flocking to the Saltpietre Hospital in Paris to study with the great Charcot, conversion reactions were called "hysterical neuroses." The classic examples of hysterical neuroses in those days were young female patients who had "glove anesthesia," a loss of sensation in an entire hand which is not compatible with the known neuroanatomy of the arm and hand. Today the diagnosis of conversion disorder is more often encountered in developing countries: for example, at a psychiatric clinic in India, Chandrasekaran et al. [1994] undertook a follow-up study of 51 patients who'd been diagnosed with hysterical neurosis over a one-year period. They found that the presenting complaint for more than half of these patients (30/51= 59%) was seizures or "dissociative convulsions." I also remember having once seen an article published shortly after the end of World War II in a British medical or psychiatric journal—an article which, unfortunately, I've been unable to relocate—where the authors reported the prevalences of various kinds of combat-related medical conditions that had been diagnosed among Indian troops serving in that war: in that article, one of the most frequent diagnosis was conversion reaction. And of course the Indian subcontinent is the region where the techniques of meditation practiced by adepts all over the world were invented and standardized.

The ecstatic seizure that I've described would seem to constitute a classic case of conversion reaction where a psychological state is "converted" into a somatic seizure, but the DSM-IV explicitly excludes a diagnosis of the *disorder* called "conversion" if either of two criteria are present: (1) if the conversion symptoms do not "cause clinically significant distress or impairment in social, occupational, or other important areas of functioning or warrant medical evaluation," and/or (2) if the behaviors take place in an setting in which a conversion reaction constitutes "culturally sanctioned behavior or experience (p. 457)." These exclusions mean the diagnosis of conversion disorder will seldom, if ever, apply to cases where meditators cultivate phosphene imagery with the goal of triggering ecstatic seizures because in most instances the ecstatic seizures are pursued precisely because they are recommended as a spiritual goal by some religious tradition. There are two other subtypes of dissociative disorders that might potentially apply in my case, both excluded for similar reasons: "Depersonalization," defined as a "feeling of detachment or estrangement from one's self [DSM-IV, §300.6, p. 490]," would aptly describe some of what I felt during the ecstatic paroxysm (although it was not a dominant symptom), but this diagnosis cannot be applied to "voluntarily induced experiences [that] . . . form part of mediative and trance practices that are prevalent in many religions (p. 488)." The category of "Dissociation Disorder Not Otherwise

Specified," defined as a "narrowing of awareness of immediate surroundings or stereotyped behaviors or movements that are experienced as being beyond one's control" that occurs as "single or episodic disturbances in the state of consciousness, identity, or memory [DSM-IV, §300.15, p. 490]," looks as if it could be used as a catch-all category, but this diagnosis, like the others, is excluded if the practice of inducing trance states is determined to be "a normal part of a broadly-accepted collective cultural or religious practice (p. 490)."

Are these exclusions justified? The answer is—it depends. The goal of the DSM-IV is to determine who needs psychiatric treatment, so it is understandable that the authors, writing in an era dominated by the philosophy of cultural relativism and the expedient of political correctness, would want to avoid being accused of cultural imperialism, but in the realm of basic neuroscientific research, where the goal is not to administer medical treatment to unwilling subjects but rather to identify the causal mechanisms associated with human behaviors, this agnostic strategy is not only not relevant but also presents an obstacle to scientific progress. A better understanding of the neural mechanisms underlying meditation and hypnosis will foster an improvement in experimental designs for future research studies, and those future studies might well discover that some types of meditation practices pose a significant risk of self-injury, as the phosphene evidence we've examined here clearly implies. Informing meditators and religious communities about the potential risks entailed by certain practices (and the absence of risk in the case of alternative practices) might eventually allow followers of a traditional meditation practice to make adjustments that remove or ameliorate the risk.

There is another type of dissociative disorder worth mentioning here because a surprisingly large number of patients who come to epilepsy clinics complaining of seizures are eventually discovered to be merely *simulating* what they think a seizure should look like. For these patients, the diagnosis is "psychogenic non-epileptic seizure" (PNES), a contemporary label that replaces what was formerly known by more pejorative names like "pseudoseizure" and "hysterical seizure." To diagnose PNES, a physician has to weigh several criteria. Is the EEG test is normal? Is there is evidence of organic lesions? If these tests turn out to be normal, which can often happen even when patients do have epilepsy, the physician considers other factors. When asked to demonstrate what happens during their seizures, do the patients perform behaviors that are not typical of real epileptic seizures but quite typical for PNES patients—for example, do they keep thrusting their pelvis about? Is there is a personal or family history of psychiatric problems? And, finally, is there evidence that patients are currently struggling with social or environmental stressors, and that, consciously or unconsciously, they want to avoid those stressors by mobilizing somatic symptoms and taking on a sick role [Ettinger et al., 1999; Frances et al., 1999; Bowman and Markhand, 1996; Roy, 1989; Theodore, 1989]? The differential diagnosis of PNES versus epileptic seizures can be particularly challenging when patients who have already been diagnosed with epilepsy (and who are therefore better informed about what epileptic symptoms look like) come into an epilepsy clinic with complaints that cause the physicians to suspect PNES. Reports estimating the prevalence of PNES vary considerably from a low of 9% of patients who come to a clinic with complaints of seizure to a high of 50% [Frances et al., 1999; Bowman and Markhand, 1996].

Might a diagnosis of PNES apply to my case? Trying to be objective, I would say that there is some evidence to support both sides of that question. Obviously my seizure was "psychogenic," and the neurological work-up did not find any evidence of epileptiform activity in the EEG nor were any organic lesions detected in the CAT scan. Did I attempt to *simulate* a seizure? Well, it's true that during the EEG test I did not comply with the instructions I'd been given and instead indulged my desire to show the neurologist what happened in the brain when I meditated, and I suppose this noncompliance might qualify as "simulating" something, but it involved a simulation of meditation, not the kind of bizarre physical behaviors typically associated with the performances of PNES patients. Since I was seeing a psychiatrist at the time, I can't deny that, technically speaking, I had a personal history of psychiatric problems, but, on the other hand, my diagnosis was "atypical dysphoria," a relatively mild type of mood disorder, not a full-scale clinical depression, and thus the psychotherapy focused primarily on mood regulation. Did my meditation-induced, phosphene experiences represent an attempt to escape social or environmental stressors? Throughout the period during which these events occurred I continued to function normally, participating in family life as a loving husband and father and executing a number of professional writing projects without incident, so I think it would not apply. If these several observations constituted the only evidence available, I would conclude that the diagnosis of PNES probably does not apply in my case, although I would be open to counter-arguments. But there is another reason why a diagnosis of PNES would not apply in my case: the "reverse-engineering" analysis of phosphene images demonstrates that *the light visions I saw could not have appeared in the visual field unless I did experience a real seizure, a seizure that activated the same neural mechanisms activated by seizures that clearly qualify as "epileptic."*

Epileptic seizures can be generated by either of two mechanisms: by hypersynchronous discharges that engage large groups of neurons but preserve the inhibitory processes of the brain, or, alternatively, by paroxysmal discharges of small groups of neurons that result from a failure of inhibition at the location where the seizure begins [Engel, Jr., et al., 1997; Williamson and Engel, Jr., 1997]. The phosphene evidence documents a tandem activation of both types of mechanisms: first the onset of hypersynchronous discharges in the corticothalamic, then a gradual build-up of hypersynchronous activity in subfield CA3 of one hippocampus, then an outbreak of paroxysmal discharges in the contralateral hippocampus that propagated bilaterally without affecting those regions of the brain that support conscious awareness.

Epileptic Auras and Subclinical Seizures

A seizure that produces only subtle alterations of consciousness is called a simple partial seizure; if consciousness is more significantly impaired but not lost, the diagnosis is complex partial seizure. Partial seizures are generated by focal disturbances in the temporolimbic regions. By contrast, generalized seizures are generated by disturbances in corticothalamic circuits that expand ("generalize") to incorporate cortical regions that support consciousness. In a generalized tonic-clonic seizure, the victim loses consciousness, collapses, and has convulsions. Sometimes a simple partial seizure initiates a generalized seizure ("secondary generalization"), and this kind of premonitory simple partial seizure is often called an "aura," a name derived from the ancient Greek word for "breeze," as in a *warning* breeze that heralds the imminent arrival of something ominous.) The meaning of aura has also been expanded by common usage to include simple partial seizures that occur independently, i.e., without secondary generalization.

Most epileptic auras involve symptoms that are experienced as unsettling, unpleasant, or frightening, so it is rare to find reports of epileptic auras described as "pleasant," much less to encounter reports of auras that would qualify as "ecstatic" [Lennox and Cobb, 1933; Gastaut, 1978]. In recent years a number of case studies purporting to describe "ecstatic auras" have been published in the medical literature—cases that we'll review later in this chapter—and there is an on-going debate among neurologists as to what criteria should be used to make this diagnosis.

Simple partial seizures (epileptic auras) can overlap with a relatively new diagnostic category, the "subclinical seizure." In subclinical seizures the symptoms are so subtle that the person is typically unaware that anything is amiss [Sperling and O'Connor, 1990]. A subcategory of subclinical seizure is the "subictal-dysphoric disorder" where a person experiences many intermittent episodes of depressed mood with variable symptoms that are not recognized as being a problem until the symptoms of depression become significantly worse [Blumer, 2000; Blumer et al., 2004]. In this discussion, my references to subclinical seizures will assume inclusion of the subictal-dysphoric disorder.

To determine how the patterns of electrographic activity associated with epileptic auras compare with the patterns observed during subclinical seizures, Sperling and O'Connor [1990] studied 42 patients awaiting surgery for intractable epilepsy. They implanted depth-electrodes to measure electrographic activity taking place in subcortical regions and compared this with brainwaves registering in a scalp EEG that had extra electrodes placed below the normal 10-20 array. Twenty-three of the patients (23/42 = 58%) experienced subclinical seizures; in this subgroup, *99.1% of the subclinical seizures originated in the hippocampus, and almost all of these subclinical seizures remained confined within the hippocampus.* The authors note that they would not have detected any of those subclinical seizures if they had not placed the extra scalp electrodes below the normal array. Twenty patients experienced epileptic auras (20/42 = 48%), but only half of the auras generated ictal discharges in the scalp EEG (11/20 = 55%). When the researchers focused on those auras for which they did have EEG documentation, they found that *almost all of these auras (10/11 = 90.9%) were generated by ictal discharges in the hippocampal-amygdala complex*. Based on these findings, Sperling and O'Connor concluded that subclinical seizures are "simply more restricted versions of auras and CPSs [complex partial seizures], and do not appear to be intrinsically different (p. 326; emphasis added)." The reason why the patient's consciousness is impaired in a complex partial seizure is because the paroxysmal activity spreads out of the hippocampal-amygdala complex into regions of the brain that subserve conscious awareness. The results of the Sperling and O'Connor study are so important for our investigation of meditation-induced, phosphene-mediated seizures that they bear repeating: *subclinical seizures, simple partial seizures (auras), and complex partial seizures are usually initiated by the same neural mechanism—the outbreak of ictal discharges in the hippocampus*. This finding means that it is not necessary to choose one of these diagnoses and reject the others in order to explain what happened in my case; any one of the three might apply, and all three of these diagnoses point to the same conclusion we reached independently in the "reverse-engineering" analysis of the meditation-induced phosphene imagery: that the culminating event in the progression of meditation-induced light visions is a partial seizure—an "ecstatic aura"—even though it is not, technically speaking, an *epileptic* aura. Seizures with hippocampal onset have distinctive EEG signatures which were documented in the depth-electrode study by Pacia and Ebersole [1997], discussed in the previous chapter: if the seizure remains confined within the hippocampus, this will not produce any significant changes in the scalp EEG, even if extra electrodes have been placed below and between a normal array, but if that seizure then spreads into adjacent temporal cortex, the EEG will register high-amplitude surges that generate an "earmuff" and/or "table-top" pattern. Almost all of the EEG studies of expert meditators reviewed in the previous chapter reported one of these patterns, indicating that the meditator was most likely exploiting an epileptogenic "sensory-limbic hyperconnection" that had been created long before the study by the meditator's repeat inductions of hippocampal-onset temporolimbic seizure. If I had been monitored by EEG when my seizure occurred, it seems likely that one of these tell-tale patterns would have also appeared in my EEG.

When the hippocampus initiates a seizure, it is usually because there has been a significant amount of cell loss (sclerosis) in subfield CA1 [Williamson and Engel, Jr., 1990; Gates and Gumnit, 1990]. While there is no evidence of hippocampal sclerosis in my case, an absence of evidence is not evidence of absence; therefore, it remains theoretically possible that hippocampal sclerosis did play some contributing role that facilitated the build-up of rhythmical activity in the right hippocampus. Since the seizure has already occurred, there is no way to test this hypothesis. But even when there is little or even no pre-existing sclerosis, hippocampal seizures can still occur: in a recent study of patients with mesotemporal epilepsy, Cohen-Gadol et al. [2005] found that hippocampal seizures can occur in patients whose temporal lobe epilepsy is "paradoxical" in that their hippocampal cell loss averaged only 20% (with a range varying from a low of zero cell loss to a high of 59%) compared to the more typical sclerosis pattern observed in the control group of patients with temporal lobe epilepsy where cell loss averaged 75% (with a range varying from a low of 41% to a high of 90%). It may be easier to trigger a seizure if the hippocampus has substantial pre-existing sclerosis, but sclerosis is not a prerequisite.

The meditation-induced simple partial seizure of hippocampal origin produces symptoms that would seem to qualify as being "ecstatic," and certainly that is how these experiences are regarded by the religious traditions that prize them as mystical transports of the highest order. To better understand the nature of the meditation-induced, phosphene-mediated simple partial seizures and to determine where this mystical experience fits in the spectrum of epileptiform phenomena, we need to learn more about the "ecstatic auras" of temporolimbic epilepsy.

THE ECSTATIC AURA IN TEMPOROLIMBIC EPILEPSY

Dostoevsky's Epilepsy and the "Ecstatic Aura" Debate

The famous Russian writer, Fyodor Dostoevsky, began to suffer generalized tonic-clonic seizures while imprisoned in a Siberian labor camp. Later in his novels he would sometimes include characters who suffered epileptic seizures, the most famous being Prince Myshkin in *The Idiot*. Dostoevsky describes Myshkin's "fits" as beginning with lightning-like flashes that brought a moment of ecstasy just before Myshkin lost consciousness and collapsed in a generalized tonic-clonic seizure:

> He pondered, among other things, the fact that there was a stage in his epileptic condition just before the fit itself (if it occurred during the waking hours) when all of a sudden, amid the sadness, spiritual darkness, and oppression, there were moments when his brain seemed to flare up momentarily and all his vital forces tense themselves at once in an extraordinary surge. The sensation of being alive and self-aware increased almost tenfold in those lightning-quick moments. His mind and heart were bathed in *an extraordinary illumination.* . . . [T]hese *flashes,* were merely the prelude to that final second (never more than a second) which marked the onset of the actual fit. That second was, of course, unendurable. Reflecting on that moment afterwards when he had recovered, he often used to tell himself that *all these gleams and lightning-flashes of heightened self-awareness, and hence also of "higher existence,"* were nothing more than the illness itself, violating the normal state of things as it did, and thus it was not a higher mode

of existence at all—on the contrary, it should be regarded as the lowest. And yet he arrived at length at a paradoxical conclusion: "What if it is the illness then?" he decided finally. "What does it matter if it is some abnormal tension, if the end-result, the instant of apprehension, recalled and analyzed during recovery, turns out to be the highest pitch of harmony and beauty, conferring a sense of some hitherto-unknown and unguessed completeness, proportion, reconciliation, an ecstatic, prayerful fusion with the supreme synthesis of life?" . . . . If in that second, in the final conscious moment before the attack, he could have managed to tell himself clearly and deliberately: "Yes, for this moment one could give one's whole life!" then of course, that moment on its own would be worth one's whole life [Dostoevsky, 1992 (1868), p. 237; emphasis added].

Most of the references to seizures in the records kept by Dostoevsky's own physician and in accounts written by his friends describe their having observed symptoms typical of generalized tonic-clonic seizure—a sudden loss of consciousness, a physical collapse, and tonic-clonic muscle spasms. But was this all he experienced? Might Dostoevsky have experienced the same kind of ecstatic aura he attributed to Prince Myshkin, or was that depiction merely the novelist's exercise of poetic license? A debate about "ecstatic auras" was initiated by neurologist Norman Geschwind in 1963 when he proposed that Dostoevsky could have experienced a complex partial seizure before the onset of his generalized tonic-clonic seizure, and that, if this were so, it would mean that the novelist's description of Myshkin's ecstatic aura might well reflect his own personal experience [Geschwind, 1963]. Geschwind's hypothesis was immediately challenged by neurologist Henri Gastaut, one of the leading epileptologists in Europe: Gastaut insisted that never once in his thirty-five years of practice with epileptic patients had he ever encountered a single patient who claimed to have experienced an ecstatic aura, nor had he ever heard of such a case, nor could he find such a case reported in the medical literature [Gastaut, 1963, 1978]. Gastaut concluded that the diagnosis of primary generalized epilepsy assigned by Dostoevsky's personal physician was more credible than Geschwin's proposal and that this diagnosis would exclude the possibility that the novelist could have retained consciousness for even the briefest moment once the seizure was underway. Not only was it impossible, in Gastaut's view, for Dostoevsky to have experienced an ecstatic aura, but it was also unlikely that ecstatic auras actually exist.

The debate about Dostoevsky's aura was revitalized in 1983 when a Dutch neurologist, Piet Voskuil, published an article that showed how a slight revision in Geschwin's hypothesis could account for Dostoevsky's symptoms and also bridge the gap between Geschwin and Gestaut [Voskuil, 1983]. Voskuil pointed out that Gastaut had not explicitly addressed the possibility that Dostoevsky might have experienced a complex partial seizure that immediately triggered a secondary generalization. He cited a number of incidents reported by the novelist's physician and by friends in support this hypothesis: (1) before Dostoevsky learned of the epileptic nature of his episodes, he often referred to them as "strokes with a little breeze," which implies that there was some kind of aura preceding the main seizure; (2) before he was diagnosed with epilepsy, the novelist reported having many different kinds of seizures; and, (3) a friend described having observed one seizure in which Dostoevsky suddenly cried out, "God exists, He exists . . . ," just before the novelist lost consciousness and collapsed. These observations were not really new—they'd been mentioned by other commentators—but Voskuil was able to cite a new case which changed the course of the debate. The patient described in a case study by Cirignotta et al. [1980] was a male in his early thirties who was referred to the epilepsy clinic after he suffered his first generalized tonic-clonic seizure while asleep at night. He told his physicians that since the age of 13 he had often experienced brief alterations in consciousness lasting no more than 20 to 30 seconds with symptoms that included psychomotor arrest, a slight lapse of consciousness, erotic sensations, and feelings of ineffable joy:

> Seizures generally come on when he is *relaxed or drowsy*. The subjective symptoms are defined by the patient himself as "indescribable," . . . . However, he says that *the pleasure he feels is so intense that he cannot find its match in reality*. . . . His mind, his whole being, is pervaded by a *sense of bliss*. / All attention to his surroundings is suspended; he almost feels as if this *estrangement from the environment* were a sine qua non for the onset of seizures. He insists that the only comparable pleasure is that conveyed by music. *Sexual pleasure is completely different*: once he happened to have an attack during sexual intercourse, which he carried on mechanically, being totally absorbed in his utterly mental enjoyment [Cirignotta et al., Ibid., pp. 709; emphasis added].

When the patient was awake, his EEG was usually normal, but when he was asleep it would occasionally register some epileptiform spikes in the right temporal lobe. Then one day while he was being monitored by EEG the patient happened to experience one of his typical auras, producing the first EEG record of an ecstatic aura. Based on this new study by Cirignotta et al., and on his own reassessment of Dostoevsky's medical history, Voskuil concluded that the novelist most likely experienced an ecstatic aura—a complex partial seizure—which then triggered a secondary generalization. "Although I share Gastaut's doubts to a great extent," Voskuil writes, "I think it is not possible, with any confidence, to reject the classification (in Dostoevsky's case) of partial complex epilepsy with a majority of secondarily generalized nocturnal attacks (p. 664-5)." This article convinced Gastaut to revise his opinion:

> Perhaps the most reasonable hypothesis is an eclectic one, wherein both etiologies are associated. Accordingly, Dostoevsky may have presented both of the following: a temporal lesion of very limited magnitude and thus devoid of mental or somatic expression in interictal periods; and a constitutional predisposition to epilepsy of sufficient magnitude to render epileptogenic this otherwise silent temporal lesion and to induce an almost immediate secondary generalization of each seizure [Gastaut, 1984., p. 409].

Recent Cases of Ecstatic Auras

Since the Geschwind-Gastaut-Voskuil exchange, a number of new cases involving ecstatic auras have been reported in the medical literature. Naito and Matsui [1988] describe the case of a Japanese woman who kept voluminous, detailed diaries of her paroxysmal experiences:

> At age 60, she experienced, while awake, a peculiar attack lasting several minutes, during which she said, "A halo appeared around god. Thank my god! Oh! Thank my god! She then stared with motor arrest. She failed to respond to shouts from her family. Later, she was unable to recollect this experience. . . . / In April 1980, at her place of employment she suddenly cried out, "I saw my god!" and shed happy tears. She was then 61 and had no memory loss of the joyous experience and insisted even after that she felt extreme happiness, as if she had been in paradise. / One early morning in May, 1980, she watched the sun rising, and had a sudden complex yet pleasant experience. She related, "Triple halos appeared around the sun. Suddenly the sunlight became intense. I experienced a revelation of god and all creation glittering under the sun. The sun became bigger and engulfed me. My mind, my whole being was pervaded by a feeling of delight (p.123).

When the patient was tracked by 24-hour EEG monitoring, it was found that she experienced a complex partial seizure with gestural automatisms while she was asleep. The EEG recorded epileptic spikes in her temporal lobes during this nocturnal seizure, but since the patient was not conscious at the time, it was not possible to link the EEG documentation with her subjective experience of ecstatic auras.

Diaguiji [1990] describes the case of a thirty-five-year-old Japanese man who experienced his first generalized convulsion while a university student. The patient said he often experienced a premonitory aura of numbness just before a seizure that caused him to lose consciousness and collapse. After graduation, the man joined a new religious cult called the T-Society. He then began to interpret his epileptic aura of numbness as his receiving non-verbal communications from the cult's founder. One evening while attending a meeting of the T-Society, he saw "something white float up above the carpet of the exercise hall and wondered that others could not see it (p. 177)." This vision of light convinced him to go into seclusion at a cult retreat called "the Mountain" where he remained for seven years before seeking medical treatment.

Morgan [1990] describes a 35-year-old man who returned to the epilepsy clinic when the anticonvulsive medications that controlled his nocturnal clonic-tonic seizures eventually stopped working. The patient reported that, in addition to the recurrence of his nocturnal seizures, he had now begun to experience a new type of seizure, one that was "joyful and pleasurable" and that made him feel content and fulfilled. This new seizure occurred several times a day:

A typical fit began suddenly with a feeling of irritation followed promptly by a sense of detachment. He would see *a bright but not glaring light. He sensed that the light was the source of knowledge and understanding.* He occasionally heard soft music. In about half of these cases a young bearded man would appear.... The entire episode lasted only a second or two, but to the patient it seemed much longer. His family reported that during these fits he seemed in another world and would not respond normally to them. *At first the patient was frightened after these episodes but gradually came to see them as joyful and pleasurable. During the fit he felt at ease with himself and his environment. He sensed an ineffable contentment and fulfillment.* Occasionally these ecstatic seizures were followed by a grand mal convulsion (p. 414; emphasis added).

In the neurological work-up, a CAT scan detected a tumor in the anterior temporal lobe of the right hemisphere. When the tumor was surgically removed along with the anterior hippocampus and amygdala, the pathologist examining the resected temporal lobe tissue found an epileptic lesion that confirmed the results of the CAT scan. This is the first case of an ecstatic aura to document the exact site of the epileptogenic lesion.

In a recent study by Hansen and Brodtkorb [2003], the authors discussed the types of symptoms that occurred during auras reported by 11 patients, all diagnosed with temporolimbic epilepsy, who ranged in age from 23 to 62. Half of their patients (6/11 = 54.5%) described their seizures as involving a "dreamy state" that coexists with normal consciousness. Hansen and Brodtkorb called this state of consciousness "mental diplopia." The majority of patients enjoyed their auras (8/11 = 72.7%), and almost half of them were suspected of self-inducing their seizures (5/11 = 45.5%). Four patients (4/11 = 36%), including two men and two women, reported erotic sensations. Hansen and Brodtkorb described the experiences of several patients in more detail, including those of a young man who, when he was still a teenager, began to experience brief episodes of an "indefinable" feeling when he listened to concert music. The patient did not seek medical treatment until many years later when the brief episodes of altered consciousness he typically experienced became a premonitory aura that triggered a secondary generalization. Sometimes this aura occurred without the secondary generalization, allowing him to appreciate its ecstatic qualities:

He characterizes these emotions as "a trance of pleasure." "It is like an emotional wave striking me again and again. I feel compelled to obey a sort of phenomenon. These sensations are outside the spectrum of what I have ever experienced outside a seizure." He also describes cold shivering, increased muscle tension, and a delicious taste, and he swallows repeatedly. He enjoys the sensations and is absorbed in them in a way that he can barely hear when spoken to. When in a particular, relaxed mood, he can sometimes induce seizures by "opening up mentally" and contracting muscles. He denies any religious aspects of the symptoms. . . . It lasts a few minutes and afterward he is tired with difficulties expressing himself for about 1 hour [Hansen & Brodtkorb, Ibid., p. 668].

What Counts as "Ecstatic"?

Even though a number of case studies that purport to describe "ecstatic auras" have been published in the medical literature, the debate continues as to whether or not there is any such entity. The most recent challenge to the concept of ecstatic auras appears in an article by neurologist John Hughes [2005]. He objects that the term, "ecstasy," has been defined too broadly in the existing studies: it is not enough for an aura to be merely "pleasant;" the aura must, in addition, present some attribute that can be easily distinguished from the other kinds of psychic symptoms that are commonly reported in temporolimbic auras. Then, assuming that the proponents of ecstatic auras are able to better define what constitutes an "ecstatic" symptom, these symptoms must also be *caused by the seizure* and *experienced during the seizure*. But it is the third objection posed by Hughes that presents the most formidable challenge: in depth-electrode studies that stimulate the amygdala and other limbic areas, researchers have demonstrated that *only low-amplitude stimulation generates auras are experienced as pleasant, whereas, by contrast, high-amplitude stimulation produces auras that are experienced as unpleasant and aversive. These studies also show that there is only one structure in the limbic system where this correlation between high-amplitude discharges and aversive experiences does not hold—in the septum.* High-amplitude activity erupts in the septum during sexual orgasm and also in experiments where subjects are allowed to self-stimulate the pleasure centers of their brains:

> The lateral septal nucleus (to and from the hippocampus) was one of the most sensitive areas for this phenomenon [of brain reward effects in self-stimulation experiments]. . . . it was the septal nucleus that was special. All other areas with a "pleasure-inducing" stimulation that "felt good" in these patients had an aversive effect with high currents, except one, the septal area. This area continued to be pleasure-inducing up to a maximum current of 12.5 mA [Hughes, Ibid., p. 535].

The case studies of ecstatic auras published in the medical literature were not designed to monitor high-amplitude activity in the septal nucleus, so there is no way, in retrospect, to determine if those auras were associated with high-amplitude discharges in the septum. But the "reverse-engineering" analysis of the meditation-induced light visions does provide this evidence: it localizes the outbreak of ictal discharges to the right hippocampus, traces the propagation of those ictal discharges, and describes sensorimotor and psychic symptoms, most notably the orgasmic sensations, that are consistent with activation of high-amplitude discharges in the septum.

Case studies in which seizures generate sexual sensations are rarely reported in the medical literature, but they are not unknown. Stoffels et al. [1980] describe 15 patients who experienced "genital and sexual paroxystic manifestations" that were accompanied by spiking in the scalp EEG. One male experienced a penile erection and one female experienced sexual orgasm. Remillard et al. [1983] describe 12 female patients with temporal lobe epilepsy who experienced sexual sensations during partial seizures. Jacome and Risko [1983] describe a middle-aged man who displayed sexual automatisms during absence seizures. Janszky et al. [2002] describe a patient with an orgasmic epileptic aura and ictal onset in the right mesotemporal region. Finally, in a retrospective study of patients with drug-resistant epilepsy, Mascia et al. [2005] described 24 patients who experienced genital automatisms during their seizures. The authors emphasize that these movements did not bear any resemblance to the pelvic thrusting typically displayed by patients with psychogenic non-epileptic seizures: "the most frequent genital automatisms consist in subtle phenomena while hypermotoric behavior, such as pelvic rhythmic movements, are quite rare." They conclude that the genital automatisms were most likely generated by discharges in the temporal lobes.

Evidence of patients self-inducing seizures with sexual symptoms can also be found in the medical literature on photosensitive seizures, a subject likely to be of special interest given that our investigation focuses on a seizure triggered by the same neural mechanisms that are implicated in photosensitive epilepsy, except for the fact that the phosphene images do not require external light stimuli.

ECSTATIC AURAS IN PHOTOSENSITIVE EPILEPSY

The Elements of Photosensitivity

Photosensitive epilepsy is a type of "reflex" epilepsy in which exposure to certain kinds of light energy—to certain frequencies, colors, or patterns of light—triggers *generalized* seizures [Wilkins et al., 1980; Harding and Jeavons, 1994]. These seizures can range from brief, relatively minor episodes with "absence" symptoms to complete loss of consciousness and physical collapse with tonic-clonic convulsions. The characteristics of the epileptogenic light stimulus can vary from person to person. The likelihood that a patient with photosensitivity will experience a photosensitive seizure is significantly increased by sleep deprivation [Wilkins et al., 1980, p. 87; Scollo-Lavozzi and Scollo-Lavozzi, 1974].

Estimating the prevalence of photosensitivity is complicated by the fact that there are two competing theories about how to interpret the results of the the photo-stimulation test which is the primary diagnostic tool used to determine if a patient is photosensitive. A patient stares through goggles at a screen inside the photostimu-lation machine where a very bright white strobe light flashes. Some physicians are only prepared to diagnose photosensitive epilepsy if the patient experiences a "photoconvulsive response," that is, a paroxysmal response that is not phase-locked to the flashes of the strobe light and does not stop even after the strobe light is turned off. When this strict criterion is used, only about 5% of subjects tested are diagnosed with photosensitive epilepsy. But some clinicians will consider giving a diagnosis of photosensitivity if the patient's responses to the photostimulation test are sufficiently unusual, even if the responses never become convulsive and even if they stop when the strobe light stops. Using this broader definition of photosensitivity, a neurologist might diagnose photosensitivity if the subject experienced rhythmic contractions of head and neck muscles ("photomyoclonus"), and if, in addition, there were also signs of epileptiform activity in the scalp EEG—either synchronous delta waves distributed over both hemispheres or epileptiform spiking in the occipital regions. In studies that use this broader definition, the prevalence of photosensitivity in adult patients ranges from 5% to 10% and from 16% to 33% in children [Wilkins et al., 1980]. Some commentators object to these prevalence figures on the grounds that the existing studies are not rigorous enough and set their estimates too high [de Bittencourt, 2004].

Case Studies of Self-Induced Photosensitive Seizures

Among patients with photosensitive epilepsy, the most interesting, given the subject of our investigation, are those patients who *self-induce* seizures, who actively seek out situations or repeat behaviors that they know will expose them to the light stimuli that triggered their seizures in the past. The proportion of patients with photosensitive epilepsy who self-induce seizures is surprisingly high with estimates ranging from 26% to 30% [Laidlaw et al., 1993, p. 317; Trenite, 1989, p. 13]. It is often assumed that self-induction of photosensitive seizures occurs primarily in patients with mental and emotion problems, but this is not correct: in a study of children who self-induced photosensitive seizure, Trenité [1989] found that 71% of these patients were normal and intelligent.

Patients seldom admit to self-inducing seizures. Often they practice self-stimulation out of the sight of other family members (who might inform a physician), and often they hide the fact that they are not taking their anticonvulsive medications. Sometimes the only evidence that patients are self-inducing seizures is their failure to improve despite the supposed implementation of a treatment plan. Koutroumanidis et al. [1998] describes the case of a 20-year-old male patient who had a history of photosensitive seizures triggered by looking at flickering light who went to the trouble of retraining himself to respond to an internally-generated trigger so he could persist in his self-inductions without being caught. He learned how to induce seizures by "concentrating on upsetting things in the school," or by thinking about his father—"Like the time I spent with him, also the time he was in hospital . . . ."—and thus was able to continue self-inducing seizures without being detected.

Another problem in cases of self-induced photosensitive epilepsy is the difficulty of obtaining EEG documentation. For example, Ames and Saffer [1983] describe the case of a 13-year-old girl with photosensitive epilepsy who felt compelled from time to time to interrupt whatever she was doing and stare at the sun, waving her hands in front of her face to trigger a seizure:

She said that, when exposed a glaring overcast sort of sunlight, her gaze became riveted to the white centre of the sun and her head was forced back. She then felt dizzy, saw blue, green and occasionally red lights, her right hand waved in front of her eyes and she ultimately felt faint. / Her mother and sister . . . described her as suddenly riveting with her head tilted backwards and her eyes directed towards the sun. Her eyelids were half-closed and her eyes deviated upwards, while her right hand (with fingers abducted) waved in front of her right eye sometimes brushing the right side of her forehead. Her body sometimes rocked backwards and forwards. Her face often became flushed. She looked remote and out of touch. Her attention could only be gained by shouting or touching her, ... Attacks lasted several seconds but might occur up to 5 times an hour if she remained in sunlight. She had amnesia for many of them especially those provoked by sudden transition from shadow to sunlight when her hand went up automatically and waved (Ibid., p. 2).

During a five year period during which the young girl continued to experience her attacks, Ames and Saffer administered many EEG tests but failed to obtain "conclusive or convincing" EEG evidence that their patient actually had photosensitive epilepsy.

The most dramatic case study of a patient with self-induced photosensitive epilepsy is the report by Faught et al. [1986] of a 32-year-old mother who felt compelled to "go to the window," the euphemism she used to refer to her practice of staring at the sun while waving her hand in front of her face. This patient was diagnosed as epileptic at the age of eight, but she did not begin to practice the sun-seeking, hand-waving behaviors until she was a teenager. As the woman matured, the problems caused by her heliotropic compulsion grew more persistent and more disruptive, so that, by the time she was 30 years old, her self-inductions were so frequent and so absorbing that she often failed to carry out her normal maternal responsibilities—she would forget to pick up her children after school or ignore her family even when they were present. The woman described her episodes as being dreamy, pleasurable, relaxing, and erotic:

The patient reported that this behavior, when performed while gazing at strong light, resulted in a dreamy state characterized by "time standing still" and feelings of pleasure, followed on awakening by a feeling of relaxation. / By the age of 26 she had developed a strong craving to stand before windows through which sunlight was streaming. She would wave her hands before her eyes, stare and blink at the light, then after a few minutes repeat the hand waving, sometimes engaging in this activity for many hours. Her husband observed her to be masturbating during many of these episodes. Often, fecal and urinary incontinence occurred and the patient fell to the floor; occasionally generalized tonic-clonic activity was observed. These latter phenomena did not dissuade her from her compulsion to "go to the window," as she termed it. / This compulsion dominated the patient's life by the age of 30 years; . . . . Once she passed a strong light bulb, stopped abruptly to stare at it, and became violent at attempts to remove her, and was 30 minutes late for her job. . . . Clonazepam was prescribed, which resulted in abolition of the absence and tonic-clonic seizures as well as the heliotropic compulsion.

However, she became depressed, stopped taking the drug, and resumed the previous behavior. . . . She refused to take medications or to wear dark glasses. / . . . . She was amnesic for events during the seizures except for recollections of feeling "dreamy and happy" [Faught et al., Ibid., p. 408].

When the patient was given an EEG test, no epileptiform activity was detected; however, during the photostimulation test she had a paroxysmal response to the strobe light which she found to be intensely pleasant, so much so that, after the test was over, she expressed her "strong desire" to have the strobe turned back on again.

In a case study reported by Panayiotopoulos [1996], the patient's photosensitive seizures began as spike-wave complexes in corticothalamic visual circuits—the typical pattern observed at the onset of most generalized seizures—but then it did not spread across the cortical mantle, as would be expected in most photosensitive seizures, but rather it remained confined within the occipital cortices. A similar phenomenon occurred in my case: the sleep rhythm oscillators destabilized, triggering hypersynchronous spike-waves in corticothalamic circuits (which generated the phosphene image of dark, fast-moving rings), then there was a shift to cortical fast-runs that produced an "expanding epileptic penumbra" of hypersynchronous discharges (which generated the phosphene image of a radiating spray of tiny light-flecks).

Photosensitive Seizures in Religious Mysticism

Some religious traditions attempt to induce mystical states by engaging in practices that resemble the behaviors used by patients with photosensitive epilepsy to self-induce seizures. The Sun Dance ritual practiced by a number of Native American tribes in the American West presents a good example of the spiritual use of sun-gazing. Tribal members who've taken a vow to participate dance in toward a tall pole sunk into the center of the ceremonial circle and dance back again, all the while staring at the sun (or rather just to one side of the sun) and blowing occasionally on a small bone whistle [personal observation; also see Mails, 1978]. On the third and final day of the Sun Dance, when the dancers are exhausted because they've been moving almost continuously for three days without sleep and without food, taking only a little water when necessary, those who have chosen to be "pierced" have Eagle claws or skewers inserted beneath the skin of their chests and then fastened to a rope tied to the central pole. The "piercers" then begin to dance again, blowing on their whistles and staring toward the sun while they pull back against the rope until their skin rips apart, releasing them to collapse on the ground in an altered state of consciousness. This combination of physical exhaustion, fasting, severe pain, and sun-gazing overloads the physiological systems of the body, triggering what anthropologists call a "paradoxical collapse" of the sympathetic "flight or fight" system that leaves the parasympathetic systems that govern quiescent states in full control [Winkleman, 1992]. During the paradoxical collapse and the altered state of consciousness it engenders, mystical visions often appear. A Sioux sun dancer who saw such a vision told his informant that, after collapsing and then regained consciousness, he saw colored disks of light in front of his eyes that he used to diagnose the ailments of tribal members who regarded him as having acquired mystical powers [Mails, 1978, pp. 144-145].

In Renaissance Europe, Jewish rabbis who celebrated the secret disciplines of the mystical Kabbalah recommended the practice of setting a bowl of water with oil spread over its surface at an angle to the sun so that brilliant sunbeams reflected off the oil and directly into one's eyes. The bright light that flooded the visual field was considered to be only a hint of the true radiance of God's Glory [see Moses de Leon's *Zohar*, verse 1:41b, in Matt, 1983, pp. 34-36; *Zohar* verse 1:10b, in Wolfson, 1994, re Rabbi Gikatilla, pp. 276, 831; re Rabbi Eleazar ben Judah, p. 266].

In Protestant Europe during the 16th-Century, Jacob Boehme, a shoemaker's apprentice, was confirmed in his choice to begin a new career as an itinerant mystic when he happened to look at a pewter dish reflecting beams of sunlight and triggered a photosensitive seizure with ecstatic qualities :

> [S]itting one day in his room, his eye fell upon burnished pewter dish which reflected the sunshine with such marvelous splendor that he fell into a deep inward ecstasy and it seemed to him that he could now look into the principles and deepest foundations of things. He believe it was only a fancy, and in order to banish it from his mind he went out upon the green. But here he remarked that he gazed into the very heart of things; . . " [Boehme, *Dialogues*, p. ix].

Another more recent example of the cultivation of photosensitive reactions was sponsored by the French "Phosphenisme" movement led by Francis Lefebure [1982]. One of Lefebure's followers designed a egg-like shell large enough for a human to recline on the soft cushion inside and look up at the tiny tensor lights arrayed along the inside ceiling of the shell. A person seeking a spiritual experience would wait in the sound-proofed darkness until the tiny, bright, colored lights began to glow briefly and then fade and then glow once again. As each light vanished, it left in its wake a disk-shaped afterimage that changed from the color of the stimulus to a complementary color. I was invited to try the device, which I did, and I can testify that it was very effective at realizing the claims that the designer made for it: in response to the light stimuli, I quickly fell into a state of deep relaxation and dissociation similar to what I induce by meditating or by hypnotizing myself, but the machine elicited this response much faster and without my having to do anything.

Experimental Induction of Photosensitivity as a Model

Photosensitive seizures can be induced experimentally in cats and baboons by stimulating one eye several times a day with a low-intensity light pulse too weak at the outset to provoke a paroxysmal response. The intermittent repetition of the weak light stimulus gradually lowers the firing thresholds and reorganizes the connections linking the neuron networks that discharge in concert in response to the light stimulus. As the firing thresholds of the participating neurons gradually drop, they eventually reach a critical threshold; once that happens, the next administration of the low-intensity light stimulus triggers hypersynchronous spike-waves, the signature rhythm of generalized seizures and of photosensitive seizures in particular [Killiam et al., 1967; Shouse and Ryan, 1984; Wada et al., 1984; Fukuda et al., 1988]. Once a vulnerability to the light stimulus is established and a seizure ensues, the effects can be long-lasting:

> Once an animal is kindled, the reduction in seizure threshold may last for more than 6 months, suggesting that a relatively permanent synaptic reorganization has occurred. . . . Most noteworthy for our purposes is the finding that the kindling phenomenon is not dependent on the manifestation of generalized seizures. The threshold for localized after-discharges unaccompanied by motor phenomena is also lowered following repetitive electrical stimulation. . . . *Thus seizures may serve as a marker for the kindling process but are not themselves a prerequisite.* / A final note particularly relevant for later clinical interpretations of the kindling data is the finding that *a chronically kindled animal may eventually exhibit spontaneous seizures, i.e. the kindling process may so facilitate neuronal pathways and seizure mechanisms that they discharge autonomously* [Post and Kopanda, 1989, p. 629; emphasis added].

If bilateral spike-wave seizures can be induced in animal models by intermittently stimulating the animal's retina with a low-intensity light stimulus, might a similar chain of events be instigated by a meditator repeatedly inducing phosphene images? When meditators induce phosphenes, the phosphene light sensations are generated by the discharges of vision-relay neurons in the LGN, not by the discharges of retinal light receptors, but once the vision-relay cells in the LGN send their signals forward, just as they would do if they were relaying signals that had originated in the retina, from then on neurons in the visual cortices do not distinguish between those visual signals that originated in the retina and those that originated in the thalamus. Therefore, the intermittent induction of the same kinds of phosphene light sensations over a long enough time interval will very likely produce the same effect as the intermittent stimulation of retinal receptors using a low-intensity light stimulus in the animal experiments—a gradual lowering of the firing thresholds for those neurons that participate in the discharges that eventually register in consciousness as phosphene images.

The first phosphene image in the paradigm meditation-induced progression is a green light-ring, so it is interesting to note that *light stimuli shaped like rings are optimally effective for triggering photosensitive seizures, significantly more effective than disk-shapes* [Wilkins et al., 1980]. The second phosphene image in the meditation-induced sequence is the amorphous swirling wave with dark blue or purple colors. Harding and Fylan [1999] report that *blue intermixed with black is the optimal color for triggering photosensitive seizures*. The reason for this is that blue light intermixed with black activates the color-processing ("parvocellular") components of the visual system—a prerequisite for evoking a photoconvulsive response—but does so without also activating the spatially opponent networks in the retina that would normally inhibit or modulate the expression of the S-cone "blue-on" receptors. To control the epileptogenic effect of blue light, patients with photosensitive epilepsy are advised to wear polarized sunglasses with blue lens that deflect those light energies that would generate "blue" sensations away from the eyes [Takahashi and Takahashi, 1992; Kepecs et al., 2004].

Does the intermittent induction of green phosphene rings and dark blue nebulae swirling in the dark visual field have the effect of lowering the firing threshold of those neurons that generate the phosphenes? There is one important observation that demonstrates that this is indeed the case: early in the book I described how the green light-rings suddenly acquire a dark blue central disk after many intermittent phosphene inductions. In order for this change to take place—for a dark blue disk to fill in the center of the light-ring at precisely 2 seconds into the ring's 4-second trajectory—there must be a significant decrease in the time that was formerly required to complete the intracortical amplification of S-cone "blue-on" signals. In the beginning, before the appearance of the blue disk, it must have taken at least 4 seconds longer for the S-cone "blue-on" signals to register in the cortical lightness record than was required to process the rest of the color-related signals that generated the green light-ring. Because of the delay interposed by the intracortical amplification of S-cone "blue-on" signals, these signals did not register in consciousness while the green light-ring was still moving through the visual field. But after repeated inductions of this phosphene image, the time required to process S-cone "blue-on" signals decreased by half, taking only 2 seconds to register in the cortical lightness record and appear in the visual field, which allowed the blue-colored disk to appear inside the light-ring 2 seconds before the light-ring disappeared. The most likely cause of this decrease in processing time is a kindling effect produced by the intermittent induction of light-rings which lowered the firing thresholds of neurons in intracortical amplification networks.

Photosensitive Seizures and Meditation-Induced Seizures

Photosensitive seizures share some important characteristics with meditation-induced, phosphene-mediated seizures, which can be summarized as follows:

1. The central role played by the visual system;
2. The prevalence of self-induction;
3. The facilitating effect of sleep loss;

4. The special sensitivity to ring-shapes and to blue light intermixed with black;

5. The vulnerability of the visual pathways to intermittent stimulation that kindles a lowering of neuron firing thresholds;

6. The initial seizure is triggered by one type of seizure mechanism—by hypersynchronous spike-wave complexes in corticothalamic circuits, the hallmark rhythm of a generalized seizure—but can then switch to a second type of seizure mechanism—to ictal discharges in the hippocampus, the same mechanism involved in simple partial seizures of temporolimbic origins; and,

7. The activation of a temporolimbic partial seizure generates the distinctive cluster of sensorimotor and psychic symptoms that constitute the ecstatic aura, which may include orgasmic sensations if paroxysmal activity spreads from the hippocampus to the septum.

WHAT KIND OF SEIZURE IS IT?

We began this chapter with the goal of determining if any of the diagnoses used by neurologists or psychiatrists can encompass the meditation-induced, phosphene-mediated, ecstatic seizure I've described in this book. From the beginnings of Western medicine, practitioners have recognized that hypnosis, hysteria, dissociation, sleep, epilepsy, and mystical experience present many common features and thus are likely to share some common causal mechanisms [Thornton, 1976; Mavromatis, 1987; Temkin, 1994]. Neurologists suspect that many experiences the general public regards as "mystical" will eventually be linked to simple partial seizures (auras) of temporolimbic origin. In a review of the neurological origins of mystical experience, psychiatrists Saver and Rabin [1997] describe a variety of psychological symptoms that neurologists attribute to onset of simple partial seizures:

> Among individuals with partial complex seizures, the frequency of auras ranges from 23% to 83%, and up to one-quarter of the auras are psychic in content. The most common psychic or experiential ictal manifestations of temporal lobe epilepsy are fear, déjà vu, jamais vu, memory recall, and visual and auditory hallucinations. / Hughlings Jackson was among the first to identify and characterize less common ictal "intellectual auras" ("dreamy states," "cognitive auras") in which the experience of the immediacy and liveliness of one's own or external reality is altered. Depersonalization auras produce an alteration or loss of the sense of one's own reality, often accompanied by a sense of detachment from others and the environment, or acting like an automaton. Derealization auras

generate an alteration or loss of the sense of reality of the external environment; for example, the feeling that the external surround is just a dream - and also are often associated with a sense of detachment. Double consciousness ("mental diplopia") auras create a simultaneous experience of persisting remnants of one's normal consciousness and of a new quasi-parasitical consciousness with a different perception of reality. Auras of depersonalization, derealization, and dream state account for approximately one-quarter of psychic auras (p. 197).

The psychiatric diagnoses that we considered as most appropriate for the meditation-induced, phosphene-mediated seizure—the dissociative disorders of conversion and depersonalization—were specifically excluded because meditation is a "culturally-sanctioned" practice in most contexts, and other candidate diagnoses that initially seemed relevant ultimately had to be excluded on equally technical grounds, but now I think we are now in a position to make a diagnosis: the meditation-induced, phosphene-mediated seizure most closely resembles the self-induced photosensitive seizures that begin as generalized seizures but then fail to generalize and instead trigger simple (or complex) partial seizures of temporolimbic origin. It is this temporolimbic activation that generates the "ecstatic" symptoms that are so reinforcing. The ecstatic qualities of the meditation-induced, phosphene-mediated seizure meet all of the criteria for an "ecstatic" aura proposed by Hughes, including the specification that there must be high-amplitude activity in the septum. In effect, a meditator's success at inducing the full progression of phosphene images culminating in the lightning-like flashes and an ecstatic aura is evidence of an *acquired phosphene-sensitivity*, a meditation-acquired phosphene-sensitivity, which suggests MAPS as a handy acronym.

11

A CONCLUDING, UNSCIENTIFIC POSTSCRIPT

ISSUES UNRESOLVED

Mechanism and Meaning

In this book I have presented a thoroughly reductionist approach to meditation, attempting to explain a psychological state in exclusively materialist terms. My theory that "empty-mind" meditation—the state called *turiya* in Hindu India, *dhyana* in Buddhist Tibet, and *shou-i* in Daoist China—is installed by activation of slow wave sleep rhythms provides a simple, comprehensive, and *necessary* explanation of this phenomenon, but my theory does not provide a *sufficient* explanation because it omits a discussion of the range of meanings that humans in many different cultures and many different historical eras have ascribed to meditational states and meditation-induced light visions. What is the relationship between neuroscientific theories that propose materialist explanations of psychological states and human ascriptions of meaning? Several years ago a friend provided me with a useful analogy that I often use to structure my own thoughts on this issue: she pointed out that scientists can explain many of the physiological processes that take place when a baby is born, but this materialist explanation, while it is undeniably important in many situations, does not and cannot account for the emotional significance that a new birth has for everyone involved—for the mother and father, for siblings and grandparents, perhaps for the community as well, and, if one were to adopt an Olympian perspective, the significance of an individual's birth can have important implications for an entire society, perhaps even for humanity as a whole. I think this apt and useful analogy is most instructive for those of us who study the neuro-scientific underpinnings of human behaviors: it helps us remember that we humans have to create a sense of selfhood by telling ourselves stories—stories about where and when we came into being, stories about our early lives, stories about who we have now become, and stories about where we're going. As scientists, we can propose a theory about how the brain's mechanisms install and maintain an altered state of consciousness like meditation and hypnosis, and, based on that theory, we might predict that the practice will produce some outcomes that benefit the practitioner but also will produce other outcomes that threaten the meditator's health, but, in the human realm these predictions about the neural correlates and the neural consequences of certain behaviors cannot be regarded as having encompassed all aspects of the behavioral phenomenon.

How Much Meditation Is Too Much?

If my theory about the neural correlates of light visions is correct, then a meditator who succeeds at inducing the lightning-like flashes, tremors, and ecstatic raptures so highly-prized by mystics in the world's major religious traditions will almost certainly damage some neurons in the hippocampus, neurons that the mystic can ill afford to lose. The loss of hippocampal neurons is thought to play an important role in temporolimbic epilepsy and is also associated with the compromise of short-term memory that occurs in Alzheimer's disease and other forms of dementia. It would seem likely, then, that repeated inductions of paroxysmal light visions constitute a form of self-injury. I would not be surprised to read someday in the latest bulletins that some meditators who have achieved recognition and influence based on their demonstrated abilities to induce ecstatic visionary raptures have been found to suffer premature memory loss as a result of their having incurred significant neuron damage in the hippocampus. Is the prospect of neuronal damage a good reason to abandon the dedicated pursuit of meditation-induced light visions? I would think so, especially for someone who must continue to make his or her own way in the world, for someone who does not have a coterie of followers ready to assume responsibility for obtaining the requisite finances to support their group and to carry out the normal tasks of daily life so the meditator can continue to meditate undisturbed. As for myself, I made the decision to stop inducing phosphenes as soon as I discovered what was happening inside my brain while I was enjoying the lightning-like flashes and the ecstatic raptures that accompanied them, but will other people react in the same way? And will those religions that have developed elaborate meditation traditions celebrating the virtues of ecstatic visionary experiences be open to making some adjustments in the meditational practices they prescribe so as to make it safer for those adherents who meditate? Perhaps, but, then again, perhaps not: I suspect that there will always be individuals who are obsessed with transcending mundane reality by triggering the very kind of ecstatic rapture that we've discussed in this book, or something quite similar, and, for those individuals, warnings that some risks are involved might serve as lures rather than deterrents; obviously the same dynamic occurs in many other high-risk activities—rock-climbing, sport parachuting, and the like. And then for those with a spiritual inclination there is always the existential paradox that Dostoevsky expressed so well in the words of his fictional protagonist, the epileptic Prince Myshkin—the paradox that the most intense mystical rapture might be inextricably linked with a illness:

> He pondered, among other things, the fact that there was a stage in his epileptic condition just before the fit itself (if it occurred during the waking hours) when all of a sudden, amid the sadness, spiritual darkness, and oppression, there were moments when his brain seemed to flare up momentarily and all his vital forces tense themselves at once in an extraordinary surge. The sensation of being alive and self-aware increased almost tenfold in those lightning-quick moments. His mind and heart were bathed in an extraordinary illumination. . . . these flashes, were merely the prelude to that final second (never more than a second) which marked the onset of the actual fit. . . . Reflecting on that moment afterwards when he had recovered, he often used to tell himself that all these gleams and lightning-flashes of heightened self-awareness, and hence also of "higher existence," were nothing more than the illness itself, violating the normal state of things as it did, and thus it was not a higher mode of existence at all—on the contrary, it should be regarded as the lowest. And yet he arrived at length at a paradoxical conclusion: "What if it is the illness then?" he decided finally. "What does it matter if it is some abnormal tension, if the end-result, the instant of apprehension, recalled and analyzed during recovery, turns out to be the highest pitch of harmony and beauty, conferring a sense of some hitherto-unknown and unguessed completeness, proportion, reconciliation, an ecstatic, prayerful fusion with the supreme synthesis of life?" . . . . If in that second, in the final conscious moment before the attack, he could have managed to tell himself clearly and deliberately: "Yes, for this moment one could give one's whole life!" then of course, that moment on its own would be worth one's whole life [Dostoevsky, 1992 (1868), p. 237].

For some people the chance of experiencing a moment of true ecstasy and having one's life seemingly showered with transcendent meaning will remain an irresistible challenge, a goal made even more alluring by the dangers involved. For meditators who want to continue meditating without the risks that we've discussed here, an alternative course of action has already been charted by Theravadan and Zen Buddhist sects: in these traditions, when meditators learn how to induce the state of "empty-mind consciousness," they begin to see a spontaneous flow of light visions, and that is considered to be the prerequisite for making further progress, but then, once the light visions have appeared, indicating the attainment of a "beginner's samadhi," the meditator is counseled to ignore these inner lights, to regard them as yet another form of illusion, as a form of apparitional reality that is so pleasant to contemplate that beginners are often seduced into believing that they've arrived at their goal when in fact they have departed from the path that leads ultimately to True Insight. As for myself, this is the discipline that I now practice: I

234

continue to meditate on some occasions, but I avoid my former practice of fixing attention on the play of phosphene imagery. If, as often happens, the early "sleep rhythm" phosphenes begin to flow spontaneously—the green rings, then the blue nebulae—I don't try to suppress these images, but at the same time I make a point of not trying to push beyond these early images into the paroxysmal sequences which generate the ecstatic raptures. If there is any hint that this might happen—if, for example, I see hints of a faint, bluish white cloud and begin to feel euphoric—I immediately back off, divert my attention, and prepare to move on to some other activity. This modest practice brings the benefits of meditation without imposing costs that I haven't already incurred.

So how much meditation is too much? It depends—it depends on the type of meditation one practices, on the strength of one's attraction to the lure of mystical ecstasies, and on one's tolerance for high-risk behaviors.

Light Visions, Hypnotizability and Human Evolution

If meditation-induced light visions are initiated by activation of slow wave sleep rhythms, and if the activation of sleep rhythm oscillators imposes significant constraints on how much variation can occur in the spatial and temporal characteristics of meditation-induced light visions, then it is reasonable to infer that meditation-induced phosphene sensations will manifest the same characteristics whenever and wherever they appear. There are two important implications of this proposition. First, the conclusion that there are neurologically-imposed constraints that limit the variability of meditation-induced light visions implies that mystics visionaries in all of the organized religions (and shamans who practice among tribal peoples) must all see essentially the same progression of light visions if and when they induce those visions by some form of meditation (as opposed, say, to ingesting hallucinogenic drugs or dancing themselves to the point of physical collapse). The second implication is this: if the neural mechanisms that generate meditation-induced light visions are the same mechanisms that put humans to sleep every night, and if it is relatively easy—even without instruction—to learn how to manipulate sleep rhythms in a way that produces a spontaneous flow of light visions, then this capability could have been, and most likely was, discovered independently by many different individuals living in many different cultures and in many different historical eras. If so, then references to meditation-induced light visions should be ubiquitous in human culture, surfacing time and time again—in the symbols of prehistoric rock art, in the shamanic practices of contemporary tribal cultures, in traditional accounts of the lives of the founders of the world's major religious traditions, even in modern industrialized societies, and, indeed, we should expect that the phenomenon of meditation-induced light visions giving rise to metaphysical claims will surface yet again at some future time in a form that would strike us as both familiar and also strange.

If meditation-induced light visions are a by-product of neurophysiological and neuropsychological processes that are universal in humans, it should not be surprising to discover that they have a universal distribution, and, if this is indeed the case, then activation of sleep rhythms by meditating would likely have played some role in human evolution. In this regard, I am fascinated by James McClenon's theories about the role of meditation's twin, hypnosis, in human evolution presented in his book, *Wondrous Healing* [McClenon, 2004]: he proposes that the neuropsychological capacity to hypnotize oneself (or to be hypnotized by others) is a trait that conferred significant survival advantages during the early stages of human evolution on those individuals who learned how to use this inward shift of attention to ameliorate the pain of conditions for which there was no other remedy available by mobilizing the body's natural healing resources. In this view, women who could hypnotize themselves (or be hypnotized by others) during the pain of childbirth would acquire some survival advantage over those who could not, and, similarly, those hunters and warriors who could respond to wounds by mobilizing their body's resources through hypnosis would acquire some survival advantage over those who could not. If there was indeed a survival advantage conferred by the ability to become hypnotized, then natural selection would likely cause this useful neuropsychological trait to become more widely distributed in the human population. It is this trait of hypnotizability—the ability to dissociate with relative ease—that enables many humans (but not all) to learn how to induce the trance states that generate a spontaneous flow of phosphene images.

In many tribal hunter/gather cultures that have survived into modern times, the ability to induce visions of strange, unworldly lights is a prerequisite for becoming a shaman/healer. Once the shaman achieves recognition, the induction of light visions continues to serve as one of the most important tools in the shaman's repertoire. Those who have seen visions of an eerie, inner light that does not match any type of light seen in the external world are able to claim that they have seen convincing evidence for the existence of a hidden "spirit" world "with their own eyes." Having experienced such a vision, and having experienced the disorientation of having one's consciousness seemingly pulled out of the physical body—an "ecstasy" in the literal meaning of the word, "ex-stasis"—and then having returned to their bodies unharmed, seers are apt to acquire a unshakable belief in their having been "chosen" by supernatural entities to provide their community with a new metaphysical interpretation of the meaning of life—in some cases, by offering a new myth, and, in others, offering personal testimony that validates the efficacy of the existing myths that are prized by that culture. Those who see light visions *need* myths to explain why the light visions appeared and what they mean, and, conversely, the cultural myth-systems *need* some individuals to see otherworldly light visions so that they can testify in the continued potency of the prevailing myths. A shaman's ability to self-induce light visions is particularly effective at enhancing the practitioner's confidence in the efficacy of his or her ritual performances, first, because this is a criterion for efficacy that remains within the personal control of the shaman, and, second, because it is a criterion of effectiveness that does not depend on actually bringing about the intended effect in the external environment. In a scientific method, a failed prediction casts doubt on the underlying hypothesis, but the failed prediction of a shaman can be attributed to other causes—to mistakes that might have been made in the performance of the prescribed rituals, or to the black magic of some other shaman who wants to prevent a good outcome. So for shamans the induction of light visions turns out to be valuable indeed: light visions increase a shaman's confidence in his or her powers, and that display of self-confidence embues a shaman with charismatic authority that impresses clients. As McClenon points out in his study of healing rituals, it is precisely this fact—that the client believes in the efficacy of a healer and the healer's ritual—that increases the likelihood that the performance will indeed produce some beneficial results, most notably in those clients whose inborn trait of hypnotizability renders them susceptible to ritual-induced hypnosis and the placebo effects that hypnosis can mobilize. I believe McClenon's analysis is spot-on, that the psychological trait of hypnotizability is the root of meditation, and that the root of hypnotizability is an ability to activate slow wave sleep rhythms while retaining consciousness.

Is There a "God Module" in the Human Brain?

Is there a "specialized neural circuitry for the sole purpose of mediating religious experience," as V. S. Ramachandran suggested in a presentation at the Annual Meeting of the Society for Neuroscience in 1997 [Bower, *Science News* 2001;159(97): 104 – 106; Ramachandran and Blakeslee, 1997]? The "reverse-engineering" analysis of meditation-induced light visions presented in this book suggests that there is indeed a set of neural mechanisms that can function as a "god module," but it reveals that these particular mechanisms, far from being "specialized . . . for the sole purpose of mediating religious experience," are the very same mechanisms that put humans to sleep every night. It seems likely, given the diversity of human mystical experiences, that there are many "god modules" in the brain, not just one, and I rather suspect that when researchers uncover the existence of new "god modules," they will discover that, as in the present case where sleep rhythms are responsible for generating ecstatic light visions, the new "god modules" activate regions of the brain that also have more normal functions, that the common thread is that the mundane can be transformed, temporarily, into a vehicle of transcendence—into a "god module."

BIBLIOGRAPHY

Abramov I. 1994. Color appearance: On seeing red - or yellow, or green, or blue. *Annual Review of Psychology* 45: 451 - 485.

Acsády L, Kamondi A, Sík A, Freund Tamás and Buzsáki G. 1998. GABAergic cells are the major postsynaptic targets of mossy fibers in the rat hippocampus. *Journal of Neuroscience* 18(9): 3386 - 3403.

Aguirre GK, Detre JA, Alsop DC and D'Esposito M. 1996. The parahippocampus subserves topographical learning in man. *Cerebral Cortex* 6: 823 - 829.

Amaral DG and Kutz J. 1985. An analysis of the origins of the cholinergic and noncholinergic septal projections to the hippocampal formation of the rat. *Journal of Comparative Neurology* 240: 37 - 59.

Amaral DG, Insausti R and Cowan WM 1984 The commissural connections of the money hippocampal formation. *Journal of Comparative Neurology* 225: 307-306.

Amaral DG, Price JL, Pitkänen A and Carmichael. 1992. Anatomical organization of the primate amydaloid complex. In: Aggleton JP, editor, *The Amydala* (New York: Wiley-Liss, p. 1 - 66)

Ames FR and Saffer D. 1983. The sunflower syndrome: A new look at "self-induced" photosensitive epilepsy. *Journal of the Neurological Sciences* 59: 1-11.

Anand BK, Chhina GS and Singh B. 1961. Some Aspects of Electroencephalographic Studies in Yogis. *Electroencephalography and Clinical Neurophysiology* 13: 452 - 456.

Andersen RA 1989. Visual and eye movement functions of the posterior parietal cortex. *Annual Reviews of Neuroscience* 12: 377-403.

Andersen RA and Mountcastle VB. 1983. The influence of the angle of gaze upon the excitability of the light-sensitive neurons of the posterior parietal cortex. *Journal of Neuroscience* 3(3): 532-548.

Andersen RA, Essick GK and Siegel RM 1987. Neurons of area 7 activated by both visual stimuli and oculomotor behavior. *Experimental Brain Research* 67: 316-322;

Andersen RA, Bracewell RM, Barash S, Gnadt JW and Fogassi L 1990. Eye position effects on visual, memory, and saccade-related activity in areas LIP and 7a of the macaque. *Journal of Neuroscience* 10(4): 1176-1196.

Andersen P, Soleng A and Raastad M. 2000. The hippocampal lamella hypothesis revisited. *Brain Research* 886: 165- 171.

Arambula P, Peper E, Kawakami M and Gibney K. 2001. The physiological correlates of Kundalini Yoga meditation: a study of a yoga master. *Applied Psychophysiology and Biofeedback* 26(2): 147 - 153.

Austin JH. 1999. *Zen and the Brain: Toward an Understanding of Meditation and Consciousness* (MIT Press: Cambridge, MA).

Baloh RW and Honrubia V. 1990. *Clinical Neurophysiology of the Vestibular System* (F.A. Davis & Co.: Philadelphia).

Barbarosie M and Avoli M. 1997. CA3-driven hippocampal-entorhinal loop controls rather than sustains in vitro limbic seizures. *Journal of Neuroscience* 17(23): 9308 - 9314.

Barbarosie M, Louvel J, Kurcewicz I and Avoli M. 2000. CA3-released entorhinal seizures disclose dentate gyrus epileptogenicity and unmask a temporoammonic pathway. *Journal of Neurophysiology* 83: 1115 -1124.

Barbas H and Blatt GJ. 1995. Topographically specific hippocampal projections target functionally distinct prefrontal areas in the rhesus monkey. *Hippocampus* 5(6): 511-533.

Bare M, Burnstine TH, Fisher R and Lesser R. 1994. Electroencephalographic Changes During Simple Partial Seizures. *Epilepsia* 35, 4, pp. 715 - 720.

Barlow JS. 1993. *The Electroencephalogram: Its Patterns and Origins* (MIT Press: Cambridge).

Bartegashi R and Gessi T. 2003. Activation of perforant path neurons to field CA1 by hippocampal projections. *Hippocampus* 13: 235 – 249.

Bausch SB and Chavkin C. 1997. Changes in hippocampal circuitry after pilocarbine-induced seizures as revealed by opoid receptor distribution and activation. *Journal of Neuroscience* 17(1): 477 - 492.

Bazier JS, Ungerleider LG and Desimone R. 1991. Organization of inputs to the inferior temporal and posterior parietal cortex in macaques. *Journal of Neuroscience* 11(1): 168-190.

Bazil C and Walczak T. 1997. Effects of Sleep and Sleep Stage on Epileptic and Nonepileptic Seizures. *Epilepsia* 38(1): 56-62.

Bear D. 1979. Temporal lobe epilepsy: A syndrome of sensory-limbic hyperconnection. Cortex 15(3): 357-384.

Bear D. 1986. Hemispheric Asymmetries in Emotional Function: A Reflection of Lateral Specialization in Cortical-Limbic Connections. In Doane BK and Livingston KE, eds., *The Limbic System: Functional Organization and Clinical Disorders* (Raven Press: New York, pp. 29 - 41.

Bear D and Fedio P. 1977. Quantitative Analysis of Interictal Behavior in Temporal Lobe Epilepsy. *Archives of Neurology* 34: 454 - 467.

Beauregard M and O'Leary D. 2007. *The Spiritual Brain: A Neuroscientist's Case for the Existence of the Soul* (HarperCollins: New York).

Bender D and Youakim M. 2001. Effect of attentive fixation in macaque thalamus and cortex. *Journal of Neurophysiology* 85: 219 - 234.

Bennie CD, Estevez O, Kasteleijn-Nolst Trenite DG and Peters A. 1984. Colour and photosensitive epilepsy. *Electroencephalography and Clinical Neurophysiology* 58(5): 387-391.

Benson D. 1991. The Geschwind Syndrome. *Advances in Neurology* 55: 406 - 421.

Benson H. 1975. *The Relaxation Response* (Morrow: New York).

Benson H, Malhotra M, Goldman R, Jacobs G and Hopkins P. 1990. Three case reports of the metabolic and electroencephalograpic changes during advanced Buddhist meditation techniques. *Behavioral Medicine* 16(2): 90-95.

Bernard C, Cannon RC, Ben Ari Y and Wheal HV. 1997. Model of spatio-temporal propagation of action potentials in the Schaffer collateral pathway of the CA1 area of the rat hippocampus. *Hippocampus* 7: 58-72.

Bernasconi N, Bernasconi A, Caramanos Z, Antel SB, Andermann F and Arnold DL. 2003. Mesial temporal damage in temporal lobe epilepsy: a volumetric MRI study of the hippocampus, amygdala and parahippocampal region. *Brain* 126(Pt 2): 462 – 469.

Bertram EH, Mangan PS, Zhang DX, Scott CA and Williamson JM. 2001. The midline thalamus: alterations and a potential role in limbic epilepsy. *Epilepsia* 42(8): 967-978.

Bertram EH, Zhang DX and Williamson JM. 2008. Multiple roles of midline dorsal thalamic nuclei in induction and spread of limbic seizures. *Epilepsia* 49(2): 256-268.

Bettendorf L, Sallanon-Moulin M, Touret M, Wins P, Margineanu I and Schoffeniels E. 1996. Paradoxical sleep deprivation increases content of glutamate and glutamine in rat cerebral cortex. *Sleep* 19(1): 65 - 71.

Bhawe SS. 1957, 1960, 1962. *The Soma Hymns of the Rig Veda, Parts I - III*, as quoted in Wasson RG. *Soma: Divine Mushroom of Immortality* (Harcourt Brace Jovanovich: New York, 1971).

Bishop MP, Elder ST and Heath RG. Intracranial self-stimulation in man. *Science* 140: 394-396.

Blatt G and Rosene D. 1998. Organization of direct hippocampal efferent projections to the cerebral cortex of the Rhesus monkey: projections from CA1, prosubiculum, and subiculum to the temporal lobe. *Journal of Comparative Neurology* 392: 92 - 114.

Blumenfeld H and McCormick D. 2000. Corticothalamic inputs control the pattern of activity generated in thalamocortical networks. *Journal of Neuroscience* 20(13): 5153 - 5162.

Blumer D. 2000. Dysphoric disorders and paroxysmal effects: recognition and treatment of epilepsy-related psychiatric disorders. *Harvard Review of Psychiatry* 8(1): 8-17.

Blumer D, Montouris G and Davies K. 2004. The interictal dysphoric disorder: recognition, pathogenesis, and treatment of a major psychiatric disorder of epilepsy. *Epilepsy and Behavior* 5(6): 826 – 840.

Boehme J. No date. *Dialogues on the Suprasensual Life*, William Law, transl. (Frederick Ungar Publ Co: New York).

Bokenkamp SR. 1996. Declarations of the Perfected. In: Lopez DS, Jr. *Religions of China in Practice* (Princeton University Press: Princeton, NJ, pp. 166-179).

Bokenkamp SR. 1997. *Early Daoist Scriptures* (University of California Press: Berkeley and Los Angeles).

Bonhila L, Kobayashi E, Rorden C, Cendes F and Li LM. 2003. Medial temporal lobe atrophy in patients with refractory temporal lobe epilepsy. *Journal of Neurology, Neurosurgery and Psychiatry* 74(12): 1627 – 1630.

Boston Globe, October 29, 1997, p. A14, "A Study on the 'God Module': Finding Faith in the Brain."

Bower B. 2001. Into the Mystics: Scientists Confront the Hazy Realm of Spiritual Enlightenment. *Science News* 159(7): 104 - 106.

Bowman ES and Markhand ON. 1996. Psychodynamics and psychiatric diagnoses of pseudoseizure patients. *American Journal of Psychiatry* 153(1): 57-63.

Boylan LS, Labovitz DL, Jackson SC, Starner K and Devinsky O. 2006. Auras are frequent in idiopathic generalized epilepsy. *Neurology* 67: 343-345.

Bragin A, Jandó G, Nádasdy Z, van Landeghen M and Buzsáki G. 1995. Dentate EEG spikes and associated interneuronal population bursts in the hippocampal hilar region of the rat. *Journal of Neurophysiology* 73(4): 1691 - 1705.

Bragin A, Csicsvari J, Penttonen M and Buzsáki G. 1997. Epileptic afterdischarge in the hippocampal-entorhinal system: current source density and unit studies. *Neuroscience* 76(4): 1187 - 1203.

Bragin A, Csicsvári J, Penttonen M and Buzsáki G. 1997. Epileptic afterdischarge in the hippocampal-entorhinal system: current density and unit studies. *Neuroscience* 76(4): 1187 – 1203.

Bragin A, Engel J Jr., Wilson CL, Fried I and Buzsáki G. 1999a. High-frequency oscillations in human brain. *Hippocampus* 9: 137 - 142.

Bragin A, Engel J Jr, Wilson C, Vizentin E and Mathern G. 1999b. Electrophysiologic analysis of a chronic seizure model after unilateral hippocampal KA injection. *Epilepsia* 40(9): 1210 - 1221.

Bragin A, Engel J Jr, Wilson, CL, Vizentin E and Mathern GW. 1999c. Electrophysiologic analysis of a chronic seizure model after unilateral hippocampal KA injection. *Epilepsia* 40(9): 1210 – 1221.

Bragin A, Wilson CL and Engel J Jr. Chronic epileptogenesis requires development of a network of pathologically interconnected neuron clusters: a hypothesis. *Epilepsia* 2000; 41 (Suppl. 6): S144-S152).

Bragin A, Wilson C and Engel J Jr. 2002. Local generation of fast ripples in the epileptic brain. *Journal of Neuroscience* 22(5): 2012 - 2021.

Braun A, Balkin T, Wesensten N, Gwadry F, Carson R, Varga M, Baldwin P, Belenky G and Herscovitch P. 1998. Dissociated Pattern of Activity in Visual Cortices and Their Projections During Human Rapid Eye Movement Sleep. *Science* 279, 2, pp. 91 -95.

Bremmer F. 2000. Eye position effects in macaque V-4. *Neuroreport* 11(6): 1277 - 1283.

Bremner J. 2001. Hypotheses and controversies related to effects of stress on the hippocampus: an argument for stress-induced damage to the hippocampus in patients with posttraumatic stress disorder. *Hippocampus* 11: 75 - 81.

Bremner J, Randall P, Scott TM, Bronen RA, Seibyl JP, Southwick SM, Delaney RC, McCarthy G, Charney DS and Innis RB. 1995. MRI-based measurement of hippocampal volume in patients with combat-related posttraumatic stress disorder. *American Journal of Psychiatry* 152: 973 - 981.

Broughton R and Hasan J. 1995. Quantitative Topographic Electroencephalographic Mapping During Drowsiness and Sleep Onset. *Journal of Clinical Neurophysiology* 12, 4, pp. 372 - 386.

Brown D. 1986. The Stages of Meditation in Cross-Cultural Perspective. In: K. Wilber K., Engler J and Brown D. *Transformations of Consciousness* (Shambhala Press: Boston).

Brunner DP, Dijk D-J and Borbély AA. 1993. Repeated partial sleep deprivation progressively changes the EEG during sleep and wakefulness. *Sleep* 16(2): 100 - 113.

Buchsbaum M, Hazlett E, Wu J and Bunney W Jr. 2001. Positron emission tomography with deoxyglucose-F18 imaging of sleep. *Neuropsychopharmacology* 25 (5 Suppl): S50 - 56.

Buckley MJ, Booth MC, Rolls ET and Gaffan D. 2001. Selective perceptual impairments after perirhinal cortex ablation. *Journal of Neuroscience* 21(24): 9824 – 9836.

Buhusi C and Schmajuk NA. 1996. Attention, configuration, and hippocampal function. *Hippocampus* 6: 621 - 642.

Bundesen C, Larsen A, Kyllingsbaek S, Paulson OB and Law I. 2002. Attentional effects in the visual pathways: a whole-brain PET study. *Experimental Brain Research* 147(3): 394 - 406.

Bussey TJ and Saksida LM. 2002. The organization of visual object representation: a connectionist model of effects of lesions in perirhinal cortex. *European Journal of Neuroscience* 15(2): 355 – 364.

Buzsáki G. 1986. Generation of hippocampal EEG patterns. In: Issacson and Pribham. *The Hippocampus, Vol. 3* (New York: Plenum Press, pp 137 - 167).

Buzsáki G. 1989. Two-stage model of memory trace formation: a role for "noisy" brain states. *Neuroscience* 31(3): 551 - 570.

Buzsáki G. 1996. The hippocampal-neocortical dialogue. *Cerebral Cortex* 6: 81 - 92.

Buzsáki G, Penttonen M, Bragin A, Nádasdy Z and Chrobak JJ. 1995. Possible physiological role of the perforant path-CA1 projection. *Hippocampus* 5: 141 - 146.

Chagmé K with Gyatrul Rinpoche and Wallace A. 2000. *Naked Awareness: Practical Instructions on the Union of Mahamudra and Dzogchen* (Snow Lion Publications: Ithaca, NY).

Chandrasekaran R, Goswami U, Sivakumar V and Chitralekha. 1994. Hysterical neurosis - a follow-up study. *Acta Psychiatrica Scandinavia* 89: 78-80.

Chatterjee S and Callaway EM. 2002. *Neuron* 35(6): 1135 - 1146.

Chatterjee S and Callaway EM. 2003. Parallel colour-opponent pathways to primary visual cortex. *Nature* 426: 6888 - 5002.

Chen W, Zhu XH, Thulborn KR and Ugurbil K. 1999. Retinotopic mapping of lateral geniculate nucleus in humans using functional magnetic resonance imaging. *Proceedings of the National Academy of Sciences* 96: 2340 - 2434.

Chow TW and Cummings JL. 1999. In: Miller BL and Cummings JL, eds. *The Human Frontal Lobes* (Guilford Press: New York).

Chrobak JJ and Buzsáki G. 1994. Selective activation of deep layer (V - VI) retrohippocampal cortical neurons during hippocampal sharp waves in the behaving rat. *Journal of Neuroscience* 14(10): 6160-6170.

Churchland PS, Ramachandran VS and Sejnowski TJ. 1994. A critique of pure vision. In: Koch, C., and Davis, J., eds. *Large-Scale Neuronal Theories of the Brain* (Cambridge: MIT Press, pp. 23-61).

Cirignotta F, Todesco CV and Lugaresi L. 1980. Temporal lobe epilepsy with ecstatic seizures (co-called Dostoevsky epilepsy). *Epilepsia* 21: 705-710.

Coghill RC, Talbot JD, Evans AC, Meyer E, Gjedde A, Bushnell MC and Duncan GH. 1994. Distributed processing of pain and vibration by the human brain. *Journal of Neuroscience* 14(7): 4095-4108.

Cohen-Gadol AA, Bradley CC, Williamson A, Kim JH, Westerveld M, Duckrow RB and Spencer DD. 2005. Normal magnetic resonance imaging and medial temporal lobe epilepsy: the clinical syndrome of paradoxical temporal lobe epilepsy. *Journal of Neurosurgery* 102(5): 902-9.

Colder BW, Frysinger RC, Wilson CL, Harper RM and Engel J Jr. 1996a. Decreased neuronal burst discharge near site of seizure onset in epileptic human temporal lobes. *Epilepsia* 37(2): 113 - 121.

Colder BW, Wilson CL, Frysinger RC, Chao LC, Harper RM and Engel J Jr. 1996b. Neuronal synchrony in relation to burst discharge in epileptic human temporal lobes. *Journal of Neurophysiology* 75(6): 2496 - 2508.

David Coming. 2007. *Did Man Create God: Is Your Spiritual Brain at Peace with Your Thinking Brain?* (Hope Press: Duarte, CA).

Connolly M and Van Essen D. 1984. Representation of the visual field in parvicellular and magnocellular layers of the lateral geniculate nucleus in the macaque monkey. *Journal of Comparative Neurology* 226: 544 - 564.

Contreras D and Steriade M. 1995. Cellular basis of EEG slow rhythms: A study of dynamic corticothalamic relationships. *Journal of Neuroscience* 15(1): 604-622.

Contreras D and Steriade M. 1997. State-dependent fluctuations of low-frequency rhythms in cortico-thalamic networks. *Neuroscience* 76(1): 25 - 38.

Contreras D, Destexhe A, Sejnowski TJ and Steriade M. 1997. Spatiotemporal patterns of spindle oscillations in the cortex and thalamus. *Journal of Neuroscience* 17(3): 1179 - 1196.

Conway B. 2001. Spatial structure of cone inputs to color cells in alert macaque primary visual cortex (V-1). J Neurosci 21(8): 2768 - 2783.

Corbetta M, Miezin FM, Dobmeyer S, Shulman GL and Petersen SE. 1991. Selective and divided attention during visual discriminations of shape, color, and speed: functional anatomy by positron emission tomography. *Journal of Neuroscience* 11(8): 2383-2402.

Corbetta M, Miezin FM, Shulman GL and Petersen SE. 1993. A PET study of visuospatial attention. *Journal of Neuroscience* 13(3): 1202-1226.

Corby J, Roth W, Zarcone V Jr and Kopell B. 1978. Psychophysiological Correlates of the Practice of Tantric Yoga Meditation. *Archives of General Psychiatry* 35: 571-577.

Corsi-Cabrera M, Guevara M, Del Rio-Portilla Y, Arce C and Villaneuva-Hernandez Y. 2000. EEG Bands During Wakefulness, Slow-Wave and Paradoxical Sleep as a Result of Principle Component Analysis in Man. *Sleep* 23, 6, pp. 738 - 744.

Cortez M, McKerlie C and Snead OC. 2001. A model of atypical absence seizures: EEG, pharmacology, and developmental characterization. *Neurology* 56: 341 - 349.

Cottaris NP and De Valois RL. 1998. Temporal dynamics of chromatic tuning in macaque primary visual cortex. *Nature* 396: (6705): 896-900.

Coulter DA. 1997. Thalamocortical anatomy and physiology. In: Engel J Jr and Pedley TA. *Epilepsy: A Comprehensive Textbook, Vol. I.* (Philadelphia: Lippincott-Raven Publishers, pp. 341-351).

Cowen R, Frederick B, Rainey M, Levin J, Maas L, Bang J, Hennen J, Lukas S and Renshaw P. 2000. Sex differences in response to red and blue light in human primary visual cortex: a bold fMRI study. *Psychiatry Research: Neuroimaging* 100: 129-138.

Cozort D. 1986. *Highest Yoga Tantra: An Introduction to the Esoteric Buddhism of Tibet* (Snow

Lion Publications: Ithaca, NY)

Crawford HJ and Gruzelier JH. 1992. A midstream view of the neuropsychophysiology of hypnosis: recent research and future directions. In: Fromm E & Nash M, eds. *Contemporary Perspectives in Hypnosis Research* (New York: Guilford Press, pp. 227-266) .

Crawford HJ, Brown AM and Moon CE. 1993. Sustained attentional and disattentional abilities: differences between low and highly hypnotizable persons. *Journal of Abnormal Psychology* 102(4): 534-543.

Creutzfeld OD. 1993. The neurophysiological correlates of colour induction, colour and brightness contrast. *Progress in Brain Research* 95: 45-53.

Cross CG. 2000. Coding for visual categories in the human brain. *Nature Neuroscience* 3: 855 – 856.

Cruetzfield O, Grunewald G, Simonova O and Schmiz H. 1969. Changes of the basic rhythms of the EEG during the performance of mental and visuomotor tasks. In: Evans CR and Mulholland TB, eds. *Attention in Neurophysiology* (Butterworths: London, pp. 148-168).

Dacey DM. 2000. Parallel pathways for spectral coding in primate retina. *Annual Review of Neuroscience* 23: 743-775.

Dacey DM and Packer OS. 2003. Colour coding in the primate retina: diverse cell types and cone-specific circuitry. *Current Opinion in Neurology* 13(4): 421-427.

Daiguiji M. 1990. Significance of the affinity of the epileptic to somatesthetic religion. *Psychopathology* 23: 176-180.

Dange SA. 1992. *Divine Hymns and Ancient Thought, Vol. I: RgVeda Hymns and Ancient Thought* (N. Singal, NAVRANG: New Delhi).

D'Antuono M, Benini R, Biagni G, D'Arcangelo G, Barbarosie MK, Tancredi V and Avoli M. 2001. Limbic network interactions leading to hyperexcitability in a model of temporal lobe epilepsy. *Journal of Neurophysiology* 87: 634 - 639.

d'Aquili E and Newberg A. 1993. Religious and Mystical States: A Neuropsychological Model. *Zygon* 28: 177 -199.

d'Aquili E and Newberg A. 1999. *The Mystical Mind: Probing the Biology of Religious Experience* (Fortress Press: Minneapolis, MN).

Darian-Smith C, Darian-Smith I and Cheema SS. 1990. Thalamic projections to sensorimotor cortex in the macaque monkey: use of multiple retrograde fluorescent tracers. *Journal of Comparative Neurology* 299: 17 - 46.

Das N and Gastaut H. 1995. Variations De L'Activite Electrique Du Cerveau, Du Coeur, Et Des Muscles Squelettiques Au Cours De La Meditation Et De L'Extase Yogique, *Electroencephalography and Clinical Neurophysiology* (Supplement 6), pp. 211 - 219.

Datta S. 1995. Neuronal activity in the peribrachial area: relationship to behavioral state control. *Neuroscience and Biobehavioral Reviews* 19(1): 67-84.

Daurat A, Aguirre A, Foret J and Benoit O. 1997. Disruption of sleep recovery after 36 hours of exposure to moderately bright light. *Sleep* 20(5): 352 - 358.

De Valois R, Cottaris N, Elfar S, Mahon L and Wilson JA. 2000. Some transformations of color information from lateral geniculate nucleus to striate cortex. *Proceedings of the National Academy of Sciences USA* 97(9): 4997 - 5002.

Deadwyler SA and Hampson RE. 1999. Anatomical model of hippocampal encoding of spatial information. *Hippocampus* 9: 397-412.

Deadwyler SA, West JR, Cotman CW and Lynch GS. 1975a. A neurophysiological analysis of commissural projections to dentate gyrus of the rat. *Journal of Neurophysiology* 38: 167-184.

Deadwyler SA, West JR, Cotman CW and Lynch G. 1975b. Physiological studies of the reciprocal connections between the hippocampus and entorhinal cortex. *Experimental Neurology* 49: 35 - 57.

de Bettencourt PR. 2004. Photosensitivity: the magnitude of the problem. *Epilepsia* 45 Suppl 1: 30 – 34.

DeLuca JW. 2005. Generating Wisdom and Compassion: QEEG and LORETTA Findings. Presentation delivered at a September conference sponsored by the International Society for Neuronal Regulation. Abstract available in PDF format at DeLuca's website: <www.fearlessheart.com>.

DeLuca JW and Daly R. 2003. The inner alchemy of Buddhist Tantric meditation: a QEEG case study using low resolution electromagnetic tomography (LORETA). *Subtle Energies and Energy Medicine* 13(2): 155-208.

Demeter S, Rosene DL and Van Hoesen GW. 1985. Interhemispheric pathways of the hippocampal formation, presubiculum, and entorhinal and posterior parahippocampal cortices in the rhesus monkey: the structure and organization of the hippocampal commissures. *Journal of Comparative Neurology* 233: 30-47.

Derrington AM, Krauskopf J and Lennie P. 1984. Chromatic mechanisms in lateral geniculate nucleus of macaque. *Journal of Physiology.* 357: 241 - 265.

Detre JA, Alsop DC, Aguirre GK and Sperling MR. 1996. Coupling of cortical and thalamic ictal activity in human partial epilepsy: demonstration by functional magnetic resonance imaging. *Epilepsia* 37(7): 657 - 661.

Diagnostic and Statistical Manual of Mental Disorders, Fourth Edition. 1994. (American Psychiatric Association: Washington, DC).

Dolorfo C and Amaral D. 1998. Entorhinal cortex of the rat: topographic organization of the cells of origin of the perforant path projection to the dentate gyrus. *Journal of Comparative Neurology* 398: 25 - 48.

Donaldson IML and Dixon RA. 1980. Excitation of units in the lateral geniculate and contiguous nuclei of the cat by stretch of the extrinsic ocular muscles. *Experimental Brain Research* 38: 245-255.

Doniger-O'Flaherty W. 1971. *The Rig Veda: An Anthology* (Penguin Books: London).

Dostoevsky F. 1992 [1868]. *The Idiot.* Myers A, Transl. (Oxford University Press: Oxford).

Dow BM. 1990. Nested maps in macaque monkey visual cortex. In: Leibovic KN, ed., *Science of Vision* (Springer-Verlag: New York), pp. 84 - 124.

Dow BM. 2002. Orientation and color columns in monkey striate cortex. *Cerebral Cortex.* 12: 1005 - 1015.

Drevets WC, Burton H, Videen TO, Snyder AZ, Simpson JR and Raichle ME. 1995. Blood flow changes in human somatosensory cortex during anticipated stimulation. *Nature* 373: 249-252.

Duvernoy H. 1988. *The Human Hippocampus: An Atlas of Applied Anatomy* (J.F. Bergmann Verlag: Munich).

Edelman GM. 1987. *Neural Darwinism: the Theory of Neuronal Group Selection* (New York, NY: Basic Books).

Edelman GM. 1992. *Bright Air, Brilliant Fire: On the Matter of the Mind* (Basic Books: New York).

Edelman R. 1990. *Discussions in Neuroscience, Vol 7(1): Magnetic Resonance Imaging of the Nervous System* (Elsevier Science: Amsterdam).

Elton M, Winter O, Heslenfeld D, Loewy D, Campbell K and Kok A. 1997. Event-related potentials to tones in the absence and presence of sleep spindles. *Journal of Sleep Research* 6: 78 – 83.

Engel J Jr and Rocha LL. 1992. Interictal disturbances: a search for molecular substrates. *Epilepsy Research Supplement* 9: 342-349 (Discussion 350).

Engel J Jr, Dichter M and Schwartzkroin P. 1997. Basic mechanisms of human epilepsy. In: Engel J Jr and Pedley TA, editors, *Epilepsy: A Comprehensive Textbook, Vol. I.* (Lippincott-Raven Publishers: Philadelphia), pp. 499 - 512.

Ettinger AB, Devinsky O, Weisbrot DM, Ramakrishna RK and Goyal A. 1999. A comprehensive profile of clinical, psychiatric and psychosocial characteristics of patients with psychogenic non-epileptic seizures. *Epilepsia* 40(9): 1292-1298.

Evans-Wentz WY, Ed. 1958. *Tibetan Yoga and Secret Doctrines*. Lama Kazi Dawa-Samdup, Transl. (Oxford University Press: New York).

Fahrion S. 1996. Commentary in Dialogue: Phosphene Images of Thalamic Sleep Rhythms Induced by Self-Hypnosis. *Journal of Subtle Energies and Energy Medicine* 7(3): 268 - 272.

Fahrion S, Wirkus M and Pooley P. 1992. EEG Amplitude, Brain Mapping, & Synchrony In & Between A Bioenergy Practitioners & Client During Healing. *Journal of Subtle Energies and Energy Medicine* 3, 1, pp. 19 - 52.

Faught E, Falgout J, Nidiffer FD and Dreifuss FE. 1986. Self-induced photosensitive absence seizures with ictal pleasure. *Archives of Neurology* 43: 408-410.

Ferlazzo E, Zifkin BG, Andermann E and Andermann F. 2005. Cortical triggers in generalized reflex seizures and epilepsies. *Brain* 128(4): 700-710.

Ferrillo F, Beelke M and Nobili L. 2000a. Sleep EEG Synchronization Mechanisms and Activation of Interictal Epileptic Spikes. *Clinical Neurophysiology* 11(Suppl 2): S65 - S73.

Ferrillo F, Beelke M, De Carli F, Cossu M, Munari C, Rosadini G and Nobili L. 2000a. Sleep-EEG Modulation of Interictal Epileptiform Discharges in Adult Partial Epilepsy: A Spectral Analysis Study. *Clinical Neurophysiology* 11, pp. 916 - 923.

Feuerstein, G.. 1989. *The Yoga-Sutra of Patañjali: A New Translation and Commentary* (Inner Traditions International: Rochester, VT).

Fish D. 1997. Psychic seizures. In: Engel J, Jr., and Pedley, TA. *Epilepsy: A Comprehensive Textbook, Vol. I.* (Lippincott-Raven Publishers: Philadelphia), pp. 543 - 548.

Frances PL, Baker GA and Appleton PL. 1999. Stress and avoidance in pseudoseizures: testing the assumptions. *Epilepsy Research* 34: 241-249.

Friedman B (1911) Observations of entoptic phenomena. *Archives of Opthalmology* 28: 285-307.

Friis M. 1990. Stress convulsions. In: Dam M and Gram L, *Comprehensive Epileptology* (Ravens Press: New York), pp. 247 - 250.

Friis M and Lund M. 1974. Stress convulsions. *Archives of Neurology* 31: 155 -159.

Fukumoto S, Tanaka S, Tojo H, Akaike K and Takigawa M. 2002. Perirhinal cortical lesion suppresses secondary generalization in kainic acid-induced limbic seizure. *Psychiatry and Clinical Neuroscience* 56(5): 561 – 567.

Gastaut H. 1978. F.M. Dostoevsky's involuntary contribution ot the symptomatology and prognosis of epilepsy. *Epilepsia* 19: 186-201..

Gastaut H. 1984. New comments on the epilepsy of Fyodor Dostoevsky. *Epilepsia* 25(4): 408-411.

Gastaut H and Tassarini CA. 1966. Triggering mechanisms in epilepsy: the electroclinical point of view. *Epilepsia* 7: 85-138.

Gates JR and Gumnit RJ. 1990. Partial seizures of temporal lobe origin. In: Dam M and Gram L. *Comprehensive Epileptology* (Raven Press: New York).

Gates JR, Ramani V, Whalen S and Loewenson R. 1985. Ictal characteristics of pseudoseizures. *Archives of Neurology* 42: 1183-1187.

George M, Ketter T, Parekh B, Horwitz B, Herscovitch P and Post R. 1995. Brain activity during transient sadness and happiness in healthy women. *American Journal of Psychiatry* 152: 341 - 351.

Geschwind N. 1983. Interictal changes in epilepsy. *Epilepsia* 24 [Suppl.1]: S23-S30.

Geschwind N. 1984 [1961]. Dostoievsky's Epilepsy. In: Blumer D. *Psychiatric Aspects of Epilepsy* (American Psychiatric Press: Washington, D.C.), pp. 325-333.

Gheorghiu E and Kingdom FA. 2007. Chromatic tuning of contour-shape mechanisms revealed through the shape-frequency and shape-amplitude after-effects. *Vision Research* 47(14): 1935-1949.

Gloor P. 1986. Consciousness as a neurological concept in epileptology: a critical review. *Epilepsia* 27 (Suppl. 2): S14 - S26.

Gloor P. 1991. Neurobiological substrates of ictal behavioral changes. In: Smith D, Trieman D, and Trimble M, eds. *Advances in Neurology* 55: 11-32.

Gloor P. 1997. *The Temporal Lobe and Limbic System* (Oxford University Press: London).

Gloor P, Olivier A, Quesney LF, Andermann F and Horowitz S. 1982 The role of the limbic system in experiential phenomena of temporal lobe epilepsy. *Annals of Neurology* 12: 129-144.

Gloor P, Avoli M and Kostopoulos G. 1990. Thalamocortical relationships in generalized epilepsy with bilaterally synchronous spike-and-wave discharge. In: Avoli M, Gloor P, Kostopoulos and Naquet R, editors. *Generalized Epilepsy* (Birkhäuser: Boston), pp. 190-212.

Gloor P, Salanova V, Olivier A and Quesney LF. 1993. The human dorsal hippocampal commissure: an anatomically identifiable and functional pathway. *Brain* 116: 1249-1273.

Goetz D and Morley SG. 1950. *Popol Vuh: The Sacred Book of the Ancient Quiché Maya* (University of Oklahoma: Norman).

Goldberg M and Wurtz R. 1972. Activity of superior colliculus in behaving monkey: I. Visual receptive fields of single neurons. *Journal of Neurophysiology* 35: 553-586.

Gonda J. 1963. *The Vision of the Vedic Poets* (Mouton & Co.: The Hague, Netherlands).

Gotman J. 1983. Measurement of small time differences between EEG channels: method and application to epileptic seizure propagation. *Electroencephalogy and Clinical Neurophysiology* 56: 501 - 514.

Gotman J. 1987. Interhemispheric interactions in seizures of focal onset: data from human intracranial recordings. *Electroencephalogy and Clinical Neurophysiology* 67: 120-133.

Gouras P. 2003. The role of S-cones in human vision. *Documenta Opthalmologica* 106(1): 5-11.

Gove A, Grossberg S and Mingolla E. 1995. Brightness perception, illusory contours, and cortico-geniculate feedback. *Visual Neuroscience* 12: 1027-1052.

Grant JA and Rainville P. 2005. Hypnosis and meditation: similar experiential changes and shared brain mechanisms. *Medical Hypotheses* 2005;65(3): 625-626.

Green E, Parks P, Guyer P, Fahrion S and Coyne L. 1995. Anomalous Electrostatic Phenomena in Exceptional Subjects. *Journal of Subtle Energies and Energy Medicine* 2 (3): 69-94.

Griffith RTH. 1971[1889]. *The Hymns of the Rig Veda, Vols. I - II* (Chowkhamba Series: Varanasi, India).

Gulyás AI, Seress L, Tóth K, Acsády L, Antal M and Freund TF. 1991. Septal GABAergic neurons innervate inhibitory interneurons in the hippocampus of the macaque monkey. *Neuroscience* 41(2/3): 381 - 390.

Gunderson CH, Dunne PB and Feyer TL. 1973. Sleep deprivation seizures. *Neurology* 23: 679 - 686.

Hájos N, Papp ECS, Acsády L, Levey AI and Freund TF. 1998. Distinct interneuron types express m2 muscarinic receptor immunoreactivity on their dendrites or axon terminals in the hippocampus. *Neuroscience* 82(2): 355 - 376.

Halász P. Filakovszky J, Vargha A and Bagdy G. 2002. Effect of sleep deprivation on spike-wave discharges in idiopathic generalised epilepsy: a 4 x 24 h continuous long term EEG monitoring study. *Epilepsy Research* 51: 123 – 132.

Hallet M. 1997. Myoclonus and myoclonic syndromes. In: Engel J Jr and Pedley TA, editors, *Epilepsy: A Comprehensive Textbook, Vol. I.* (Lippincott-Raven Publishers: Philadelphia), pp. 2717 - 2723.

Hampson R, Hedberg T and Deadwyler S. 2000. Differential information processing by hippocampal and subicular neurons. *Annals of the New York Academy of Sciences* 911: 151 - 165.

Hanazawa A, Komatsu H and Murakami I. 2000. Neural selectivity for hue and saturation of color in the primary visual cortex of the monkey. *European Journal of Neuroscience* 12: 1753 - 1763.

Hansen BA and Brodtkorb E. 2003. Partial epilepsy with "ecstatic" seizures. *Epilepsy and Behavior* 4: 667-673.

Harding GFA and Fylan F. 1999. Two visual mechanisms of photosensitivity. *Epilepsia* 40(10): 1446-1451.

Harding GFA and Jeavons PM. 1994. *Clinics in Developmental Medicine No. 133: Photosensitive Epilepsy, 2nd Ed* (MacKeith Press: Birmingham, UK).

Heath R. 1972. Pleasure and brain activity in man. J Nerv Mental Dis 154(1): 3 - 18.

Henn V, Baloh RW and Hepp K. 1984. The sleep-wake transition in the oculomotor system. *Experimental Brain Research* 54: 166-176.

Henze DA, Wittner L and Buzsáki G. 2002. Single granule cells reliably discharge targets in the hippocampal CA3 network in vivo. *Nature Neuroscience* 5(8): 790 – 795.

Herzog H, Lee V, Kuwert T, Langen K, Kops E and Feinendegen L. 1990-1991. Changed Pattern of Regional Glucose Metabolism During Yoga Meditative Relaxation. *Neuropsychobiology* 23, pp. 182 - 187.

Hesdorffer DC and Verity CM. 1997. Risk factors. In: Engel J, Jr., and Pedley, TA, editors. *Epilepsy: A Comprehensive Textbook, Vol. I* (Lippincott-Raven: Philadelphia), pp. 59 - 67.

Heynen A and Bear M. 2001. Long-term potentiation on thalamocortical transmission in the adult visual cortex in vivo. *Journal of Neuroscience* 21(24): 9801-9813.

Hirase H, Leinekugel X, Csicsvari J, Czurko A and Buzsaki G. 2001. Behavior-dependent states of the hippocampal network affect functional clustering of neurons. *Journal of Neuroscience* 21(10): RC 145 (1- 4).

Hofle N, Paus T, Reuten, D, Fiset P, Gotman J, Evans A and Jones B. 1997. Regional Cerebral Blood Flow Changes as a Function of Delta and Spindle Activity During Slow Wave Sleep in Humans. *Journal of Neuroscience* 17(12): 4800 - 4808.

Holmes MD, Brown M and Tucker DM. 2004. Are "generalized" seizures truly generalized? Evidence of localized mesial frontal and frontopolar discharges in absence. *Epilepsia* 45(12): 1568-1579.

Horgan J. 2003. *Rational Mysticism: Dispatches From the Border Between Science and Spirituality* (Houghton Mifflin Co.: Boston).

Horii A, Takeda N, Mochizuki T, Okakura-Mochizuki K, Yamamoto Y and Yamatodani A. 1994. Effects of vestibular stimulation on acetylcholine release from rat hippocampus: an in vivo microdialysis study. *Journal of Neurophysiology* 72: 605 - 611.

Horowitz MJ. 1978. Image formation and cognition (Appleton-Century-Crofts: New York).

Horvath Z, Hsu M, Pierre E, Vadi D, Gallyas F and Buzsáki G. 1992. Structural impairment in hippocampal neurons following a single epileptic afterdischarge. *Society of Neuroscience Abstracts* 18: 553.

Hughes JR. 2005. The ideosyncratic aspects of the epilepsy of Fyodor Dostoevsky. *Epilepsy and Behavior* 7: 531-538.

Hume L. 1992. *Ancestral Power: The Dreaming, Consciousness and Aboriginal Australians* (Melbourne University Press: Victoria, Australia).

Inoue Y and Mihara T. 1998. Awareness and responsiveness during partial seizures. *Epilepsia* 39 (Suppl. 5): 7 - 10.

Insausti R and Muñoz M. 2001. Cortical projections of the non-entorhinal hippocampal formation in the cynomolgus monkey (*Macaca fascicularis*). *European Journal of Neuroscience* 14: 435 – 425.

Ishizuka N, Weber J and Amaral DG. 1990. Organization of intrahippocampal projections originating from CA3 pyramidal cells in the rat. *Journal of Comparative Neurology* 295: 580 - 623.

Jacobson E. 1938. *Progressive Relaxation* (University of Chicago Press: Chicago).

Jacome DE and Risko MS. 1983. Absence status manifested by compulsive masturbation. *Ar-*

chives of Neurology 40(8): 523-524.

James W. 1961(1902). *The Varieties of Religious Experience: A Study in Human Nature* (Collier MacMillan: New York).

Janszky J, Szucs A, Halasz P, Borbely C, Hollo A, Barsi P and Mirnics Z. 2002. Orgasmic aura originates from the right hemisphere. *Neurology* 58(2): 302-304.

Jaseja H. 2005. Meditation may predispose to epilepsy: an insight into the alteration of brain environment induced by meditation. *Medical Hypotheses* 2005;64(3): 464-467.

Jaseja H. 2006a. A brief study of a possible relation of epilepsy associated with meditation. *Medical Hypotheses* 66: 1036-49.

Jaseja H. 2006b. Meditation potentially capable of increasing susceptibility to epilepsy - a follow-up hypothesis. *Medical Hypotheses* 66(5): 925-8.

Jaseja H. 2007. Meditation and epilepsy: The ongoing debate. *Medical Hypotheses* 68(4): 916-7.

Jensen MS and Yaari Y. 1997. Role of the intrinsic burst firing, potassium accumulation, and electrical coupling in the elevated potassium model of hippocampal epilepsy. *Journal of Physiology* 77: 1224 - 1233.

John of the Cross. 1958 Edition. *Ascent of Mount Carmel* (Doubleday Image Books, NY)

John of the Cross. 1973 [Reprint of 3rd Edition (1903)]. *The Dark Night of the Soul* (Attic Press: Greenwood, SC)

Johnson E, Hawken M and Shapley R. 2001. The spatial transformation of color in the primary visual cortex of the macaque monkey. *Nature Neuroscience* 4(4): 409 - 416.

Jones AKP, Brown WD, Friston KJ, Qi LY and Frackowiack RSJ. 1991. Cortical and subcortical location of response to pain in man using positron emission tomography. *Proceedings of the Royal Society of London, Series B: Biological Sciences* 244: 39-44.

Jung MW, Wiener SI and McNaughton BL. 1994. Comparison of spatial firing characteristics of units in dorsal and ventral hippocampus of the rat. *Journal of Neuroscience* 14: 7347 - 7356.

Jutila L, Ylinen A, Partanen K, Alafuzoff I, Mervaala E, Partanen J, Vapalahti M, Vainio P and Pitkanen A. 2001. MR volumetry of entorhinal, perirhinal, and temporopolar cortices in drug-refractory temporal lobe epilepsy. *American Journal of Neuroradiology* 22(3): 1490 – 1501.

Kahle W, Leonhardt H and Platzer W. 1993. *Color Atlas/Text of Human Anatomy, Vol. 3: Nervous System and Sensory Organs* (Georg Thieme Verlag: Stuttgart).

Kamondi A, Acsády L and Buzsáki G. 1998. Dendritic spikes are enhanced by cooperative network activity in the intact hippocampus. *Journal of Neuroscience* 18(10): 3919 - 3928.

Kandel A, Bragin A, Carpi D and Buzsáki G. 1996. Lack of hippocampal involvement in a rat model of petit mal epilepsy. *Epilepsy Research* 23: 123 - 127.

Kanner A and Balabanov A. 2002. Depression and epilepsy: how closely related are they? *Neurology* 58 (8 Suppl 5): S27 - S39.

Kasamatsu A, Okuma T, Takenaka S, Koga E, Ikeda K and Sugiyama H. 1957. The EEG of "Zen" and "Yoga" Practitioners. *Electroencephalography and Clinical Neurophysiology* (Supplement 9), pp. 51 - 52.

Kasamatsu A and Hirai. T. 1966. An Electroencephalographic Study on the Zen Meditation (Zazen), *Folia Psychiatrica et Neurologica Japonica* 20, 4, pp. 315 - 336.

Kasteleijn-Nolst Trenité, DGA. 1989. Photosensitivity in epilepsy: electrophysiological and clinical correlates. *Acta Neurologia Scandinavia.* 125 Suppl.: 3-149.

Kavanaugh K, Ed. 1987. *John of the Cross: Selected Writings* (Paulist Press, NY)

Kellogg R, Knoll M and Kugler J. 1965. Form-Similarity Between Phosphenes of Adults and Pre-School Children's Scribblings. *Nature* 208:1129-130.

Kepecs MR, Boro A, Haut S, Kepecs G and Moshé SL. 2004. A novel nonpharmacological treatment for photosensitive epilepsy: a report of three patients tested with blue cross-polarized sunglasses. *Epilepsia* 45(9): 1158 - 1162.

Ketter TA, Andreason PJ, George MS, Lee C, Gill DS, Parekh PI, Willis MW, Herscovitch P and Post RM. 1996. Anterior paralimbic mediation of procaine-induced emotional and psychosensory experiences. *Archives of General Psychiatry* 53: 59 - 69.

Kieffer G. 1988. *Kundalini for the New Age: Selected Writings by Gopi Krishna* (Bantam Books: NY).

Killiam KF, Killiam EK and Naquet R. 1967. An animal model of light sensitive epilepsy. *Electroencephalography and Clinical Neurophysiology* 22: 497-513.

Kilpatrick L and Cahill L. 2003. Amygdala modulation of parahippocampal and frontal regions during emotionally influenced memory storage. *Neuroimage* 20(4): 2091 – 2099.

Kim U, Bal T and McCormick D. 1995. Spindle waves are propagating synchronized oscillations in the ferret LGN in vitro. *Journal of Neurophysiology* 74(3): 1301 - 1323.

Kinsley DR. 1993. *Hinduism: A Cultural Perspective, 2nd edition* (Prentice Hall: Englewood Cliffs, New Jersey).

Kjaer T, Bertelsen C, Piccini P, Brooks, D, Alving J and Lou H. 2002. Increased dopamine tone during meditation-induced change of consciousness. *Brain Research: Cognitive Brain Research* 13(2): 255 - 259.

Kloosterman F, Witter MP and van Haeften T. 2003. Topographical and laminar organization of the subicular projections to the parahippocampal region of the rat. *Journal of Comparative Neurology* 455(2): 156 – 171.

Klueva J, Munsch T, Albrecht D and Pape HC. 2003. Synaptic and non-synaptic mechanisms of amygdala recruitment into temporolimbic epileptiform activities. *European Journal of Neuroscience* 18(10): 2779 – 2791.

Klüver, H. 1966 [1942]. *Mescal and Mechanisms of Hallucinations* (University of Chicago Press: Chicago).

Knoll M. 1958. Anregung geometrischer Figuren und anderer subjektiver Lichtmuster in elektrischen Feldern. *Schweizerische Zeitschrift für Psychologie und Ihra Anwendungen* 17:110-26.

Knoll, M. 1959. Subjective light pattern spectroscopy in the encephalographic frequency range. Nature 184: 1823-1824.

Knoll M and Kugler J. 1959. Subjective Light Pattern Spectroscopy in the Encephalographic Frequency Range. *Nature* 184:1823-1824.

Knoll M, Kugler J, Eichmeier J and Höfer O. 1962. Note on the Spectroscopy of Subjective Light Patterns. *The Journal of Analytical Psychology* 7:55-69.

Knoll M, Kugler J, Höfer O and Lawder SD. 1963. Effects of Chemical Stimulation of Electrically-Induced Phosphenes on their Bandwidth, Shape, Number and Intensity. *Confinia Neurologica* 23: 201-226.

Kohn L. 1993. *The Taoist Experience: An Anthology* (State University of New York Press: Albany).

Kosslyn S, Thompson W, Kim I and Alpert N. 1995. Topographical Representations of Mental Images in Primary Visual Cortex. *Nature* 378, pp. 496 - 498.

Kostopoulos G. 2001. Involvement of the thalamocortical system in epileptic loss of consciousness. *Epilepsia* 42 (Suppl 3): 13 - 19.

Kotagal P and Lüders HO. 1997. Simple motor seizures. In: Engel J, Jr., and Pedley, TA, editors. *Epilepsy: A Comprehensive Textbook, Vol. I.* (Lippincott-Raven: Philadelphia), pp. 525-532.

Koutroumanidis M, Agathonikou A and Panayiotopoulos CP. 1998. Self-induced noogenic seizures in a photosensitive patient. *Journal of Neurology, Neurosurgery and Psychiatry* 64: 139-140.

Kreiman G, Koch C and Fried I. 2000. Category-specific visual responses of single neurons in the human medial temporal lobe. *Nature Neuroscience* 3(9): 946-953.

Krishna, G. 1971 [1967]. *Kundalini: The Evolutionary Energy in Man, 2nd edition* (Shambhala Publications: Boulder, CO).

Kroll PW. 1996. Body Gods and Inner Vision: The Scripture of the Yellow Court. In: Lopez DS, Jr. *Religions of China in Practice* (Princeton University Press: Princeton), pp. 149 -155.

Krug M, Brödemann R, Matthies R, Rüthrich H and Wagner M. 2001. Activation of the dentate gyrus by stimulation of the contralateral perforant pathways: Evoked potentials and long-term potentiation after ipsa- and contralateral induction. *Hippocampus* 11: 157–167.

Laidlaw J, Richens A and Chadwick D. 1993. *A Textbook of Epilepsy* (Churchill Livingstone: New York).

Lancel M, van Reizen H and Glatt A 1992. The time course of sigma activity and slow-wave activity during NREMS in cortical and thalamic EEG of the cat during baseline and after 12 hours of wakefulness. *Brain Research* 596: 285-295.

Lansky EP and St. Louis EK. 2006. Transcendental meditation: A double-edged sword in epilepsy? *Epilepsy & Behavior* 9(3): 394-400.

Laroche S, Davis S and Jay TM. 2000. Plasticity at hippocampal to prefrontal cortex synapses: Dual roles in working memory and consolidation. *Hippocampus* 10: 438 – 446.

Lavanex P and Amaral DG. 2000. Hippocampal-neocortical interaction: A hierarchy of associativity. *Hippocampus* 10: 420 – 430.

Lavanex P, Suzuki WA and Amaral DG. 2002. Perirhinal and parahippocampal cortices of the macaque monkey: projections to the neocortex. *Journal of Comparative Neurology* 447(4): 394 – 420.

Lazar S, Bush G, Gollub R, Fricchione G, Khalsa G and Benson H. 2000. Functional brain mapping of the relaxation response and meditation. *Neuroreport* 11: 1581-1585.

Lazar S, Kerr CE, Wasserman RH, Gray JR, Greve DN and Treadway MT, McGarvey M, Quinn BT, Dusek JA, Benson H, Rauch SL, Moore CI and Fischl B. 2005. Meditation experience is associated with increased cortical thickness. *Neuroreport* 16(17): 1893-1897.

Le Gros Clark WE. 1940-41. The laminar organization and cell content of the lateral geniculate body in the monkey. *Journal of Anatomy* 75: 419 - 433.

Lefebure F. 1982. *Phosphenisme et Origine des Religions* (Edition Dereume: Bruxelles).

Lehmann D, Faber P, Achermann P, Jeanmonod D, Gianotti L and Pizzagalli D. 2001. Brain sources of EEG gamma frequency during volitionally meditation-induced, altered states of consciousness, and experience of self. *Psychiatry Research: Neuroimagining Section* 108: 111- 121.

Lennox WG and Cobb S. 1933. Epilepsy XIII, Aura in epilepsy: A statistical review of 1,359 cases. *Archives of Neurology and Psychiatry* 30: 374-387.

Lenz FA, Seike M, Lin YC, Baker FH, Rowland LH, Gracely RH and Richardson RT 1993. Neurons in the area of the human thalamic nucleus ventralis caudlis respond to painful heat stimuli. *Brain Research* 623: 235-240.

Leproult R, Copinschi G, Buxton O and Van Cauter E. 1997. Sleep loss results in an elevation of cortisol levels the next evening. *Sleep* 20(10): 865 - 870.

Li X-G, Somogyi P, Ylinen A and Buzsáki G. 1994. The hippocampal CA3 network: an in vivo intracellular labeling study. *Journal of Comparative Neurology* 339: 181 - 208.

Lieb JP and Babb TL. 1986. Interhemispheric propagation time of human hippocampal seizures. II. Relationship to pathology and cell density. *Epilepsia* 27: 294 - 300.

Lieb JP, Engel J and Babb TL. 1986. Interhemispheric propagation time of human hippocampal seizures. I. Relationship to surgical outcomes. *Epilepsia* 27: 286 - 293.

Lieb JP, Babb TL, Engel J and Darcey T. 1987. Propagation pathways of interhemispheric seizure discharges in human versus animal hippocampal epilepsy. In: Engel J, Jr., Ojemann GA, Luders HO, Williamson PD, editors. *Fundamental Mechanisms of Human Brain Function: Opportunities for Direct Investigation in Association with the Surgical Treatment of Epilepsy* (Raven Press: New York), pp. 165-170.

Liporace JD and Sperling MR. 1997. Simple autonomic seizures. In: Engel J, Jr., and Pedley, TA,

Editors. *Epilepsy: A Comprehensive Textbook, Vol. I.* (Lippincott-Raven: Philadelphia), pp. 549-555.

Little S and Eichman S. 2000. *Taoism and the Arts of China* (The Art Institute of Chicago and the University of Chicago Press: Berkeley).

Loiseau P. 1997. Seizure precipitants. In: Engel J, Jr., and Pedley, TA, Editors. *Epilepsy: A Comprehensive Textbook, Vol. I.* (Lippincott-Raven: Philadelphia), pp. 93-97.

Lopez da Silva FH. 1987. Dynamics of EEGs as signals of neuronal populations: models and the theoretical considerations. In: Niedermeyer E and Lopes da Silva FH, eds. *Electroencephalography* (Schwartzenberg: Baltimore & Munich, pp. 15-28).

Lopez da Silva FH, Vos JE, Mooibroek J and van Rotterdam A. 1980. Partial coherence analysis of thalamic and cortical alpha rhythms in the dog. A contribution towards a general model of the cortical organization of rhythmical activity. In: Pfurscheller G, Buser P and Lopez da Silva FH, eds. *Rhythmic EEG Activities and Cortical Functioning* (Elsevier/North-Holland: Amsterdam, pp. 33-59).

Lorenzo I, Ramos J, Arce C, Guevara MA and Corsi-Cabrera M. 1995. Effect of total sleep deprivation on reaction time and waking EEG activity in man. *Sleep* 18(5): 346 - 354.

Lothman EW, Bertram EH, III and Stringer JL. 1991. Functional anatomy of hippocampal seizures. *Progress in Neurobiology* 37: 1 - 82.

Lothman EW. 1997. Biological consequences of repeated seizures. In: Engel J Jr and Pedley TA, Editors. *Epilepsy: A Comprehensive Textbook, Vol. I.* (Lippincott-Raven: Philadelphia), pp. 481-497.

Lou H, Kjaer T, Friberg L, Wildschiodtz G, Holm S and Nowak M. 1999. A ^{15}O-H$_2$O PET Study of Meditation and the Resting State of Normal Consciousness. *Human Brain Mapping* 7: 998-105.

Lutz A, Greischar LL, Rawlings NB, Matthieu R and Davidson RJ. 2004. Long-term meditators self-induce high-amplitude gamma synchrony during mental practice. *Proceedings of the National Academy of Science* 2004; 101(46): 16369-16373.

Lytton WW, Contreras D, Destexhe A and Steriade M. 1997. Dynamic interactions determine partial thalamic quiescence in a computer network model of spike-and-wave seizures. *Journal of Neurophysiology* 77: 1679 - 1696.

Maeda E, Robinson HPC and Kwana A. 1995. The mechanisms of generation and propogation of synchronous bursting in developing networks of cortical neurons. *Journal of Neuroscience* 15(10): 6834-6845.

Magariños AM, Verdugo JMG and McEwen BS. 1997. Chronic stress alters synaptic terminal structure in hippocampus. *Proceedings of the National Academy of Science USA (Neurobiology)* 94: 14002 - 14008.

Malpelli JG and Baker RH. 1975. The representation of the visual field in the lateral geniculate nucleus of the macaca mulatta. *Journal of Comparative Neurology* 161: 569 - 594.

Mandel AJ. 1980. Toward a Psychobiology of Transcendence: God in the Brain. In: Davidson JM and Davidson RJ, Editors. *The Psychobiology of Consciousness* (Plenum Press: New York), pp. 379–463

Maquet P. 1995. Sleep Functions and Cerebral Metabolism. *Behavioral Brain Research* 69: 75-83.

Maquet P. 2000. Functional neuroimaging of normal human sleep by positron emission tomography. *Journal of Sleep Research* 9(3): 207-231.

Maquet P, Dive D, Salmon E, Sadzot B., Franco G, Poirrier R and Franck G. 1992. Cerebral Glucose Utilization During Stage 2 Sleep in Man. *Brain Research* 571: 149-153.

Maquet P, Degueldre C, Delfiore G, Aerts J, Peters J, Luxen A and Franck G. 1997. Functional anatomy of human slow wave sleep. *Journal of Neuroscience* 17(8): 2807-2812.

Maquet P, Faymonville ME, Degueldre C, Delfiore G, Franck G, Luxen A and Lamy M. 1999a.

Functional Neuroanatomy of the Hypnotic State. *Biological Psychiatry* 45: 327 - 333.

Maquet P, Peters J-M, Aerts J, Delfiore G, Degueldre C, Luxen A and Franck G. 1999b. Functional Neuroanatomy of Human Rapid-Eye-Movement Sleep and Dreaming, *Nature* 383, pp. 163 - 166.

Marks W, Dobelle W and MacNichol E. 1961. Visual pigments of simple primate cones. *Science* 143: 1181.

Mars NJI and Lopes da Silva FH. 1983. Propagation of seizure activity in kindled dogs. *Electro-encephalogy and Clinical Neurophysiology* 56: 194-209.

Mars NJI, Thompson PM and Wilkens RJ. 1985. Spread of epileptic seizure activity in humans. *Epilepsia* 26: 85 - 94.

Marsella A, Friedman M, Gerrity E and Scurfield R. 1996. *Ethnocultural Aspects of Posttraumatic Stress Disorder* (American Psychiatric Press: Washington, D.C.).

Martin PR, White AJR, Goodchild AK, Wilder HD and Selfton AE. 1997. Evidence that blue-on cells are part of the third geniculocortical pathways in primates. *European Journal of Neuroscience* 9: 1536-1541.

Mascia A, Di Gennaro G, Esposito V, Grammaldo LG, Meldolesi GN, Giampa T, Sebastiano F, Falco C, Onorati P, Manfredi M, Cantore G and Quarato PP. 2005. Genital and sexual manifestations in drug-resistant partial epilepsy. *Seizure* 14(2): 133-138.

Matt DC, Transl. 1983. *Moses de Leon's Zohar: The Book of Enlightenment* (Paulist Press: Ramsey, NJ, 1983).]

Mavromatis A. 1987. *Hypnagogia: The unique state of consciousness between wakefulness and sleep* (Routledge & Kegan Paul: London).

McAlonan K and Brown VJ. 2002. The thalamic reticular nucleus: more than a sensory nucleus? *Neuroscientist* 8(4): 302-305.

McClenon J. 2002. *Wondrous Healing: Shamanism, Human Evolution and the Origin of Religion* (Northern Illinois University Press: Dekalb, Illinois).

McClurkin JW, Optican LM and Richmond BJ. 1994. Cortical feedback increases visual information transmitted by monkey parvocellular lateral geniculate nucelus neurons. *Visual Neuroscience* 11: 601-617.

McCormick DA and Pape HC. 1990. Properties of a hyperpolarization-activated cation current and its role in rhythmic oscillation in thalamocortical relay neurons. *Journal of Physiology (London)* 431: 291 - 318.

McDaniel J. 1989. *The Madness of the Saints: Ecstatic Religion in Bengal* (University of Chicago Press: Chicago).

McKenna JT and Vertes RB. 2004. Afferent projections to nucleus reuniens of the thalamus. *Journal of Comparative Neurology* 480(2): 115-142.

McLachlan RS, Gloor P and Avoli M. 1984. Differential participation of some "specific" and "nonspecific" thalamic nuclei in generalized spike and wave discharges of feline generalized penicillin epilepsy. *Brain Research* 307: 277 - 287.

Meeren H, Pijn J, Luijtelaar E, Coenen A and Lopes da Silva F. 2002. Cortical focus drives widespread corticothalamic networks during spontaneous absence seizures in rats. *Journal of Neuroscience* 22(4): 1480-1495.

Mehta A, Ulbert I and Schroeder C. 2000. Intermodal selective attention in monkey. I: distribution and timing of effects across visual areas. *Cerebral Cortex* 10(4): 343-358.

Mello LEA and Covolan L. 1996. Spontaneous seizures preferentially injury interneurons in the pilocarpine model of chronic spontaneous seizures. *Epilepsy Research* 26: 123 - 129.

Mishra R S. 1987. *The Textbook of Yoga Psychology: The Definitive Translation and Interpretation of Patanjali's Yogasutras* (Crown Publishers, New York, NY).

Mizumori SJY, Ragozzino KE, Cooper BG and Leutgeb S. 1999. Hippocampal representational organization and spatial context. *Hippocampus* 9: 444-451.

Monaco F, Mula M and Cavanna AE. 2005. Consciousness, epilepsy and emotional qualia. *Epilepsy & Behavior* 7: 150-160.

Montero V. 2000. Attentional activation of the visual thalamic reticular nucleus depends on 'top-down' inputs from the primary visual cortex via corticogeniculate pathways. *Brain Research* 864: 95 - 104.

Morgan H. 1990. Dostoevsky's epilepsy: A case report and comparison. *Surgical Neurology* 33: 413-416.

Motter BC, Steinmetz MA, Duffy CJ and Mountcastle VB. 1987. Functional properties of properties of parietal visual neurons: mechanisms of directionality along a single axis. *Journal of Neuroscience* 7(1): 154 - 176.

Mountcastle VB, Andersen RA and Motter BC. 1981. The influence of attentive fixation upon the excitability of the light-sensitive neurons of the posterior parietal cortex. *Journal of Neuroscience* 1(11): 1218-1235.

Moutoussis K and Zeki S. 2001. The relationship between cortical activation and perception investigated with invisible stimuli. *Proceedings of the National Academy of Sciences* 99(14): 9527–9532.

Muktananda S. 1978. *Play of Consciousness, 4th Edition* (SYDA Foundation: South Fallsburg, NY).

Mullin GH. 1996. *Tsongkhapa's Six Yogas of Naropa* (Snow Lion: Ithaca, NY).

Mullen KT, Dumoulin SO, McMahon KL, de Zuibicaray GI and Hess RF. 2007. Selectivity of human retinotopic visual cortex to S-cone-opponent, L/M-cone-opponent and achromatic stimulation. *European Journal of Neuroscience* 25(2): 491-502.

Myslobodsky MS. 1993. Pro- and anticonvulsant effects of stress: the role of neuroactive steroids. *Neuroscience and Biobehavioral Reviews* 17: 129-139.

Naber P, Lopes de Silva F and Witter M. 2001. Reciprocal connections between the entorhinal cortex and hippocampal fields CA1 and the subiculum are in register with the projections from CA1 to the subiculum. *Hippocampus* 11: 99-104.

Naito H and Matsui N. Temporal lobe epilepsy with ictal ecstatic state and interictal behavior of hypergraphia. *Journal of Nervous and Mental Disease* 176(2): 123-124.

Nanamoli B. 1991[1975]. *The Path of Purification (Visuddhimagga) by Bhudantacariya Buddhaghosa, 5th edition* (Buddhist Publishing Co.: Kandy, Sri Lanka).

Neckelmann D, Amzica F and Steriade M. 1998. Spike-wave complexes and fast components of cortically generated seizures. III. Synchronizing mechanisms. *Journal of Neurophysiology* 80(3): 1480 - 1494.

Nelson JS, Meredith MA and Stein BE 1989. Does an extraocular proprioceptive signal reach the superior colliculus? *Journal of Neuroscience* 62(6): 1360-1374.

Newberg A and d'Aquili E. 2001. *Why God Won't Go Away: Brain Science and the Biology of Belief* (Ballantine Books: NY).

Newberg AB and Iversen J. 2003. The neural basis of the complex mental task of meditation: neurotransmitters and neurochemical considerations. *Medical Hypotheses.* 61(2): 282-291.

Newberg AB and Lee BY. 2005. The neuroscientific study of religious and spiritual phenomena: Or why God doesn't use biostatistics. *Zygon* 40(2): 469-489.

Newberg A, Alavi A, Baime M, Mozley P and d'Aquili E. 1997. Measurement of Cerebral Blood Flow During the Complex Cognitive Task of Meditation Using HMPAO-SPECT Imaging: A Preliminary Study. *Journal of Nuclear Medicine* 38: 95P.

Newberg A, Alavi A, Baime M and Pourdehnad M. 2000. Cerebral Blood Flow During Meditation: Comparison of Different Cognitive Tasks. *European Journal of Nuclear Medicine* 27, 8, p. 1104 (PS. 375).

Newberg A, Alavi A, Baime M, , Santanna J and d'Aquili E. 2001. The Measurement of Regional Cerebral Blood Flow During the Complex Cognitive Task of Meditation: A Preliminary SPECT Study. *Psychiatry Research: Neuroimaging* 106: 113-122.

Newberg A, Pourdehnad M, Alavi A and d'Aquili E. 2003. Cerebral blood flow during meditative prayer: preliminary findings and methodological issues. *Perceptual and Motor Skills* 97: 625-630.

Newhouse J and Wiener J. 1991. *Understanding MRI* (Little, Brown & Company: Boston).

Newman J and Grace A. 1999. Binding across time: the selective gating of frontal and hippocampal systems modulating working memory and attentional states. *Consciousness & Cognition* 8: 196-212.

Newmark ME and Penry JK. 1979. *Photosensitivity and Epilepsy: A Review* (Raven Press, NY).

Nicholson P. 1992. Dissociation, Dream-Sleep, and Self-Induction of Thalamo-Occipital Seizures with Ecstatic Auras and Interictal Behavior, *Proceedings of the 4th International Montreux Congress on Stress* (American Institute of Stress), February 16-20, pp. 82-83.

Nicholson P. 1996a. Phosphene images of thalamic sleep rhythms induced by self-hypnosis. *Journal of Subtle Energies and Energy Medicine* 7(2): 111-148.

Nicholson P. 1996b. Dialogue: Phosphene images of thalamic sleep rhythms induced by self-hypnosis. *Journal of Subtle Energies and Energy Medicine* 7(3): 273-283.

Nicholson P. 1999. Phosphene Epiphenomena of Hypersynchronous Activity Emerging in Thalamocortical Circuits and Triggering a Hippocampal Seizure. *Epilepsia* 40 [Suppl 2]: 27 & 203.

Nicholson P. 2002a. The Soma Code, Part I: Luminous Visions in the Rig Veda. Electronic Journal of Vedic Studies. *The Electronic Journal of Vedic Studies* 8(3): 31-52.

Nicholson P. 2002b. The Soma Code, Part II: Soma's Birth, Purification, and Transformation into Indra. *The Electronic Journal of Vedic Studies* 8(3): 53-69.

Nicholson P. 2002c. The Soma Code, Part III: Visions, Myths, and Drugs. *The Electronic Journal of Vedic Studies* 8(3): 70-92.

Nicholson P. 2002d. Meditation, Slow Wave Sleep, and Ecstatic Seizures: The Etiology of Kundalini Visions. *Journal of Subtle Energies and Energy Medicine* 12(3): 186-227.

Nicholson P. 2002e. Empirical Studies of Meditation: Does a Sleep Rhythm Hypothesis Explain the Data? *Journal of Subtle Energies and Energy Medicine* 13(2): 109-129.

Nicholson P. 2006. Does Meditation Predispose to Epilepsy? EEG Studies of Expert Meditators Self-Inducing Simple Partial Seizures. *Medical Hypotheses* 66(3): 674-676.

Nicholson P and Firnhaber RP. 2003 [2001]. Autohypnotic Induction of Sleep Rhythms Generates Visions of Light With Form-Constant Patterns. In: Leete A & Firnhaber RP, eds., *Shamanism in the Interdisciplinary Context* (BrownWalker Press: Boca Raton, Florida).

Nicholson P. In Press. Restoring the One: Meditation and Light Visions in Early Daoist Texts. In: Bai Gengsheng, ed., *Papers from the 7th International Conference of the International Society for Shamanistic Research* (Changchun, China, August, 2004).

Nicholson P. In Press. Light Visions, Shaman Control Fantasies and the Creation of Myths. In: Witzel M, Editor, *Papers from the Harvard-Peking University International Conference on Comparative Mythology* (Beijing, China, May, 2006).

Nobili L, Baglietoo M, Beelke M, De Carli F, Veneselli E and Ferrillo F. 2001. Temporal relationship of generalized epileptiform discharges to spindle frequency activity in childhood absence epilepsy. *Clinical Neurophysiology* 112: 1912 - 1916.

O'Flaherty WD (nee Doniger). 1971. *The Rig Veda: An Anthology* (Penguin Books: London).

O'Mara SM, Rolls ET, Berthoz A and Kesner RP. 1994. Neurons responding to whole-body motion in the primate hippocampus. *Journal of Neuroscience* 14(11): 6511 - 6523.

Pacia S and Ebersole J. 1997. Intracranial Substrates of Scalp Ictal Patterns From Temporal Lobe Foci. *Epilepsia* 38, 6, pp. 642-654.

Panayiotopoulos CP. 1996. Epilepsies characterized by seizures with specific modes of precipitation (reflex epilepsies). In: Wallace S, Editor. *Childhood Epilepsy* (Chapman and Hall: London), pp. 355-37.

Paré D and Steriade M. 1993. The reticular thalamic nucleus projects to the contralateral dorsal thalamus in macaque monkeys. *Neuroscience Letters* 154: 96-100

Paré D, deCurtis M and Llinás R. 1992. Role of the hippocampal-entorhinal loop in temporal lobe epilepsy: extra- and intracellular study in the isolated guinea pig brain in vitro. *Journal of Neurology* 12(5): 1867 - 18l81.

Penfield W and Jasper H. 1954. *Epilepsy and the Functional Anatomy of the Human Brain* (Little, Brown and Company: Boston).

Penttonen M, Kamondi A, Sik A, Acsády L and Buzsáki G. 1997. Feed-forward and feed-back activation of the dentate gyrus in vivo during dentate spikes and sharp wave bursts. *Hippocampus* 7: 437-450.

Persinger MA. 1984. "Striking EEG Profiles from Single Episodes of Glossolalia and Transcendental Meditation," *Perceptual and Motor Skills* 58(1):127-133.

Persinger MA. 1987. *Neuropsychological Basis of God Beliefs* (Praeger Press: New York).

Persinger MA. 1993a. Transcedental meditation (TM) and general meditation are associated with enhanced complex partial epileptic-like signs: evidence for "cognitive kindling"? *Perceptual and Motor Skills* 76: 80-2.

Persinger, M. 1993b. Paranormal and Religious Beliefs May Be Mediated Differentially By Subcortical and Cortical Phenomenological Processes of the Temporal (Limbic) Lobes, *Perceptual and Motor Skills* 76(11): 247-251.

Persinger MA. 2001. The neuropsychiatry of paranormal experiences. *Journal of Neuropsychiatry and Clinical Neuroscience* 13(4): 515-523.

Persinger MA and Fisher S. 1990. Elevated Specific Temporal Lobe Signs in a Population Engaged in Psychic Studies. *Perceptual and Motor Skills* 71(3 Pt 1): 817-818.

Persinger MA and Makarec K. 1993. Complex Partial Epileptic Signs as a Continuum from Normals to Epileptics: Normative Data and Clinical Populations. *Journal of Clinical Psychology* 49(1): 33-45.

Pihlajamäki M, Tanila H, Hänninen T, Könönen M, Mikkonen M, Jalkanen V, Partanen K, Aronen HJ and Soininen H. 2003. Encoding of novel picture pairs activates the perirhinal cortex: An fMRI study. *Hippocampus* 13: 67–80.

Pitman R. 2001. Hippocampal diminuition in PTSD: more (or less?) than meets the eye. *Hippocampus* 11: 73-74.

Posner M. 1995. Modulation by instruction. *Nature* 373: 198-199.

Posner M and Rothbart M. 1994. Constructing neuronal theories of mind. In: Koch C and Davis JL, Editors. *Large-Scale Neuronal Theories of the Brain* (MIT Press: Cambridge), pp. 183-200.

Post RM and Kopanda RT. 1989. Cocaine, Kindling, and Psychosis. *American Journal of Psychiatry* 133(6): 627-634.

Prince DA and Farrell D. 1963. 'Centrencephalic' spike-wave discharges following parenteral penicillin injection in the cat. *Neurology* 19: 309 - 310.

Radhakrishnan S. 1992. *The Principal Upanishads* (Humanities Press International: Atlantic Highlands, NJ).

Rainville P. 2003. Hypnosis phenomenology and the neurobiology of consciousness. *The International Journal of Clinical and Experimental Hypnosis.* 51(2): 105-129.

Rainville P, Hofbauer RK, Paus T, Duncan GH, Bushnell MC and Price DD. 1999. Cerebral mechanisms of hypnotic induction and suggestion. *Journal of Cognitive Neuroscience* 11(1): 110-25.

Rajna P and Veres J. 1993. Correlations between night sleep duration and seizure frequency in temporal lobe epilepsy. *Epilepsia* 34(3): 574 - 579.

RamachandranV and Blakeslee S. 1997. *Phantoms in the Brain: Probing the Mysteries of the Human Mind* (William Morrow & Co.: New York).

Raos V and Bentivoglio M. 1993. Crosstalk between the two sides of the thalamus through the reticular nucleus: a retrograde and anterograde tracing study in the rat. *Journal of Comparative Neurology* 332: 145-154.

Rauch SL, van der Kolk BA, Fisler RE, Alpert NM, Orr SP, Savage CR, Fischman AJ, Jenike MA and Pitman RK. 1996. A symptom provocation study of posttraumatic stress disorder using positron emission tomography and script-driven imagery. *Archives of General Psychiatry* 53: 390 - 387.

Ray RA. 1994. *Buddhist Saints in India: A Study of Buddhist Values and Orientations* (Oxford University Press: New York).

Ray WJ and Cole HW. 1985. EEG activity reflects attentional demands and beta activity reflects emotional and cognitive processes. *Science* 228: 750-752.

Raybourn MS and Keller EL. 1977. Colliculoreticular organization in primate oculomotor system. *Journal of Neurophysiology* 40(4): 861-878.

Redding FK. 1967. Modification of sensory cortical evoked potentials by hippocampal stimulation. *Electroencephalography & Clinical Neurophysiology* 22: 74-83.

Redecker C, Bruehl C, Hagemann G, Binus O and Witte OW. 1997. Coupling of cortical and thalamic metabolism in experimentally induced visual and somatosensory focal epilepsy. *Epilepsy Research* 27: 127-137.

Reece LJ and Schwartzkroin PA. 1991. Effects of cholinergic agonists on two non-pyramidal cell types in rat hippocampal slices. *Brain Research* 566: 115-126.

Reissenweber J, David E and Pfotenhauer M. 1992. Investigations of psychological aspects of the perception of magnetophosphenes and electrophosphenes. *Biomedizinische Tecknik* 37(3): 42-45.

Remillard GM, Andermann F, Testa GF, Gloor P, Aube M, Martin JB, Feindel W, Guberman A and Simpson C. 1983. Sexual ictal manifestations predominate in women with temporal lobe epilepsy: a finding suggesting sexual dimorphism in the human brain. *Neurology* 33(3): 323-330.

Reza. 1996. Pilgrimage to China's Buddhist Caves. *National Geographic* 189(4): 53-63.

Rich AN, Williams MA, Puce A, Syngeniotis A, Howard MA, McGlone F and Mattingley JP. 2006. Neural correlates of imagined and synaesthetic colours. *Neuropsychologia* 44(14): 2918-2925.

Robinet I. 1993. *Taoist Meditation: The Mao-Shan Tradition of Great Purity* (State University of New York Press: Albany, New York).

Robinet I. 1997 [1992]. *Taoism: The Growth of a Religion* (Stanford University Press: Stanford, California).

Rodin E and Schmaltz S. 1984. The Bear-Fedio personality inventory and temporal lobe epilepsy. *Neurology* 34: 591-6.

Roland PE and Gulyas B. 1995. Visual memory, visual imagery, and visual recognition of large field patterns by the human brain: functional anatomy by positron emission tomography. *Cerebral Cortex* 5(1): 79-93.

Roll WG, Persinger MA, Webster DL, Tiller SG and Cook CM. 2002. Neurobehavioral and neurometabolic (SPECT) correlates of paranormal information: involvement of the right hemisphere and its sensitivity to weak complex magnetic fields. *International Journal of Neuroscience* 112: 197-224.

Rolls ET. 1989. Functions of neuronal networks in the hippocampus and neocortex in memory. In: Byrne JH and Berry WO, Editors. Neural models of plasticity: experimental and theoretical approaches (Academic Press: San Diego), pp. 240 – 265.

Rolls ET. 1999. Spatial view cells and the representation of space in the primate hippocampus. *Hippocampus* 9: 467-480.

Rolls ET. 2000. Hippocampal-cortical and cortico-cortical backprojections. *Hippocampus* 10: 380–388.

Rosene DL and Van Hoesen GW. 1987. The hippocampal formation of the primate brain. In: Jones EG and Peters A, Editors. *Cerebral Cortex, Vol. 6: Further Aspects of Cortical Function, Including Hippocampus* (Plenum Press: New York), pp. 345-457.

Sato Y, Fukuoka Y, Minamitani H and Honda K. 2007. Sensory stimulation triggers spindles during sleep stage 2. *Sleep* 30(4): 511-518.

Satyewarananda Giri. 1991 [1983]. *Babaji, Vol. 2: Lahiri Mahasay, 3rd Edition* (The Sanskrit Classics: P.O. Box 5368, San Diego, California).

Saver JL and Rabin JR. 1997. The Neural Substrates of Religious Experience. In: Salloway S, Malloy P and Cummings JL, eds., *The Neuropsychiatry of Limbic and Subcortical Disorders* (American Psychiatric Press: Washington, D.C.), pp. 195-207.

Schiller P and Malpelli J, 1978. Functional specificity of lateral geniculate nucleus laminae of the rhesus monkey. *Journal of Neurophysiology* 41: 788-797.

Schipper K. 1993. *The Taoist Body* (University of California Press: Berkeley).

Schultz JH and Luthe W. 1969. *Autogenic Training: a Physiological Approach to Psychotherapy* (Grune & Stratton: New York, NY).

Schultz S and Rolls E. 1999. Analysis of information transfer in the Schaffer collaterals. *Hippocampus* 9: 582 - 598.

Schwartzkroin PA and McIntyre DC. 1997. Limbic anatomy and physiology. In: Engel J, Jr., and Pedley, TA, Editors. *Epilepsy: A Comprehensive Textbook, Vol. I.* (Lippincott-Raven: Philadelphia), pp. 323-337.

Scollo-Lavizzari G and Scollo-Lavizzari GR. 1974. Sleep, sleep deprivation, photosensitivity and epilepsy. *European Journal of Neurology* 11: 1-21.

Sharp PE. 1999. Complimentary roles for hippocampal versus subicular/entorhinal place cells in coding place, context, and events. *Hippocampus* 9: 432-443.

Sharp PE, Blair HT, Etkin D andTzanetos DB. 1995. Influences of vestibular and visual motion information on the spatial firing patterns of hippocampal place cells. *Journal of Neuroscience* 15: 173-189.

Shen B and McNaughton BL. 1996. Modeling the spontaneous reactivation of experience-specific hippocampal cell assemblies during sleep. *Hippocampus* 6: 685 – 692.

Shouse MN and Ryan W. 1984. Thalamic kindling: electrical stimulation of the lateral geniculate nucleus produces photosensitive grand mal seizures. *Experimental Neurology* 86: 18-32.

Siapas AG and Wilson MA. 1998. Coordinated Interactions Between Hippocampal Ripples and Cortical Spindles During Slow-Wave Sleep. *Neuron* 21: 1123-1128.

Silburn L. 1988. *Kundalini: The Energy of the Depths*. Gontier J, Transl. (State University of New York Press: Albany).

Simmons ML and Chavkin C. 1996. Endogenous opoid regulation of hippocampal function. *International Review of Neurobiology* 39: 145-196.

Sirota A, Csicsvári J, Buhl D and Buzsáki G. 2003. Communication between neocortex and hippocampus during sleep in rodents. *Proceedings of the National Academy of Sciences USA* 100(4): 2065–2069.

Sorensen AS and Bolwig TG. 1987. Personality and epilepsy: new evidence for a relationship? A review. *Comprehensive Psychiatry* 28(5): 369-83.

Spencer SS. 1988a. Substrates of localization-related epilepsies: biologic implication of localization findings in humans. *Epilepsia* 39(2): 114 - 123.

Spencer SS. Cortical and intercortical seizure spread. 1988b. In: Meldrum BC, Ferrendelli JA and Weiser HG. *Anatomy of Epileptogenesis* (John Libbey & Co.: London), pp. 139-154.

Spencer SS and Spencer DD. 1994. Entorhinal-hippocampal interactions in medial temporal lobe epilepsy. *Epilepsia* 35(4): 721 - 727.

Spencer SS, Williamson PD, Spencer DD and Mattson RH. 1987. Human hippocampal seizure spread studied by depth and subdural recording: the hippocampal commissure. *Epilepsia* 28(5): 479-89.

Spencer SS, Marks D, Katz A, Kim J and Spencer D. 1992. Anatomic correlates of interhippocampal seizure propagation time. *Epilepsia* 33(5): 862-873.

Sperling MR and O'Connor MJ. 1990. Auras and subclinical seizures: characteristics and prognostic significance. *Annals of Neurology* 28: 320-328.

St. Louis EK and Lansky EP. 2006. Meditation and epilepsy: A still hung jury. *Medical Hypotheses* 67(2): 247-250.

Staba RJ, Wilson CL, Bragin A, Fried I and Engel J Jr. 2002a. Sleep states differentiate single neuron activity recorded from human epileptic hippocampus, entorhinal cortex, and subiculum. *Journal of Neuroscience* 22(13): 5694–5704.

Staba RJ, Wilson CL, Fried I and Engel J Jr. 2002b. Single neuron burst firing in the human hippocampus during sleep. *Hippocampus* 12: 724–734.

Stabell U & Stabell B. 1993. Mechanisms of chromatic rod vision in scotopic illumination. *Vision Research* 34(8): 1019-1027.

Stefano G. 2002. Molecular processes that have the potential to be part of the placebo effect and the relaxation response. *Proceedings of Science and Mind/Body Medicine Course* (Harvard School of Medicine, Department of Continuing Education: Course met on May 3, 2002).

Steinmetz MA, Motter BC, Duffy CJ and Mountcastle VB. 1987. Functional properties of parietal visual neurons: radial organization of directionalities within the visual field. *Journal of Neuroscience* 7(1): 177-191.

Steriade M. 1991. Alertness, quiet sleep, and dreaming. In: Peters A and Jones EG, Editors. *Cerebral Cortex, Vol. 9* (Plenum Press: New York), pp. 279-357.

Steriade M. 1993. Cellular substrates of brain rhythms. In: Niedermeyer E and Lopez da Silva F, Editors. *Electroencephalography: Basic Principles, Clinical Applications, and Related Fields, 3rd Edition* (Williams and Wilkins: Baltimore), pp. 27-92.

Steriade M and McCarley RW. 1990. *Brainstem Control of Wakefulness and Sleep* (Plenum Press: New York).

Steriade M and Contreras D. 1995. Relations between cortical and thalamic cellular events during transition from sleep patterns to paroxysmal activity. *Journal of Neuroscience* 15(1): 623-642.

Steriade M and Contreras D. 1998. Spike-wave complexes and fast components of cortically generated seizures. I. Role of the neocortex. *Journal of Neurophysiology* 80(3): 1439-1455.

Steriade M and Timofeev I. 2003. Neuronal Plasticity in Thalamocortical Networks during Sleep and Waking Oscillations. *Neuron* 37: 563 – 576.

Steriade M, Contreras D, Curro Dossi R and Nunez A. 1993a. The slow (< 1 Hz) oscillation in reticular thalamic and thalamocortical neurons: scenario of sleep rhythm generation in interacting thalamic and neocortical networks. *Journal of Neuroscience* 13(8): 3284-3299.

Steriade M, McCormick DA and Sejnowski T. 1993b. Thalamocortical oscillations in the sleeping and aroused brain, *Science* 262: 679-685

Steriade M, Nuñez A and Amzica F. 1993c. Intracellular analysis of relations between the slow (< 1 Hz) neocortical oscillation and other sleep rhythms of the electroencephalogram. *Journal of Neuroscience* 13(8): 3266-3283.

Steriade M, McCormick DA and Sejnowski T. 1993d. Thalamocortical Oscillations in the Sleeping and Aroused Brain, *Science* 262: 679-685.

Steriade M, Contreras D, Amzica F and Timofeev I. 1996. Synchronization of fast (30 - 40 Hz) spontaneous oscillations in intrathalamic and thalamocortical net-works. *Journal of Neuroscience* 16(8): 2788 - 2808; see also Contreras D and Steriade M. (1997) State-dependent fluctuations of low-frequency rhythms in corticothalamic networks. *Neuroscience* 76(1): 25 - 38.

Steriade M, Amzica F, Neckelmann D and Timofeev I. 1998. I. Spike-wave complexes and fast components of cortically generated seizures. II. Extracellular patterns. *Journal of Neurophysiology* 80(3): 1456 -1479.

Steriade M, Timofeev I and Grenier F. 2001. Natural waking and sleep states: a view from inside neocortical neurons. *Journal of Neurophysiology* 85: 1969–1985.

Stern CE, Corkin S, Gonzalez RG, Guimaraes AR, Baker JR, Jennings PJ, Carr CA, Sugiura RM, Vendatham V and Rosen BR. 1996. The hippocampal formation participates in novel picture encoding: Evidence form functional magnetic resonance imaging. *Proceedings of the National Academy of Sciences USA* 93: 8660–8665.

Stern CE and Hasselmo ME. 1999. Bridging the gap: integrating cellular and functional magnetic resonance imaging studies of the hippocampus. *Hippocampus* 9: 45-53.

Stevens JR, Mark VH, Erwin R, Pacheco and Suematsu K. 1969. Deep temporal stimulation in man. *Archives of Neurology* 21: 157-169.

Stoffels C, Munari C, Bonis A, Bancaud J and Talairach J. 1980. Genital and sexual manifestations occurring in the course of partial seizures in man. *Revue d'electroencephalographie et de neurophysiologie clinique* 10(4): 386-392.

Stoop R and Pralong E. 2000. Functional connections and epileptic spread between hippocampus, entorhinal cortex and amygdala in a modified horizontal slice preparation of the rat brain. *European Journal of Neuroscience* 12(10): 3651–3663.

Stringer JL and Lothman EW. 1992. Reverberatory seizure discharges in hippocampal-parahippocampal circuits. *Experimental Neurology* 116: 198-203.

Stringer JL, Williamson JM and Lothman EW. 1989. Induction of paroxysmal discharges in the dentate gyrus: frequency dependence and relationship to afterdischarge production. *Journal of Neurophysiology* 62(1): 126-135.

Suarez H, Koch C and Douglas R. 1995. Modeling direction selectivity of simple cells in striate visual cortex within the framework of the canonical microcircuit. *Journal of Neuroscience* 15(10): 6700-6719.

Suzuki WA and Amaral DG. 2003. Perirhinal and parahippocampal cortices of the macaque monkey: Cytoarchitectonic and chemoarchitectonic organization. *Journal of Comparative Neurology* 463: 67–91.

Szechtman H, Woody E, Bower, K and Nahmias C. 1998. Where the imaginal appears real: a positron emission tomography study of auditory hallucinations. *Proceedings of the National Academy of Sciences USA* 95: 1956-1960.

Takahashi T and Tsukahara Y. 1976. Influence of color on the photoconvulsive response. *Electroencephalography and Clinical Neurophysiology.* 41: 124-136.

Takahashi T and Tsukahara Y. 1992. Usefulness of blue sunglasses in photosensitive epilepsy. *Epilepsia* 33(3): 517 – 521.

Talbot JD, Marrett S, Evans AC, Meyer E, Bushnell MC and Duncan GH. 1991. Multiple representations of pain in the human cerebral cortex. *Science* 251: 1355-1358.

Tamamaki N and Nojyo Y. 1991. Crossing fiber arrays in the rat hippocampus as demonstrated by three-dimensional reconstruction. *Journal of Comparative Neurology* 303: 435-442.

Tanaka H, Hayashi M and Hori T. 1996. Statistical Features of Hypnagogic EEG Measured by a New Scoring System. *Sleep* 19, 9, pp. 73 -738.

Tanaka H, Hayashi M and Hori T. 2000. Topographical Characteristics of Slow Wave Activities During the Transition from Wakefulness to Sleep. *Clinical Neurophysiology* 111, pp. 417-427.

Tanaka K. 1996. Inferotemporal cortex and object vision. *Annual Reviews of Neuroscience* 19: 109–139.

Tassarini CA, Rubboli G and Michelucci R. 1990. Reflex epilepsy. In: Dam M and Gram L. *Comprehensive Epileptology* (Raven Press: New York).

Temkin O. 1994. *The Falling Sickness: A History of Epilepsy from the Greeks to the Beginnings of Modern Neurology, 2nd Edition* (John Hopkins University Press: Baltimore).

Theodore WH. 1989. Pseudoseizures: Differential diagnosis. *Journal of Neuropsychiatry* 1(1): 67-71.

Thomas S, Sing H, Belenky G, Holcomb H, Mayberg H, Dannals R, Wagner H, Thorne D, Popp K, Rowland L, Welsh A, Balwinski S and Redmond D. 2000. *Journal of Sleep Research* 9(4): 335-352.

Thornton EM. 1976. *Hypnotism, Hysteria and Epilepsy* (William Heinemann Medical Books, Ltd.: London).

Thorpe J, Barker G, Jones S, Moseley I, Losseff N, MacManus D, Webb S, Mortimer C, Plummer D, Tofts P, McDonald W and Miller D. 1995. Magnetisation transfer ratios and transverse magnetisation decay curves in optic neuritis: correlation with clinical findings and electrophysiology. *Journal of Neurology, Neurosurgery, and Psychiatry* 59: 487-492.

Timofeev I, Contreras D and Steriade M. 1996. Synaptic responsiveness of cortical and thalamic neurons during various phases of slow oscillation in cats. *Journal of Physiology* 494: 265–278.

Timofeev I, Grenier F and Steriade M. 1998. Spike-wave complexes and fast components of cortically generated seizures. IV. Paroxysmal fast runs in cortical and thalamic neurons. *Journal of Neurophysiology* 80(3): 1495-1513.

Tisher PW, Holzer JC, Greenberg M, Benjamin S, Devinsky O and Bear DM. 1993. Psychiatric presentations of epilepsy. *Harvard Review of Psychiatry* 1(4): 219-228.

Travis F and Wallace RK. 1999. Autonomic and EEG Patterns During Eyes-Closed Rest and Transcendental Meditation (TM) Practice: The Basis for a Neural Model of TM Practice. *Consciousness and Cognition* 3: 302-328.

Uchida S, Atsumi Y and Kojima T. 1994. Dynamic relationships between sleep spindles and delta waves during a NREM period. *Brain Research Bulletin* 33: 351-355.

Ulrich DJ, Manning KA and Feig SL. 2003. *Journal of Comparative Neurology* 458(2): 128-143.

Vaitl D, Birbaumer N, Gruzelier J, Jamieson GA, Kotchoubey B, Kubler A, Lehmann D, Miltner WHR, Ott U, Putz P, Sammer G, Strauch I, Strehl U, Wackermann J and Weiss T. 2005. Psychobiology of altered states of consciousness. *Psychological Bulletin* 131(1): 98-127.

Van Ness PC, Lesser RP and Duchowny MS. 1997. Simple sensory seizures. In: Engel J, Jr., and Pedley, TA, Editors. *Epilepsy: A Comprehensive Textbook, Vol. 1* (Lippincott-Raven: Philadelphia), pp. 533-542.

Vannucci M, Dietl T, Pezer N, Viggiano MP, Helmstaedter C, Schaller C, Elger CE and Grunwald T. 2003. Hippocampal function and visual object processing in temporal lobe epilepsy. *Neuroreport* 14(11): 1489–1492.

Velasco AL, Wilson CL, Babb TL and Engel J Jr. 2000. Functional and anatomic correlates of two frequently observed temporal lobe seizure-onset patterns. *Neural Plasticity* 7(1-2): 49–63.

Vertes RP, Hoover WB, Szigeti-Buck K and Leranth C. 2007. Nucleus reuniens of the midline thalamus: Link between the medial prefrontal cortex and the hippocampus. *Brain Research Bulletin* 71(6): 601-609.

Vibert N, De Waele C, Serafin M, Babalian A, Muhlethaler M and Vidal PP. 1997. The vestibular system as a model of sensorimotor transformations. A combined in vivo and in vitro approach to study the cellular mechanisms of gaze and posture stabilization in mammals. *Progress in Neurobiology* 51: 243-286.

Vinogradova O. 2001. The hippocampus as comparator: role of the two input and two output systems of the hippocampus in selection and registration of information. *Hippocampus* 11: 578-598.

Vitek JL, Ashe J, DeLong MR and Kaneoke Y. 1996. Microstimulation of primate motor thalamus: somatotopic organization and differential distribution of evoked responses among subnuclei. *Journal of Neurophysiology* 75(6): 2486-2495.

Vitte E, Derosier C, Caritu Y, Berthoz A, Hasboun D and Soulie D. 1996. Activation of the hippocampal formation by vestibular stimulation: a functional magnetic resonance imaging study. *Experimental Brain Research* 112: 523-526.

Von Bohlen und Halbach O and Albrecht D. 2002. Reciprocal connections of the hippocampal area CA1, the lateral nucleus of the amygdala and cortical areas in a combined horizontal slice preparation. *Neuroscience Research* 44(91): 91–100.

von Krosigk M, Bal T and McCormick DA. 1993. Cellular mechanisms of a synchronized oscillation in the thalamus. *Science* 291: 361-364.

Voskuil PHA. 1983. The epilepsy of Fyodor Mikhailovitch Dostoevsky (1821-1881). *Epilepsia* 24: 658-667.

Wada Y, Minabe Y, Okuda H, Jibiki I, Yoshida K and Yamaguchi N. 1984. Lateral geniculate kindling and long-lasting photosensitivity in the cat. *Experimental Neurology* 91: 343-354.

Wallace BA, Ed. 2003. *Buddhism and Science: Breaking New Ground* (Cambridge University Press: New York).

Wasson RG. 1971. *Soma: Divine Mushroom of Immortality* (Harcourt Brace Jovanovich: New York).

Waxman S and Geschwind N. 1975. The Interictal Behavioral Syndrome of Temporal Lobe Epilepsy. *Archives of General Psychiatry* 32: 1580-1586.

Wilkins AJ, Binnie CD and Darby CE. 1980. Visually-induced seizures. *Progress in Neurology* 15: 85-117.

Wilkus RJ, Dodrill CB, and Thompson PM. 1984. Intensive EEG monitoring and psychological studies of patients with pseudoepileptic seizures. *Epilepsia* 25(1): 100-107.

Williamson A, Patrylo PR, and Spencer DD. 1999. Decrease in inhibition in dentate granule cells from patients with medial temporal lobe epilepsy. *Annals of Neurology* 45: 92-99.

Williamson PD and Engel J Jr. 1997. Complex partial seizures. In: Engel J Jr and Pedley TA, Editors. *Epilepsy: A Comprehensive Textbook, Vol. I* (Lippincott-Raven: Philadelphia), pp. 557 - 566.

Wilson CL, Isokawa M, Babb TL, Engle J, Jr., Cahan LD and Crandall PH. 1987. A comparative view of local and interhemispheric limbic pathways in humans: an evoked potential analysis. In: Engel J, Jr., Ojemann GA, Luders HO, Williamson PD, Editors. *Fundamental Mechanisms of Human Brain Function: Opportunities for Direct Investigation in Association with the Surgical Treatment of Epilepsy* (Raven Press: London), pp. 27-38.

Wilson CL, Isokawa M, Babb TL and Crandall PH. 1990. Functional connections in the human temporal lobe. I. Analysis of limbic system pathways using neuronal responses evoked by electrical stimulation. *Experimental Brain Research* 82: 279-292.

Wilson CL, Isokawa M, Babb TL, Crandall PH, Levesque MF and Engle J Jr. 1991. Functional connections in the human temporal lobe. II. Evidence for a loss of functional linkage between contralateral limbic structures. *Experimental Brain Research* 85: 174-187.

Wilson HH. 1888. *Rig-Veda Samhita: A Collection of Ancient Hindu Hymns, Vols. I - VI* (Trubner & Co.: London).

Wilson E. 1994. The Transits of Consciousness. *Journal of Subtle Energies and Energy Medicine* 4(2): 171-185.

Witter MP, Naber PA, van Haeften T., Machielsen WCM, Rombouts SARB, Barkhof F, Scheltens P and Lopes da Silva FH. 2000. Cortico-hippocampal communication by way of parallel parahippocampal-subicular pathways. *Hippocampus* 10: 398–410.

Wolf P. 1997. Isolated seizures. In: Engel J, Jr., and Pedley, TA, Editors. *Epilepsy: A Compre-*

hensive Textbook, Vol. 1 (Lippincott-Raven: Philadelphia), pp. 2475-2481.

Wolfson ER. 1994. *Through a Speculum that Shines: Vision and Imagination in Medieval Jewish Mysicism* (Princeton University Press: Princeton).

Wright K Jr, Badia P and Wauquier A. 1995. Topographical and Temporal Patterns of Brain Activity During the Transition from Wakefulness to Sleep. *Sleep* 18(10): 880-889.

Wu K, Canning KJ and Leung LS. 1998. Functional interconnections between CA3 and the dentate gyrus revealed by current source density analysis. *Hippocampus* 8: 217-230.

Wurtz RH and Mohler CW 1976. Enhancement of visual responses in monkey striate cortex and frontal eye fields. *Journal of Neurophysiology* 39: 766-772.

Xue J-T, Kim CBY, Moore RJ and Spear PD 1994. Influence of the superior colliculus on responses of lateral geniculate neurons in the cat. *Visual Neuroscience* 11: 1059-1076.

Yeckel MF and Berger TW. 1998. Spatial distribution of potentiated synapses in hippocampus: dependence on cellular mechanisms and network properties. *Journal of Neuroscience* 18(1): 438-450.

Yehuda R. 2001. Are glucocortoids responsible for putative hippocampal damage in PTSD? How and when to decide. *Hippocampus* 11: 85-89.

Yen CT and Shaw FZ. 2003. Reticular thalamic responses to nociceptive inputs in anesthesized rats. *Brain Research* 968: 179-191.

Yukie M. 2000. Connections between the medial temporal cortex and the CA1 subfield of the hippocampal formation in the Japanese monkey. *Journal of Comparative Neurology* 432: 282-299.

Zalesky C. 1987. *Otherworldly Journeys: Accounts of Near Death Experiences in Medieval and Modern Times* (Oxford University Press: New York).

Zeki S. 1993. *A Vision of the Brain* (Blackwell Scientific Publications: London).

Zhang DX and Bertram EH. 2002. Midline thalamic region: widespread excitatory input to the entorhinal cortex and amygdala. *Journal of Neuroscience* 22: 3277-3284.

Zironi I, Iacovelli P, Aicardi G, Liu P and Bilkey DK. 2001. Prefrontal cortex lesions augment the location-related firing properties of area TE/perirhinal neurons in a working memory task. *Cerebral Cortex* 11(11): 1093–1100.

LIST OF FIGURES & TABLES

INDEX

f = figure; t = table

acetylcholine (ACh), 130-137, 144, 183-185
alpha frequency brainwaves, 190-196, 207
    meditation and, 190-196
    resting occipital alpha and, 187-196
    sleep rhythms and, 190-194
Amaraughasasana, 25-26, 28f
amorphous expanding waves, 81-85,
    83f, 89f, 91f-92, 97
amygdala, 177-178, 214, 219-220
analgesia, 56-57, 76
angle of gaze, 47, 51, 75, 92
Anguttara-Nikaya, 35
anterior cingulate, 77
arousal, effects of, 9, 52, 57, 123, 191, 204
attention, 51-52, 75-79, 81, 84-85, 95-97,
    123, 130f, 132-138, 145, 165, 185
auto-suggestion, 170

Book of Great Profundity
    (*Ta-tung jing*), 12, 44-49
Book of the Yellow Court
    (*Huang-ting jing*), 12, 46, 49
brahmarandhra, 25-26, 33
brightening and bluing visions of, 16, 100,
    103, 110-119, 114f
    origins of, 115-132, 131f, 138-
        140
bubble images, visions of, 97
bulbospongiosus muscle, 163-164,
    168-169, 176
bulbous images
    visions of, 17, 20, 25-26, 41, 47-49
    entorhinal-hippocampal complex and,
        115-118, 123,
    origins, 132-138, 141-145, 162-167
Buddha, Gotama Sakyamuni, 11, 34-36
Buddhaghosa, 36-38f
Buddhism:

Mahayana, 12, 36-41
Theravadan, 12, 37-38f, 202, 233
Vajrayana (Tibetan), 12, 33, 39-42f, 202
Buzsáki G, 118-120, 124, 130, 145, 178

CA1, 118-138, 153-162, 184-185, 214
CA3, 118-138, 144-160, 182-188, 212
CA3/4 neurons, 134-135, 182, 184
calcium spikes, 59, 86-90, 95, 98, 104,
    108, 193
caksus ("Inner Eye"), 25, 35
Chu-ci ("Elegies of Chu"), 44
circadian rhythms, 92-93
circumstantiality, 171
collaterals, Schaffer, 118, 130, 153-158, 160
commissures
    dorsal hippocampal commissure (DHC),
        119-139
    ventral hippocampal commissure (VHC),
        119-130, 145-147f, 152, 182
    monkey VHC, trajectory, 147f
comparator theory. *See* Vinogradova.
computer simulation (Bernard et al.),
    153-161, 155f, 159f
conditioning, 122
cone density patterns, 88-92, 88f, 91f
cone receptors, types of, 67-73, 88-90
cone response profiles, 69f
conversion disorder, 210, 229
cortical fast-runs, 105, 112, 125, 224
cortical lightness record, composition,
    66-74, 88-92, 138-140, 162
cortical slow (<1 Hz) waves, 85-90,
    89f, 97-98
cun-jian (Daoist "retentive visualization"), 43
current of energy, 163-168, 177

Daoism (Taoism), 43-50, 48f, 202
dark rings
    in near-death experiences, 111-112

About the Author

Philip Nicholson has published articles on the neural correlates of meditation-induced light visions in medical journals (*Epilepsia*, *Medical Hypotheses*, *The Journal of Subtle Energies and Energy Medicine*) and academic publications (*The Electronic Journal of Vedic Studies*; *Shamanism in the Interdisciplinary Context*; *Proceedings of the 7th International Conference of the International Society for Shamanistic Research, Changchun, China, 2004 [in press]*; *Proceedings of the 2006 Harvard-Peking University International Conference on Comparative Mythology, Beijing, China [in press]*). His research on the neural correlates of meditation and meditation-induced light visions originally published in those sources has been incorporated—in revised form—in this book. The author's other projects encompass a wide range of subjects, including an examination of ethical dilemmas facing military psychiatrists (*Archives of General Psychiatry*); a high school psychology text (Grace et al., *Your Self: An Introduction to Psychology*); film-

scripts for a "Dilemmas in Legal Ethics" series commissioned by the American Bar Association; videoscripts for programs used in the continuing education of physicians (sponsored by The American Cancer Society, The National Heart Lung & Blood Institute, and myriad pharmaceutical companies); and articles on the cumulative psychological impact of living and working in fast-paced, computer-driven environments ("Technostress at the Top: Work, Morale, and Self-Scrutiny," *Leaders Magazine*). More information is available online at <www.philipnicholson.com>.

NOTES

Made in the USA
Las Vegas, NV
09 February 2022

43476661R10155